CLEP

College Level Examination Program

CLEP 33

Copyright © 2016 XAMonline, Inc.

All rights reserved. No part of the material protected by this copyright notice may be reproduced or utilized in any form or by any means, electronic or mechanical, including photocopying, recording or by any information storage and retrievable system, without written permission from the copyright holder.

To obtain permission(s) to use the material from this work for any purpose including workshops or seminars, please submit a written request to

> XAMonline, Inc.
> 21 Orient Avenue
> Melrose, MA 02176
> Toll Free 1-800-301-4647
> Email: info@xamonline.com
> Web: www.xamonline.com
> Fax: 1-617-583-5552

Library of Congress Cataloging-in-Publication Data

Wynne, Sharon A.

CLEP 33: College Level Examination Program / Sharon A. Wynne.
   ISBN: 978-1-60787-575-8

1. CLEP   2. Study Guides.

Disclaimer:

The opinions expressed in this publication are the sole works of XAMonline and were created independently from The College Board, or any State Department of Education, National Evaluation Systems or other testing affiliates. Between the time of publication and printing, state specific standards as well as testing formats and website information may change that are not included in part or in whole within this product. XAMonline develops sample test questions, and they reflect similar content as on real tests; however, they are not former tests. XAMonline assembles content that aligns with state standards but makes no claims nor guarantees candidates a passing score. Numerical scores are determined by testing companies such as The College Board.

Cover photo provided by © Can Stock Photo Inc./zimmytws

Printed in the United States of America   œ-1
CLEP 33
ISBN: 978-1-60787-575-8

TABLE OF CONTENTS

About CLEP i

American Literature 1

Analyzing and Interpreting Literature 24

College Composition 51

College Composition Modular 70

English Literature 99

Humanities 123

French 153

German 157

Spanish 161

American Government 190

History of the United States I: Early Colonization to 1877 212

History of the United States II: 1865 to the Present 241

Human Growth and Development 272

Introduction to Educational Psychology 304

Principles of Macroeconomics 309

Principles of Microeconomics 335

Introductory Psychology 361

Introductory Sociology 383

Social Sciences and History 403

Western Civilization I: Ancient Near East to 1648 437

Western Civilization II: 1648 to the Present 465

Biology	470
Calculus	495
Chemistry	508
College Algebra	514
College Mathematics	528
Natural Sciences	545
Precalculus	572
Financial Accounting	578
Information Systems	583
Introductory Business Law	607
Principles of Management	631
Principles of Marketing	660

I. The College-Level Examination Program

How the Program Works

CLEP exams are administered at over 1,800 institutions nationwide, and 2,900 colleges and universities award college credit to those who perform well on them. This rigorous program allows many self-directed students of a wide range of ages and backgrounds to demonstrate their mastery of introductory college-level material and pursue greater academic success. Students can earn credit for what they already know by getting qualifying scores on any of the 33 examinations.

The CLEP exams cover material that is taught in introductory-level courses at many colleges and universities. Faculty at individual colleges review the exams to ensure that they cover the important material currently taught in their courses.

Although CLEP is sponsored by the College Board, only colleges may grant credit toward a degree. To learn about a particular college's CLEP policy, contact the college directly. When you take a CLEP exam, you can request that a copy of your score report be sent to the college you are attending or planning to attend. After evaluating your score, the college will decide whether or not to award you credit for a certain course or courses, or to exempt you from them.

If the college decides to give you credit, it will record the number of credits on your permanent record, thereby indicating that you have completed work equivalent to a course in that subject. If the college decides to grant exemption without giving you credit for a course, you will be permitted to omit a course that would normally be required of you and to take a course of your choice instead.

The CLEP program has a long-standing policy that an exam may not be taken within the specified wait period. This waiting period provides you with an opportunity to spend additional time preparing for the exam or the option of taking a classroom course. If you violate the CLEP retest policy, the administration will be considered invalid, the score canceled, and any test fees will be forfeited. If you are a military service member, please note that DANTES will not fund retesting on a previously funded CLEP exam. However, you may personally fund a retest after the specified wait period.

The CLEP Examinations

CLEP exams cover material directly related to specific undergraduate courses taught during a student's first two years in college. The courses may be offered for three, four, six or eight semester hours in general areas such as mathematics, history, social sciences, English composition, natural sciences and humanities. Institutions will either grant credit for a specific course based on a satisfactory score on the related exam, or in the general area in which a satisfactory is earned. The credit is equal to the credit awarded to students who successfully complete the courses. See the Table of Contents for a complete list of all exam titles.

About CLEP

What the Examinations Are Like

CLEP exams are administered on computer and are approximately 90 minutes long, with the exception of College Composition, which is approximately 120 minutes long. Most questions are multiple-choice; other types of questions require you to fill in a numeric answer, to shade areas of an object, or to put items in the correct order. Questions using these kinds of skills are called zone, shade, grid, scale, fraction, numeric entry, histogram and order match questions.

CLEP College Composition includes a mandatory essay section, responses to which must be typed into the computer.

Some of the examinations have optional essays. You should check with the individual college or university where you are sending your score to see whether an optional essay is required for those exams. These essays are administered on paper and are scored by faculty at the institution that receives your score.

Where to Take the Examinations and How to Register

CLEP exams are administered throughout the year at over 1,800 test centers in the United States and select international sites. Once you have decided to take a CLEP examination, you can log into My Account at https://clepportal.collegeboard.org/myaccount to create and manage your own personal accounts, pay for CLEP exams and purchase study materials. You can self-register at any time by completing the online registration form.

Through My Account you can also access a list of institutions that administer CLEP and locate a test center in your area. **After paying for your exam through My Account, you must still contact the test center to schedule your CLEP exam.**

If you are unable to locate a test center near you, call 800-257-9558 for more information.

ACE's College Credit Recommendation Service

The College Credit Recommendation Service (CREDIT) of the American Council on Education (ACE) enables you to put all of your educational achievements on a secure and universally accepted ACE transcript. All of your ACE-evaluated courses and examinations, including CLEP, appear in an easy-to-read format that includes ACE credit recommendations, descriptions and suggested transfer areas. The service is perfect for candidates who have acquired college credit at multiple ACE-evaluated organizations or credit-by-examination programs. You may have your transcript released at any time to the college of your choice. There is a one-time setup fee of $40 (includes the cost of your first transcript) and a fee of $15 for each transcript requested after release of the first. ACE has an additional transcript service for organizations offering continuing education units.

The College Credit Recommendation Service is offered through ACE's Center for Lifelong Learning. For more than 50 years, ACE has been at the forefront of the evaluation of education and training attained outside the classroom. For more information about ACE CREDIT, contact:

About CLEP

ACE CREDIT
One Dupont Circle, NW
Suite 250
Washington, DC 20036

ACE's Call Center is open Monday to Friday, 8:45 a.m. to 4:45 p.m., and can be reached at 866-205-6267 or CREDIT@ace.nche.edu. Staff are able to assist you with courses and certifications that carry ACE recommendations for both civilian organizations and training obtained through the military.

If you are already registered for an ACE transcript, you can access your records and order transcripts using the ACE Online Transcript System: https://www.acenet.edu/transcripts/.

ACE's Center for Lifelong Learning can be found on the Internet at: http://www.acenet.edu/higher-education.

How Your Score Is Reported

You have the option of seeing your CLEP score immediately after you complete the exam, except in the case of College Composition, for which scores are available four to six weeks after the exam date. Once you choose to see your score, it will be sent automatically to the institution you have designated as a score recipient; it cannot be canceled. You will receive a candidate copy of your score before you leave the test center. If you have tested at the institution that you have designated as a score recipient, it will have immediate access to your test results.

If you do not want your score reported, you may select that as an option at the end of the examination *before the exam is scored*. Once you have selected the option to not view your score, the score is canceled.

The score will not be reported to the institution you have designated, and you will not receive a candidate copy of your score report. You will have to wait the specified wait period before you can take the exam again.

CLEP scores are kept on file for 20 years. During this period, for a small fee, you may have your transcript sent to another college or to anyone else you specify. Your score(s) will never be sent to anyone without your approval.

II. Approaching a College about CLEP

The following sections provide a step-by-step guide to learning about the CLEP policy at a particular college or university. The person or office that can best assist you may have a different title at each institution, but the following guidelines will lead you to information about CLEP at any institution.

Adults and other nontraditional students returning to college often benefit from special assistance when they approach a college. Opportunities for adults to return to formal learning in the classroom are now widespread, and colleges and universities have worked hard to make this a smooth process for older students. Many colleges have established special offices that are staffed with trained professionals who understand the kinds of problems facing adults returning to college. If you think you might benefit from such assistance, be sure to find out whether these services are available at your college.

How to Apply for College Credit

Step 1. *Obtain, or access online, the general information catalog and a copy of the CLEP policy from each college you are considering.*

Information about admission and CLEP policies can be obtained on the college's website at clep.collegeboard.org/search/colleges, or by contacting or visiting the admissions office. Ask for a copy of the publication in which the college's complete CLEP policy is explained. Also, get the name and the telephone number of the person to contact in case you have further questions about CLEP.

Step 2. If you have not already been admitted to a college that you are considering, look at its admission requirements for undergraduate students to see whether you qualify.

Whether you're applying for college admission as a high school student, transfer student or as an adult resuming a college career or going to college for the first time, you should be familiar with the requirements for admission at the schools you are considering. If you are a nontraditional student, be sure to check whether the school has separate admissions requirements that might apply to you. Some schools are very selective, while others are "open admission."

It might be helpful for you to contact the admissions office for an interview with a counselor. State why you want the interview and ask what documents you should bring with you or send in advance. (These materials may include a high school transcript, transcript of previous college work or completed application for admission.) Make an extra effort to have all the information requested in time for the interview.

During the interview, relax and be yourself. Be prepared to state honestly why you think you are ready and able to do college work. If you have already taken CLEP exams and scored high enough to earn credit, you have shown that you are able to do college work. Mention this achievement to the admissions counselor because it may increase your chances of being accepted. If you have not taken a CLEP exam, you can still improve your chances of being accepted by describing how your job training or independent study has helped prepare you for college-level work. Discuss with the counselor what you have learned from your work and personal experiences.

Step 3. *Evaluate the college's CLEP policy.*

Typically, a college lists all its academic policies, including CLEP policies, in its general catalog or on its website. You will probably find the CLEP policy statement under a heading such as Credit-by-Examination, Advanced Standing, Advanced Placement or External Degree Program.

About CLEP

These sections can usually be found in the front of the catalog. You can also check out the institution's CLEP Policy by visiting clep.collegeboard.org/search/colleges.

Many colleges publish their credit-by-examination policies in separate brochures, which are distributed through the campus testing office, counseling center, admissions office or registrar's office. If you find a very general policy statement in the college catalog, seek clarification from one of these offices.

Review the material in the section of this chapter entitled "Questions to Ask about a College's CLEP Policy." Use these guidelines to evaluate the college's CLEP policy. If you have not yet taken a CLEP exam, this evaluation will help you decide which exams to take. Because individual colleges have different CLEP policies, a review of several policies may help you decide which college to attend.

Step 4. *If you have not yet applied for admission, do so as early as possible.*

Most colleges expect you to apply for admission several months before you enroll, and it is essential that you meet the published application deadlines. It takes time to process your application for admission. If you have yet to take a CLEP exam, you may want to take one or more CLEP exams while you are waiting for your application to be processed. Be sure to check the college's CLEP policy beforehand so that you are taking exams your college will accept for credit. You should also find out from the college when to submit your CLEP score(s).

Complete all forms and include all documents requested with your application(s) for admission. Normally, an admission decision cannot be reached until all documents have been submitted and evaluated. Unless told to do so, do not send your CLEP score(s) until you have been officially admitted.

Step 5. *Arrange to take CLEP exam(s) or to submit your CLEP score(s).*

CLEP exams can be taken at any of the 1,800 test centers world-wide. To locate a test center near you. clep.collegeboard.org/search/test-centers.
If you have already taken a CLEP exam, but did not have your score sent to your college, you can have an official transcript sent at any time for a small fee. Fill out the Transcript Request Form included on the same page as your exam score. If you do not have the form, visit clep.collegeboard.org/about/score to download a copy, or call 800-257-9558 to order a transcript using a major credit card. Completed forms should be faxed to 610-628-3726 or sent to the following address, along with a check or money order made payable to CLEP for $20 (this fee is subject to change).

CLEP Transcript Service
P.O. Box 6600
Princeton, NJ 08541-6600

Transcripts will only include CLEP scores for the past 20 years; scores more than 20 years old are not kept on file.

About CLEP

Your CLEP scores will be evaluated, probably by someone in the admissions office, and sent to the registrar's office to be posted on your permanent record once you are enrolled. Procedures vary from college to college, but the process usually begins in the admissions office.

Step 6. *Ask to receive a written notice of the credit you receive for your CLEP score(s).*

A written notice may save you problems later, when you submit your degree plan or file for graduation. In the event that there is a question about whether or not you earned CLEP credit, you will have an official record of what credit was awarded. You may also need this verification of course credit if you meet with an academic adviser before the credit is posted on your permanent record.

Step 7. *Before you register for courses, seek academic advising.*

A discussion with your academic adviser can help you to avoid taking unnecessary courses and can tell you specifically what your CLEP credit will mean to you. This step may be accomplished at the time you enroll. Most colleges have orientation sessions for new students prior to each enrollment period. During orientation, students are usually assigned academic advisers who then give them individual help in developing long-range plans and course schedules for the next semester. In conjunction with this counseling, you may be asked to take some additional tests so that you can be placed at the proper course level.

Questions to Ask about a College's CLEP Policy

Before taking CLEP exams for the purpose of earning college credit, try to find the answers to these questions:

1. *Which CLEP exams are accepted by the college?*

   A college may accept some CLEP exams for credit and not others — possibly not the exams you are considering. For this reason, it is important that you know the specific CLEP exams for which you can receive credit.

2. *Does the college require the optional free-response (essay) section for exams in composition and literature as well as the multiple-choice portion of the CLEP exam you are considering? Will you be required to pass a departmental test such as an essay, laboratory or oral exam in addition to the CLEP multiple-choice exam?*

   Knowing the answers to these questions ahead of time will permit you to schedule the optional free-response or departmental exam when you register to take your CLEP exam.

3. *Is CLEP credit granted for specific courses at the college? If so, which ones?*

   You are likely to find that credit is granted for specific courses and that the course titles are designated in the college's CLEP policy. It is not necessary, however, that credit be granted for a specific course for you to benefit from your CLEP credit. For instance, at many liberal

About CLEP

arts colleges, all students must take certain types of courses; these courses may be labeled the core curriculum, general education requirements, distribution requirements or liberal arts requirements. The requirements are often expressed in terms of credit hours. For example, all students may be required to take at least six hours of humanities, six hours of English, three hours of mathematics, six hours of natural science and six hours of social science, with no particular courses in these disciplines specified. In these instances, CLEP credit may be given as "6 hrs. English Credit" or "3 hrs. Math Credit" without specifying for which English or mathematics courses credit has been awarded. To avoid possible disappointment, you should know before taking a CLEP exam what type of credit you can receive or whether you will be exempted from a required course but receive no credit.

4. *How much credit is granted for each exam you are considering, and does the college place a limit On the total amount of CLEP credit you can earn toward your degree?*

Not all colleges that grant CLEP credit award the same amount for individual exams. Furthermore, some colleges place a limit on the total amount of credit you can earn through CLEP or other exams. Other colleges may grant you exemption but no credit toward your degree. Knowing several colleges' policies concerning these issues may help you decide which college to attend. If you think you are capable of passing a number of CLEP exams, you may want to attend a college that will allow you to earn credit for all or most of them. Check out if your institution grants CLEP policy by visiting clep.collegeboard.org/search/colleges.

5. *What is the required score for earning CLEP credit for each exam you are considering?*

Most colleges publish the required scores for earning CLEP credit in their general catalogs or in brochures. The required score may vary from exam to exam, so find out the required score for each exam you are considering.

6. *What is the college's policy regarding prior course work in the subject in which you are considering taking a CLEP exam?*

Some colleges will not grant credit for a CLEP exam if the candidate has already attempted a college-level course closely aligned with that exam. For example, if you successfully completed English 101 or a comparable course on another campus, you will probably not be permitted to also receive CLEP credit in that subject. Some colleges will not permit you to earn CLEP credit for a course that you failed.

7. *Does the college make additional stipulations before credit will be granted?*

It is common practice for colleges to award CLEP credit only to their enrolled students. There are other stipulations, however, that vary from college to college. For example, does the college require you to formally apply for or to accept CLEP credit by completing and signing a form? Or does the college require you to "validate" your CLEP score by successfully completing a more advanced course in the subject? Getting answers to these and other questions will help to smooth the process of earning college credit through CLEP.

About CLEP

III. Preparing to Take CLEP Examinations

Test Preparation Tips

1. Familiarize yourself as much as possible with the test and the test situation before the day of the exam. It will be helpful for you to know ahead of time:

   a. how much time will be allowed for the test and whether there are timed subsections. (This information is included in the examination guides and in the CLEP Tutorial video.)

   b. what types of questions and directions appear on the exam. (See the examination guides.)

   c. how your test score will be computed.

   d. in which building and room the exam will be administered.

   e. the time of the test administration.

   f. direction, transit and parking information to the test center.

2. Register and pay your exam fee through My Account at https://clepportal.collegeboard.org/myaccount and print your registration ticket. Contact your preferred test center to schedule your appointment to test. Your test center may require an additional administration fee. Check with your test center and confirm the amount required and acceptable method of payment.

3. On the day of the exam, remember to do the following.

   a. Arrive early enough so that you can find a parking place, locate the test center, and get settled comfortably before testing begins.

   b. Bring the following with you:

      - completed registration ticket
      - any registration forms or printouts required by the test center. Make sure you have filled out all necessary paperwork in advance of your testing date.
      - a form of valid and acceptable identification. Acceptable identification must:

         - Be government-issued
         - Be an original document — photocopied documents are not acceptable
         - Be valid and current — expired documents (bearing expiration dates that have passed) are not acceptable, no matter how recently they may have expired
         - Bear the test-taker's full name, in English language characters, exactly as it appears on the
         - Registration Ticket, including the order of the names.

About CLEP

- Middle initials are optional and only need to match the first letter of the middle name when present on both the ticket and the identification.
- Bear a recent recognizable photograph that clearly matches the test-taker
- Include the test-taker's signature
- Be in good condition, with clearly legible text and a clearly visible photograph

Refer to the Exam Day Info page on the CLEP website (http://clep.collegeboard.org/exam-day-info) for more details on acceptable and unacceptable forms of identification.

- military test-takers, bring your Geneva Convention Identification Card. Refer to clep.collegeboard.org/military for additional information on IDs for active duty members, spouses, and civil service civilian employees.
- two number 2 pencils with good erasers. Mechanical pencils are prohibited in the testing room.

    c. Leave all books, papers and notes outside the test center. You will not be permitted to use your own scratch paper; it will be provided by the test center.

    d. Do not take a calculator to the exam. If a calculator is required, it will be built into the testing software and available to you on the computer. The CLEP Tutorial video will have a demonstration on how to use online calculators.

    e. Do not bring a cell phone or other electronic devices into the testing room.

4. When you enter the test room:

    a. You will be assigned to a computer testing station. If you have special needs, be sure to communicate them to the test center administrator *before* the day you test.

    b. Be relaxed while you are taking the exam. Read directions carefully and listen to all instructions given by the test administrator. If you don't understand the directions, ask for help before the test begins. If you must ask a question that is not related to the exam after testing has begun, raise your hand and a proctor will assist you. The proctor cannot answer questions related to the exam.

    c. Know your rights as a test-taker. You can expect to be given the full working time allowed for taking the exam and a reasonably quiet and comfortable place in which to work. If a poor testing situation is preventing you from doing your best, ask whether the situation can be remedied. If it can't, ask the test administrator to report the problem on a Center Problem Report that will be submitted with your test results. You may also wish to immediately write a letter to CLEP, P.O. Box 6656, Princeton, NJ 08541- 6656. Describe the exact circumstances as completely as you can. Be sure to include the name of the test center, the test date and the name(s) of the exam(s) you took.

About CLEP

Accommodations for Students with Disabilities

If you have a disability, such as a learning or physical disability, that would prevent you from taking a CLEP exam under standard conditions, you may request accommodations at your preferred test center. Contact your preferred test center well in advance of the test date to make the necessary arrangements and to find out its deadline for submission of documentation and approval of accommodations. Each test center sets its own guidelines in terms of deadlines for submission of documentation and approval of accommodations.

Accommodations that can be arranged directly with test centers include:

- ZoomText (screen magnification)
- Modifiable screen colors
- Use of a reader, amanuensis, or sign language interpreter
- Extended time
- Untimed rest breaks

If the above accommodations do not meet your needs, contact CLEP Services at clep@info.collegeboard.org for information about other accommodations.

IV. Interpreting Your Scores

CLEP score requirements for awarding credit vary from institution to institution. The College Board, however, recommends that colleges refer to the standards set by the American Council on Education (ACE). All ACE recommendations are the result of careful and periodic review by evaluation teams made up of faculty who are subject-matter experts and technical experts in testing and measurement. To determine whether you are eligible for credit for your CLEP scores, you should refer to the policy of the college you will be attending. The policy will state the score that is required to earn credit at that institution. Many colleges award credit at the score levels recommended by ACE. However, some require scores that are higher or lower than these.

Your exam score will be printed for you at the test center immediately upon completion of the examination, unless you took College Composition. For this exam, you will receive your score four to six weeks after the exam date. Your CLEP exam scores are reported only to you, unless you ask to have them sent elsewhere. If you want your scores sent to a college, employer or certifying agency, you must select this option through My Account. This service is free only if you select your score recipient at the time you register to take your exam. A fee will be charged for each score recipient you select at a later date. Your scores are kept on file for 20 years. For a fee, you can request a transcript at a later date.

The pamphlet *What Your CLEP Score Means*, which you will receive with your exam score, gives detailed information about interpreting your scores. A copy of the pamphlet is in the appendix of this Guide. A brief explanation appears below.

About CLEP

How CLEP Scores Are Computed

In order to reach a total score on your exam, two calculations are performed.

First, your "raw score" is calculated. This is the number of questions you answer correctly. Your raw score is increased by one point for each question you answer correctly, and no points are gained or lost when you do not answer a question or answer it incorrectly.

Second, your raw score is converted into a "scaled score" by a statistical process called *equating*. Equating maintains the consistency of standards for test scores over time by adjusting for slight differences in difficulty between test forms. This ensures that your score does not depend on the specific test form you took or how well others did on the same form. Your raw score is converted to a scaled score that ranges from 20, the lowest, to 80, the highest. The final scaled score is the score that appears on your score report.

How Essays Are Scored

The College Board arranges for college English professors to score the essays written for the College Composition exam. These carefully selected college faculty members teach at two- and four-year institutions nationwide. The faculty members receive extensive training and thoroughly review the College Board scoring policies and procedures before grading the essays. Each essay is read and scored by two professors, the sum of the two scores for each essay is combined with the multiple-choice score, and the result is reported as a scaled score between 20 and 80. Although the format of the two sections is very different, both measure skills required for expository writing. Knowledge of formal grammar, sentence structure and organizational skills are necessary for the multiple-choice section, but the emphasis in the free-response section is on writing skills rather than grammar.

Optional essays for CLEP Composition Modular and the literature examinations are evaluated and scored by the colleges that require them, rather than by the College Board. If you take an optional essay, it will be sent to the institution you designate when you take the test. If you did not designate a score recipient institution when you took an optional essay, you may still select one as long as you notify CLEP within 18 months of taking the exam. Copies of essays are not held beyond 18 months or after they have been sent to an institution.

American Literature

Description of the Examination

The American Literature examination covers material that is usually taught in a semester survey course (or the equivalent) at the college level. It deals with the prose and poetry written in the United States from colonial times to the present. It is primarily a test of knowledge about literary works — their content, their background, and their authors — but also requires an ability to interpret poetry, fiction, and nonfiction prose, as well as a familiarity with the terminology used by literary critics and historians. The examination emphasizes fiction and poetry and deals to a lesser degree with the essay, drama, and autobiography.

In both coverage and approach, the examination resembles the chronologically organized survey of American literature offered by many colleges. It assumes that candidates have read widely and developed an appreciation of American literature, know the basic literary periods, and have a sense of the historical development of American literature.

The test contains approximately 100 questions to be answered in 90 minutes. Some of these are pretest questions that will not be scored. Any time candidates spend on tutorials and providing personal information is in addition to the actual testing time.

An optional essay section can be taken in addition to the multiple-choice test. The essay section requires that two essays be written during a total time of 90 minutes. For the first essay, a common theme in American literature and a list of major American authors are provided. Candidates are asked to write a well-organized essay discussing the way that theme is handled in works by any two of those authors. For the second essay, candidates are asked to respond to one of two topics — one requiring analysis of a poem, the other requiring analysis of a prose excerpt. In each case, the specific poem or prose excerpt is provided and questions are offered for guidance.

Candidates are expected to write well-organized essays in clear and precise prose. The essay section is graded by faculty at the institution that requests it and is still administered in paper-and-pencil format. There is an additional fee for taking this section, payable to the institution that administers the exam.

Knowledge and Skills Required

Questions on the American Literature examination require candidates to demonstrate one or more of the following abilities in the approximate proportions indicated.

45%-60%   **Knowledge of particular literary works, including:**
- Authors
- Characters
- Plots
- Setting
- Style
- Themes

25%-40%   **Ability to understand and interpret:**
- Short poems
- Excerpts from long poems
- Excerpts from prose works

10%-15%   **Knowledge of:**
- The historical and social settings of specific works
- Relations between literary works

- Relations of specific works to literary traditions
- Influences on authors

5%-10% **Familiarity with:**
- Critical terms
- Verse forms
- Literary devices

The subject matter of the American Literature examination is drawn from the following chronological periods. The percentages indicate the approximate percentage of exam questions from each period.

15% **The Colonial and Early National Period (Beginnings-1830)**

25% **The Romantic Period (1830-1870)**

20% **The Period of Realism and Naturalism (1870-1910)**

25% **The Modernist Period (1910-1945)**

15% **The Contemporary Period (1945-Present)**

SAMPLE TEST

1. *"Does this safari guarantee I come back alive?"* The reply: *"We guarantee nothing!"*

   What literary device best describes this quote?

   A. Foreshadowing

   B. Call-back

   C. Science fiction

   D. Cliffhanger

   E. Epilogue

2. *Moby Dick's* **Ishmael is an example of what?**

   A. Antagonist

   B. Raconteur

   C. Deus ex Machina

   D. Red herring

   E. Prolepsis

3. **What were two major characteristics of the first American literature?**

   A. Vengefulness and arrogance

   B. Oral delivery and reverence for the land

   C. Maudlin and self-pitying egocentrism

   D. Bellicosity and derision

   E. Satire and humor

4. **"Assonance" describes:**

   A. rhyming poetry

   B. repetition of a letter or sound at the beginning of close words

   C. a piece of literature with a clear metaphorical meaning.

   D. a clue used to deceive the reader

   E. repetition of internal vowel sounds

American Literature

5. **Which of the following best describes a parable?**

   A. A short, entertaining account of some happening, usually using talking animals as characters

   B. A slow, sad song or poem expressing lamentation

   C. An extended narrative work expressing universal truths regarding domestic life

   D. A short, simple story of a familiar occurrence, from which a moral or religious lesson may be drawn

   E. An oral telling passed down through generations

6. *"Whirl up, Sea-*
   Whirl your pointed pines,
   Splash your great pines
   On our rocks,
   Hurl your green over us-
   Cover us with your pools of fir."

   What is the title of the above poem?

   A. "Gulls" by William Carlos Williams

   B. "Nature is what we see" by Emily Dickinson

   C. "Oread" by Hilda "H.D." Doolittle

   D. "A Clear Midnight" by Walt Whitman

   E. "April Rain Song" by Langston Hughes

7. **Which of these sentences best describes the poem?**

   A. A metaphor, comparing the sea and a forest

   B. A parable, warning of the dangers inherent in nature

   C. A ballad, exploring the beauty of creation

   D. A dirge, a lamentation on something that was lost

   E. A satire, parodying florid prose styles

8. **The second and third lines contain an example of what poetic device?**

   A. A slant rhyme

   B. An epistrophe

   C. A stanza

   D. A muse

   E. An assonance

American Literature

9. **What is an untrue statement about theme in literature?**

   A. It is the central idea of a literary work

   B. All aspects of a work (plot, characters, etc.) should contribute to the theme in some way

   C. It is always stated directly in the text

   D. It can be inferred through close analysis of the text

   E. It is often open to interpretation

10. **Jack Kerouac was credited with giving a voice to which cultural movement?**

    A. Hipsters

    B. Generation X

    C. Pacifist and conscientious objectors

    D. The Beat Generation

    E. Hippy culture

11. *"The thousand injuries of Fortunato I had borne as best I could, but when he ventured on insult I vowed revenge."*

    This quote begins what famous short story?

    A. Murders in the Rue Morgue

    B. A Sound of Thunder

    C. The Cask of Amontillado

    D. An Occurrence at Owl Creek Bridge

    E. The Story of an Hour

12. **Arthur Miller's *The Crucible* parallels which historical event?**

    A. The Cold War

    B. The fall of the Berlin Wall

    C. Sen. McCarthy's House un-American Activities Committee hearings

    D. The Persian Gulf War

    E. The Great Depression

American Literature

13. In *The Scarlet Letter*, Hester Prynne must wear the titular letter after she is found guilty of...

    A. Murder

    B. Theft

    C. Prostitution

    D. Adultery

    E. Witchcraft

14. Who wrote "A Good Man is Hard to Find"?

    A. Ernest Hemingway

    B. Nathaniel Hawthorne

    C. John Updike

    D. Flannery O'Connor

    E. Zora Neal Hurston

15. Neil Simon won the Pulitzer Prize for which play?

    A. Biloxi Blues

    B. The Sunshine Boys

    C. Brighton Beach Memoirs

    D. Lost in Yonkers

    E. The Odd Couple

16. Which of the following novels features an African American protagonist?

    A. The Invisible Man

    B. Gone With the Wind

    C. To Kill a Mockingbird

    D. The Age of Innocence

    E. A Good Man is Hard To Find

17. In Mark Twain's *Adventures of Huckleberry Finn*, what is the name of Huckleberry's primary traveling companion?

    A. Boo

    B. Jim

    C. Tom

    D. George

    E. Pap

18. "Prolepsis" is another term for what literary device?

    A. Flash-forward

    B. Frame story

    C. MacGuffin

    D. Comic relief

    E. Protagonist

American Literature

19. **The title of *To Kill a Mockingbird* refers to:**

    A. a Biblical passage.

    B. a poem by Robert Burns

    C. a line spoken in the novel by Atticus Finch.

    D. a Shakespearian sonnet.

    E. a Southern proverb.

20. **"Mark Twain" was the pen name of which author?**

    A. August Wilson

    B. Samuel Clemens

    C. Horace Greeley

    D. Nathaniel Hawthorne

    E. Thomas Paine

21. *so much depends*
    upon

    a red wheel
    barrow

    glazed with rain
    water

    beside the white
    chickens.

    Who authored the above poem?

    A. Walt Whitman

    B. William Carlos Williams

    C. Robert Frost

    D. Wallace Stevens

    E. Emily Dickinson

22. **The poem's curious format makes use of what poetic technique?**

    A. Free verse

    B. Slant

    C. Enjambment

    D. Metaphor

    E. Haiku

American Literature

23. **This poem is a prime example of what literary movement?**

    A. Imagism

    B. Realism

    C. Avant-garde

    D. Absurdism

    E. Post-modernism

24. **Ezra Pound is also famous for which poetry collection?**

    A. The Waste Land

    B. Ripostes

    C. Four Quartets

    D. Absalom, Absalom

    E. A Further Range

25. **What occurs at the end of John Steinbeck's *Of Mice and Men*?**

    A. Lenny runs away from home, leaving George morose

    B. George is acquitted of all charges after a lengthy legal battle

    C. George shoots Lenny to spare him a painful lynching

    D. Candy dies, leaving George a sizable inheritance

    E. The farm becomes insolvent, leaving the ranch hands unemployed

26. **The short story collection *The Things They Carried* depicts what war?**

    A. The Civil War

    B. World War II

    C. The Korean War

    D. The Vietnam War

    E. World War I

27. **Raymond Chandler is best known for his work in what literary genre?**

    A. Science fiction

    B. Historical fiction

    C. Mystery

    D. Horror

    E. Magical realism

28. **American colonial writers were primarily:**

    A. naturalists

    B. romanticists

    C. neoclassicists

    D. realists

    E. atheists

American Literature

29. Herman Melville's *Moby Dick* is an example of what literary movement?

A. Romanticism

B. Americanism

C. Magical Realism

D. Neoclassicism

E. Allegory

30. Mark Twain's *Adventures of Tom Sawyer* takes places during which period in American history?

A. Antebellum South

B. Manifest Destiny

C. The Civil War

D. Reconstruction

E. Jim Crow

31. Who is the protagonist of Ernest Hemingway's *For Whom the Bell Tolls?*

A. Tom Joad

B. Robert Jordan

C. Santiago

D. Nick Carraway

E. Jake Barnes

32. Which elements are least applicable to all types of poetry?

A. Setting and audience

B. Theme and tone

C. Pattern and diction

D. Diction and rhyme scheme

E. Plot and historicity

33. What was an early alternative title for *The Great Gatsby*?

A. Trimalchio in West Egg

B. The Spectacular Gatsby

C. The Star-Spangled Banner

D. Satyricon

E. Citizen Gatsby

34. Which short story was not written by William Faulkner?

A. Red Leaves

B. Dry September

C. Uncle Willy

D. To Build a Fire

E. Barn Burning

American Literature

35. Which play by Eugene O'Neill did not win the Pulitzer Prize for Drama?

    A. The Iceman Cometh

    B. Anna Christie

    C. Long Day's Journey Into Night

    D. Beyond the Horizon

    E. Strange Interlude

36. Who is the protagonist of Zora Neale Hurston's *Their Eyes Were Watching God*?

    A. Tituba

    B. Janie Crawford

    C. Calpurnia

    D. Maude Atkinson

    E. Phoebe Watson

37. In *The Glass Menagerie*, which character possesses the titular collection?

    A. Amanda

    B. Laura

    C. Blanche

    D. Steven

    E. Stella

38. e. e. Cummings was best known for writing poetry in what style?

    A. Romantic

    B. Absurdist

    C. Elegy

    D. Pastoral

    E. Avant-Garde

39. *"I'll tell you God's truth." His right hand suddenly ordered divine retribution to stand by. "I am the son of some wealthy people in the middle-west--all dead now. I was brought up in America but educated at Oxford because all my ancestors have been educated there for many years. It is a family tradition."*

    Which American literary character describes himself with the above quote?

    A. Atticus Finch

    B. Rabbit Angstrom

    C. Jay Gatsby

    D. Ignatius Reilley

    E. Philip Marlowe

40. What occurs at the end of Richard Wright's *Native Son*?

    A. Bigger escapes the city with the help of his brother, Buddy.

    B. Bigger defends himself in court, and his fate is left ambiguous.

    C. Jack betrays Bigger to the police.

    D. Bigger is convicted of murder, eventually accepting his fate.

    E. Bigger's gang is killed in a firefight, leaving him the only survivor.

41. Which author wrote *A Raisin in the Sun*?

    A. Ida B. Wells

    B. Lorraine Hansbury

    C. Langston Hughes

    D. Richard Wright

    E. Toi Derracotte

42. Which Native American author wrote *House Made of Dawn*?

    A. N. Scott Momaday

    B. Sherman Alexie

    C. Louise Erdrich

    D. Clarence Alexander

    E. Sandra Birdsell

43. What autobiographical event does Kurt Vonnegut describe in his novel, *Slaughterhouse-Five*?

    A. His mother's suicide

    B. The sinking of the USS Indianapolis

    C. The bombing of Dresden

    D. His time publishing short stories in Playboy Magazine

    E. His addiction to morphine

44. *"By now, pull in your ladder road behind you*
    And put a sign up CLOSED to all but me.
    Then make yourself at home. The only field
    Now left's no bigger than a harness gall.
    First there's the children's house of make-believe,
    Some shattered dishes underneath a pine,
    The plaything's in the playhouse of the children.
    Weep for what little things could make them glad.
    Then for the house that is no more a house,
    But only a belilaced cellar hole,
    Now slowly closing like a dent in dough.
    This was no playhouse but a house in earnest.

The excerpt is written in what meter?

A. Iambic pentameter

B. Free

C. Enjambed

D. Quantitative

E. Pyrrhic

45. Who wrote the above excerpt?

A. Walt Whitman

B. Henry David Thoreau

C. Robert Frost

D. Joyce Carol Oates

E. Wallace Stevens

46. What does the author think about the "children's playhouse" mentioned in the excerpt?

A. It's a real, physical location, now destroyed by the ravages of time.

B. It was a flight of fancy, now gone because the children have matured.

C. It was a lie, and it is important to understand it as such.

D. It was imagined, but the joy the children felt there made it real.

E. It was a poor substitution for a real house.

47. *"My father brought to conversations a cavernous capacity for caring that dismayed strangers."*

What poetic device does this quote display?

A. Assonance

B. Unreliable narrator

C. Censure

D. Alliteration

E. Hyperbole

48. O. Henry's works are known for what two features?

A. Witty narration and twist endings

B. Nature imagery and social themes

C. Neoclassical prose and extensive dialogue

D. Poetic interludes and political allegory

E. Tragic characters and abrupt conclusions

American Literature

49. Which poem contains the line *"I have measured out my life in coffee spoons"*?

    A. "Song of Myself" by Walt Whitman

    B. "The Love Song of J. Alfred Prufrock" by T. S. Eliot

    C. "Middle Passage" by Robert Hayden

    D. "To My Dear and Loving Husband" by Ann Bradstreet

    E. "Memories of West Street and Lepke" by Robert Lowell

50. Which of these writers is not associated with the Southern Gothic style?

    A. Harry Crews

    B. Cormac McCarthy

    C. Erskine Caldwell

    D. Harriet Beecher Stowe

    E. William Faulkner

51. Studs Terkel is primarily remembered as a chronicler of…

    A. Race relations and the Civil Rights movement

    B. Oral histories of the common man

    C. The rise of political parties in the United States

    D. Governmental corruption in Chicago

    E. Sports culture in the American Midwest.

52. What is a "red herring"?

    A. An attack on someone's character

    B. A piece of information that misleads the reader

    C. A fallacious argument

    D. An objective for a character to fulfill

    E. A primary antagonist

53. What is the setting of the novel, *Native Son*?

    A. The Bronx

    B. Atlanta, Georgia

    C. Chicago's South Side

    D. Pre-Civil War Mississippi

    E. The Cherokee Indian Reservation

American Literature

54. *In Medias Res* describes a story that:

   A. ends suddenly

   B. ends somber note

   C. is written in the present tense

   D. begins in the middle of a sequence of events

   E. is very old

55. Theodore Dreiser is best associated with which American city?

   A. St. Louis

   B. Chicago

   C. Boston

   D. New York

   E. Philadelphia

56. In *The Old Man and the Sea*, the protagonist struggles with what kind of fish?

   A. Swordfish

   B. Shark

   C. Marlin

   D. Musky

   E. Sailfish

57. "The New Colossus" by Emma Lazarus is an example of what type of poetic form?

   A. Iambic pentameter

   B. Free verse

   C. Allegory

   D. Ballad

   E. Sonnet

58. What is the name of the foreign-born harpooner Ishmael befriends in *Moby Dick*?

   A. Pequod

   B. Kokovoko

   C. Queequeg

   D. Starbuck

   E. Santiago

59. *The Piano Lesson* is part of August Wilson's:

   A. Pittsburgh Cycle

   B. Millennium Trilogy

   C. Roots Saga

   D. Chicago Trilogy

   E. Pulitzer Plays

American Literature

60. What was the name of the fictional county in which William Faulkner set many of his works?

A. Lafayette

B. Hannibal

C. Yoknapatawpha

D. Arkham

E. Flathead

61. Booker T. Washington's autobiography, *Up From Slavery*, contains a speech he'd written containing what primary message?

A. African American social equality will be accomplished by any means necessary.

B. The economic factors behind slavery have proven insurmountable.

C. Blacks must reconnect with their African roots.

D. White and black Americans must work together to develop commercial and industrial opportunities for both communities.

E. Until white Americans accept the reality of their privileged position, no progress can be made.

62. What American orator was noted for both their staunch abolitionism and support of women's rights?

A. Frederick Douglass

B. Ida B. Wells

C. Langston Hughes

D. Dred Scott

E. Margaret Mitchell

63. Charles W. Chestnutt's *The House Behind the Cedars* deals with what central theme?

A. Woman's suffrage and emancipation

B. Race relations in the post-Civil War South

C. The role of religion in American colonial society

D. Class immobility for the working poor

E. The grieving process after losing a loved one

American Literature

64. **Which of these stories is considered an early piece of American feminist literature?**

    A. The Yellow Wallpaper

    B. The Lottery

    C. A Good Man is Hard to Find

    D. Where Are You Going, Where Have You Been?

    E. I Know Why the Caged Bird Sings

65. **In Mark Twain's *Adventures of Huckleberry Finn*, the King and the Duke are:**

    A. slave owners

    B. confidence men

    C. aristocrats

    D. boat workers

    E. tradesmen

66. ***A Raisin in the Sun* gets its title from what poem?**

    A. A Dream Deferred

    B. I Know Why The Caged Bird Sings

    C. Dreams

    D. from Citizen, I

    E. A Negro Love Song

67. *"They were hungry, and they were fierce. And they had hoped to find a home, and they found only hatred. Okies--the owners hated them because the owners knew they were soft and the Okies strong, that they were fed and the Okies hungry; and perhaps the owners had heard from their grandfathers how easy it is to steal land from a soft man if you are fierce and hungry and armed. The owners hated them."*

    Which novel contains the above passage?

    A. A Farewell to Arms

    B. Absalom, Absalom

    C. Oil!

    D. The Grapes of Wrath

    E. The Adventures of Augie March

68. **Which novel exposed the horrid working conditions of Chicago meat packers?**

    A. Upton Sinclair's *The Jungle*

    B. Mike Royko's *Boss*

    C. Langston Hughes's *Not Without Laughter*

    D. Carl Sandburg's *The People, Yes*

    E. Theodore Dreiser's *An American Tragedy*

69. **Which Upton Sinclair novel became highly controversial for its motel sex scene?**

    A. The Jungle

    B. The Brass Check

    C. Sylvia

    D. Oil!

    E. Between Two Worlds

70. **Which Revolutionary era work was directly inspired by Thomas Paine's *Common Sense*?**

    A. Benjamin Franklin's "The Way to Wealth"

    B. John Adams's autobiography

    C. The Declaration of Independence

    D. Freneau's "On the Causes of Political Degeneracy"

    E. Crevecoeur's *Letters from an American Farmer*

71. **Which of Edgar Allen Poe's short stories is considered to be the first popular piece of detective fiction?**

    A. The Mystery of Marie Roget

    B. Murders in the Rue Morgue

    C. The Purloined Letter

    D. The Fall of the House of Usher

    E. The Tell-Tale Heart

72. **Mark Twain's *Adventures of Tom Sawyer* takes place in what fictional town?**

    A. St. Petersburg

    B. Hannibal

    C. Arkham

    D. Joliet

    E. Springfield

73. **"Climax" describes what part of a story?**

    A. The ending

    B. The falling action

    C. The point of highest tension

    D. The resolution

    E. The call to action

74. **What was the "unpardonable sin" committed by Ethan Brand in Nathaniel Hawthorn's short story?**

    A. Loss of faith in a Christian God

    B. Murder

    C. The hubris of setting oneself above God

    D. To value intellect over brotherhood

    E. Any sin committed without repentance

75. **Which of these authors achieved great success with an abolitionist novel?**

    A. Harriet Beecher Stowe

    B. Louisa May Alcott

    C. Sarah Orne Jewett

    D. Rebecca Harding Davis

    E. Mary Wilkins Freeman

76. **Which of the following is not a characteristic of a fable?**

    A. Animals that talk and feel like humans

    B. Happy solutions to human dilemmas

    C. Teaches a moral or standard for behavior

    D. Illustrates specific people or groups without directly naming them

    E. Passed down orally from generation to generation

77. **In Henry James's *Daisy Miller*, the title character dies as a result of:**

    A. suicide, specifically by ingesting poison

    B. tuberculosis, contracted while sailing

    C. "Roman Fever", caught after spending a night in the Colosseum

    D. complications during the birth of her son

    E. a beating she receives from Winterbourne

78. **"I would prefer not to" is a common refrain from what literary character?**

    A. Nick Carraway

    B. Bartleby

    C. Ethan Brand

    D. Tom Sawyer

    E. Bigger Thomas

79. **"So it goes" is a phrase repeated often in which novel?**

    A. Slaughterhouse-Five

    B. A Confederacy of Dunces

    C. The Old Man and the Sea

    D. East of Eden

    E. The Road

American Literature

80. **Which literary movement is noted for its early exploration of the inner lives of women and female desires?**

    A. Romantic

    B. Weird

    C. Gothic

    D. Realist

    E. Neoclassical

81. ***The Grapes of Wrath* is a powerful indictment of the Great Depression, focusing its most aggressive critique on:**

    A. illegal immigrants who took jobs away from American farmers

    B. the greed of the upper class, specifically bankers

    C. Roosevelt's New Deal, which failed spectacularly

    D. religious institutions that exploited a desperate working class

    E. irresponsible Wall Street moneylenders

82. **Who wrote *How I Learned to Drive?***

    A. Tony Kushner

    B. Paula Vogel

    C. August Wilson

    D. Amy Freed

    E. David Lyndsay-Abaire

83. **Which colonial American author did not write in an autobiographical style?**

    A. Edward Taylor

    B. Benjamin Franklin

    C. Samson Occom

    D. Mary Rowlandson

    E. Elizabeth Ashbridge

84. ***The Great Gatsby* was written as a satire and critique of what era in American history?**

    A. The Roaring 20s

    B. The Red Scare

    C. Manifest Destiny

    D. The New Deal

    E. The Great Depression

85. **Truman Capote was strongly identified with what social scene?**

    A. Working class laborers

    B. New York social elite

    C. East coast academia

    D. Far left political intelligentsia

    E. Religious scholars

86. **H. P. Lovecraft became a seminal figure in which literary subgenre?**

    A. Gothic fiction

    B. High fantasy

    C. Hardboiled mystery

    D. Weird fiction

    E. Political satire

87. **William S. Borroughs was considered a major voice for which artistic movement?**

    A. Postmodern

    B. Horror

    C. Surreal

    D. Modern

    E. Pop

88. **Margaret Mitchell's *Gone with the Wind* ends with:**

    A. Scarlett selling the homestead to pay her debts

    B. Rhett abandoning Scarlett

    C. Scarlett's daughter dying of fever, leaving her in mourning

    D. Rhett and Scarlett marry

    E. the Civil War's cessation, leaving the family hopeful

89. **Which term best describes the form of the following poetic excerpt?**

    Because I could not stop for Death -
    He kindly stopped for me -
    The Carriage held but just Ourselves -
    And Immortality.

    We slowly drove - He knew no haste
    And I had put away
    My labor and my leisure too,
    For His Civility -

    We passed the School, where Children strove
    At Recess - in the Ring -
    We passed the Fields of Gazing Grain -
    We passed the Setting Sun –

    A. Ballad

    B. Lyrical

    C. Gothic

    D. Rhyming

    E. Imagist

90. **Who wrote the above poem?**

    A. Harriet Beecher Stowe

    B. Edgar Allen Poe

    C. Emily Dickinson

    D. Sylvia Plath

    E. Mabel Loomis Todd

91. **The poem characterizes Death using what poetic technique?**

    A. Allegory

    B. Metaphor

    C. Personification

    D. Simile

    E. Synecdoche

92. **Tim O'Brien is most famous for which short story collection?**

    A. The Things They Carried

    B. The Good War

    C. The Guns of August

    D. The Rising Sun

    E. The Golden Apples

93. **Which is the best definition of *vers libre*?**

    A. Poetry that consists of an unaccented syllable followed by an accented one

    B. Short lyrical poetry with an instructive purpose

    C. Poetry that does not have a uniform pattern of rhythm

    D. Poetry that tells a story and has a plot

    E. Overly romantic or sentimental prose

94. ***Deus ex Machina* occurs in a story that:**

    A. is short

    B. continues after the main characters have died

    C. is religious in tone

    D. is resolved by new forces not introduced earlier in the story

    E. is overly complicated

95. **What becomes of the titular item in John Steinbeck's *The Pearl*?**

    A. It is sold off, bringing much wealth to the family

    B. It is stolen by trackers who pursue Kino over the mountains

    C. It is lost when a large wave shakes Kino's boat

    D. It is thrown back into the sea after the death of Kino's son

    E. It is smashed to dust by Kino's wife, Juana

96. **"Satire" describes:**

    A. broad comedy

    B. intensely political literature

    C. humor intended to critique

    D. an ironic turn of events

    E. esoteric writing

97. **Which of the following is the best definition of imagism?**

    A. A poetic style that makes use of florid prose and universal themes

    B. A movement in poetry characterized by precise images, free verse, and suggestion over complete statement

    C. A counter-movement in literature rejecting postmodern surrealism

    D. A style of prose that focuses largely on the divinity of nature

    E. A satirical kind of poetry that lampooned the inscrutable style of the intellectual elite

98. **What is "sprung rhythm"?**

    A. Rhythm designed to mimic natural speech

    B. Meter consisting of five-syllable poetic feet

    C. Poetry that suggests a musical cadence

    D. Avant-garde rhythm, in a strange meter

    E. Exuberant rhythm designed to suggest joy

99. *"Sing we for love and idleness,*
    Naught else is worth the having.

    Though I have been in many a land,
    There is naught else in living.

    And I would rather have my sweet,
    Though rose-leaves die of grieving,

    Than do high deeds in Hungary
    To pass all men's believing."

    What is the main message of this poem, Ezra Pound's "An Immortality"?

    A. Though love is nice, it cannot last.

    B. You must travel the world to find what makes you happy.

    C. Great deeds make a man immortal.

    D. Love is all that matters in life.

    E. In the end, all things are forgotten.

100. **What is the rhyme scheme of this poem?**

    A. abcbdbeb

    B. aabbccdd

    C. ababcdcd

    D. abcbabcb

    E. ababcdcd

American Literature

ANSWER KEY

Question Number	Correct Answer	Your Answer	Question Number	Correct Answer	Your Answer	Question Number	Correct Answer	Your Answer
1	A		36	B		71	B	
2	B		37	B		72	A	
3	C		38	E		73	C	
4	E		39	C		74	D	
5	D		40	D		75	A	
6	C		41	B		76	B	
7	A		42	A		77	C	
8	B		43	C		78	B	
9	C		44	A		79	A	
10	D		45	C		80	C	
11	C		46	D		81	B	
12	C		47	D		82	B	
13	D		48	A		83	A	
14	D		49	B		84	A	
15	D		50	D		85	B	
16	A		51	B		86	D	
17	B		52	B		87	A	
18	A		53	C		88	B	
19	C		54	D		89	B	
20	B		55	B		90	C	
21	B		56	C		91	C	
22	C		57	E		92	A	
23	A		58	C		93	C	
24	B		59	A		94	D	
25	C		60	C		95	D	
26	D		61	D		96	C	
27	C		62	A		97	B	
28	C		63	B		98	A	
29	A		64	A		99	B	
30	A		65	B		100	A	
31	B		66	A				
32	A		67	D				
33	A		68	A				
34	D		69	D				
35	A		70	C				

Analyzing and Interpreting Literature

Description of the Examination

The Analyzing and Interpreting Literature examination covers material usually taught in a general undergraduate course in literature. Although the examination does not require familiarity with specific works, it does assume that candidates have read widely and perceptively in poetry, drama, fiction and nonfiction. The questions are based on passages supplied in the test. These passages have been selected so that no previous experience with them is required to answer questions. The passages are taken primarily from American and British literature.

The examination contains approximately 80 multiple-choice questions to be answered in 98 minutes. Some of these are pretest questions that will not be scored. Any time candidates spend taking tutorials and providing personal information is additional to actual testing time.

An optional essay section can be taken in addition to the multiple-choice test. The essay section requires that two essays be written during a total time of 90 minutes. For the first essay, candidates are asked to analyze a short poem. For the second essay, candidates are asked to apply a generalization about literature (such as the function of a theme or a technique) to a novel, short story, or play that they have read.

Knowledge and Skills Required

Questions on the Analyzing and Interpreting Literature examination require candidates to demonstrate the following abilities.

- Ability to read prose, poetry, and drama with understanding
- Ability to analyze the elements of a literary passage and to respond to nuances of meaning, tone, imagery and style
- Ability to interpret metaphors, to recognize rhetorical and stylistics devices, to perceive relationships between parts and wholes, and to grasp a speaker's or author's attitudes
- Familiarity with the basic terminology used to discuss literary texts

The examination emphasizes comprehensions, interpretation and analysis of literary works. A specific knowledge of historical context (authors and movements) is not required, but a broad knowledge of literature gained through reading widely and a familiarity of basic literary terminology is assumed. The following outline indicates the relative emphasis given to the various types of literature and the periods from which the passages are taken. The approximate percentage of exam questions per classification is noted within each main category.

Genre
35% - 45%   **Poetry**
35% - 45%   **Prose (fiction & nonfiction)**
15% - 30%   **Drama**

National Tradition
50% - 65%   **British Literature**
30% - 45%   **American Literature**
5% - 15%   **Works in Translation**

Period
3% - 7%   **Classical & pre-Renaissance**
20% - 30%   **Renaissance & 17th Century**
35% - 45%   **18th & 19th Centuries**
25% - 35%   **20th & 21st Centuries**

Analyzing and Interpreting Literature

CLEP Practice Exam: Analyzing and Interpreting Literature

INSTRUCTIONS

This exam gives passages from known writings (fiction, poems, non-fiction/history, biographies, drama and more) over the past five hundred years. While the student taking the exam is not expected to have read the material or have familiarity with the passage prior to the exam, the test taker is expected to have the knowledge of an undergraduate English and writing class.

TIP: As the writing changes and the time periods change, it's important for a student to note the author and time period as that may assist in answering questions by either eliminating unlikely answers or allow the student to recall items about the author.

At the end of the test passages and answers, there is an answer key and a "rationale" key for each question. Take the test without referencing these guides. For questions that you guess the answers or get wrong, the rationale is provided to help you see how test makers frame answers to questions or explain pieces of information with which you are unfamiliar.

There are 80 questions on this particular practice test, and the CLEP also uses around 80 for the credit exam. As with the CLEP exam, the passages are taken primarily from American and British Literature - though at least once question, just as in the actual exam, is taken from another area of literature. Within the questions of the CLEP, the mixture of genre types falls typically almost 80-90% between poetry and prose (both fiction and non-fiction within the prose selections) and the remaining on drama. The entire test is balanced between three main eras - Renaissance/17th Century, 18th/19th Century, as well as 10th/21st Century; in the past, there is a slightly heavier emphasis on 18th/19th work, and usually there is one passage from the Classical/pre-Renaissance period.

The CLEP allows 98 minutes to take the exam of approximately 80 questions. Time yourself during the exam, but as you practice, focus more attention on accurately answering questions as the total number of correct answers impacts your score, not how many you skip or get wrong. If you skip any questions, make sure that you also skip that line on the answer sheet - or you may spend a lot of time erasing and redoing your answer key.

These passages do not actually appear on the CLEP exam, but are meant to show how the exam is written and the various range of questions, answers, and key knowledge points required in order to pass the CLEP exam. Read each question carefully and provide the best answer choice. Good luck.

Analyzing and Interpreting Literature

SAMPLE TEST

PASSAGE 1
(Prose fiction, American, 21st century)

Mornings, he likes to sit in his new leather chair by his new living room window, looking out across the rooftops and chimney pots, the clotheslines and telegraph lines and office towers. It's the first time Manhattan, from high above, hasn't crushed him with desire. On the contrary the view makes him feel smug. All those people down there, striving, hustling, pushing, shoving, busting to get what Willie's already got. In spades. He lights a cigarette, blows a jet of smoke against the window. Suckers.
~J.R. Moehriger, 2012 p120

1. The subject in this passage is:

   A. a character, and seems to be the lead of the story

   B. a supporting character

   C. someone with an attitude of a criminal

   D. female

   E. has been poor his whole life

2. What kind of description is the author providing of this scene?

   A. Backstory of the character

   B. A characterization of what the character is like

   C. A narrative, with the end of the selection giving thoughts in the first person

   D. The unreliable narrative about a character

   E. The author is using a persuasive argument

3. What types of words are "striving, hustling, pushing, shoving, bustling"?

   A. Adjectives

   B. Adverbs

   C. Nouns

   D. Gerunds

   E. Verbs

26

4. If you had to explain the phrase "crushed him" in the paragraph above and context of the paragraph, what would be the best appropriate explanation?

   A. The city sustained him with all the opportunity available.

   B. The city called to him to be part of its life.

   C. The city complimented him for everything he has achieved.

   D. The city had energized him to get what he felt he deserved.

   E. The city smothered him with all its offerings.

5. The author portrays the attitude of the character toward the people on the street below as:

   A. condescending

   B. sarcastic

   C. affectionate

   D. tolerant

   E. encouraged

PASSAGE 2
(Poetry, American, 19th century)

There is no frigate like a book
To take us lands away,
Nor any coursers like a page
Of prancing poetry;
This traverse may the poorest take
Without oppress of toll;
How frugal is the chariot
That bears the human soul!
~Emily Dickinson (1830-1886)

6. Authors use particular literary structures for descriptions. What best explains the one that Emily Dickinson employs in this poem?

   A. A literary allegory

   B. Personification

   C. Idioms

   D. Similes

   E. Flashbacks

7. How many types of transport types does the author incorporate?

   A. Two

   B. Three

   C. Four

   D. Five

   E. None

8. If the words 'frigate, coursers, and chariot' were replaced with synonyms, what would the best choice of the following options include?

   A. Train, car, carriage
   B. Train, horse, carriage
   C. Ship, car, carriage
   D. Ship, car, train
   E. Ship, horse, carriage

9. Which of the following descriptions more closely describes the author's intended meaning of poem?

   A. Difficulties at work
   B. The importance of books
   C. Confessions for the soul
   D. Poverty makes things difficult
   E. Describing modes of transportation

10. There are very descriptive and strong feelings conveyed by the poet. Which of the following is not a feeling that this poem expresses?

    A. Enjoyment of reading
    B. Excitement of where reading can take you
    C. Encouragement to get others to read
    D. Fascination with topics in books
    E. Discouragement for new readers

11. What is a good paraphrase of "To take us lands away" that Ms. Dickinson writes in this poem?

    A. War makes it unsafe to travel, so we can just read about places.
    B. Poems will drive us to save our souls.
    C. Books can engage us to see new things.
    D. Authors can show us how to go on vacation.
    E. It shows poems are short and fun.

PASSAGE 3
(Poetry, British, 17th century)

Since brass, nor stone, nor earth, nor boundless sea,
But sad mortality o'ersways their power,
How with this rage shall beauty hold a plea,
Whose action is no stronger than a flower? (line 4)
O how shall summer's honey breath hold out
Against the wrackful siege of batt'ring days,
When rocks impregnable are not so stout,
Nor gates of steel so strong, but Time decays? (line 8)
O fearful meditation! where, alack,
Shall Time's best jewel from Time's chest lie hid?
Or what strong hand can hold his swift foot back?
Or who his spoil of beauty can forbid? (line 12)
O none, unless this miracle have might,
That in black ink my love may still shine bright.

~William Shakespeare, 1609

12. **In line four, what is the strength of a flower describing?**

    A. Beauty (beauty line above)

    B. Time

    C. Summer's honey breath

    D. Strong hand

    E. Meditation

13. **The first line of the poem tries to explain _____.**

    A. that there are a lot of things discussed in the poem.

    B. that the strongest natural things are no match for beauty.

    C. where you can find love.

    D. what the author went through to write this poem.

    E. that prayer can solve any problems.

14. **"Black ink" references what in the last line?**

    A. Written poems

    B. Street signs

    C. Black diamonds

    D. Summer flowers dying

    E. Graffiti

15. **The main idea of this poem is describing all of the following except:**

    A. hope

    B. time, aging and death overthrow beauty

    C. marriage

    D. things that time cannot destroy

    E. the author's victory

16. **Shakespeare creates emotions in this poem, and expresses all of the following except:**

    A. rage

    B. defeat

    C. love

    D. devotion

    E. mortality

Analyzing and Interpreting Literature

PASSAGE 4
(Prose non-fiction, American, 20th century)

When rays of light pass through a prism, they undergo a change of direction: they are always deflected away from the refractive edge. It is possible to conceive an assembly of prisms whose refractive surfaces progressively become more nearly parallel to each other towards the middle: light rays passing through the outer prisms will undergo the greatest amount of refraction, with consequent deflection of their path towards the center, whereas the middle prism with its two parallel surfaces causes no deflection at all. When a beam of parallel rays passes through these prisms, the rays are all deflected towards the axis and converge at one point. Rays emerging from a point are also deflected by the prisms that they converge. A lens can be conceived as consisting of a large number of such prisms placed close up against one another, so that their surfaces merge into a continuous spherical surface. A lens of this kind, which collects the rays and concentrates them at one point, is called a convergent lens. Since it is thicker in the middle than at the edge, it is known as a convex lens.

In the case of a concave lens, which is thinner in the middle than at the edge, similar considerations show that all rays diverge from the center. Hence such a lens is called a divergent lens. After undergoing refraction, parallel rays appear to come from one point, while rays remerging from a point will, after passing through the lens, appear to emerge from another point. Lenses have surfaces in the same direction but having a different radii of curvature, these are known as meniscus lenses and are used more particularly in spectacles.
~The Way Things Work, ©1963

17. According to the passage above, light rays hit convex mirror and:

   A. the rays pass straight through

   B. the rays bounce only straight back to the light source

   C. bend together to cross at a single point on the other side

   D. are refracted to open outward on the other side

   E. are reflected outward at angles back toward the light source

18. Light rays hit a concave surface. As the passage explains, light:

   A. travels through the prism's surface, angling together to a point

   B. moves in the same direction but has a different radii of curvature

   C. the light merges to a point on the continuous spherical surface

   D. is always reflected away from the refractive edge

   E. experiences no deflection

19. Spectacles use meniscus lenses, which are explained by the author that these lenses are:

   A. flat

   B. concave lenses

   C. convex lenses

   D. round on both sides of the lens, meaning they have double refraction

   E. always convergent lenses

PASSAGE 5
(Prose fiction, British, 18th century)

There is likewise another diversion, which is only shown before the Emperor and Empress, and first minister, upon particular occasions. The Emperor lays on a table three fine silken threads of six inches long. One is blue, the other red, and the third green. These threads are proposed as prizes for those persons whom the Emperor hath a mind to distinguish by a peculiar mark of his favor. The ceremony is performed in his Majesty's great chamber of state; where the candidates are to undergo a trial of dexterity very different from the former, and such as I have not observed the least resemblance of in any other country of the old or the new world. The Emperor holds a stick in his hands, both ends parallel to the horizon, while the candidates, advancing one by one, sometimes leap over the stick, sometimes creep under it backwards and forwards several times, according as the stick is advanced or depressed. Sometimes the Emperor holds one end of the stick, and his first minister holds the other; sometimes the minister has it entirely to himself. Whoever performs his part with most agility, and holds out the longest in *leaping* and *creeping,* is rewarded with the blue-colored silk; the red is given to the next, and the green is given to the third, which they all wear girt twice round the middle; and you see few great persons about this court who are not adorned with one of these girdles.
~Jonathan Swift, 1704

20. The stick game described by the author in this passage is an allusion to what?

   A. Jumping to the tune of the Emperor's (his boss') direction

   B. Baseball

   C. War games

   D. A circus

   E. Tennis

21. Why are the silk threads highly valued?

   A. Silk is a common material.

   B. Green is the Empress' favorite color.

   C. People don't give gifts very often.

   D. Silk was very expensive in the 1700s, when the story was written.

   E. All great persons wear silk.

22. Using the information only in the passage, are the colors of the silk threads significant?

   A. Yes, because they are royal colors.

   B. Yes, because they represent places of winners.

   C. No, because everyone has them.

   D. No, because hardly everyone has them.

   E. You cannot determine from the passage if the colors are important.

PASSAGE 6
(Prose non-fiction, 20th century)

On the other hand, however, we have no intention whatever of maintaining such a foolish and doctrinaire thesis as that the spirit of capitalism could only have arisen as the result of certain effects of Reformation, or even that of capitalism as an economic system is a creation of the Reformation. In itself, the fact that certain important forms of capitalistic business organizations are known to be considerably older than the Reformation is a sufficient refutation of such a claim. On the contrary, we only wish to ascertain whether and to what extent religious forces have taken part in the qualitative formation and the quantitative expansion of that spirit over the world. Furthermore, what concrete aspects of our capitalistic culture can be traced to them. In the view of the tremendous confusion of interdependent influences between the material basis, the forms of social and political organization, and the ideas current in the time of Reformation, we can only proceed by investigating whether and at what points certain correlations between forms of religious belief and practical ethics can be worked out. At the same time, we shall as far as possible clarify the manner and the general direction which, by virtue of those relationships, the religious movements have influenced development of material culture. Only when this has been determined with reasonable accuracy can the attempt be made to estimate to what extent the historical development of modern culture can be attributed to those religious forces and to what extent others.
~Max Weber, 1904

23. Capitalism is what type of system according to this passage?

   A. Democratic

   B. Economic

   C. Religious

   D. Cultural

   E. Expansionist

24. When the author compares capitalism to the Reformation, what were the main ideas of the Reformation?

   A. Democratic

   B. Economic

   C. Religious

   D. Cultural

   E. Expansionist

Analyzing and Interpreting Literature

25. What word or phrase originating at least in part in the above passage best describes the goal or target of capitalism?

    A. Ethics based

    B. Culture driven

    C. Historical application

    D. Material accumulation

    E. Force of nature

26. From the passage above, which of the following phrases best describes the author's attitude toward capitalism?

    A. The author approves of capitalism if it involves religion.

    B. The author approves of capitalism when it is driven by "qualification expansion of spirit".

    C. The author disapproves of capitalism when it involves modern culture.

    D. The author disapproves of capitalism when Reformation is involved.

    E. The author disapproves of capitalism but wants to investigate why it is wrong.

PASSAGE 7
(Prose non-fiction, 20th century)

I'd like to say here, that I wasn't the only important one. I was part of a family, just like all of my brothers and sisters. The whole community was important. We used to discuss many of the community's problems together, especially when someone was ill and we couldn't buy medicine, because we were getting poorer and poorer. We'd start discussing and heaping insults on the rich who'd made us suffer for so long. It was about then I began learning about politics. I tried to talk to people who could help me sort my ideas out. I wanted to know what the world was like on the other side. I knew the *finca*, I knew the *Altiplano*. But what I didn't know was about the other problems of the Indians in Guatemala. I didn't know the problems the other groups had to holding onto their land. I knew there were lots of other Indians in other parts of the country, because I'd been meeting them in the *finca* since I was a child, but though we all worked together, we didn't know any of the names of the towns they came from, or how they lived, or what they ate. We just imagined that they were like us.
~Rigoberta Menchu, Nobel Peace Prize Winner 1992

27. From the context of the passage, what is a *finca*?

    A. A farm

    B. A village or town

    C. A mountain range

    D. A house

    E. It cannot be determined

28. The author is telling a story about her own life. What is this kind of document called?

    A. Autobiography

    B. Mystery

    C. Biography

    D. Narrative

    E. Romance

29. Given the information in the passage, the author most likely worked as:

    A. a washer woman

    B. a seamstress

    C. a farmer

    D. a teacher

    E. it cannot be determined from the passage

30. The author describes who is the most important. She defines it as:

    A. herself

    B. her family

    C. her community

    D. the rich people that employed them

    E. the *finca*

PASSAGE 8
(Poetry, British, 18th century)

Tyger! Tyger! burning bright
In the forests of the night,
What immortal hand or eye
Could frame thy fearful symmetry?

In what distant deeps or skies
Burnt the fire of thine eyes?
On what wings dare he aspire?
What the hand dare seize the flame?

And what shoulder, & what art,
Could twist the sinews of they heart?
And when thy heart began to beat,
What dread hand? & what dread feet?
~Excerpt, William Blake, 1794

31. Which of the topics below is this best description of the poem's main idea?

    A. Strength, as sinews of the heart are strong.

    B. Creationism, and the author asks what immortal being created the tiger.

    C. Flying, because it talks about wings.

    D. Fire, with references to flames and burning forests.

    E. Love, describing the heart and how it beats.

Analyzing and Interpreting Literature

32. **Sinews, in the third stanza, can be best compared to:**

    A. thread

    B. a cage

    C. rope

    D. heart strings or emotions

    E. burnt fire, from the second stanza

33. **Another phrase for "deeps or skies" that would fit in this poem could be:**

    A. caves or planes

    B. trees or forests

    C. seas or air

    D. waves or wind

    E. oceans or lakes

34. **What is personified in the poem?**

    A. A lion

    B. Birds

    C. Candle

    D. A tiger

    E. The sky

35. **In line 7 of this poem, what word below most nearly means "aspire"?**

    A. Soar

    B. Plunge

    C. Scheme

    D. Travel

    E. Admire

36. **The poet, William Blake, uses all of the following literary tools to convey his message, except:**

    A. metaphors

    B. rhymed couplets

    C. personification

    D. symbols

    E. lyrics

PASSAGE 9
(Prose fiction, British, 19th century)

"Without their visits you cannot hope to shun the path I tread. Expect the first tomorrow night, when the bell tolls One. Expect the second on the next night at the same hour. The third, upon the next night, when the last stroke of Twelve has ceased to vibrate Look to see me no more; and look that, for your own sake, you remember what has passed between us!"

It walked backward from him; and at every step it took, the window raised itself a little, so that, when the apparition reached it, it was wide open.

35

Analyzing and Interpreting Literature

Scrooge closed the window, and examined the door by which the Ghost had entered. It was double-locked, as he had locked it with his own hands, and the bolts were undisturbed. Scrooge tried to say "Humbug!" but stopped at the first syllable. And being, from the emotion he had undergone, or the fatigues of the day, or his glimpse of the invisible world, or the dull conversation of the Ghost, or the lateness of the hour, much in need of repose, he went straight to bed, without undressing, and fell asleep on the instant.
~Charles Dickens, 1843

37. What quality of the Ghost is the most likely trait that Scrooge dislikes the most?

    A. The Ghost's old fashioned speech bothers Scrooge the most.

    B. The authoritative nature the Ghost takes with Scrooge is the quality disliked the most.

    C. The fact that the Ghost could break into his house is the trait that Scrooge dislikes.

    D. The Ghost is taller than Scrooge, and that bothers him.

    E. Scrooge dislikes that his bedtime was later than usual.

38. The way Scrooge's reaction to the Ghost is portrayed could mean that according to this passage that Scrooge is:

    A. tired

    B. angry

    C. looking for excuses

    D. forgetful

    E. planning to ignore the Ghost

39. The Ghost's remarks listed in the passage can most likely be inferred as:

    A. a warning to Scrooge

    B. the Ghost is talking to the wrong person

    C. Scrooge is hallucinating

    D. a friend was playing a joke on Scrooge

    E. no inference can be made

40. Scrooge's reaction to the Ghost in this passage leads a reader to conclude:

    A. that Scrooge was just conducting a normal nighttime house-check

    B. when the Ghost comes back for him, Scrooge will go along willingly

    C. even wealthy people like Scrooge lock their houses

    D. that Scrooge does not believe in the supernatural

    E. Scrooge is likely overcome with exhaustion

41. The tone of the passage is intended to:

    A. serve as a warning to Scrooge about things he will be shown

    B. serve as a reminder that Scrooge has forgotten appointments

    C. describe how disconcerted Scrooge felt after the warning was given by the Ghost

    D. provide backstory

    E. explain why Scrooge is so stingy

PASSAGE 10
(Prose, non-fiction, American, 20th century)

Using the Constitution to protect the minorities, James Madison's system of government is largely an attempt to divide and frustrate the majority. Madison envisioned a political system with the broadest possible power base. For example, he rejected the common belief that a democracy could work only in a very small area, arguing that it could succeed in a large country like the United States. A large population spread over a huge area would make it very difficult to force a permanent majority. Such a society would probably divide into varied and fluctuating minorities, making a long lasting majority unlikely. Instead, majorities would be created out of combinations of competing minorities. Thus, any majority would be temporary, and new ones would be elusive. This system, political scientists now term *pluralism*.
~Leon Baradat, 1973

42. According to the passage, what is pluralism?

    A. Majorities created out of combinations of competing minorities

    B. A new division of political science

    C. A political system with the smallest possible power base

    D. A new name for a permanent majority

    E. The system for democracy to work in a very small area

43. The Constitution mentioned in the first line, in context to this passage, is:

   A. James Madison's document to create a permanent majority

   B. the document creating the United States

   C. the personality of James Madison

   D. the health of the majority

   E. instructions on how to create combinations of competing minorities

44. The passage talks about democracy. Another phrase for a democracy is:

   A. the rule of a few over the many

   B. the welfare state

   C. a laissez-faire economy

   D. an elected government system

   E. an appointed government by a monarch

PASSAGE 11
(Prose non-fiction, British, 21st century)

American black music was going along like an express train. But white cats, after Buddy Holly died and Eddie Cochran died, and Elvis was in the army gone wonky, white American music when I arrived was the Beach Boys and Bobby Vee. They were still stuck in the past. The past was six months ago; it wasn't a long time. But things changed. The Beatles were the milestone. And then they got stuck inside their own cage. "The Fab Four." Hence, eventually, you got the Monkees, all this ersatz stuff. But I think there was a vacuum somewhere in white American music at the time.

When we first got to America and to LA, there was a lot of Beach Boys on the radio, which was pretty funny to us - it was before *Pet Sounds* - it was hot rod songs and surfing songs, pretty lousily played, familiar Chuck Berry licks going on. "Round, round get around / I get around," I though that was brilliant. It was later on, but Brian Wilson had something. "In My Room," "Don't Worry Baby." I was more interested in their B-sides, the ones he slipped in. There was no particular correlation with what we were doing so I could just listen to it on another level. I thought these are very well-constructed songs. I took easily to the pop song idiom. I'd always listened to everything, and America opened it all out - we were hearing records there that were regional hits. We'd get to know local labels and local acts, which is how we came across "Time Is on My Side," in LA, sung by Irma Thomas. It was a B-side of a record on Imperial Records, a label we'd have been aware of because it was independent and successful and based on Sunset Strip.
~Keith Richards, 2010

Analyzing and Interpreting Literature

45. **How many unique singers versus unique bands, respectively, are named in the passage above?**

    A. Seven and Four

    B. Six and Three

    C. Eight and Three

    D. Seven and Three

    E. Six and Four

46. **How many songs are referenced in the passage above?**

    A. Two

    B. Three

    C. Four

    D. Five

    E. Six

47. **In the context of the selection's first paragraph, how many white singers or groups are named by the author?**

    A. Four

    B. Five

    C. Three

    D. Seven

    E. One

48. **Given what the author says about the B-side of a record, which of the following sentences is closest to the author's opinion?**

    A. The B-side had more creativity and outlets for artists, making it unique.

    B. It was called the B-side because the songs were generally not as good.

    C. Only regional labels took the time to press B-sides.

    D. The B-side was where all the surfing songs were recorded.

    E. Labels were strict about the contents of the B-sides.

49. **When the author talks about the Beatles and says "they got stuck inside their own cage," the author most likely means:**

    A. that the Beatles always had to hide in hotels because they were so famous

    B. that successful musical groups could never enjoy the publicity

    C. that the Beatles were trapped on planes all the time

    D. that the Beatles couldn't perform with anyone outside of their four members

    E. the Beatles outgrew the standard previously set for successful musicians, and were trapped in their own famous sensation

50. Given the descriptions in the passage, the author's profession is likely:

    A. a roadie

    B. a writer

    C. a singer

    D. a photographer

    E. a teacher

PASSAGE 12
(Prose fiction, British, pre-Ren/Classic)

A marvelous case is it to hear, either the warnings of that he should have voided, or the tokens of that he could not void. For the self night next before his death, the lord Stanley sent a trusty secret messenger unto him at midnight in all the haste, requiring him to rise and ride away with him, for he was disposed utterly no longer to bide; he had so fearful a dream, in which him thought that a boar with his tusks so raced them both by the heads, that the blood ran about both their shoulders. And forasmuch as the protector gave the boar for his cognizance, this dream made so fearful an impression in his heart, that he was thoroughly determined no longer to tarry, but had his horse ready, if the lord Hastings would go with him to ride so far yet the same night, that they should be out of danger ere day. Ay, good lord, quoth the lord Hastings to this messenger, leaneth my lord thy master so much to such trifles, and hath such faith in dreams, which either his own fear fantasieth or do rise in the night's rest by reason of his day thoughts? Tell him it is plain witchcraft to believe in such dreams; which if they were tokens of things to come, why thinketh he not that we might be as likely to make them true by our going if we were caught and brought back (as friends fail fleers), for then had the boar a cause likely to race us with his tusks, as folk that fled for some falsehood, wherefore either is there no peril (nor none there is indeed), or if any be, it is rather in going than biding. And if we should, needs cost, fall in peril one way or other, yet had I livelier that men should see it were by other men's falsehood, than think it were either our own fault or faint heart. And therefore go to thy master, man, and commend me to him, and pray him be merry and have no fear: for I ensure him I am as sure of the man that he wotteth of, as I am of my own hand. God send grace, sir, quoth the messenger, and went his way.

~Sir Thomas More, 1513

51. The beginning of the passage is describing what?

    A. An injury sustained by the main character

    B. A rider that is trying to escape injury

    C. The main character's dream

    D. A witch's story

    E. The boar that the character will grill for dinner

52. **What is the cautionary message that the rider gets when he reaches his destination?**

    A. Dreams are witchcraft if you believe in them.

    B. Dreams can come true if you believe in them.

    C. God sends His grace.

    D. Those faint of heart do not have dreams.

    E. Men cannot fall for other men's falsehoods.

53. **Did the main character in this passage believe he could out run bad visions?**

    A. No, the passage makes it clear you always get what's coming in a dream.

    B. No, dreams mean nothing, so the main character didn't pay any attention to it.

    C. Yes, it was possible to escape bad visions on horseback.

    D. Yes, the main character thought dancing would rid himself of bad dreams.

    E. There is nothing in the passage that assists in answering this question.

PASSAGE 13
(Prose fiction, British, 19th century)

To go into solitude, a man needs to retire as much from his chamber as from society. I am not solitary whilst I read and write, though nobody is with me. But if a man would be alone, let him look at the stars. The rays that come from those heavenly worlds, will separate between him and what he touches. One might think the atmosphere was made transparent with this design, to give man, in the heavenly bodies, the perpetual presence of the sublime. Seen in the streets of cities, how great they are! If the stars should appear one night in a thousand years, how would men believe and adore; and preserve for many generations the remembrance of the city of God which had been shown! But every night come out these envoys of beauty, and light the universe with their admonishing smile.
~Ralph Waldo Emerson, 1836

54. **The first two lines of this passage imply what?**

    A. A man is never alone.

    B. A man is always alone.

    C. A man can be alone if he turns his back on people.

    D. A man can be alone if he makes his mind focus.

    E. A man who is lonely is considered alone.

55. Given the whole passage, which of the following is the best match for the author's opinion about nature?

   A. The author prefers to seek to retire in his chamber.

   B. The author sees wonder in the sky and beauty at night.

   C. The author does not like trees.

   D. The author can only see stars one night in a thousand years.

   E. You cannot tell the author's opinion from this passage.

56. The phrase "light the universe with their admonishing smile" is an example of:

   A. personification

   B. a simile

   C. a metaphor

   D. irony

   E. satire

PASSAGE 14
(Poetry, American, 20th century)

Two roads diverged in a yellow wood,
And sorry I could not travel both
And be one traveler, long I stood
And looked down one as far as I could
To where it bent in the undergrowth;

Then took the other, as just as fair,
And having perhaps the better claim,
Because it was grassy and wanted wear;
Though as for that the passing there
Had worn them really about the same,

And both that morning equally lay
In leaves no step had trodden black.
Oh, I kept the first for another day!
Yet knowing how way leads on to way,
I doubted if I should ever come back.

I shall be telling this with a sigh
Somewhere ages and ages hence:
Two roads diverged in a wood, and I—
I took the one less traveled by,
And that has made all the difference.
~Robert Frost, 1920

57. When the author uses the phrase "wanted wear" in the third stanza, what does that mean?

   A. It looked just as fair as the other path.

   B. It was not as inviting.

   C. The path didn't go the same way as the other one.

   D. The path was less traveled than the other one.

   E. You cannot determine what the author means.

58. The author says that he "took the one less traveled by"; what does that mean?

    A. The other path looked like it was used more.

    B. He did the right thing when others chose the wrong one.

    C. He took the one on the left.

    D. He took the one on the right.

    E. It cannot be determined what the author meant by this short selection.

59. What is another way the author states his path was the "one less traveled by"?

    A. "both that morning equally lay"

    B. "no step had trodden black"

    C. "Somewhere ages and ages hence"

    D. "bent in the undergrowth"

    E. "having perhaps the better claim"

60. What does the author imply since he took the path less traveled?

    A. He has run into fewer people that try to bully him into doing what they want.

    B. Life is tougher getting to see the light.

    C. He was sorry he didn't chose to go the more well-trod path.

    D. He didn't make as much money as the people that took the other path.

    E. His life is better for choosing to go his own path.

PASSAGE 15
(Prose fiction, American, 20th century)

His memories of the Boston Society Contralto were nebulous and musical. She was a lady who sang, sang, sang in the music room on their house on Washington Square - sometimes with guests all about her, the men with their arms folded, balanced breathlessly on the edges of sofas, the women with their hands in their laps, occasionally making little whispers to the men and always clapping very briskly and uttering cooing cries after each song - and she often sang to Anthony alone, in Italian or French or in a strange and terrible dialect...

Oblivious to the social system, he lived for a while alone and unsought in a high room in Beck Hall - a slim dark boy of medium height with a shy sensitive mouth. His allowance was more than liberal. He laid the foundations for a library by purchasing from a wandering bibliophile first editions of Swinburne, Meredith, and Hardy, and a yellowed

illegible autograph letter of Keats', finding later he had been amazingly overcharged. He became an exquisite dandy, amassed a rather pathetic collection of silk pajamas, brocaded dressing-gowns, and neckties too flamboyant to wear; in this secret finery he would parade before a mirror in his room or lie stretched in satin along the window-seat looking down on the yard and realizing this clamor, breathless and immediate, in which it seemed he was to never have a part.
~F. Scott Fitzgerald, 1922

61. Based on the information in the passage, what is a "contralto"?

    A. A Boston slang term for a high class man

    B. A female singer

    C. A female dancer

    D. A writer

    E. A bibliophile

62. Based on the information in the passage, an "exquisite dandy" refers to:

    A. the first editions of the books listed in the passage

    B. anyone who wears silk pajamas

    C. a gentleman who has money to spend extravagantly on fancy things

    D. someone who likes to parade before a mirror

    E. someone who likes candy

63. Why would the social system be important in this reading selection?

    A. Richer classes don't have dandies, so the main character can't be dandy.

    B. A rich man with no female friends is called a dandy, and it helps explain the story.

    C. The character seems ostracized and that can't happen in certain social classes.

    D. If the main character was of a lower class, he could not live the life described.

    E. No one lives the luxurious life described in the passage.

PASSAGE 16
(Prose fiction, American, 20th century)

These are morning matters, pictures you dream as the final wave heaves you up on the sand in the bright light and drying air. You remember pressure, and a curved sleep you rested against, soft, like a scallop in its shell. But the air hardens your skin; you stand; you leave the lighted shore to explore some dim headland, and soon you're lost in the leafy interior, intent, remembering nothing.

I still think of that old tomcat, mornings, when I wake. Things are tamer now; I sleep with the window shut. The cats and our rites are gone and my life is changed, but the memory remains of something powerful playing over me. I wake expectant, hoping to see a new thing. If I'm lucky I might be jogged awake by a strange bird call. I dress in a hurry,

imagining the yard flapping with auks, or flamingos. This morning it was a wood duck, down at the creek. It flew away.
~Annie Dillard, 1975 Pulitzer Prize

64. The tone of the selection is:

   A. reflective

   B. indulgent

   C. indifferent

   D. dishonest

   E. ironic

65. The author uses _____ to describe the setting.

   A. personification

   B. ambivalence

   C. satire

   D. allusion

   E. clichés

66. The phrase, "like a scallop in its shell" is an example of:

   A. irony

   B. a simile

   C. a metaphor

   D. personification

   E. euphemism

67. The author describes many of her feelings and situations by focusing the conversation on animals. Based on the information in the passage, one reason could be:

   A. animals are comforting and relax the reader

   B. birds are flighty and the center of her story

   C. the setting of this story is a farm

   D. the lead character doesn't have many human friends

   E. it is the backstory of how animals and nature are always present in the character's life

68. The phrase "the air hardens your skin" within the context of the passage most likely refers to what?

   A. The morning air woke the character up from dreaming.

   B. The scallop shell bed the character sleeps in has opened.

   C. The air dries out the character's skin.

   D. The coldness of the room turns off the brain of the character.

   E. The air turns the character's skin cold when the cat leaves the bed.

Analyzing and Interpreting Literature

PASSAGE 17
(Drama, British, 16th century/classical)

Bernardo : Welcome, Horatio: welcome, good Marcellus.
Marcellus : What, has this thing appear'd again to-night?
Bernardo : I have seen nothing.
Marcellus : Horatio says 'tis but our fantasy,
And will not let belief take hold of him
Touching this dreaded sight, twice seen of us:
Therefore I have entreated him along
With us to watch the minutes of this night;
That if again this apparition come,
He may approve our eyes and speak to it.
Horatio : Tush, tush, 'twill not appear.
Bernardo : Sit down awhile;
And let us once again assail your ears,
That are so fortified against our story
What we have two nights seen.
      ~William Shakespeare, 1599-1602

69. The three men in the play can be said, in this passage:

   A. to disagree about a ghost that was seen

   B. to disagree that two days ago they saw people meeting "twice seen of us"

   C. that Horatio and Bernardo are trying to persuade Marcellus they saw something

   D. that Horatio and Marcellus are trying to persuade Bernardo they saw something

   E. to meet for a drink for "fortification"

70. When Marcellus speaks of "approving our eyes", what is he saying?

   A. Marcellus and Bernardo need glasses.

   B. Bernardo didn't believe what Marcellus saw.

   C. Horatio believes what Marcellus saw.

   D. Horatio should see what Bernardo and Marcellus saw.

   E. Marcellus should believe what Bernardo saw.

71. When Bernardo says "once again assail your ears", what does he mean?

   A. He wants to repeat himself to Marcellus to make him believe him.

   B. He wants to repeat himself to Horatio to make him believe him.

   C. He wants to repeat himself to help all three of them believe the story.

   D. He wants Marcellus and Horatio to poke holes in the story.

   E. None of these are the meaning of that phrase in the passage.

72. **In the context of the passage, entreated means:**

    A. invited

    B. engaged

    C. demanded

    D. refused

    E. ignored

PASSAGE 18
(Drama, American, 20th century)

Edmund : That's foolishness. You know it's only a bad cold.
Mary : Yes, of course, I know that!
Edmund : But listen, Mama. I want you to promise me that even if it turns out to be something worse, you'll know I'll soon be alright again, anyway, and don't worry yourself sick, and you'll keep on taking care of yourself -
Mary : I won't listen when you talk so silly! There's absolutely no reason to talk as if you expect something dreadful! Of course, I promise you I give you my sacred word of honor! But I suppose you're remembering I've promised before on my word of honor.
Edmund : No!
Mary : I'm not blaming you, dear. How can you help it? How can any one of us forget? That's what makes it so hard - for all of us. We can't forget.
Edmund : Mama! Stop it!
Mary : All right, dear. I didn't beam to be so gloomy. Don't mind me. Here. Let me feel your head. Why, it's nice and cool. You certainly don't have any fever now.
~Eugene O'Neill, 1955

73. **It can be said that this passage of the drama:**

    A. puts American dream against American nightmare

    B. describes the normal American family

    C. portrays Americans in a very resilient fashion

    D. was likely written during a war so obviously has negative overtones

    E. has the mother remembering the death of another child

74. **Mary changes the direction of the conversation by:**

    A. stopping Edmund from talking by taking his temperature

    B. making Edmund feel badly about the death of his brother

    C. walking out of the room

    D. tucking the covers up to his chin

    E. ignoring him

75. **This portion of the play is a:**

    A. monologue

    B. dialogue

    C. soliloquy

    D. entendre

    E. stichomythia

76. Mary talks about Edmund expecting something dreadful. What's a literary term for that action?

   A. Oxymoron

   B. Dissonance

   C. Foreshadowing

   D. Stream of consciousness

   E. Understatement

PASSAGE 19
(Prose fiction, British, 18th century)

But though thus largely indebted to fortune, to nature she had yet greater obligation: her form was elegant, her heart was liberal. Her countenance announced the intelligence of her mind, her complexion varied with every emotion of her foul, and her eyes, the heralds of her speech, now beamed with understanding and now glistened with sensibility.

For the short period of her minority, the management of her fortune and the care of her person, had by the Dean been entrusted to three guardians, among whom her own choice was to settle to her residence: but her mind, saddened by the lots of all her natural friends, coveted to regain its serenity in the quietness of the country, and in the bosom of an aged and maternal counsellor, whom she loved as her mother, and to whom she had been known from her childhood.
Fanny Burney, 1782

77. From the context of this passage, which of the following statements is the most likely to be true?

   A. The main character is poor.

   B. The main character is an orphan.

   C. The setting of the story is in England.

   D. The main character is going to live with her aunt.

   E. The main character doesn't like to live in town.

78. In the quote, "her heart was liberal", what is the author trying to express?

   A. The author implies that the main character is of loose morals.

   B. The author implies that while ladylike, she has a wild streak.

   C. The author alludes that the woman is more open than her demeanor.

   D. The author makes it clear that she is alone.

   E. The author shows how she was older than her natural friends.

Analyzing and Interpreting Literature

79. **What does the word "minority" mean in the context of the passage?**

    A. The woman in the passage is a Native American.

    B. The character is not yet an adult.

    C. The group of people in the story are members of the minority political party.

    D. The character has less money than her friends.

    E. None of the given options explain "minority" in this passage.

80. **What is another word for serenity in this passage?**

    A. Peacefulness

    B. Counsellor

    C. Bosom

    D. Rambunctiousness

    E. Prayerful

Analyzing and Interpreting Literature

ANSWER KEY

Question Number	Correct Answer	Your Answer
1	A	
2	C	
3	E	
4	D	
5	A	
6	A	
7	B	
8	E	
9	B	
10	E	
11	C	
12	A	
13	B	
14	A	
15	C	
16	B	
17	E	
18	A	
19	B	
20	A	
21	D	
22	B	
23	B	
24	C	
25	D	
26	E	
27	B	

Question Number	Correct Answer	Your Answer
28	A	
29	C	
30	C	
31	B	
32	D	
33	C	
34	D	
35	A	
36	C	
37	B	
38	C	
39	A	
40	D	
41	C	
42	A	
43	B	
44	D	
45	D	
46	C	
47	D	
48	A	
49	E	
50	C	
51	C	
52	A	
53	C	
54	D	

Question Number	Correct Answer	Your Answer
55	B	
56	A	
57	D	
58	A	
59	B	
60	E	
61	B	
62	C	
63	D	
64	A	
65	D	
66	C	
67	E	
68	A	
69	A	
70	D	
71	B	
72	A	
73	E	
74	A	
75	B	
76	C	
77	B	
78	C	
79	B	
80	A	

College Composition

Description of the Examination

The CLEP College Composition examinations assess writing skills taught in most first-year college composition courses. Those skills include analysis, argumentation, synthesis, usage, ability to recognize logical development and research. The exams cannot cover every skill (such as keeping a journal or peer editing) required in many first-year college writing courses. Candidates will, however, be expected to apply the principles and conventions used in longer writing projects to two timed writing assignments and to apply the rules of standard written English.

College Composition contains approximately 50 multiple-choice items to be answered in approximately 50 minutes and two essays to be written in 70 minutes (with 30 minutes to write the first essay and 40 minutes to read the two sources and write the second essay), for a total of approximately 120 minutes testing time. Essays must be typed on the computer.

The actual examination contains multiple-choice items and two mandatory, centrally scored essays. The essays are scored twice a month by college English faculty from throughout the country via an online scoring system. Each of the two essays is scored independently by two different readers, and the scores are then combined. This combined score is weighted approximately equally with the score from the multiple-choice section. These scores are then combined to yield the candidate's score. The resulting combined score is reported as a single score between 20 and 80. Separate scores are not reported for the multiple-choice and essay sections.

Knowledge and Skills Required

The subject matter of the College Composition examination is drawn from the following topics. The percentages next to the main topics indicate the approximate percentage of exam questions on that topic for the 50 multiple-choice items.

10% Conventions of Standard English
- measures the awareness of logical, structural and grammatical relationships within sentences. Questions relate to syntax, punctuation, concord/agreement, modifiers, active versus passive voice and additional areas

40% Revision Skills
- measures revision skills in the context of early essays, such as organization, level of detail, awareness of audience or tone, sentence variety and structure, main ideas, transitions, point of views

25% Ability to Use Source Material
- measures familiarity with basic reference and research skills via the use of reference materials, evaluation of sources, integration of resources and documentation

25% Rhetorical Analysis
- measures ability to analyze writing primarily using passage based questions reviewing appeals, tone, structure, rhetorical effects

College Composition

SAMPLE TEST

There are 50 questions that you must answer in less than 50 minutes. Then, there are essay questions that you must answer in a timed fashion: the first essay has 30 minutes and the second essay has 40 minutes to read two passages and complete and essay.

Remember, your goals for this test are those questions you answer accurately; it is not based on how many are incorrect. Take your time, and good luck.

CONVENTIONS OF STANDARD WRITTEN ENGLISH
DIRECTIONS: Read each item carefully, paying attention to the underlined portions. If there is an error, it will be underlined. Assume that elements of the sentence not underlined are correct. If there is an error, select the one underlined part and enter that letter on the answer sheet. If there is no error, choose E.

1. On a long day in October, the rain <u>fell</u> so hard that it <u>causes</u> flooding all <u>along</u> the highway, <u>bringing</u> traffic to a stop. <u>No error</u>.

   A. fell

   B. causes

   C. along

   D. bringing

   E. No error

2. <u>Their</u> attempts are almost always comical, not <u>being able</u> to move supplies without <u>loosing</u> at least one package on the <u>route</u>. <u>No error</u>.

   A. Their

   B. being able

   C. loosing

   D. route

   E. No error

3. At least two of the seven <u>defendents</u> <u>want</u> a delay, <u>saying</u> they need more time <u>to prepare</u> for trial. <u>No error</u>.

   A. defendents

   B. want

   C. saying

   D. to prepare

   E. No error

4. The surfer <u>was bit</u> by a shark, but <u>got</u> his revenge when he <u>caught</u> him and <u>ate</u> it for dinner. <u>No error</u>

   A. was bit

   B. got

   C. caught

   D. ate

   E. No error

5. A portrait of a <u>women</u> <u>had been</u> painted onto an iceberg, which was precariously <u>perched</u> on the edge of a melting <u>piece</u> of glacier. <u>No error</u>

   A. women

   B. had been

   C. perched

   D. piece

   E. No error

REVISION SKILLS

Read the following paragraph and answer the questions that follow.

   There was a steaming mist in all the hollows, and it roamed in its forlornness up the hill, like an evil spirit, seeking rest and finding none. A clammy and intensely cold mist, it made its way through the air in ripples that visibly followed and overspread one another, as the waves of an unwholesome sea might do. It was dense enough to shut out everything from the light of the coach-lamps but these its own workings, and a few yards of road; and the reek of the laboring horses steamed into it, as if they had made it at all.

6. The description of this scene gives the impression that it is:

   A. an oppressive journey.

   B. an enlightening route.

   C. a contemplative traveling discussion.

   D. an entertaining troupe making way to the next show.

   E. None of these things is true.

7. What is the main idea of this passage?

   A. Weather sets the stage in any narrative.

   B. The coach horses were not up to the task of the road.

   C. It was a dark and cold night, relatively unsuitable for travel.

   D. One of the coach-lamps was unlit, making it difficult to see.

   E. An English countryside scene is perfect for a scary setting.

8. The author's purpose is to:

   A. Inform

   B. Entertain

   C. Persuade

   D. Narrate

   E. Analyze

Read the following passage and answer the questions that follow.

Everyone called him Pop Eye. Even in those days when I was a skinny thirteen-year-old I thought he probably knew about his nickname but didn't care. His eyes were too interested in what lay up ahead to notice us barefoot kids.

He looked like someone who had seen or known great suffering and hadn't been able to forget it. His large eyes in his large head stuck out further than anyone else's - like they wanted to lave the surface of his face. They made you think of someone who can't get out the house quickly enough.

Pop Eye wore the same white linen suit every day. His trousers snagged onto hi sony knees in the sloppy heat. Some days he wore a clown's nose. His nose was already big. he didn't need that red light bulb. But for reasons we couldn't think of he wore the red nose on certain days that may have meant something to him. We never saw him smile. And on those days he wore the clowns nose you found yourself looking away because you never saw such sadness.

9. **What is the main idea of the passage?**

   A. The main character was a generally sad man, disinterested in the scene around him.

   B. The main character cannot remember the thirteen-year-old kid.

   C. The physical appearance of the main character was awkward.

   D. The main character was so poor that he only had one suit.

   E. None of these represent the main idea of the passage.

10. **From the passage, one can infer that:**

    A. Pop Eye is surrounded by family.

    B. Pop Eye works as a clown.

    C. The narrator is related to Pop Eye.

    D. Pop Eye lives a lonely life.

    E. The narrator has done well for himself.

11. What is the author's purpose in writing this passage?

   A. To entertain

   B. To narrate

   C. To describe

   D. To persuade

   E. To make demands

12. The author implies that :

   A. the main character had secret talents.

   B. the main character had great sadness.

   C. the narrator was related to the main character.

   D. the main character was generally neat and tidy.

   E. the narrator was homeless.

Read the following passage excerpted from Biography.com and choose the best answer to the questions that follow.

    A prolific artist, Austrian composer Wolfgang Mozart created a string of operas, concertos, symphonies and sonatas that profoundly shaped classical music. Over the years, Mozart aligned himself with a variety of European venues and patrons, composing hundreds of works that included sonatas, symphonies, masses, concertos and operas, marked by vivid emotion and sophisticated textures.
    During the time when he worked for Archbishop Hieronymus von Colleredo, young Mozart had the opportunity to work in several different musical genres composing symphonies, string quartets, sonatas and serenades and a few operas. He developed a passion for violin concertos producing what came to be the only five he wrote.
    In 1776, he turned his efforts toward piano concertos, culminating in the Piano Concerto Number 9 in E flat major in early 1777. In Salzburg in 1779, Wolfgang Amadeus Mozart produced a series of church works, including the Coronation Mass. He also composed another opera for Munich, Ideomeneo in 1781.

13. Who is the target audience of this passage?

   A. Artists.

   B. Austrians.

   C. Catholics.

   D. A person interested in classical music.

   E. None of these are accurate.

College Composition

14. **What is the main idea of the previous passage?**

    A. Mozart had a sister that also performed with him.

    B. Mozart's father was his promoter.

    C. The Catholic church was supportive of Mozart's talent.

    D. Many operas and other pieces were composed by Mozart before he was 25 years old.

    E. The rapid development and appreciation of Mozart's music.

15. **What is the author's purpose in writing this?**

    A. To describe

    B. To narrate

    C. To entertain

    D. To inform

    E. To argue

16. **From reading this passage, we can conclude that:**

    A. Mozart wrote several complex pieces of music at a young age.

    B. There were not many composers as young and talented as Mozart.

    C. There was a special relationship between the Catholic church and Mozart's family.

    D. There were not as many composers in Austria as other countries.

    E. None of these are accurate.

17. **Which of the following is not a musical genre?**

    A. Opera

    B. Sonnet

    C. Symphony.

    D. Concerto.

    E. Quartet.

College Composition

Read the following paragraph and answer the questions that follow.

(1) Outside, the late afternoon sun slanted down in the yard, throwing into gleaming brightness the dogwood trees that were solid masses of white blossoms against the background of new green. (2) The twins' horses were hitched in the driveway, big animals, red as their masters' hair; and around the horses' legs quarreled the pack of lean, nervous possum hounds that accompanied Stuart and Brent wherever they went. (3) A little aloof, as became and aristocrat, lay a black-spotted carriage dog, puzzle on paws, patiently waiting for the boys to go home to supper.

18. What is the main idea of this passage?

   A. The passage is describing an afternoon outdoor setting.

   B. The twins had very poised animals.

   C. Certain concessions should be made for dogs.

   D. The difficulties of travel in thick blossoming forests.

   E. None of these covey the main idea of the passage.

19. What is the author's main purpose?

   A. To inform

   B. To entertain

   C. To describe

   D. To narrate

   E. To record

20. What type of sentence is the second sentence?

   A. Simple

   B. Compound

   C. Complex

   D. Complex-Compound

   E. Dependent clause

Read the following paragraph from Wikipedia and answer the question that follows.

Isaac Newton built the first practical reflecting telescope and developed a theory of colour based on the observation that a prism decomposes white light into the many colors of the visible spectrum. He formulated an empirical law of cooling, studied the speed of sound, and introduced the notion of a Newtonian fluid. In addition to his work on calculus, as a mathematician Newton contributed to the study of power series, generalized the binomial theorem to non-integer exponents, developed a method for approximating the roots of a function, and classified most of the cubic plane curves.

21. What is the main idea of this passage?

    A. Power series is an important part of scientific discovery.

    B. Fluid engineering is about the empirical law of cooling.

    C. Through telescopes, scientists have made discoveries that have helped many people.

    D. Newton was a mathematician and a scientist.

    E. None of the above.

Read the following paragraph from *Popular Mechanics* and answer the question that follows.

We've been finding planets beyond our solar system for two decades now, but there are good reasons why it's taken so long to find the first forming world. For one thing, Stephanie Sallum says, planets spend only a brief period of their long lives in formation. Simply looking at the the odds, "it's unlikely that you'll come across a planet when it's still forming," she says.

22. The author's purpose is to

    A. Describe

    B. Inform

    C. Persuade

    D. Narrate

    E. Summarize

Read the following paragraph from National Geographic and answer the question.

So far, more than 150 countries – from Sudan to Suriname and from Kiribati to Kyrgyzstan – have outlined for United Nations negotiators just how, when, and by how much each would cut carbon dioxide over the next several decades. If an agreement is reached, it would mark the first serious global commitment to reduce the pollution that is warming the planet, souring the oceans, and causing seas to rise.

23. What type of organizational pattern is the author using?

   A. Comparison and Contrast

   B. Generalization

   C. Cause and Effect

   D. Simple Listing

   E. Analogy

Read the following paragraph from *Antiques and Fine Art* and answer the following question.

Since the colonial period, the Atlantic Ocean has operated both as a barrier between America and Europe and as a conduit for international exchanges of peoples, goods, and ideas. It spurred commerce and enterprise that was the basis for both national economic activity and personal fortune. The activities in America's great harbors and port cities also supported the nation's cultural development, prompting the rise of schools of maritime and landscape painting, as well as portraiture.

24. Which organizational pattern does the author use?

   A. Comparison and Contrast

   B. Simple Listing

   C. Cause and Effect

   D. Definition

   E. Description

Read the following quote and answer the following question.

> "I don't think about whether people will remember me or not. I've been an okay person. I've learned a lot. I've taught people a thing or two. That's what's important." – Julia Child

25. The quote primarily:

    A. describes.

    B. informs.

    C. entertains.

    D. narrates.

    E. lists.

26. Addressing someone absent or something inhuman as though present and able to respond describes a figure of speech known as:

    A. personification

    B. synecdoche

    C. metonymy

    D. apostrophe

    E. rhetorical strategy

Read the following paragraphs and answer the questions that follows.

At the end of the period, the artistic temperament of the painter undergoes a profound modification; it reflects a set of assimilated romantic ideas, expands the grandeur of classical art, and, while in the early works the love for the antique style throughout the popular subjects with inanimate edifice with the classic treatment as well as characterless, mythological subjects in the frescoes. The painter's figures assume heroic proportions, exude solemn expressions, and everything seems to come alive in a life more lush, more monumental and simple at the same time...

Overall, we find an artist's determined personality, animated by a continuous and rapid progress, the result of a clear conscience and scrupulous study fiery aspects of reality with which can be sympathized, of an intense search of technical development, the assimilation of many and beautiful expressions of art. So he states, from the beginning of his artistic activity, a teacher of exceptional importance, which rises with noble means and personal and solid, without resorting to defiant rage, the glitz, the stylism that characterize so remarkable part of the art of his time.

Serra, Luigi. Domenico Zampieri detto Il Domenichino. Rome: Casa Editrice del Bollettino d'Arte, Del Ministero Della P. Istruzione. 1909. pp11-12.

27. Where does the excerpt originate?

A. Webster's Dictionary

B. Luigi Serra

C. Domenico Zampieri

D. World Book Encyclopedia

E. Wikipedia

28. In the second paragraph, the second sentence can best be described as:

A. compound.

B. complex.

C. run-on.

D. a fragment.

E. compound-complex.

29. This, H. (2006). Food for Tomorrow? How the Scientific Discipline of Molecular Gastronomy Could Change the Way We Eat. *EMBO Reports*, 7(11), 1062-1066.

In the citation, 1062 provides what information?

A. Date printed

B. Date accessed

C. First page of reference

D. Last page of reference

E. None of these are correct

30. In the citation above, the (11) refers to:

A. the eleventh article in the magazine.

B. the eleventh article published by this author.

C. there are eleven articles on gastronomy in this issue.

D. there are eleven authors.

E. This is the eleventh issue in the series, in volume seven.

31. In the *EMBO* citation above, 7 refers to what?

A. The number of volumes this has magazine has published in 2006.

B. How many articles have discussed gastronomy in the magazine's history.

C. The seventh report for this issue.

D. Pagination.

E. Tagnemics

32. **Bernstein, M. (2002). 10 tips on writing the living Web.** *A List Apart: For People Who Make Websites, 149.* **Retrieved from http://www.alistapart.com/articles/writeliving is a citation example of a:**

    A. newspaper.

    B. book.

    C. online periodical.

    D. abstract.

    E. none of these selections are accurate.

33. **2. Weinstein, "Plato's** *Republic*,**" 452–53.**

    This is an example of:

    A. note style.

    B. duplicate style.

    C. bibliography.

    D. APA style.

    E. MLA style.

34. **Kossinets, Gueorgi, and Duncan J. Watts. "Origins of Homophily in an Evolving Social Network."** *American Journal of Sociology* **115 (2009): 405–50. Accessed February 28, 2010. doi:10.1086/599247.**

    Which style is this?

    A. MLA

    B. APA

    C. Chicago

    D. New York

    E. None of these

35. **Maxmen, Amy. "How Ebola Found Fertile Ground in Sierra Leone's Chaotic Capital." National Geographic. 27 January, 2015. Web. 16 November, 2015.**

    This is an example of what kind of citation format?

    A. MLA

    B. APA

    C. Chicago

    D. Turabian

    E. None of these

36. In the citation above, what does 27 January 2015 reference?

    A. Reference date

    B. Publication date

    C. Editing date

    D. Web upload date

    E. None of these

37. Treverton, Gregory F. "The Changed Target." *Intelligence for an Age of Terror*. Cambridge: Cambridge UP, 2009. 24-25. Print. What does print reference?

    A. Magazine article

    B. Newspaper article

    C. Printed web source

    D. Book

    E. None of these

Read the following paragraph from the *National Independent Schools Magazine* and answer the questions that follow.

   The bias against introverted students is embedded in our educational system: years of unrelenting focus on cooperative learning, thinking aloud, and talking-as-learning, with grades for class participation, required public speaking (often now as a disproportionate pedagogical focus displacing more traditional forms of scholarship and substantive mastery), and a pervasive, almost normative, value placed on being social and well liked, particularly in a large-group context. In sum, the classroom focus is now too often on "doing," in sacrifice to "thinking."

38. What is meant by the word "unrelenting" in the first sentence?

    A. Continuing

    B. Protective

    C. Pervasive

    D. Cautious

    E. Reckless

39. What is the author's tone?

    A. Aseptic

    B. Analytical

    C. Disbelieving

    D. Disapproving

    E. Scornful

40. What type of organizational pattern is the author using?

    A. Classification

    B. Explanation

    C. Comparison and Contrast

    D. Cause and Effect

    E. Entertaining

41. Who would be the intended audience of this excerpt?

    A. Politicians, for funding purposes.

    B. Social workers, for counseling purposes.

    C. Teachers, for refocusing efforts.

    D. Parents, for normative adjustments.

    E. None of these are applicable.

Read the following passage from Roll of Thunder, Hear My Cry and answer the questions that follow.

> My youngest brother paid no attention to me. Grasping more firmly his newspaper-wrapped notebook and his tin-can lunch of cornbread and oil sausages, he continued to concentrate on the dusty road. He lagged several feet behind my other brothers, Stacey and Christopher-John, and me, attempting to keep the rusty Mississippi dust from swelling with each step and drifting back upon his shiny black shoes and the cuffs of his corduroy pants by lifting each foot high before setting it gently down again. Always meticulously neat, six-year-old Little Man never allowed dirt or tears or stains to mar anything he owned. Today was no exception.
> "You keep it up and make us late for school, Mama's gonna wear you out," I threatened, pulling with exasperation at the high collar of the Sunday dress Mama had made me wear for the first day of school - as if that event were something special. It seemed to me that showing up at school all on a bright August-like October morning made for running the cool forest trails and wading barefoot in the forest pond was concession enough; Sunday clothing was asking too much. Christopher-John and Stacey were not too pleased about the clothing or school either. Only Little Man, just beginning his school career, found the prospects of both intriguing.

42. What is the meaning of the word "meticulously" in the next to last sentence in the first paragraph?

    A. Many

    B. Very

    C. Exceptionally

    D. Rarely

    E. Fairly

43. What is the overall organizational pattern used in this passage?

    A. Generalization

    B. Cause and Effect

    C. Addition

    D. Descriptive

    E. Informational

College Composition

44. What is the author's tone?

    A. Disbelieving

    B. Exasperated

    C. Informative

    D. Optimistic

    E. None of these are correct.

Read the following passage from Pride and Prejudice and answer the questions that follow.

    Mr. Bennet was so odd a mixture of quick parts, sarcastic humour, reserve, and caprice, that the experience of three-and-twenty years had been insufficient to make his wife understand his character. Her mind was less difficult to develop. She was a woman of mean understanding, little information, and uncertain temper. When she was discontented, she fancied herself nervous. The business of her life was to get her daughters married; its solace was visiting and news.

    Mr. Bennet was among the earliest of those who waited on Mr. Bingley. He had always intended to visit him, though to the last always assuring his wife that he should not go; and till the evening after the visit was paid she had no knowledge of it. It was then disclosed in the following manner. Observing his second daughter employed in trimming a hat, he suddenly addressed her with:

    "I hope Mr. Bingley will like it, Lizzy."

45. What is the overall organizational pattern of this passage?

    A. Generalization

    B. Cause and Effect

    C. Addition

    D. Summary

    E. Informational

46. What is the meaning of the phrase "uncertain temper" in the third sentence?

    A. Hot tempered

    B. Quixotic emotions

    C. Unusually morose

    D. Generally happy

    E. None of these apply

47. What is the organizational pattern of the second paragraph?

    A. Cause and Effect

    B. Classification

    C. Addition

    D. Explanation

    E. None of these things

Read the following passage from Wuthering Heights and answer the questions that follow.

Before passing the threshold, I pause to admire a quantity of grotesque carving lavished over the front, and especially about the principal door; above which, among a wilderness of crumbling griffins and shameless little boys, I detected the date '1500,' and the name 'Hareton Earnshaw.' I would have made a few comments, and requested a short history of the plane from the surly owner; but his attitude at the door appeared to demand my speedy entrance, or complete departure, and I had no desire to aggregate his impatience previous to inspecting the penetralium.

48. **What is the author's overall organizational pattern?**

    A. Classification

    B. Cause and Effect

    C. Definition

    D. Comparison and Contrast

    E. None of these things

49. **The author's tone in the passage is one of:**

    A. Inquisition

    B. Excitement

    C. Surliness

    D. Concern

    E. Impatience

50. **The most similar way to rephrase "I had no desire to aggregate his impatience" in context of the passage would be:**

    A. I wanted to keep him happy

    B. I didn't want to make him mad

    C. I didn't want to stay around

    D. I wanted him to quickly inspect the penetralium

    E. None of these are approximations

College Composition

SAMPLE TEST ESSAY 1

As a reminder, you have 30 minutes to compose your essay and type it on the computer.

Directions: Write an essay in which you discuss the extent to which you agree or disagree with the statement below. Support your discussion with specific reasons and examples from your reading, experience or observations.

Topic: *Beauty is in the eye of the beholder.*

Readers will assign scores based on a matrix, or scoring guide. Here is an example outline of how both student essays will be graded on a six point scale.

SCORE OF 6 - The 6 essay presents a thesis that is coherent and well-developed. The writer's ideas are detailed, intelligent, and thoroughly elaborated. The writer's use of language and structure is correct and meaningful.

SCORE OF 5 - The 5 essay presents a thesis and offers persuasive support. The writer's ideas are usually new, mature, and thoroughly developed. A command of language and a variety of structures are evident.

SCORE OF 4 - The 4 essay presents a thesis and frequently offers a plan of development, which is usually demonstrated. The writer offers sufficient details to achieve the purpose of the essay. There is capable use of language and varied sentence structure. Errors in sentence structure and usage don't interfere with the writer's main purpose.

SCORE OF 3 - The 3 essay gives a thesis and offers a plan of development, which is usually demonstrated. The writer gives support that leans toward generalized statements or a listing. Overall, the support in a 3 essay is neither adequate nor coherent enough to be convincing. There are errors in sentence structure and usage that frequently interfere with the writer's ability to state the purpose.

SCORE OF 2 - The 2 essay usually states a thesis. The writer offers support that may be incomplete. Simple and disconnected sentence structure is present. Mistakes in grammar and usage often thwart the writer's ability to state the purpose.

SCORE OF 1 - The 1 essay has a thesis that is pointless or poorly articulated. Support is shallow. The language is muddled and confusing. Many mistakes in grammar and usage.

SAMPLE ESSAY 2

As a reminder, you have 40 minutes to read these two passages and type your essay on the computer.

Directions: Write an essay in which you incorporate the two sources of information provided below. You must use both sources and you must use appropriate citation for both sources using the author's last name, the title or by any other means that adequately identifies it. Support your discussion with specific reasons and examples from your reading, experience or observations.

Assignment: Read the following sources carefully. Then write an essay in which you develop a position on whether people or communities express devotion differently.

Introduction: Devotion, according to Oxford's Dictionary, is "love, loyalty or enthusiasm for a person, activity, or cause."

Source 1: Shakespeare, William. *Romeo and Juliet.* England: 1595.

"But, soft! what light through yonder window breaks?

It is the east, and Juliet is the sun.
Arise, fair sun, and kill the envious moon,
Who is already sick and pale with grief,
That thou, her maid, art far more fair than she.
Be not her maid, since she is envious;
Her vestal livery is but sick and green
And none but fools do wear it; cast it off.
It is my lady, O, it is my love!
Oh, that she knew she were!"

Source 2: Heller, Joseph. "Catch 22." United States: 1961.

"What is a country? A country is a piece of land surrounded on all sides by boundaries, usually unnatural."

College Composition

ANSWER KEY

Question Number	Correct Answer	Your Answer
1	B	
2	C	
3	A	
4	A	
5	A	
6	A	
7	C	
8	D	
9	A	
10	D	
11	C	
12	B	
13	D	
14	E	
15	D	
16	A	
17	B	

Question Number	Correct Answer	Your Answer
18	A	
19	C	
20	D	
21	D	
22	B	
23	C	
24	A	
25	B	
26	A	
27	B	
28	C	
29	C	
30	E	
31	A	
32	C	
33	B	
34	C	

Question Number	Correct Answer	Your Answer
35	A	
36	B	
37	D	
38	A	
39	D	
40	D	
41	C	
42	C	
43	D	
44	B	
45	A	
46	B	
47	D	
48	E	
49	A	
50	B	

College Composition Modular

Description of the Examination

The CLEP College Composition examinations assess writing skills taught in most first-year college composition courses. Those skills include analysis, argumentation, synthesis, usage, ability to recognize logical development and research. The exams cannot cover every skill (such as keeping a journal or peer editing) required in many first-year college writing courses. Candidates will, however, be expected to apply the principles and conventions used in longer writing projects to two timed writing assignments and to apply the rules of standard written English.

College Composition contains approximately 50 multiple-choice items to be answered in approximately 50 minutes and two essays to be written in 70 minutes (with 30 minutes to write the first essay and 40 minutes to read the two sources and write the second essay), for a total of approximately 120 minutes testing time. Essays must be typed on the computer.

The actual examination contains multiple-choice items and two mandatory, centrally scored essays. The essays are scored twice a month by college English faculty from throughout the country via an online scoring system. Each of the two essays is scored independently by two different readers, and the scores are then combined. This combined score is weighted approximately equally with the score from the multiple-choice section. These scores are then combined to yield the candidate's score. The resulting combined score is reported as a single scared score between 20 and 80. Separate scores are not reported for the multiple-choice and essay sections.

The College Composition Modular exam allows institutions to administer and/or score test-takers' essays after approximately 90 multiple choice questions are completed in 90 minutes (with the two essay questions to be completed in 70 minutes to complete both essay answers), for a total of approximately 160 minutes. The knowledge and skills assessed are the same as those measured by College Composition, but the format and timing allow a more extended indirect assessment of test-takers' knowledge and skills. The percentages of exam questions on each topic are the same in the College Composition exam as well as this sample College Composition Modular sample test.

Knowledge and Skills Required

The subject matter of the College Composition examination is drawn from the following topics. The percentages next to the main topics indicate the approximate percentage of exam questions on that topic for the multiple-choice items.

10% Conventions of Standard English

- measures the awareness of logical, structural and grammatical relationships within sentences. Questions relate to syntax, punctuation, concord/agreement, modifiers, active versus passive voice and additional areas

40% Revision Skills

- measures revision skills in the context of early essays, such as organization, level of detail,

awareness of audience or tone, sentence variety and structure, main ideas, transitions, point of views
- Modular format includes questions that require sentence restructuring/word replacement to improve comprehension

25% Ability to Use Source Material
- measures familiarity with basic reference and research skills via the use of reference materials, evaluation of sources, integration of resources and documentation

25% Rhetorical Analysis
- measures ability to analyze writing primarily using passage based questions reviewing appeals, tone, structure, rhetorical effects

On the next page, the sample test begins. **There are 87 questions that you must answer in less than 90 minutes. Then, there are essay questions that you must answer in a timed fashion: the first essay has 30 minutes and the second essay has 40 minutes to read two passages and complete and essay.**

Remember, your goals for this test are those questions you answer accurately; it is not based on how many are incorrect. Take your time, and good luck.

College Composition Modular

SAMPLE TEST

CONVENTIONS OF STANDARD WRITTEN ENGLISH

DIRECTIONS: Read each item carefully, paying attention to the underlined portions. If there is an error, it will be underlined. Assume that elements of the sentence not underlined are correct. If there is an error, select the one underlined part and enter that letter on the answer sheet. If there is no error, choose E.

1. A <u>fearful</u> man, all in grey, <u>were</u> down by the river <u>standing</u> by the bunches of <u>rushes</u>. <u>No error</u>.

    A. fearful

    B. were

    C. standing

    D. rushes

    E. No error

2. When our group of <u>friends</u> goes to Italy next year, we will be <u>seeing</u> many of the <u>countries</u> famous <u>landmarks</u>. <u>No error</u>.

    A. friends

    B. seeing

    C. countries

    D. landmarks

    E. No error

3. <u>Their</u> are no walls high enough, no <u>valleys</u> deep enough, <u>to</u> keep the warriors <u>from</u> attacking the city. <u>No error</u>.

    A. Their

    B. valleys

    C. to

    D. from

    E. No error

4. <u>Whenever</u> the phone rings, the dog <u>likes</u> to run to the front door to <u>see</u> who <u>has come</u> to visit. <u>No error</u>

    A. Whenever

    B. likes

    C. see

    D. has come

    E. No error

72

5. **Every one** must pass **through** Vanity Fair in order to get to the **celestial** city and receive **their** three golden eggs. **No error**

   A. Every one

   B. through

   C. celestial

   D. their

   E. No error

6. Suffering **has been** stronger than all other teaching, and **have** taught me to understand what **your** heart **use** to be. **No error**

   A. has been

   B. have

   C. your

   D. use

   E. No error

7. The loneliest moment in **someone's** life is when they are watching **their hole** world fall apart, and all they can do is **stare** blankly. **No error**

   A. someone's

   B. their

   C. hole

   D. stare

   E. No error

8. I have not **broken** your heart - you have **broke** it; and in **breaking** it, you **have** broken mine. **No error**

   A. broken

   B. broke

   C. breaking

   D. have

   E. No error

Read the following paragraph and answer the questions that follow.

   Mr. Smith gave instructions for the painting to be hung on the wall. And then it leaped forth before his eyes: the little cottages on the river, the white clouds floating over the valley and the green of the towering mountain ranges which were seen in the distance. The painting was so vivid that it seemed almost real. Mr. Smith was now absolutely certain that the painting had been worth money.

9. From the last sentence, one can infer that:

   A. the painting was expensive.

   B. the painting was cheap.

   C. Mr. Smith was considering purchasing the painting.

   D. Mr. Smith thought the painting was too expensive and decided not to purchase it.

   E. None of these things is true.

10. What is the main idea of this passage?

   A. The painting that Mr. Smith purchased is expensive.

   B. Mr. Smith purchased a painting.

   C. Mr. Smith was pleased with the quality of the painting he had purchased.

   D. The painting depicted cottages and valleys.

   E. Mr. Smith was looking to buy some paintings.

11. The author's purpose is to:

   A. Inform

   B. Entertain

   C. Persuade

   D. Narrate

   E. Analyze

Read the following passage and answer the questions that follow.

One of the most difficult problems plaguing American education is the assessment of teachers. No one denies that teachers ought to be answerable for what they do, but what exactly does that mean? The Oxford American Dictionary defines accountability as: the obligation to give a reckoning or explanation for one's actions.

Does a student have to learn for teaching to have taken place? Historically, teaching has not been defined in this restrictive manner; the teacher was thought to be responsible for the quantity and quality of material covered and the way in which it was presented. However, some definitions of teaching now imply that students must learn in order for teaching to have taken place.

As a teacher who tries my best to keep current on all the latest teaching strategies, I believe that those teachers who do not bother even to pick up an educational journal every once in a while should be kept under close watch. There are many teachers out there who have been teaching for decades and refuse to change their ways even if research has proven that their methods are outdated and ineffective. There is no place in the profession of teaching for these types of individuals. It is time that the American educational system clean house, for the sake of our children.

12. What is the main idea of the passage?

   A. Teachers should not be answerable for what they do.

   B. Teachers who do not do their job should be fired.

   C. The author is a good teacher.

   D. Assessment of teachers is a serious problem in society today.

   E. Defining accountability.

13. From the passage, one can infer that:

    A. The author considers herself a good teacher.

    B. Poor teachers will be fired.

    C. Students have to learn for teaching to take place.

    D. The author will be fired.

    E. All of these are characteristics of fables

14. What is the author's purpose in writing the passage on the previous page?

    A. To entertain

    B. To narrate

    C. To describe

    D. To persuade

    E. To make demands

15. The author states that teacher assessment is a problem for:

    A. Elementary schools

    B. Secondary schools

    C. American education

    D. Families

    E. Teachers

Read the following passage and answer the questions that follow.

Disciplinary practices have been found to affect diverse areas of child development such as the acquisition of moral values, obedience to authority, and performance at school. Even though the dictionary has a specific definition of the word "discipline," it is still open to interpretation by people of different cultures.

There are four types of disciplinary styles: assertion of power, withdrawal of love, reasoning, and permissiveness. Assertion of power involves the use of force to discourage unwanted behavior. Withdrawal of love involves making the love of a parent conditional on a child's good behavior. Reasoning involves persuading the child to behave one way rather than another. Permissiveness involves allowing the child to do as he or she pleases and face the consequences of his/her actions.

16. Name the four types of disciplinary styles.

    A. Reasoning, power assertion, morality, and permissiveness.

    B. Morality, reasoning, permissiveness, and withdrawal of love.

    C. Withdrawal of love, permissiveness, power, and reasoning.

    D. Permissiveness, morality, reasoning, and power assertion.

    E. Explore, Inform, Entertain, Persuade.

17. What is the main idea of the previous passage?

    A. Different people have different ideas of what discipline is.

    B. Permissiveness is the most widely used disciplinary style.

    C. Most people agree on their definition of discipline.

    D. There are four disciplinary styles.

    E. Child development needs to focus on obedience to authority.

18. What is the author's purpose in writing this?

    A. To describe

    B. To narrate

    C. To entertain

    D. To inform

    E. To argue

19. From reading this passage, we can conclude that:

    A. The author is a teacher.

    B. The author has many children.

    C. The author has written a book about discipline.

    D. The author has done a lot of research on discipline.

    E. The author has at least two siblings.

20. What does the technique of reasoning involve?

    A. Persuading the child to behave in a certain way.

    B. Allowing the child to do as he/she pleases.

    C. Using force to discourage unwanted behavior.

    D. Making love conditional on good behavior.

    E. Distracting the child in order to get them to behave appropriately.

Each underlined portion of sentences 21-23 contains one or more errors in grammar, usage, mechanics, or sentence structure. Circle the choice that best corrects the error without changing the meaning of the original sentence. Choice E may repeat the underlined portion. Select the identical phrase if you find no error.

21. **Walt Whitman was famous for his composition, *Leaves of Grass*, serving as a nurse during the Civil War, and a devoted son.**

    A. *Leaves of Grass*, his service as a nurse during the Civil War, and a devoted son.

    B. composing *Leaves of Grass*, serving as a nurse during the Civil War, and being a devoted son.

    C. his composition, *Leaves of Grass*, his nursing during the Civil War, and his devotion as a son.

    D. serving as a nurse during the civil war, being a devoted son and *Leaves of Grass*.

    E. his composition, *Leaves of Grass*, serving as a nurse during the Civil War, and a devoted son.

22. **There were <u>fewer pieces</u> of evidence presented during the second trial.**

    A. fewer peaces

    B. less peaces

    C. less pieces

    D. not as many peaces

    E. fewer pieces

23. **Wally <u>groaned, "Why</u> do I have to do an oral interpretation <u>of "The Raven."</u>**

    A. groaned "Why … of 'The Raven'?"

    B. groaned "Why … of "The Raven"?

    C. groaned "Why … of "The Raven?"

    D. groaned, "Why … of "The Raven."

    E. groaned, "Why… of The Raven?"

Read the following paragraph and answer the question that follows.

Microbiology is the study of tiny organisms that can only be seen through a magnifying glass or microscope. Scientists have used microbiology to help prevent and cure certain diseases. It has also been important in the development of new and better foods.

24. What is the main idea of this passage?

   A. Microbiology has been used to prevent and cure certain diseases.

   B. Through microbiology, scientists have made discoveries that have helped many people.

   C. Microbiology is the study of tiny organisms.

   D. It is necessary to have a magnifying glass or microscope when engaged in a microbiological study.

   E. none of the above.

Read the following paragraph and answer the question that follows.

Many people insist on wearing "real" fur coats even though artificial furs have been available for over 30 years. It is cruel to torture animals just to be fashionable. Save an animal by wearing artificial fur coats instead of "real" ones.

25. The author's purpose is to

   A. Desccribe

   B. Inform

   C. Persuade

   D. Narrate

   E. Summarize

Read the following paragraph.

Plants are very versatile living organisms. They are constantly adapting to survive in their environments. Some plants have grown spines to protect themselves from herbivores. Plants that grow in cold regions grow close to the ground to avoid harsh winds.

26. What type of organizational pattern is the author using?

   A. Cause and Effect

   B. Generalization

   C. Comparison and Contrast

   D. Simple Listing

   E. Analogy

Read the following paragraph.

Rembrandt and Van Gogh were two Dutch painters. Both were from wealthy families. Both showed incredible talent at a young age. Van Gogh did not begin to paint seriously until he was twenty-seven. Rembrandt, on the other hand, had already completed many paintings by that age.

27. Which organizational pattern does the author use?

   A. Comparison and Contrast

   B. Simple Listing

   C. Cause and Effect

   D. Definition

   E. Description

Read the following paragraph.

Charles Lindbergh had no intention of becoming a pilot. He was enrolled in the University of Wisconsin until a flying lesson changed the entire course of his life. He began his career as a pilot by performing daredevil stunts at fairs

28. The author wrote this paragraph primarily to:

   A. describe

   B. inform

   C. entertain

   D. narrate

   E. analyze

29. Addressing someone absent or something inhuman as though present and able to respond describes a figure of speech known as:

   A. personification

   B. synecdoche

   C. metonymy

   D. apostrophe

   E. rhetorical strategy

Read the following paragraph and answer the questions below, selecting the best choice of the options presented.

(1) It was a cold and windy night. (2) Everyone was close around the fire in order to keep warm. (3) It was lonely for the little boy, who waited for his mother to bring him a marshmallow to toast on a stick. (4) His sister died just weeks ago and he really missed her.

30. In sentence (2), a better way to phrase "was close" could be:

   A. huddled

   B. gather

   C. stood

   D. left from

   E. none of these options are better

31. In sentence (4), the author is describing what emotion?

   A. hunger

   B. happiness

   C. coldness

   D. sadness

   E. anger

Read the following paragraph and answer the question below, selecting the best choice of the options presented.

    As she mused the pitiful vision of her mother's life laid its spell on the very quick of her being—that life of commonplace sacrifices closing in final craziness. She trembled as she heard again her mother's voice saying constantly with foolish insistence: Derevaun Seraun! Derevaun Seraun!

* [Derevaun Seraun means "The end of pleasure is pain!" (Gaelic)]

32. The following passage is written from which point of view?

   A. First person, narrator

   B. Second person, direct address

   C. Third person, omniscient

   D. First person, omniscient

   E. First person, direct address

Answer the following questions about important points when revising writing.

33. **To understand the origins of a word, one must study the:**

   A. synonyms

   B. inflections

   C. phonetics

   D. etymology

   E. epidemiology

34. **Which is the best definition for syntax?**

   A. The specific order of word choices by an author to create a particular mood or feeling in the reader

   B. Writing that explains something thoroughly

   C. The background or exposition for a short story or drama

   D. Word choices that help teach a truth or moral

   E. Proper elocution

35. **Which is the least true statement concerning an author's literary tone?**

    A. Tone is partly revealed through the selection of details.

    B. Tone is the expression of the author's attitude toward his or her subject.

    C. Tone can be expressed in a variety of ways by an author.

    D. Tone in literature corresponds to the tone of voice a speaker uses.

    E. Tone in literature is usually satiric or angry.

36. **Regarding the study of poetry, which elements are least applicable to all types of poetry?**

    A. Setting and audience

    B. Theme and tone

    C. Pattern and diction

    D. Diction and rhyme scheme

    E. Words and symbols

Read the following selection and answer the questions below, selecting the best choice of the options presented.

**There is no frigate like a book
To take us lands away,
Nor any coursers like a page
Of prancing poetry;
This traverse may the poorest take
Without oppress of toll;
How frugal is the chariot
That bears the human soul!**

37. **How many types of transport types does the author incorporate?**

    A. two

    B. three

    C. four

    D. five

    E. none

38. **If the words 'frigate, coursers, and chariot' were replaced with synonyms, what would the best choice of the following options include?**

    A. Train, car, carriage

    B. Train, horse, carriage

    C. Ship, car, carriage

    D. Ship, car, train

    E. Ship, horse, carriage

39. **What is a good paraphrase of "To take us lands away" that Ms. Dickinson writes in this poem?**

    A. War makes it unsafe to travel, so we can just read about places.

    B. Poems will drive us to save our souls.

    C. Books can engage us to see new things

    D. Authors can show us how to go on vacation.

    E. It shows poems are short and fun.

Read the following selection and answer the questions below, selecting the best choice of the options presented.

Tyger! Tyger! burning bright
In the forests of the night,
What immortal hand or eye
Could frame thy fearful symmetry? (line 4)

In what distant deeps or skies
Burnt the fire of thine eyes?
On what wings dare he aspire?
What the hand dare seize the
    flame? (line 8)

And what shoulder, & what art,
Could twist the sinews of they heart?
And when thy heart began to beat,
What dread hand? & what dread
    feet? (line 12)

40. **Sinews, in the third stanza, can be best compared to:**

    A. thread.

    B. a cage.

    C. rope.

    D. heart strings or emotions.

    E. burnt fire, from the second stanza.

41. **Another phrase for "deeps or skies" that would fit in this poem could be:**

    A. caves or planes.

    B. trees or forests.

    C. seas or air.

    D. waves or wind.

    E. oceans or lakes.

42. **In line 7 of this poem, what word below most nearly means "aspire"?**

    A. Soar.

    B. Plunge.

    C. Scheme.

    D. Travel.

    E. Admire.

Read the following selection and answer the questions below, selecting the best choice of the options presented.

These are morning matters, pictures you dream as the final wave heaves you up on the sand in the bright light and drying air. You remember pressure, and a curved sleep you rested against, soft, like a scallop in its shell. But the air hardens your skin; you stand; you leave the lighted shore to explore some dim headland, and soon you're lost in the leafy interior, intent, remembering nothing.

I still think of that old tomcat, mornings, when I wake. Things are tamer now; I sleep with the window shut. The cats and our rites are gone and my life is changed, but the memory remains of something powerful playing over me. I wake expectant, hoping to see a new thing. If I'm lucky I might be jogged awake by a strange bird call. I dress in a hurry, imagining the yard flapping with auks, or flamingos. This morning it was a wood duck, down at the creek. It flew away.

43. The phrase, "like a scallop in its shell" is an example of:

    A. an irony.

    B. a simile.

    C. a metaphor.

    D. personification.

    E. euphemism.

44. The phrase "the air hardens your skin" within the context of the passage most likely refers to what?

    A. The morning air woke the character up from dreaming.

    B. The scallop shell bed the character sleeps in has opened.

    C. The air dries out the character's skin.

    D. The coldness of the room turns off the brain of the character.

    E. The air turns the character's skin cold when the cat leaves the bed.

Read the following paragraph and answer the questions that follows.

One of the most difficult problems plaguing American education is the assessment of teachers. No one denies that teachers ought to be answerable for what they do, but what exactly does that mean? The Oxford American Dictionary defines accountability as: the obligation to give a reckoning or explanation for one's actions.

Does a student have to learn for teaching to have taken place? Historically, teaching has not been defined in this restrictive manner; the teacher was thought to be responsible for the quantity and quality of material covered and the way in which it was presented. However, some definitions of teaching now imply that students must learn in order for teaching to have taken place.

As a teacher who tries my best to keep current on all the latest teaching strategies, I believe that those teachers who do not bother even to pick up an educational journal every once in a while should be kept under close watch. There are many teachers out there who have been teaching for decades and refuse to change their ways even if research has proven that their methods are outdated and ineffective. There is no place in the profession of teaching for these types of individuals. It is time that the American educational system clean house, for the sake of our children

45. Where does the author get her definition of "accountability?"

   A. Webster's Dictionary

   B. Encyclopedia Brittanica

   C. Oxford Dictionary

   D. World Book Encyclopedia

   E. Wikipedia

46. **In the second paragraph, the second sentence can best be described as:**

   A. compound.

   B. complex.

   C. run-on.

   D. a fragment.

   E. compound-complex.

47. Taite, Richard. "Five Things to Know About Recovery from Alcohol." *Psychology Today*. Web. (https://www.psychologytoday.com/blog/ending-addiction-good/201510/five-things-know-about-recovery-alcohol-or-drugs) October 16, 2015.

   In the citation, 16 October 2015 provides what information?

   A. Date printed

   B. Date accessed

   C. Date placed on the Internet

   D. Date the last person accessed it

   E. None of these are correct

48. Nelson, MD., Lewis S et al. Addressing the Opioid Epidemic. *JAMA*. 13 October 2015; 314(14): 1453-1454.

   The (14) refers to:

   A. the fourteenth article in the magazine.

   B. the fourteenth article published by this author.

   C. there are fourteen articles on opioids in this issue.

   D. there are fourteen authors.

   E. This is the fourteenth issue in the series, in volume 314.

49. In the *JAMA* citation previously, 1454-1454 refers to what?

   A. The number of issues this has magazine has published.

   B. How many articles have discussed opioids in the magazine's history.

   C. Page numbers for this citation.

   D. Ongoing page numbers for the table of contents in this magazine.

   E. Tagnemics

50. The word 'print' at the end of a citation is a reference for:

   A. the article is from a newspaper.

   B. the article is from a book.

   C. the article is from a periodical.

   D. the article was not accessed online.

   E. none of these selections are accurate.

51. Ciottone, Gregory et al. Disaster Medicine, Second Edition. Elsevier, digital. September 24, 2015. ISBN-13: 978-0323286657

   The "et al" refers to:

   A. no hard cover copy is available.

   B. the content is digital only.

   C. this has been published in the United States.

   D. that Ciottone is the editor.

   E. more than one author should be listed.

52. Serra, Luigi. Domencio Zampieri, detto Il Domenichino. E. Calzone, ed. 1909. Princeton University.

   Who is the editor?

   A. Serra Luigi

   B. Luigi Serra

   C. E. Calzone

   D. Domenico Zampieri

   E. Domenichino

53. Cattong, Bruce. "Grant and Lee: A Study in Contrasts." *The Bedford Reader*. 9th ed. Ed. X. J. Kennedy et al. Boston: Bedford/St. Martin's, 2006. 258-61. Print. This is an example of what kind of citation format?

    A. MLA

    B. APA

    C. Chicago

    D. Turabian

    E. None of these

54. Aloise-Young, P. A. (1993). The development of self-presentation: Self-promotion in 6- to 10- year-old children. *Social Cognition, II*, 201-222. This is an example of what kind of citation?

    A. MLA

    B. APA

    C. Chicago

    D. Turabian

    E. None of these

55. Smith, John Maynard. "The Origin of Altruism." *Nature* 393 (1998): 639-40. This is an example of which kind of citation?

    A. MLA

    B. APA

    C. Chicago

    D. Turabian

    E. None of these

Read the paragraph and answer the questions that follow.

"(1)These good folk, who have only just begun to think and act for themselves, are slow as yet to grasp the changed conditions which should attach them to these theories. (2)They have only reached those ideas which conduce to economy and to physical welfare; in the future, if some one else carries on this work of mine, they will come to understand the principles that serve to uphold and preserve public order and justice. (3)As a matter of fact, it is not sufficient to be an honest man, you must appear to be honest in the eyes of others. (4)Society does not live by moral ideas alone; its existence depends upon actions in harmony with those ideas."

56. **The first sentence can best be described as:**

    A. compound.

    B. complex.

    C. run-on.

    D. a fragment.

    E. compound-complex.

57. **The second sentence can best be described as:**

    A. compound.

    B. complex.

    C. run-on.

    D. a fragment.

    E. compound-complex.

58. **Warren, Robert Penn.** *All The King's Men.* **New York: Harcourt, Brace, 1946. Print. p415.**

    The p415 sentence can best be described as:

    A. the number of pages in the book used.

    B. the last page the reader completed.

    C. the citation for a portion referenced in the a document.

    D. the last page of dialogue in the book.

    E. none of the choices are accurate.

59. **United States. Cong. Senate. Appropriations. Schedule of Serial Set Volumes. 112 Cong., 2 sess. S. Doc. 15383A. Washington DC: U.S. Senate, 2012. Web.**

    15383A can best be described as:

    A. amendment number.

    B. edit number.

    C. page number.

    D. volume number

    E. document number.

60. **Bell, A. G. (1876).** *U.S. Patent No. 174,465.* **Washington, DC: U.S. Patent and Trademark Office.**

    This is the patent citation for:

    A. a lightbulb.

    B. train brakes.

    C. relativity.

    D. telephone.

    E. telegraph.

61. Mozart, W. A. (1970). *Die Zauberflöte* [The magic flute], K. 620 [Vocal score]. Munich, Germany: Becksche Verlagsbuchhandlung. (Original work published 1791).

   The "K. 620" is the citation for:

   A. the 620th note in the musical score.

   B. opus, or work number.

   C. the number of instruments required.

   D. the number of performers required, including voices.

   E. none of these are correct.

62. **Harris, Ann Sutherland (PhD). Seventeenth Century Art and Architecture. Lawrence King Publishing, 2005. pxv.** The "pxv" is:

   A. the version label.

   B. the author's work number.

   C. the date in Roman numeral.

   D. the preface page number.

   E. none of these are correct.

63. "Higher education has become a central part of the process by which high-income families can seek to assure that their children are more likely to have high incomes." Taylor, Timothy. How Higher Education Perpetuates Intergenerational Inequality. March 4, 2015. http://conversableeconomist.blogspot.com/2015/03/how-higher-education-perpetuates.html Accessed August 8, 2015.

   When prefaced with "61" in superscript before this phrase and listed on the same page, it would be referred to as a(an):

   A. footnote.

   B. endnote.

   C. footer.

   D. header.

   E. none of these are correct.

Read the following paragraph and answer the questions that follow.

   This writer has often been asked to tutor hospitalized children with cystic fibrosis. While undergoing all the precautionary measures to see these children (i.e. scrubbing thoroughly and donning sterilized protective gear- for the child's protection), she has often wondered why their parents subject these children to the pressures of schooling and trying to catch up on what they have missed because of hospitalization, which is a normal part of cystic fibrosis patients' lives. These children undergo so many tortuous treatments a day that it seems cruel to expect them to learn as normal children do, especially with their life expectancies being as short as they are.

64. What is the author's main purpose?

   A. To inform

   B. To entertain

   C. To describe

   D. To narrate

   E. To record

65. What is the main idea of this passage?

   A. There is a lot of preparation involved in visiting a patient of cystic fibrosis.

   B. Children with cystic fibrosis are incapable of living normal lives.

   C. Certain concessions should be made for children with cystic fibrosis.

   D. Children with cystic fibrosis die young.

   E. The specific ways you must decontaminate yourself to visit children.

66. What is meant by the word "precautionary" in the second sentence?

   A. Careful

   B. Protective

   C. Medical

   D. Sterilizing

   E. Reckless

67. What is the author's tone in the previous passage?

   A. Sympathetic

   B. Cruel

   C. Disbelieving

   D. Cheerful

   E. Cautious

68. What type of organizational pattern is the author using in the selection about cystic fibrosis?

   A. Classification

   B. Explanation

   C. Comparison and Contrast

   D. Cause and Effect

   E. Entertaining

69. How is the author so familiar with the procedures used when visiting a child with cystic fibrosis?

    A. She has read about it.

    B. She works in a hospital.

    C. She is the parent of one.

    D. She often tutors them.

    E. She had it as a child.

Read the following passage and answer the questions that follow.

    Disciplinary practices have been found to affect diverse areas of child development such as the acquisition of moral values, obedience to authority, and performance at school. Even though the dictionary has a specific definition of the word "discipline," it is still open to interpretation by people of different cultures.
    There are four types of disciplinary styles: assertion of power, withdrawal of love, reasoning, and permissiveness. Assertion of power involves the use of force to discourage unwanted behavior. Withdrawal of love involves making the love of a parent conditional on a child's good behavior. Reasoning involves persuading the child to behave one way rather than another. Permissiveness involves allowing the child to do as he or she pleases and face the consequences of his/her actions

70. What is the meaning of the word "diverse" in the first sentence?

    A. Many

    B. Related to children

    C. Disciplinary

    D. Moral

    E. Racially disparate

71. What organizational structure is used in the first sentence of the second paragraph?

    A. Addition

    B. Explanation

    C. Definition

    D. Simple Listing

    E. Argumentative

72. What is the author's tone?

    A. Disbelieving

    B. Angry

    C. Informative

    D. Optimistic

    E. None of these are correct.

73. What is the overall organizational pattern of this passage?

    A. Generalization

    B. Cause and Effect

    C. Addition

    D. Summary

    E. Informational

Read the following passage and answer the questions that follow.

One of the most difficult problems plaguing American education is the assessment of teachers. No one denies that teachers ought to be answerable for what they do, but what exactly does that mean? The Oxford American Dictionary defines accountability as: the obligation to give a reckoning or explanation for one's actions.

Does a student have to learn for teaching to have taken place? Historically, teaching has not been defined in this restrictive manner; the teacher was thought to be responsible for the quantity and quality of material covered and the way in which it was presented. However, some definitions of teaching now imply that students must learn in order for teaching to have taken place.

As a teacher who tries my best to keep current on all the latest teaching strategies, I believe that those teachers who do not bother even to pick up an educational journal every once in a while should be kept under close watch. There are many teachers out there who have been teaching for decades and refuse to change their ways even if research has proven that their methods are outdated and ineffective. There is no place in the profession of teaching for these types of individuals. It is time that the American educational system clean house, for the sake of our children

74. What is the meaning of the word "reckoning" in the third sentence?

    A. Thought

    B. Answer

    C. Obligation

    D. Explanation

    E. Prayerful

75. What is the organizational pattern of the second paragraph?

    A. Cause and Effect

    B. Classification

    C. Addition

    D. Explanation

    E. None of these things

76. What is the author's overall organizational pattern?

    A. Classification

    B. Cause and Effect

    C. Definition

    D. Comparison and Contrast

    E. None of these things

77. **The author's tone in the passage on the previous page is one of:**

    A. Disbelief

    B. Excitement

    C. Support

    D. Concern

    E. Empathy

78. **What is meant by the word "plaguing" in the first sentence of the previous passage?**

    A. Causing problems

    B. Causing illness

    C. Causing anger

    D. Causing failure

    E. Causing unrest

Read the following paragraph and answer the question below.

(1)London was our present point of rest; we determined to remain several months in this wonderful and celebrated city. (2)Clerval desired the intercourse of the men of genius and talent who flourished at this time; but this was with me a secondary object; I was principally occupied with the means of obtaining the information necessary for the completion of my promise, and quickly availed myself of the letters of introduction that I had brought with me, addressed to the most distinguished natural philosophers.

79. **The fourth word in the second sentence, "intercourse", refers to:**

    A. intimate relations between two people

    B. interactive conversation

    C. an in-depth artist's class

    D. a secondary outcome after a gift is given in Victorian times

    E. none of these options are correct

80. **In the previous passage (referenced in question 79 also), what is the main theme of the selection?**

    A. Travel discussions that compare where the characters have been

    B. Discussions about information gathering and solving an issue

    C. Meeting gentlemen for coffee

    D. Identifying the thought-leaders of the time

    E. How the travelers were going to spend their time in the city.

Read the following paragraph and answer the two questions that follow.

"Oh, Madam Mina," he said, "how can I say what I owe to you? This paper is as sunshine. It opens the gate to me. I am dazed, I am dazzled, with so much light, and yet clouds roll in behind the light every time. But that you do not, cannot comprehend. Oh, but I am grateful to you, you so clever woman. Madame," he said this very solemnly, "if ever Abraham Van Helsing can do anything for your or yours, I trust you will let me know. It will be pleasure and delight if I may serve you as a friend, as a friend, but all I have ever learned, all I can ever do, shall be for you and those you love. There are darknesses in life, and there are lights. You are one of the lights. You are one of the lights. You will have a happy life and a good life, and your husband will be blessed in you."

81. The phase "This paper is as sunshine. It opens the gate to me." means

   A. Madam Mina was holding a light in the next sentence that made it seem as bright as day.

   B. the character speaking has been given new glasses with which to see the sunshine.

   C. the character speaking simply has new information that is helpful to him.

   D. that he is making a joke to Madam Mina.

   E. none of these things.

82. Using the information only presented in the selection, he tone used by the author suggests:

   A. Madam Mina gave Van Helsing information unwillingly.

   B. one of the characters has been drinking a love potion.

   C. Madam Mina wants nothing to do with Van Helsing.

   D. that Van Helsing is making fun to Madam Mina.

   E. Van Helsing is enamored with Madam Mina because of her helpfulness.

Read the following paragraph and answer the two questions that follow.

"Mornings, he likes to sit in his new leather chair by his new living room window, looking out across the rooftops and chimney pots, the clotheslines and telegraph lines and office towers. It's the first time Manhattan, from high above, hasn't crushed him with desire. On the contrary the view makes him feel smug. All those people down there, striving, hustling, pushing, shoving, busting to get what Willie's already got. In spades. He lights a cigarette, blows a jet of smoke against the window. Suckers."

83. **The subject in this passage is**

    A. a character, and seems to be the lead in the story.

    B. a supporting character.

    C. has the attitude of a criminal.

    D. female.

    E. has been poor his whole life.

84. **What kind of description is the author providing of this scene?**

    A. Backstory of the character.

    B. A characterization of what the character is like.

    C. A narrative, with the end of the selection giving thoughts in the first person.

    D. The unreliable narrative about a character.

    E. The author is using a persuasive argument.

85. **What types of words are "striving, hustling, pushing, shoving, bustling"?**

    A. Adjectives

    B. Adverbs

    C. Nouns

    D. Gerunds

    E. Verbs

86. **If you had to explain the phrase "crushed him" in the paragraph above and context of the para graph, what would be the best appropriate explanation?**

    A. The city sustained him with all the opportunity available.

    B. The city called to him to be part of its life.

    C. The city complimented him for everything he has achieved.

    D. The city had energized him to get what he felt he deserved.

    E. The city smothered him with all of its offerings.

87. **The author portrays the attitude of the character toward the people on the street below as:**

    A. Condescending.

    B. Sarcastic.

    C. Affectionate.

    D. Tolerant.

    E. Encouraged.

Read the following paragraph and answer the three questions that follow.

Solemnly he came forward and mounted the round gunrest. He faced about and blessed gravely thrice the tower, the surrounding country and the awaking mountains. Then, catching sight of Stephen Dedalus, he bent towards him and made rapid crosses in the air, gurgling in his throat and shaking his

head. Stephen Dedalus, displeased and sleepy, leaned his arms on the top of the staircase and looked coldly at the shaking gurgling face that blessed him, equine in its length, and at the light untenured hair, grained and hued like pale oak.

88. The likely setting for this paragraph is:

    A. a hospital.

    B. the battlefield.

    C. Stephen's bedroom.

    D. beside the river.

    E. unable to be determined.

89. The description of the main character's hair leads to the conclusion that he is:

    A. a blonde.

    B. a brunette.

    C. has black hair.

    D. has grained black and white hair.

    E. is bald.

90. The phrase "equine in its length" to describe the main character:

    A. is complementary as horses were very valuable to soldiers

    B. could be considered sarcastic.

    C. reveals the way Stephen feels about the main character, which is not fond or complementary.

    D. was a common description of the time period.

    E. is used repeatedly in this book.

College Composition Modular

SAMPLE TEST ESSAY 1

As a reminder, you have 30 minutes to compose your essay and type it on the computer.

Directions: Write an essay in which you discuss the extent to which you agree or disagree with the statement below. Support your discussion with specific reasons and examples from your reading, experience or observations.

Topic: *Communication is the key for success.*

Readers will assign scores based on a matrix, or scoring guide. Here is an example outline of how both student essays will be graded on a six point scale.

SCORE OF 6 - The 6 essay presents a thesis that is coherent and well-developed. The writer's ideas are detailed, intelligent, and thoroughly elaborated. The writer's use of language and structure is correct and meaningful.

SCORE OF 5 - The 5 essay presents a thesis and offers persuasive support. The writer's ideas are usually new, mature, and thoroughly developed. A command of language and a variety of structures are evident.

SCORE OF 4 - The 4 essay presents a thesis and frequently offers a plan of development, which is usually demonstrated. The writer offers sufficient details to achieve the purpose of the essay. There is capable use of language and varied sentence structure. Errors in sentence structure and usage don't interfere with the writer's main purpose.

SCORE OF 3 - The 3 essay gives a thesis and offers a plan of development, which is usually demonstrated. The writer gives support that leans toward generalized statements or a listing. Overall, the support in a 3 essay is neither adequate nor coherent enough to be convincing. There are errors in sentence structure and usage that frequently interfere with the writer's ability to state the purpose.

SCORE OF 2 - The 2 essay usually states a thesis. The writer offers support that may be incomplete. Simple and disconnected sentence structure is present. Mistakes in grammar and usage often thwart the writer's ability to state the purpose.

SCORE OF 1 - The 1 essay has a thesis that is pointless or poorly articulated. Support is shallow. The language is muddled and confusing. Many mistakes in grammar and usage.

College Composition Modular

SAMPLE ESSAY 2

As a reminder, you have 40 minutes to read these two passages and type your essay on the computer.

Directions: Write an essay in which you incorporate the two sources of information provided below. You must use both sources and you must use appropriate citation for both sources using the author's last name, the title or by any other means that adequately identifies it. Support your discussion with specific reasons and examples from your reading, experience or observations.

Assignment: Read the following sources carefully. Then write an essay in which you develop a position on whether communities have contracts to keep peace and fellow members free from harm.

Introduction: A contract is a legal agreement between people, companies, et cetera. Miriam-Webster Dictionary.

Source 1: Hobbes, Thomas. "Leviathan." England: 1651.

Excerpt - The final cause, end or design of men (who naturally love liberty, and dominion over others) in the introduction of that restraint upon themselves in which we see them live in Commonwealths, is the foresight of their own preservation, and of a more contented live thereby; that is to say, of getting themselves out of that miserable condition of war which is necessarily consequent, as hath been shown, to the natural passions of men when there is no visible power to keep them in awe, and tie them by fear of punishment to the performance of their covenants…"

Source 2: Golding, William. "Lord of the Flies." England: 1954.

This toy of voting was almost as pleasing as the conch. Jack started to protest but the clamor changed from the general wish for a chief to an election by acclaim of Ralph himself. None of the boys could have found good reason for this; what intelligence had been shown was traceable to Piggy while the most obvious leaders was Jack. But there was a stillness about Ralph as he sat that marked him out: there was his size, and attractive appearance; and most obscurely, yet most powerfully, there was the conch. The being that had blown that, had sat waiting for them on the platform with the delicate thing balanced on his knees, was set apart.

College Composition Modular

ANSWER KEY

Question Number	Correct Answer	Your Answer	Question Number	Correct Answer	Your Answer	Question Number	Correct Answer	Your Answer
1	B		31	D		61	B	
2	C		32	C		62	D	
3	A		33	D		63	A	
4	E		34	A		64	C	
5	A		35	E		65	C	
6	B		36	A		66	B	
7	C		37	B		67	C	
8	B		38	E		68	D	
9	A		39	C		69	D	
10	C		40	D		70	A	
11	D		41	C		71	D	
12	D		42	A		72	C	
13	A		43	C		73	E	
14	D		44	A		74	D	
15	C		45	C		75	D	
16	C		46	E		76	E	
17	A		47	B		77	D	
18	D		48	E		78	A	
19	D		49	C		79	B	
20	A		50	E		80	E	
21	B		51	E		81	C	
22	E		52	C		82	E	
23	A		53	A		83	A	
24	B		54	B		84	C	
25	C		55	C		85	E	
26	A		56	B		86	E	
27	A		57	E		87	A	
28	B		58	C		88	E	
29	A		59	E		89	A	
30	A		60	D		90	C	

English Literature

Description of the Examination

The English Literature examination covers material from the past 2,500 years. The different critical abilities and literary terms identified in a semester-long literature course are covered in this examination.

College Literature courses go beyond a general understanding of English to incorporate analytical terms as well as the ability to interpret and understand multiple genres of writing. The exam covers topics such as the identification of poetic devices and authors, appropriate application of literary devices, and the terms to describe effects in passages.

The examination contains approximately 95 questions to be answered in 90 minutes. Any time candidates spend on tutorials and providing personal information is in addition to the actual testing time.

This practice examination is intended to help the student practice at the appropriate level of difficulty to do well on the CLEP English Literature exam. These questions do not actually appear on the CLEP English Literature exam.

There is also an optional essay component of this exam; that will not be outlined in this study guide as each school decides if they will accept this portion and they grade it independently.

Knowledge and Skills Required
The subject matter of the English Literature examination is drawn from the following topics. The percentages next to the main topics indicate the approximate percentage of exam questions on that topic.

35%–40%	**Knowledge**
	• pertaining to various literary devices and content knowledge, requiring a strong understanding of English Language Arts.
50%-65%	**Ability**
	• to identify mood, context, excerpt origin, style, and understand examples of literary criticism

On the next page, the sample test begins. There are 90 questions that you must answer in less than 90 minutes. Remember, your goals for this test are those questions you answer accurately; it is not based on how many are incorrect. Take your time, and good luck.

English Literature

SAMPLE TEST

1. An example of Restoration writing is:

   A. *The New Atlantis*

   B. *Hamlet*

   C. *Leviathan*

   D. *The Principia*

   E. *Gulliver's Travels*

2. The following passage is written from which point of view?

   As she mused the pitiful vision of her mother's life laid its spell on the very quick of her being—that life of commonplace sacrifices closing in final craziness. She trembled as she heard again her mother's voice saying constantly with foolish insistence: Derevaun Seraun! Derevaun Seraun!*
   * ["The end of pleasure is pain!" (Gaelic)]

   A. First person, narrator

   B. Second person, direct address

   C. Third person, omniscient

   D. First person, omniscient

   E. First person, direct address

3. The device of personification is used in which example below?

   A. "Beg me no beggary by soul or parents, whining dog!"

   B. "We few, we happy few, we band of brothers."

   C. "O wind thy horn, thou proud fellow."

   D. "And that one talent which is death to hide."

   E. "Happiness sped through the halls cajoling as it went."

4. Which of the following is not one of the four forms of discourse?

   A. Exposition

   B. Description

   C. Rhetoric

   D. Persuasion

   E. Narration

5. **"Every one must pass through Vanity Fair to get to the celestial city" is an allusion to a:**

   A. Chinese folk tale

   B. Norse saga

   C. British allegory

   D. German fairy tale

   E. French drama

6. **To understand the origins of a word, one must study the:**

   A. synonyms

   B. inflections

   C. phonetics

   D. etymology

   E. epidemiology

Question 7

And more to lulle him in his slumber soft,
A trickling streame from high rock tumbling downe,
And ever-drizzling raine upon the loft.
Mixt with a murmuring winde, much like the sowne
Of swarming bees, did cast him in a swowne
No other noyse, nor peoples troublous cryes.
As still are wont t'annoy the walle'd towne,
Might there be heard: but careless Quiet lyes,
Wrapt in eternall silence farre from enemyes.

7. **Which term best describes the form of the poetic excerpt?**

   A. Ballad

   B. Elegy

   C. Octava rima

   D. Spenserian stanza

   E. Eulogy

English Literature

Question 8

My galley charg'ed with forgetfulness
Through sharp seas, in winter night doth
    pass
'Tween rock and rock; and eke mine enemy,
    alas,
That is my lord steereth with cruelness.
And every oar a thought in readiness,
As though that death were light in such a
    case.
An endless wind doth tear the sail apace
Or forc'ed sighs and trusty fearfulness.
A rain of tears, a cloud of dark disdain,
Hath done the wearied cords great
    hindrance,
Wreathed with error and eke with ignorance.
The stars be hid that led me to this pain
Drowned is reason that should me consort,
And I remain despairing of the poet.

8. **Which term accurately names the form of the sonnet?**

    A. Petrarchan or Italian sonnet

    B. Shakespearean or Elizabethan sonnet

    C. Romantic sonnet

    D. Spenserian sonnet

    E. Dante's sonnet

9. **Arthur Miller wrote *The Crucible* as a parallel to what twentieth-century event?**

    A. Sen. McCarthy's House Un-American Activities Committee hearings

    B. The Cold War

    C. The fall of the Berlin Wall

    D. The Persian Gulf War

    E. The Great Depression

10. **Which of the following is not a characteristic of a fable?**

    A. Animals that feel and talk like humans

    B. Happy solutions to human dilemmas

    C. Teaches a moral or standard for behavior

    D. Illustrates specific people or groups without directly naming them

    E. All of these are characteristics of fables

11. Which of the following was not written by Jonathan Swift?

    A. *A Voyage to Lilliput*

    B. *A Modest Proposal*

    C. *Samson Agonistes*

    D. *A Tale of a Tub*

    E. *Drapier's Letters*

12. Which is the best definition for diction?

    A. The specific word choices of an author to create a particular mood or feeling in the reader

    B. Writing that explains something thoroughly

    C. The background or exposition for a short story or drama

    D. Word choices that help teach a truth or moral

    E. Proper elocution

13. Which is an untrue statement about literary themes?

    A. The theme is the central idea in a literary work.

    B. A theme can be a thematic concept.

    C. All parts of the work (plot, setting, mood) should contribute to the theme in some way.

    D. By analyzing the various elements of the work, the reader should be able to arrive at an indirectly stated theme.

    E. The theme is always stated directly somewhere in the text.

14. Which is the least true statement concerning an author's literary tone?

    A. Tone is partly revealed through the selection of details.

    B. Tone is the expression of the author's attitude toward his or her subject.

    C. Tone in literature is usually satiric or angry.

    D. Tone in literature corresponds to the tone of voice a speaker uses.

    E. Tone can be expressed in a variety of ways by an author.

English Literature

15. **Regarding the study of poetry, which elements are least applicable to all types of poetry?**

    A. Setting and audience

    B. Theme and tone

    C. Pattern and diction

    D. Diction and rhyme scheme

    E. Words and symbols

16. **Which of the following definitions best describes a parable?**

    A. A short, entertaining account of some happening, usually using talking animals as characters

    B. A slow, sad song, poem or prose work expressing lamentation

    C. An extended narrative work expressing universal truths concerning domestic life

    D. A short, simple story of an occurrence of a familiar kind, from which a moral or religious lesson may be drawn

    E. A long, involved story that reveals hidden lessons after much discussion and deliberation.

17. **Which of the following is the best description of existentialism?**

    A. The philosophical doctrine that matter is the only reality and that everything in the world (including thought, will, and feeling) is rightly explained exclusively in terms of matter

    B. A philosophy that views things as they should be or as one would wish them to be

    C. A philosophical and literary movement, variously religious and atheistic, stemming from Kierkegaard and represented by Sartre

    D. The belief that all events are determined by fate and are hence inevitable

    E. The fear of losing one's identity, suspicion of activities and aggressions of others.

18. Which of the following is the best definition of imagism?

   A. A doctrine teaching that comfort is the only goal of value in life

   B. The rejection of all religious and moral principles, often in the belief that life is meaningless and just represented by images

   C. The belief that people are motivated entirely by self-centeredness

   D. The doctrine that the human mind cannot know whether there is a God, an ultimate cause, or anything beyond material phenomena

   E. A movement in modern poetry (c. 1910–1918) characterized by precise, concrete images, free verse, and suggestion rather than complete statement

19. Which choice below best defines naturalism?

   A. A belief that the writer or artist should apply scientific objectivity in his or her observation and treatment of life without imposing values or judgments

   B. The doctrine that teaches that the existing world is the best to be hoped for

   C. The doctrine teaching that God is not a personality, but that all laws, forces, and manifestations of the universe are God-related

   D. A philosophical doctrine professing that the truth of all knowledge must constantly be reexamined

   E. A belief that enhancing a character's surroundings with the environment will improve the reader's understanding

20. The tendency to emphasize and value the qualities and peculiarities of life in a particular geographic area exemplifies:

A. pragmatism

B. regionalism

C. pantheism

D. abstract expressionism

E. utilitarianism

21. The arrangement of words in sentences best describes:

A. style

B. discourse

C. thesis

D. syntax

E. none of the above

22. The substitution of "went to his rest" for "died" is an example of:

A. bowdlerism

B. jargon

C. euphemism

D. malapropism

E. simile

23. Explanatory or informative discourse is:

A. exposition

B. narration

C. persuasion

D. description

E. discussion

24. A conversation between two or more people is called a:

A. parody

B. dialogue

C. monologue

D. analogy

E. diatribe

25. "Clean as a whistle" and "easy as falling off a log" are examples of:

A. semantics

B. parody

C. clichés

D. irony

E. satire

26. Addressing someone absent or something inhuman as though present and able to respond describes a figure of speech known as:

   A. personification

   B. synecdoche

   C. metonymy

   D. apostrophe

   E. rhetorical strategy

27. Slang or jargon expressions associated with a particular ethnic, age, socioeconomic, or professional group reflect:

   A. aphorisms

   B. allusions

   C. idioms

   D. euphemisms

   E. stereotypes

Question 28

The characters of the novel also show how deeply it has been meditated; for, though none of them may excite the personal interest which clings to Sam Weller or little Dombey, they are better fitted to each other and the story in which they appear than is usual with Dickens. They all combine to produce the unity of impression which the work leaves on the mind. Individually they will rank among the most original of the author's creations.
- from a review published in *The Atlantic Monthly,* 1861

28. In line 1, the critic refers to a particular novel by Charles Dickens. Which one?

   A. *Great Expectations*

   B. *The Old Curiosity Shop*

   C. *David Copperfield*

   D. *A Christmas Carol*

   E. *Oliver Twist*

29. Which event triggered the beginning of Modern English?

   A. Conquest of England by the Normans in 1066

   B. Introduction of the printing press to the British Isles

   C. Publication of Samuel Johnson's lexicon

   D. The American Revolution

   E. Creation of the British East India Company

English Literature

30. **Which of the following is not true about the English language?**

    A. English is the easiest language to learn.

    B. English is the least inflected language.

    C. English has the most extensive vocabulary of any language.

    D. English originated as a Germanic tongue.

    E. A new word is added to the English Dictionary every two hours.

31. **Match each of the following poets to the poem that he or she wrote.**

    Maya Angelou
    e. e. cummings
    Andrew Marvell
    Sylvia Plath

    "To His Coy Mistress" _____
    "[in Just-]" _____
    "Phenomenal Woman" _____
    "Lady Lazarus" _____

32. **Children's literature became established as a distinct genre in the:**

    A. sixteenth century

    B. seventeenth century

    C. eighteenth century

    D. nineteenth century

    E. twentieth century

33. **What is the main form of discourse in this passage?**

    "It would have been hard to find a passer-by more wretched in appearance. He was a man of middle height, stout and hardy, in the strength of maturity; he might have been forty-six or seven. A slouched leather cap hid half his face, bronzed by the sun and wind, and dripping with sweat."

    A. Description

    B. Narration

    C. Exposition

    D. Persuasion

    E. Foreshadowing

English Literature

34. **Oral debate is most closely associated with which form of literary discourse?**

    A. Description

    B. Exposition

    C. Narration

    D. Persuasion

    E. Poetic

35. **Which of the following works is a satire?**

    A. Boris Pasternak's *Dr. Zhivago*

    B. Albert Camus's *The Stranger*

    C. Henry David Thoreau's "On the Duty of Civil Disobedience"

    D. Benjamin Franklin's "Rules by Which a Great Empire May Be Reduced to a Small One"

    E. C. S. Lewis' *Prince Caspian*

36. **Charles Dickens, Robert Browning, and Robert Louis Stevenson were:**

    A. Classicists

    B. Medievalists

    C. Elizabethans

    D. Absurdists

    E. Victorians

37. **Which of the following is a characteristic of blank verse?**

    A. Meter in iambic pentameter

    B. Clearly specified rhyme scheme

    C. Lack of figurative language

    D. Unspecified rhythm

    E. Presence of rhyming couplets

38. **Which of the following is the correct chronological order of authors?**

    A. Defoe, Descartes, Dumas

    B. Descartes, Dumas, Defoe

    C. Dumas, Defoe, Descartes

    D. Defoe, Descartes, Dumas

    E. Descartes, Defoe, Dumas

39. Her mother was jailed in Newgate Prison, given a reprieve and sent to America. Living with a foster mother, she grows up to be employed in a household where both brothers claim to love her, and she marries the younger brother. After the death of one of her children, she learns that her mother in law is really her biological mother - so her husband is her half-brother. What novel is described by this plot summary?

    A. *Pride and Prejudice*

    B. *Moll Flanders*

    C. *Wuthering Heights*

    D. *Novum Organum*

    E. *Sons and Lovers*

40. A passage about death and idyllic rural life is called a:

    A. ballad

    B. sonnet

    C. pastoral elegy

    D. metafiction

    E. lyric

41. The correct order of the following authors by birth is:

    A. Alexander Pope, Samuel Johnson, William Shakespeare, John Donne, William Thackeray

    B. William Shakespeare, John Donne, Samuel Johnson, Alexander Pope, William Thackeray

    C. John Donne, William Shakespeare, Alexander Pope, Samuel Johnson, William Thackeray

    D. William Shakespeare, John Donne, Alexander Pope, Samuel Johnson, William Thackeray

    E. John Donne, William Shakespeare, Samuel Johnson, Alexander Pope, William Thackeray

Question 42

A mote it is to trouble the mind's eye.
In the most high and palmy state of Rome,
A little ere the mightiest Julius fell,
The graves stood tenantless and the sheeted dead
Did squeak and gibber in the Roman streets:
As stars with trains of fire and dews of blood,
Disasters in the sun; and the moist star
Upon whose influence Neptune's empire stands
Was sick almost to doomsday with eclipse:
And even the like precurse of fierce events,
As harbingers preceding still the fates
And prologue to the omen coming on,
Have heaven and earth together demonstrated
Unto our climatures and countrymen. o
But soft, behold! lo, where it comes again!

42. Who speaks these lines?

   A. Horatio

   B. Romeo

   C. Hamlet

   D. Othello

   E. Macbeth

43. A collection of twenty stories inspired by the Hundred Years War was written by:

   A. Walter Scott

   B. John Milton

   C. John Donne

   D. William Wordsworth

   E. Geoffrey Chaucer

Question 44

These good folk, who have only just begun to think and act for themselves, are slow as yet to grasp the changed conditions which should attach them to these theories. They have only reached those ideas which conduce to economy and to physical welfare; in the future, if someone else carries on this work of mine, they will come to understand the principles that serve to uphold and preserve public order and justice. As a matter of fact, it is not sufficient to be an honest man, you must appear to be honest in the eyes of others. Society does not live by moral ideas alone; its existence depends upon actions in harmony with those ideas.

44. The passage describes:

   A. A judge's verdict

   B. A tax collector's dilemma

   C. The community view of a doctor

   D. A king's sovereign rights

   E. None of these are correct.

Questions 45-47

London was our present point of rest; we determined to remain several months in this wonderful and celebrated city. Clerval desired the intercourse of the men of genius and talent who flourished at this time; but this was with me a secondary object; I was principally occupied with the means of obtaining the information necessary for the completion of my promise, and quickly availed myself of the letters of introduction that I had brought with me, addressed to the most distinguished natural philosophers.

Line 4 is at "desired the intercourse of the men of genius"

45. **This is a passage written by:**

    A. Mary Shelley

    B. Charles Dickens

    C. Jane Austen

    D. Percy Shelley

    E. Willa Cather

46. **What is the main theme of the selection?**

    A. Travel discussions that compare where the characters have been

    B. Discussions about information gathering and solving an issue

    C. Meeting gentlemen for coffee

    D. Identifying the thought-leaders of the time

    E. How the traveler were going to select the next city they visit

47. **In line 4 of the selection, intercourse means:**

    A. crossroads

    B. relationship

    C. discussion

    D. meeting place

    E. sexual relations

48. **An example of a metaphysical poet would be:**

    A. Christopher Marlowe

    B. George Peele

    C. William Shakespeare

    D. John Donne

    E. George Cascoigne

49. **An example of a cavalier poet would be:**

    A. Richard Lovelace

    B. Mary Sidney Hebert

    C. Lancelot Andrewes

    D. John Milton

    E. Hugh Latimer

English Literature

50. An example of a Jacobean poet would be:

    A. John Bale

    B. Margaret Cavendish

    C. John Skelton

    D. John Heywood

    E. Nicolas Udall

51. Charles Darwin did not write which of the following?

    A. *The Voyage of the Beagle*

    B. *The Origin of the Species*

    C. *The Descent of Man*

    D. *Bureaucracy*

    E. He only wrote two of these.

52. Which of the following was not actually written by Lewis Carroll?

    A. *Alice's Adventures in Wonderland*

    B. *Through the Looking Glass*

    C. *The Hunting of the Snark*

    D. *Sylvie and Bruno*

    E. *After Wonderland*

53. Which of the following is not a mode of English literature?

    A. epistolary

    B. picaresque

    C. novella

    D. melodramatic

    E. chivalric

Questions 54-56

"Oh, Madam Mina," he said, "how can I say what I owe to you? This paper is as sunshine. It opens the gate to me. I am dazed, I am dazzled, with so much light, and yet clouds roll in behind the light every time. But that you do not, cannot comprehend. Oh, but I am grateful to you, you so clever woman. Madame,ds roll in behind the light every time. ed at this Helsing can do anything for your or yours, I trust you will let me know. It will be pleasure and delight if I may serve you as a friend, as a friend, but all I have ever learned, all I can ever do, shall be for you and those you love. There are darknesses in life, and there are lights. You are one of the lights. You are one of the lights. You will have a happy life and a good life, and your husband will be blessed in you."

English Literature

54. What type of novel is this?

A. Gothic

B. Renaissance

C. Jacobean

D. Medieval

E. Restoration

55. Who is the author?

A. Washington Irving

B. Margaret Fuller

C. Bram Stoker

D. Horace Greeley

E. Arthur Conan Doyle

56. The phrase, "This paper is as sunshine. It opens the gate to me," means

A. Madam Mina was holding a light in the next sentence that made it seem as bright as day.

B. The character speaking has been given new glasses with which to see the sunshine.

C. The character speaking has new information that is helpful to him.

D. He is making a joke to Madam Mina.

E. None of the above.

Questions 57-61

Strong man though he was, there is no doubt that he had behaved rather foolishly over the medicine. If he had a weakness, it was for thinking that all his life he had taken medicine boldly, and so now, when Michael dodged the spoon in Nana's mouth, he had said reprovingly, "Be a man, Michael."

57. The passage is excerpted from:

A. Little Women

B. The Adventures of Peter Pan

C. Tess of the D'Urbervilles

D. The Faerie Queene

E. Oliver Twist

58. Is this the first time the main character was used by this author?

A. Yes, there are no other references.

B. No, the author used him as a cameo in *The Little White Bird*.

C. No, the author used him in a magazine series.

D. No, the author wrote several books before this one using him.

E. No, the author used him in an advertisement first

English Literature

59. Who is talking to Michael in the passage?

A. Mrs. Darling

B. Wendy

C. Peter

D. Mr. Darling

E. John

60. In what chapter does the star of the story make his first appearance through reference and explanation?

A. Chapter 1

B. Chapter 2

C. Chapter 3

D. Chapter 4

E. Chapter 5

61. The author of this novel is:

A. J. M. Barrie

B. Louisa May Alcott

C. E. Nesbit

D. Lucy Montgomery

E. Mary Ann Evans

62. Robert Louis Stevenson's most famous novel is:

A. *Great Expectations*

B. *Treasure Island*

C. *Atonement*

D. *Pilgrim's Progress*

E. *Howard's End*

Question 63

How sweet is the Shepherd's sweet lot!
From the morn to the evening he strays;
He shall follow his sheep all the day,
And his tongue shall be filled with praise.

For he hears the lamb's innocent call,
And he hears the ewe's tender reply;
He is watchful while they are in peace,
For they know when their Shepherd is nigh.

63. The tone of the poem is:

A. peaceful.

B. argumentative.

C. mocking.

D. eclectic.

E. suspicious.

English Literature

64. **All of the following were written in the nineteenth century EXCEPT:**

    A. *Picture of Dorian Gray*

    B. *Agnes Grey*

    C. *Pickwick Papers*

    D. *David Copperfield*

    E. *Lord Jim*

65. **The following authors all published in the 1800s EXCEPT:**

    A. Jonathan Swift

    B. James Joyce

    C. Virginia Woolf

    D. Elizabeth Barrett Browning

    E. Lewis Carroll

66. **The following characteristics are true of post-colonial movement EXCEPT:**

    A. engagement with colonialism's power structures.

    B. the destabilization of ideas of homeland.

    C. a mother country's continued influence in the arts.

    D. the presentation of concepts critical of non-western cultures.

    E. the destabilization of ideas of the West

67. **Abstract imagery is:**

    A. the reaction to the Symbolist movement.

    B. a type of catachresis known as a mixed metaphor.

    C. language that cannot be perceived with the five senses.

    D. updating older language to reflect the abstract movement.

    E. the creation of a sense of removed experience from an event.

68. **Alliteration is:**

    A. addition of an extra unstressed syllable.

    B. transcription from a speaker.

    C. presentation of two alternatives in parallel structure.

    D. close proximity of repeated consonant sounds.

    E. insertion of an unnecessary vowel sound.

69. **Who wrote *Paradise Lost*?**

    A. John Ford

    B. John Milton

    C. John Webster

    D. John Fletcher

    E. John Donne

English Literature

70. Which famous author and friends dressed up in costumes in order to convince the Royal Navy they were Abyssinian Princes?

    A. Virginia Woolf

    B. Emily Bronte

    C. Charlotte Bronte

    D. Mary Shelley

    E. None of these authors did this.

71. The earliest use of "wicked" to mean "cool" was included in a novel by which of the following authors?

    A. D. H. Lawrence

    B. Hugh Lofting

    C. F. Scott Fitzgerald

    D. Jonathan Swift

    E. T. S. Eliot

72. **Ben Jonson is known for:**

    A. sonnets

    B. satirical plays

    C. medieval essays

    D. pastoral prose

    E. Elizabethan tragedy

73. Although he was a judge and legal administrator by avocation, he collected stories as a child in the Scottish highlands and began his writing career by translating German documents. This best describes:

    A. G. Bernard Shaw

    B. C. S. Lewis

    C. John Banim

    D. Robert Burns

    E. Walter Scott

74. Critics reviewed this novel and disliked "its dystopian satire of totalitarian regimes, nationalism, the class system, bureaucracy, and world leaders' power struggles," while others panned it as a "nihilistic prophesy on the downfall of humankind." Which novel does this describe?

    A. *Animal House*

    B. *1984*

    C. *South of Broad*

    D. *The Waste Land*

    E. *Culture and Anarchy*

English Literature

Question 75

While the present century was in its teens and on one sunshiny morning in June, there drove up to the great iron gate of Miss Pinkerton's academy for young ladies, on Chiswick Mall, a large family coach, with two fat horses in blazing harness, driven by a fat coachman in a three-cornered hat and wig, at the rate of four miles an hour.

75. This is the opening line of:

   A. *Vanity Fair*

   B. *The Great Gatsby*

   C. *To Kill a Mockingbird*

   D. *Hermann and Dorothea*

   E. *Fair Maid of the West*

76. The author of the passage is:

   A. John Fisher

   B. Thomas Malory

   C. Christopher Smart

   D. William Makepeace Thackeray

   E. Robert Greene

77. *Beowulf* is set in what region of the world?

   A. British Isles

   B. Scandinavia

   C. Prussia

   D. Russia

   E. Gaul

78. What is the primary focus of *Beowulf*?

   A. The Crusaders trying to return from the Middle East to Europe

   B. America's wealth, power, and influence over Russia

   C. Good over evil, with the king's funeral finishing the story

   D. The expansion of Russia towards the west and southward toward the Mediterranean Sea

   E. Examples of how the sun never sets over the British Isles

79. Which of the following is not one of the Canterbury Tales?

   A. "The Cook's Tale"

   B. "The Wife of Bath's Tale"

   C. "Sir Thopas' Tale"

   D. "The Manciple's Tale"

   E. "Sir Eduoard's Tale"

Question 80-82

To be or not to be— that is the question
Whether 'tis nobler in the mind to suffer
The slings and arrows of outrageous fortune
Or to take arms against a sea of troubles
And by opposing end them. To die, to sleep —
No more — and by a sleep to say we end
The heartache, and the thousand natural shocks
That flesh is heir to. 'Tis a consummation
Devoutly to be wished. To die, to sleep—
To sleep—perchance to dream…

80. This is an example of a:

    A. monologue

    B. soliloquy

    C. appeal

    D. benediction

    E. none of the above

81. The character that speaks these lines is:

    A. Romeo

    B. Mercutio

    C. Ceasar

    D. Hamlet

    E. Macbeth

82. The tone of this selection is:

    A. despairing

    B. joyful

    C. longing

    D. remorseful

    E. self-promotion

Question 83

Nobody wanted your dance,
Nobody wanted your strange glitter, your floundering
Drowning life and your effort to save yourself,
Treading water, dancing the dark turmoil,
Looking for something to give.

83. This passage's tone is created by using one of the following means:

    A. allegories

    B. euphemisms

    C. alliteration

    D. irony

    E. metaphors

84. **Walter Scott wrote all of the following EXCEPT:**

    A. *Rob Roy*

    B. *Ivanhoe*

    C. *Waverly*

    D. *The Talisman*

    E. *Kidnapped*

85. **H. G. Wells wrote all of the following EXCEPT:**

    A. *The Dream*

    B. *War of the Worlds*

    C. *Time Machine*

    D. *Vivian Grey*

    E. *Meanwhile*

86. **The correct order of Jane Austin's novels by publication is:**

    A. Emma, Sense & Sensibility, Pride & Prejudice, Persuasion

    B. Emma, Persuasion, Sense & Sensibility, Pride & Prejudice

    C. Persuasion, Sense & Sensibility, Pride & Prejudice, Emma

    D. Sense & Sensibility, Pride & Prejudice, Emma, Persuasion

    E. Pride & Prejudice, Sense & Sensibility, Emma, Persuasion

Question 87

All the world's a stage
And all the men and women merely players;
They have their exits and their entrances,
And one man in his time plays many parts,
His acts being seven ages.

87. **This is a passage from:**

    A. *The Tempest*

    B. *As You Like It*

    C. *Much Ado About Nothing*

    D. *Twelfth Night*

    E. *King Lear*

88. **The politician John Elwes, who had inherited a fortune but was reluctant to spend a penny - even living in empty apartments - is thought to have served as partial inspiration for which literary work?**

    A. A Christmas Carol

    B. Tale of Two Cities

    C. Pickwick Papers

    D. Mystery of Edwin Drood

    E. The Battle of Life

English Literature

89. **Events taking place on a single day, following three major characters through Dublin, describes what 20th century novel?**

    A. *A Handful of Dust*

    B. *The Third Man*

    C. *Dubliners*

    D. *Ulysses*

    E. *The Heart of the Matter*

90. **In literature, evoking feelings of pity or compassion is creating:**

    A. colloquy

    B. irony

    C. pathos

    D. paradox

    E. emphatic response.

English Literature

ANSWER KEY

Question Number	Correct Answer	Your Answer
1	D	
2	C	
3	E	
4	C	
5	C	
6	D	
7	D	
8	A	
9	A	
10	B	
11	C	
12	A	
13	E	
14	C	
15	A	
16	D	
17	C	
18	E	
19	A	
20	B	
21	D	
22	B	
23	A	
24	B	
25	C	
26	D	
27	E	
28	A	
29	B	
30	A	

Question Number	Correct Answer	Your Answer
31	***	
32	B	
33	A	
34	D	
35	D	
36	E	
37	A	
38	E	
39	B	
40	C	
41	D	
42	A	
43	E	
44	C	
45	A	
46	B	
47	C	
48	D	
49	A	
50	B	
51	D	
52	E	
53	C	
54	A	
55	C	
56	C	
57	B	
58	B	
59	D	
60	A	

Question Number	Correct Answer	Your Answer
61	A	
62	B	
63	A	
64	E	
65	A	
66	B	
67	C	
68	D	
69	B	
70	A	
71	C	
72	B	
73	E	
74	B	
75	A	
76	D	
77	B	
78	C	
79	E	
80	B	
81	D	
82	A	
83	B	
84	E	
85	D	
86	D	
87	B	
88	A	
89	D	
90	C	

*** Andrew Marvell, e.e. cummings, Maya Angelou, Sylvia Plath

Humanities

Description of the Examination

The Humanities examination tests general knowledge of literature, art and music and the performing arts. Its questions cover the periods between classical to contemporary periods in the fields of: poetry, prose, philosophy, visual art, architecture, music, dance, theater, and film. The exam requires candidates to demonstrate their understanding of the humanities through comprehension, analysis and interpretation of various works of art.

Because the exam is very broad in its coverage, it is unlikely that any one person will be highly informed about each field. The exam contains approximately 140 questions to be answered in 90 minutes. Some of these are pre-test questions that will not be scored. Any time candidates spend on tutorials or providing personal information is in addition to the actual testing time.

Colleges may grant credit toward fulfilment of a distribution requirement for students who achieve satisfactory scores on the Humanities examination. Some may grant credit for a particular course that matches the exam in content.

Note: This examination uses the chronological designations B.C.E. (before the Common Era) and CE. (Common Era). These labels correspond to B.C. (before Christ) and A.D. (anno Domini), which are used in some textbooks.

Knowledge and Skills Required

Questions on the Humanities examination require candidates to demonstrate the abilities listed below, in the approximate percentages indicated. Some questions may require more than one ability.

- Knowledge of factual information (authors, works, etc.) (50 percent of the examination)
- Recognition of techniques such as rhyme scheme, medium and matters of style, and the ability to identify characteristics of specific writers, artists, schools or periods (30 percent of the examination)
- Understanding and interpretation of literary passages and art reproductions that are likely to be unfamiliar to most candidates (20 percent of the examination)

The subject matter of the Humanities examination is drawn from the topic listed below. The percentages next to the topics indicate the approximate percentages of exam questions

50 % Literature
- 10% Drama
- 10%—15% Poetry
- 15 %—20% Fiction
- 10% Nonfiction (including philosophy)

50 % The Arts
- 20% Visual arts: painting, sculpture, etc.
- 5% Visual arts: architecture
- 15% Performing arts: music
- 10% Performing arts: film, dance, etc.

The exam questions, drawn from the entire history of art and culture, are divided among the following Western periods: Classical, Medieval, Renaissance, 17th through 21st Centuries. At least five percent of the questions draw upon non-Western cultures, such as African, Asian, and Latin American. Some of the questions cross disciplines and/or chronological periods, and a substantial number test knowledge of terminology, genre and style.

Note: Although the images that accompany some of the questions in this guide are printed in black and white, any works that are reproduced in the actual test will be in color.

Sample Test Questions

The following sample questions do not appear on an actual CLEP examination. They are intended to give potential test-takers an indication of the format and difficulty level of the examination and to provide content for practice and review.

Directions: Each of the questions or incomplete statements below is followed by five suggested answers.

Study Resources

Most textbooks used in college level humanities courses cover the topics in the outline. However, the approaches to certain topics and the emphases given to them may differ. To prepare for the Humanities exam, it is advisable to study one or more college textbooks, which can be found in most college bookstores. When selecting a textbook, check the table of contents against the knowledge and skills required for this test.
To do well on the Humanities exam, one should have general familiarity with each form of literature and fine arts from the various periods and cultures listed in the paragraph following the examination percentages. No single book covers all these areas, so it will be necessary for you to refer to college textbooks, supplementary reading, and fine arts at the college level. Two such resources are: Philip E. Bishop, *Adventures in the Human Spirit*, 5th edition, Upper Saddle River, NJ: Prentice Hall, 2007 and Henry M. Sayre, *The Humanities: Culture, Continuity, and Change*, Volumes I and II, Upper Saddle River, NJ: Prentice Hall 2007.

In addition to reading, a lively interest in the arts – attending museums and concerts, attending plays and films, watching public television programs such as *Great Performances* and *Masterpiece Theatre* and listening to radio stations that play classical music and feature discussions of the arts – will assist in preparation.

Visit clep.collegeboard.org/test-preparation for additional humanities resources. You can find suggestions for exam preparation in Chapter IV of the *Official Study Guide*. In addition, many college faculties post their course materials on their schools' websites.

Humanities

SAMPLE TESTS

1. **Plato's *Republic* centers on a discussion of _____ .**

   A. the ideal society

   B. Athenian history

   C. the teachings of Socrates

   D. a justification of politics

   E. warfare and weapons

2. **The Greek philosopher who believed that only change is real, and that the universe is in a state of flux was _____ .**

   A. Epicurus

   B. Heraclitus

   C. Socrates

   D. Cicero

   E. Thales

3. **The Renaissance author of *The Prince* was _____ .**

   A. Dante

   B. Machiavelli

   C. Mirandola

   D. Salutati

   E. Lorenzo de'Medici

4. **Stoicism is a philosophy based on the idea that _____ .**

   A. knowledge is attainable only through the use of reason

   B. the universe is mechanical

   C. knowledge is limited, so nothing can be proven

   D. all spiritual things emanate from God

   E. individual perception is the basis for absolute truth

5. **Which of the following philosophers is considered to be the founder of existentialism?**

   A. Hegel

   B. Russell

   C. Sartre

   D. Kant

   E. Hobbes

Humanities

6. **In which of the following cultures did *The Epic of Gilgamesh* originate?**

    A. Babylonian

    B. Greek

    C. Japanese

    D. Byzantine

    E. Chinese

7. **During the Renaissance, which of the following two Christian humanists advocated a return to the teachings of Jesus?**

    A. Machiavelli and Castiglione

    B. Erasmus and More

    C. Dante and Mirandola

    D. Petrarch and Bruni

    E. Saluti and Alberti

8. **The plays of William Shakespeare often focused on _____.**

    A. methods of transport

    B. fashion

    C. foreign religions

    D. supernatural forces

    E. food and drink

9. **Which of the following is the philosopher of the Enlightenment who is said to have frequently championed of civil liberties?**

    A. Hume

    B. Bentham

    C. Descartes

    D. Voltaire

    E. Bayle

10. **Dickens and Balzac can both be considered to have created works that reflect which of the following styles?**

    A. Realism

    B. Gothic Revival

    C. Penny Dreadful

    D. Socialist Realism

    E. Minimalism

11. **Which of the following is a key characteristic of a formal essay?**

    A. objectivity

    B. humor

    C. personal opinion

    D. emotion

    E. second person style

Humanities

12. The Greek philosopher who was known for his exchange and analysis of opinions was _____.

    A. Agathobulus
    B. Plato
    C. Aristotle
    D. Diogenes
    E. Epicurus

13. Which of the followings philosophers is said to have coined this well-known phrase "I think, therefore I am"?

    A. Bacon
    B. St. Augustine
    C. Descartes
    D. Locke
    E. Hegel

14. The great Roman poet Virgil can said to have been influenced by the writings of which of the following?

    A. Homer
    B. Antoninus Liberalis
    C. Quintus Smyrnaeus
    D. Nonnus
    E. Romanus the Melodist

15. Which of the following events occurred after the time that Dante wrote *The Divine Comedy*?

    A. Dante was exiled from Florence
    B. Bubonic Plague arrives in Europe
    C. His muse, Beatrice, died
    D. Holy Roman Emperor, Frederick II, died
    E. Boniface VIII was elected as Pope

16. Which of the following pairs of authors wrote during the same historical period?

    A. Tolstoy and Dickens
    B. Galsworthy and Highsmith
    C. Trollope and Orwell
    D. Kingsley and Defoe
    E. Austen and Faulkner

Humanities

17. Which of the following ideas is a major theme in ancient Greek philosophy?

    A. reason is a superior approach to decision-making

    B. behaviour is the product of conditioning

    C. man should seek Darshan

    D. man is an inferior creature created by an uncaring god

    E. man should strive to live a life in harmony with nature

18. Much of the doctrine of the medieval Roman Catholic Church, including the belief that it was the duty of the Church to find and punish heretics, was derived from the writings of which of the following influential authors?

    A. St. Boethius

    B. St. Aquinas

    C. St. Augustine

    D. St. Joan

    E. St. Jude

19. Which of the following statements is a major tenet of Humanism?

    A. human beings are not subject to God or any divine agency

    B. man's highest goal should be to serve god

    C. humans have the right of dominion over nature

    D. civil rules should be imposed by a monarchy

    E. theft of property is acceptable

20. The philosophes of the Enlightenment concerned themselves with which of the following issues?

    A. the consequences arising from a free-market economy

    B. methodology of the scientific revolution

    C. responsibility of industry toward the proletariat

    D. distribution of wealth in an ideal society

    E. animal rights

Humanities

21. Which of the following characteristics of drama is Aristotle commonly supposed to have invented?

    A. a structure based on Acts

    B. it is something performed

    C. characters are dynamic

    D. written scripts

    E. it operates within conventions

22. Which of the following authors wrote *Tales of Belkin?*

    A. Gogol

    B. Pushkin

    C. Tolstoy

    D. Derzhavin

    E. Chekhov

23. Which of the following twentieth century authors was said to be noticeably influenced by Homer's *Odyssey?*

    A. Ernest Hemingway

    B. J. D. Salinger

    C. James Joyce

    D. George Orwell

    E. Robert A. Heinlein

24. The absurdist plays of Jean Genet reflect the philosophy that _____.

    A. mankind is surrounded by a meaningless world

    B. mankind is capable of self-government

    C. human freedom leads only to terror

    D. God is existent in all living things

    E. etiquette is the most important rule of social interaction

25. Which of the following authors, is known for their examination of cultural attitudes towards gender through the use of an androgynous lead character?

    A. Ian Fleming

    B. Ernest Hemingway

    C. Virginia Woolf

    D. Tennessee Williams

    E. H. G. Wells

Humanities

26. Which of the following terms best describes the whole group actors who portray the characters in a play?

    A. ensemble

    B. Team

    C. panel

    D. cast

    E. crew

27. Which of the following terms is used to describe two or more words, which match by having the same last sound?

    A. alliteration

    B. assonance

    C. rhyme

    D. onomatopoeia

    E. repetition

28. Which of the following is the name for a form of verse, consisting of three non-rhyming lines, that traditionally invokes an aspect of nature or the seasons?

    A. Blank verse

    B. Free verse

    C. Haiku

    D. Limerick

    E. Sonnet

29. Which of the following terms describes a poem in which certain letters in each line form a word or words?

    A. acrostic

    B. couplet

    C. quatrain

    D. stanza

    E. ballad

30. Which of the following authors is frequently acclaimed as having initiated the modern detective fiction story genre?

    A. Alice Munro

    B. Joseph Conrad

    C. Edgar Allan Poe

    D. E. M. Forster

    E. M. R. James

31. In literature the "stream-of-consciousness" narrative device is otherwise known by which of the following terms?

    A. random plotting

    B. scene setting

    C. secret dialogue

    D. inspirational authoring

    E. interior monologue

32. Which of the following best describes poetry written in the "vernacular" style?

    A. using language of particular locality or region

    B. adopting florid language

    C. employing a first person narrative

    D. drawing upon historical events

    E. utilizing common buzzwords

33. Which of the following authors wrote *Treasure Island*?

    A. Arthur Conan Doyle

    B. Robert Louis Stevenson

    C. Henry James

    D. Lewis Carroll

    E. Jules Verne

34. Which of the following characters is included in the original manuscript of the *One Thousand and One Arabian Nights*?

    A. Aladdin

    B. Scheherazade

    C. Sinbad

    D. Ali Baba

    E. King Yunan

35. The British 19th Century author Mary Ann Evans wrote under which of the following pen names?

    A. Antosha Chekhonte

    B. Artemus Ward

    C. George Elliot

    D. Boz

    E. George Sand

36. Tom Stoppard's 1972 play *Jumpers* focuses on which of the following?

    A. athletes

    B. academic philosophers

    C. time travellers

    D. horse riders

    E. a knitting circle

37. The famous poem *Ozymandias* was written by which of the following Romantic poets?

    A. Byron

    B. Shelley

    C. Keats

    D. Wordsworth

    E. Coleridge

Humanities

38. Which of the following is a poem by Alfred, Lord Tennyson that includes the line "To strive, to seek, to find, and not to yield"?

    A. *Ulysses*

    B. *The Ballad of Reading Gaol*

    C. *The Lady of Shalott*

    D. *Her Voice*

    E. *Dover Beach*

39. The 19th Century poet Gerald Manley Hopkins wrote the verse "Glory be to God for dappled things" in which of the following poems?

    A. The Starlight Night

    B. The Wreck of the Deutschland

    C. Pied Beauty

    D. The Windhover

    E. Spring and Fall

40. Which of the following playwrights is said to have acted in a play by the 16th Century, British playwright, Ben Johnson?

    A. Christopher Marlowe

    B. William Shakespeare

    C. William Dunlap

    D. John Augustin Daly

    E. William Cornysh

41. The *Decameron* is a collection of stories originating in which of the following countries?

    A. Greece

    B. Italy

    C. England

    D. France

    E. Uruguay

42. Portmanteau is a literary device that best describes which of the following actions?

    A. collecting stories from around the world

    B. joining two words to make a new word

    C. using gibberish in dialogue

    D. writing in the first person style

    E. incorporating a surprise ending to a novel

Humanities

43. Which of the following correctly pairs a novelist with a work he created?

    A. Ayan Rand ... *1984*

    B. Aldous Huxley ... *Brave New World*

    C. Frank Herbert ... *Under the Volcano*

    D. Ralph Ellison ... *Slaughterhouse Five*

    E. Saul Bellow ... *Gravity's Rainbow*

44. Which of the following cities is synonymous with the Beat poetry movement of the 1950's?

    A. Miami

    B. Charlestown

    C. Minneapolis

    D. San Francisco

    E. Dallas

45. Which of the following poems tells the story of the Trojan War?

    A. The Iliad

    B. Argonautica

    C. Minyas

    D. Descent of Perithous

    E. Danaus

46. Which of the following artistic movements featured exponents of the "sound poem"?

    A. Impressionists

    B. Social Realists

    C. Dadaists

    D. Cubists

    E. Abstract Expressionists

47. Which of the following authors wrote *The Color Purple*?

    A. Toni Morrison

    B. John Steinbeck

    C. Alice Walker

    D. ZZ Packer

    E. James Baldwin

48. James Ellroy's novel *The Black Dahlia* takes its inspiration from which of the following infamous crimes?

    A. The St. Valentine's Day Massacre

    B. The murder of Elizabeth Short

    C. The Weinberger kidnapping

    D. The murder of Patty Hearst

    E. The Lindbergh kidnapping

Humanities

49. **"Anaphora" is a poetic device best described by which of the following?**

    A. Repeating consonant or vowel sounds to create rhyme

    B. Repeating vowel sounds to create a deeper meaning in a poem

    C. Repeating an opening word or phrase in a series of lines

    D. Repeating a word or phrase to affect a different meaning

    E. Repeating a single word, with no other words in between

50. **A poem that features a pair of lovers at dawn would be known as which of the following?**

    A. Serenade

    B. Nocturne

    C. Aubade

    D. Twilight poem

    E. Sonnet

51. **Which of the following are key characteristics of dramatic literature?**

    A. historical accuracy and research

    B. dialogue and performance

    C. female characters and themes of motherhood

    D. first person narrative and exotic locations

    E. fantastic plots and supernatural characters

52. **Which of the following best describes a performance space that usually features an elegant curtain and an orchestra pit?**

    A. proscenium theatre

    B. round theatre

    C. thrust theater platform

    D. amphitheatre

    E. black box theater

Humanities

53. Which of the following is a key characteristic of Commedia Dell'Arte?

    A. the authors are academics

    B. the actors wore masks

    C. the roles are performed by amateurs

    D. the performance takes place indoors

    E. the company is contracted to a specific patron

54. Which of the following terms is used to describe a fixed verse form consisting of six stanzas of six lines each?

    A. Septima

    B. Septana

    C. Sestina

    D. Serrena

    E. Pentameter

55. Molière, the French 16th Century dramatist, is famous for writing dramas in which of the following genres?

    A. Tragedy

    B. History

    C. Comedy

    D. Musicals

    E. Melodrama

56. Mummers Plays are seasonal folk plays that are commonly understood to have originated in which of the following continents?

    A. Africa

    B. Australia

    C. Asia

    D. Europe

    E. The Americas

57. Which of the following is the commonly used when discussing "meter" in poetry?

    A. Hand

    B. Head

    C. Leg

    D. Foot

    E. Arm

58. Which of the following poets wrote the poem *Esther's Tomcat?*

    A. Sylvia Plath

    B. Stevie Smith

    C. Ted Hughes

    D. T. S. Eliot

    E. John Betjeman

Humanities

59. Which of the following poets have been offered but declined the post of Poet Laureate to the Queen of the United Kingdom?

    A. Cecil Day-Lewis

    B. Philip Larkin

    C. Andrew Motion

    D. John Betjeman

    E. Carol Ann Duffy

60. Sir Walter Scott's novel *Waverley* is generally acknowledged to be which of the following?

    A. the first Romantic novel

    B. the first Historical novel

    C. the first novel to be published anonymously

    D. the first novel focusing on medicine

    E. the first novel to be written in Scotland

61. Who wrote the famous novel *The Last of the Mohicans?*

    A. Nathaniel Hawthorne

    B. James Fennimore Cooper

    C. Harriet Beecher Stowe

    D. Victor Hugo

    E. Henry David Thoreau

62. Which of the following is the title of the magazine that featured stories written by Raymond Chandler and Dashiell Hammett?

    A. Blue Cat

    B. White Mirror

    C. Black Mask

    D. Green Window

    E. Yellow Room

63. Which of the following novels by Daphne Du Maurier, was adapted into a film directed by Alfred Hitchcock?

    A. *The House on the Strand*

    B. *Don't Look Now*

    C. *Rebecca*

    D. *The Apple Tree*

    E. *The Blue Lenses*

64. Which of the following is understood to have written sonnets featuring a "dark lady"?

    A. William Shakespeare

    B. Edmund Spenser

    C. John Donne

    D. Percy Bysshe Shelley

    E. Thomas Wyatt

65. Andrew Marvell, the 17th Century poet and politician, used his political power to free which of the following poets from prison?

    A. John Dryden

    B. John Milton

    C. Richard Lovelace

    D. Alexander Pope

    E. Jonathon Swift

66. Which of the following terms is used to describe a character on stage, who is speaking their thoughts aloud when by alone or regardless of other characters?

    A. monologue

    B. soliloquy

    C. dialogue

    D. discourse

    E. aside

67. According to Aristotle, the purging of the feelings of pity and fear that occur in the audience when watching a tragic drama is known as which of the following?

    A. catharsis

    B. comic relief

    C. rising action

    D. suspense

    E. sublimation

68. Which of the following books by Charles Dickens was the first to be published in serialized form?

    A. *Hard Times*

    B. *Bleak House*

    C. *Oliver Twist*

    D. *The Pickwick Papers*

    E. *A Tale of Two Cities*

69. C. S. Lewis, author of the popular *Chronicles of Narnia* series of books, was born in which city?

    A. Dublin

    B. Paris

    C. Sydney

    D. New York

    E. Belfast

Humanities

70. Which of Shakespeare's plays is referred to as The Scottish Play, as to say its full name is supposed to bring ill luck to performers?

    A. *Hamlet*

    B. *Richard III*

    C. *Macbeth*

    D. *King Lear*

    E. *Henry V*

71. The German playwright Bertolt Brecht is known for creating which theatrical style?

    A. Theatre of Cruelty

    B. Epic Theatre

    C. Verbatim Theatre

    D. Theatre of the Absurd

    E. In Yer Face Theatre

72. Which of the following principles is used in architecture?

    A. hue

    B. tone

    C. pace

    D. time

    E. proportion

73. The genre of Handel's Messiah is _____.

    A. oratorio

    B. overture

    C. sonata

    D. suite

    E. opera

74. Which of the following would be signify a genre when discussing the visual arts?

    A. scenes of everyday life

    B. a type of tempera paint

    C. the choice of medium

    D. a type of brushstroke

    E. a historical period

75. A musical work written for one or more solo instruments with accompaniment by an orchestra is a _____.

    A. cantata

    B. symphony

    C. concerto

    D. sonata

    E. madrigal

76. **Sympathetic magic is usually associated with this style of art.**

    A. Primitive

    B. Christian

    C. Rococo

    D. Impressionism

    E. Baroque

77. **Which of the following is a key characteristic of Romanesque architecture?**

    A. glass walls

    B. white exteriors

    C. round arches

    D. flying buttresses

    E. decorative tile work

78. **A pendentive is a _____.**

    A. medieval troubadour

    B. genre of literature

    C. melancholic piece of music

    D. triangle of masonry

    E. type of doorway

79. **In which of the following countries did engraving and oil painting originate?**

    A. Italy

    B. Japan

    C. Germany

    D. Flanders

    E. Sweden

80. **A key characteristic of Baroque art is _____.**

    A. use of chiaroscuro

    B. simplicity of line

    C. cubism

    D. small scale

    E. secular subject matter

81. **The elongation of the human figure in Byzantine religious art, referred to as the hieratic style, represented _____.**

    A. spirituality

    B. original sin

    C. forgiveness

    D. a characteristic of the mosaic technique

    E. amnesty

Humanities

82. A key characteristic of a fugue is _____.

    A. solo performance

    B. lack of repetition

    C. tonic dissonance

    D. a short main theme

    E. a drum solo

83. The famous Greek sculptor known for the *Cnidian Aphrodite* was _____.

    A. Myron

    B. Polyclitus

    C. Praxiteles

    D. Scopas

    E. Phidias

84. The Flemish artist who created the painting entitled *The Arnolfini Marriage* was _____.

    A. Jan van Eyck

    B. Hugh van der Goes

    C. Hieronymus Bosch

    D. Albrecht Durer

    E. Jan Breughel

85. A key characteristic of Rococo architecture and interior design was _____.

    A. shell-like ornamentation

    B. dark marble floors

    C. heavy stone tracery

    D. scale based on human proportions

    E. form following function

86. A key characteristic of the Abstract Expressionist painting style of the 20th century was _____.

    A. non-figurative subjects

    B. fine detail

    C. social commentary

    D. delight in romantic love

    E. small canvases

87. Which of the following is used in Romantic music, which includes composers such as Chopin and Brahms, to suggest emotion?

    A. the five-tone scale

    B. key changes and dissonance

    C. contrapuntal mode

    D. weak use of percussion

    E. technical virtuosity

88. A central difference between abstract art and non-objective art is that _____.

    A. abstract art contains real subject matter

    B. abstract art has more structure

    C. non-objective art is organized by strict adherence to form

    D. non-objective art is aimed at the subliminal level of brain activity

    E. abstract art is more colorful

89. Which of the following, is a key characteristic of portrait sculpture in the Roman period?

    A. realism

    B. idealism

    C. religion

    D. scale

    E. emotion

90. Which of the following is a hallmark of twentieth century architecture?

    A. form follows function

    B. man is the measure of all things

    C. the use of natural materials

    D. picturesque appearance

    E. expensive materials

91. The 1937 painting *Guernica* by Picasso can be said to be an example of _____.

    A. historical influence in the humanities

    B. non-objective painting

    C. a painting with the emphasis is on color tension

    D. realism

    E. superrealism

92. Which of the following is a thematic motif used in art of the Realism Movement?

    A. religious subjects

    B. famous leaders

    C. everyday scenes from workers lives

    D. great battles

    E. pre-history

Humanities

93. **Which of the following lists the three main religious symbols used in painting to portray the theme of the Annunciation?**

    A. a dove, lilies, and closed book

    B. emanating rays, rainbow and goat

    C. Star of Bethlehem, keys and closed book

    D. emanating rays, keys and angels

    E. roses, servants, jewelry

94. **In Michelangelo's sculpture of *David*, the sculpture depicts the hero in the stance of _____.**

    A. hurling the rock

    B. contemplating the battle to come

    C. holding Goliath's head

    D. receiving praise after the kill

    E. hiding from Goliath

95. **Which of the following artists is known for utilizing the theme of marriage in his most famous painting?**

    A. Mark Rothko

    B. Andy Warhol

    C. Jan van Eyck

    D. Pablo Picasso

    E. Raoul Dufy

96. **The Impressionist movement of painting benefited from the scientific studies of light and which of the following?**

    A. advancements in eye surgery

    B. industrial revolution

    C. new synthetic paints

    D. new gas lighting in theaters

    E. the invention of photography

Humanities

97. **During the 1800's, musicians were able to produce more uniform sounds due to the introduction of _____.**

    A. mass production of printed music

    B. standardization in the production of musical instruments

    C. new metallic alloys

    D. increased availability of traveling conductors

    E. increased patronage of composers

98. **Twentieth century architecture was most significantly affected by which of the following?**

    A. production of structural steel

    B. restoration projects

    C. ability to control interior climate

    D. rise in property costs

    E. global migration

99. **Which of the following styles of art can be said to focus the most on light and capturing a specific moment in time?**

    A. Baroque

    B. Neoclassism

    C. Romanticism

    D. Impressionism

    E. Classicism

100. **Which of the following works, was a profound influence on Raphael, during his early career?**

    A. Caravaggio's *Calling of St. Matthew*

    B. Mirandola's *Oration on the Dignity of Man*

    C. Michelangelo's Sistine Chapel ceiling

    D. Cervantes' *Don Quixote*

    E. Donatello's *David*

101. **The technique used in art to "spotlight" the subject is known as _____.**

    A. Pointillism

    B. Color Wash

    C. Tenebrism

    D. Dry Brushing

    E. Smoothing

Humanities

102. Impressionistic art can be said to rely upon the _____.

    A. blending of complimentary colors in the eye

    B. impasto technique of painting

    C. expression of the artist's anger

    D. beauty of nature

    E. industrialization

103. Which of the following composers is most associated with the musical form of the fugue?

    A. Haydn

    B. Beethoven

    C. Bach

    D. Brahms

    E. Berlioz

104. Which of the following architects is most commonly associated with the International Style?

    A. Mies van der Rohe

    B. Frank Lloyd Wright

    C. Le Corbusier

    D. I.M. Pei

    E. Richard Rogers

105. Which of the following composers was considered as the master of spectacle in the field of opera?

    A. Wagner

    B. Puccini

    C. Mozart

    D. Vivaldi

    E. Verdi

106. Which of the following artists is associated with the concept of surrealism, and is famous for his paintings of "mindscapes"?

    A. de Kooning

    B. Miro

    C. Braque

    D. Dali

    E. Kokoschka

107. In Delacroix's painting *Liberty Leading the People*, the figure of Liberty wears which of the following type of hat?

    A. Cloche

    B. Boater

    C. Phrygian Cap

    D. Top Hat

    E. Bicorne

Humanities

108. The contemporary conceptual art of Christo lends itself to the contemplation of _____.

    A. the aesthetic

    B. modern monetary policy

    C. environmental issues

    D. religious values

    E. the history of war

109. The Hellenistic sculpture *The Dying Gaul*, was praised in poetry by which of the following poets?

    A. Shelley

    B. Tennyson

    C. Plath

    D. Wordsworth

    E. Byron

110. Which of the following sculptors is famous for his depiction of Michael Jackson and his pet, Bubbles?

    A. Jeff Koons

    B. Henry Moore

    C. Patrick Calder

    D. Barbara Hepworth

    E. Edwin Lanseer

111. In the 1931 film *M*, what does "M" stand for?

    A. Mouse

    B. Mechanic

    C. Metropolis

    D. Murderer

    E. Machine

112. The film *Gone with the Wind* is based on a novel by which of the following authors?

    A. Margaret Mitchell

    B. Mark Twain

    C. H G Wells

    D. Paul Theroux

    E. Roald Dahl

113. Which of the following is a key characteristic of Baroque Music?

    A. use of woodwind instruments

    B. complex decorative rhythms

    C. solos

    D. varied movements

    E. technical accuracy

Humanities

114. Music said to be in the classical style is typified by its use of _____.

    A. harmony, order and proportion
    B. contrapuntal motion
    C. brass sections
    D. large choirs
    E. arias

115. Which of the following painters, is known for his use of colour and his fluid draughtsman ship?

    A. Renoir
    B. Lowry
    C. Modigliani
    D. Chirico
    E. Matisse

116. The choreographer Bob Fosse is famous for his choreography of which of the following?

    A. Modern Ballet
    B. Street Dance
    C. Theatrical Jazz Dance
    D. Folk Dance
    E. Classical Ballet

117. Contemporary dance is known for which of the following?

    A. Corps de Ballet
    B. adaptions from literature
    C. frequent changes of speed and direction
    D. reliance on linear movement
    E. lavish costumes

118. Wagner's *Ride of the Valkyries* is based on creatures, which have their origins in which of the following?

    A. Japanese poetry
    B. Indian myths
    C. Australian oral traditions
    D. Norse legends
    E. Chinese fiction

119. Brass instruments are played by which of the following techniques?

    A. beating with a metal stick
    B. passing air over a reed
    C. plucking a string
    D. blowing into a tube
    E. tapping with the foot

Humanities

120. In which film from the 1930's do the following lines appear "Oh, no. It wasn't the airplanes. It was Beauty killed the Beast."?

    A. *Frankenstein* (1931)

    B. *The Adventures of Robin Hood* (1938)

    C. *King Kong* (1933)

    D. *Scarface* (1932)

    E. *Freaks* (1932)

121. *The Grand Staff* in musical notation shows which of the following?

    A. bass and treble clef combined, connected by a brace

    B. beats to a measure

    C. notes

    D. rests

    E. accidentals

122. A major scale in music consists of which of the following number of pitches or notes?

    A. Nine

    B. Ten

    C. Seven

    D. Four

    E. Five

123. Merce Cunningham is famous as a choreographer of which of the following kinds of dance?

    A. Ballet

    B. Flamenco

    C. Modern

    D. Jazz Theatre

    E. Tap

124. Which of the following composers, is most associated with the school of minimalism?

    A. Britten

    B. Elgar

    C. Handel

    D. Beethoven

    E. Cage

125. The celebrated film-score composer known by his stage name *Vangelis*, is originally from which country?

    A. The Netherlands

    B. Brazil

    C. France

    D. Greece

    E. Australia

126. The movie-making term "Spaghetti Western" became popular to describe films, which were _____.

    A. made in Italy

    B. made on a very tight budget

    C. predominantly produced and/or directed by Italians

    D. starred Italian actors

    E. adaptions of Italian literature

127. According to Hindu scripture, which of the following deities is said to have first conceived of dance as an activity?

    A. Brahma

    B. Soma

    C. Agni

    D. Pṛthivī

    E. Ganesh

128. Which of the following types of dance, developed out of the traditional forms of Japanese Kabuki theatre?

    A. Mai

    B. Kathak

    C. Sattriya

    D. Odori

    E. Kuchipudi

129. Which of the following types of signals is used in the practice of musical scales known as *Solfeggio?*

    A. Lights

    B. Flags

    C. Hands

    D. Flares

    E. Energy

130. Which of the following were commonly used from the 17th to the 19th Century to organize the melodic and harmonic parts of music?

    A. Lines

    B. Parts

    C. Modes

    D. Bars

    E. Types

131. Which of the following types of instrument are played by being struck?

    A. Woodwind

    B. Brass

    C. Percussion

    D. String

    E. Electronic

Humanities

132. In filmmaking the acronym AD is commonly applied to which job role?

    A. Actor-Director

    B. Assistant Director

    C. Associate Driver

    D. Actress-Dancer

    E. Alumni-Decorator

133. The painting *The Fighting Temeraire* by J M W Turner depicts which of the following?

    A. a battle in the Napoleonic Wars

    B. a young child

    C. heaven and hell

    D. a boat being pulled by a tug

    E. a mountain

134. The famous sculpture commonly known as the *Venus di Milo* can be found on display in which of the following museums?

    A. The Hermitage

    B. The Prado

    C. The Tate Modern

    D. The Louvre

    E. M.O.M.A

135. Which of the following types of dance originated in Brazil in the late 16th Century?

    A. Ballroom

    B. Flamenco

    C. Samba

    D. Tap

    E. Ballet

136. Which of the following musical instruments is a form of *idiophone?*

    A. Bass Drum

    B. Clarinet

    C. Oboe

    D. Castanets

    E. Bazooka

137. Which of the following is an opera by Hector Berlioz?

    A. *Carmen*

    B. *Les Troyens*

    C. *Don Giovanni*

    D. *The Magic Flute*

    E. *Madame Butterfly*

Humanities

138. Which composer is commonly believed to have invented the solo piano recital?

A. Franz Liszt

B. Claude Debussy

C. Franz Schubert

D. Richard Wagner

E. Fryderyk Chopin

139. Which of the following types of shoes are used in ballet dancing?

A. Ghillies

B. Foot thongs

C. Pointe

D. Sneakers

E. Clogs

140. Which of the following descriptions best describes the type of picture composition, commonly used in filmmaking, is known as a "Close Up"?

A. the subject takes up as much of the frame as is comfortably possible

B. shows two people

C. shows something other than the subject

D. shows a part of the subject that takes up the whole frame

E. shows a view from the subject's perspective

Humanities

ANSWER KEY

Question Number	Correct Answer	Your Answer	Question Number	Correct Answer	Your Answer	Question Number	Correct Answer	Your Answer
1	A		32	A		63	C	
2	B		33	B		64	A	
3	B		34	B		65	B	
4	A		35	C		66	B	
5	C		36	B		67	A	
6	A		37	B		68	D	
7	B		38	A		69	E	
8	D		39	C		70	C	
9	D		40	B		71	B	
10	A		41	B		72	E	
11	A		42	B		73	A	
12	B		43	B		74	A	
13	C		44	D		75	C	
14	A		45	A		76	A	
15	B		46	C		77	C	
16	A		47	C		78	D	
17	A		48	B		79	C	
18	C		49	C		80	A	
19	A		50	C		81	A	
20	B		51	B		82	D	
21	A		52	A		83	C	
22	B		53	B		84	A	
23	C		54	C		85	A	
24	A		55	C		86	A	
25	C		56	D		87	B	
26	D		57	D		88	C	
27	C		58	C		89	A	
28	C		59	B		90	A	
29	A		60	B		91	A	
30	C		61	B		92	C	
31	E		62	C		93	A	

Humanities

ANSWER KEY

Question Number	Correct Answer	Your Answer	Question Number	Correct Answer	Your Answer	Question Number	Correct Answer	Your Answer
94	B		110	A		126	C	
95	C		111	D		127	A	
96	C		112	A		128	D	
97	B		113	D		129	C	
98	A		114	A		130	C	
99	D		115	E		131	C	
100	C		116	C		132	B	
101	C		117	C		133	D	
102	A		118	D		134	D	
103	C		119	D		135	C	
104	A		120	C		136	D	
105	A		121	A		137	B	
106	D		122	C		138	A	
107	C		123	C		139	C	
108	A		124	E		140	D	
109	E		125	D				

French

Description of the Examination

The Language examination is designed to measure knowledge and ability equivalent to that of students who have completed two or three semesters of college French language study.

The examination contains approximately 121 questions to be answered in 90 minutes. Some of these are pretest questions that will not be scored. There are three separately timed sections. The three sections are weighted so that each question contributes equally to the total score. Any time candidates spend on tutorials or providing personal information in in addition to the actual testing time.

Colleges may award different amounts of credit depending on the candidate's test scores.

Knowledge and Skills Required

Candidates must demonstrate their ability to understand spoken and written French. The CLEP French Language examination tests their listening and reading skills through the various types of questions listed below. The percentages indicate the approximate percentage of exam questions devoted to each type of question.

15% **Section I:**
Listening: Rejoinders
- Listening comprehension: choosing the best responses to short spoken prompts

25% **Section II:**
Listening: Dialogues and Narratives
- Listening comprehension: choosing the answers to questions based on longer spoken selections

60% **Section III:**
Reading
- 10% Part A. Discrete sentences (vocabulary and structure)
- 20% Part B. Short cloze passages (vocabulary and structure)
- 30% Part C. Reading passages and authentic stimulus materials (reading comprehension)

French

Section I- Listening: Rejoinders
Listening comprehension: choosing the best responses to short spoken prompts

Directions for Section I: You will hear short conversations or part of conversations. You will then hear four responses, designated A, B, C and D. After you hear the four responses, choose the lettered response that lost logically continues or completed the conversation. You will have 10 seconds to choose your response before the next conversation begins. When you are ready to continue, click on the Dismiss Directions icon.

1. *(Personne A)* Où sont tes enfants? Ça fait longtemps que je ne les ai pas vus.
   (personne B)

   A. Mes enfants sont partis en vacances avec leur grand-mère

   B. Les vacances passent rapidement.

   C. Est-ce que tu as pris des vacances cette année?

   D. Combien d'heures travailles-tu par jour?

2. *(Personne A)* Il fait très beau aujourd'hui, j'aimerai aller me promener dans le parc mais j'ai beaucoup de travail à finir. J'hésite si j'y vais ou pas.
   (personne B)

   A. Est-ce que je peux t'accompagner?

   B. Je n'aime pas le soleil, je préfère la pluie.

   C. Tu peux quand même prendre une pause de cinq minutes.

   D. Je vais aller manger au parc.

3. *(Personne A)* J'ai perdu mon chat, je ne l'ai pas vu depuis ce matin. Je ne sais pas quoi faire.
   (personne B)

   A. Mes voisins ont un chat aussi.

   B. J'ai des allergies aux chats.

   C. Est-ce que tu as demandé à tes voisins s'ils l'ont vu?

   D. J'avais un chat lorsque j'étais enfant.

4. *(Personne A)* As-tu un guide touristique de Paris? Je vais passer mes vacances d'été à Paris.
   (personne B)

   A. Ma sœur en a un, je peux lui demander si elle peut te le prêter.

   B. J'ai visité Paris l'année dernière.

   C. Il pleut beaucoup à Paris.

   D. Je ne parle pas français.

5. **(Personne A)** Je pense que j'ai de la fièvre. Peux-tu me chercher un thermomètre?
(personne B)

   A. J'étais malade la semaine dernière, heureusement j'avais un thermomètre chez moi.

   B. Oui bien sûr, je vais te le chercher tout de suite.

   C. Il fait très froid dehors. Le thermomètre montre qu'il fait zéro degré

   D. Il faut faire attention lorsque les enfants ont de la fièvre.

6. **(Personne A)** Ce film a été très long, je ne l'ai pas du tout aimé. Est-ce que tu l'as aimé?
(personne B)

   A. Je n'aime pas les chansons longues.

   B. Pourquoi n'as-tu pas dit à ton frère de venir avec nous?

   C. Au contraire, c'était un très bon film, je l'ai bien aimé.

   D. Demain je vais au cinéma avec mes enfants.

7. **(Personne A)** Mon fruit préféré est l'ananas. Et toi?
(personne B)

   A. Il n'y a plus de fraises au marché.

   B. J'ai des allergies aux ananas.

   C. Moi je préfère les oranges.

   D. Mes enfants adorent les ananas.

8. **(Personne A)** Il fait très sombre au parc pendant la soirée, j'ai peur d'y aller tout seul. Est-ce que tu peux venir avec moi?
(personne B)

   A. Les voleurs se cachent au parc tous les soirs.

   B. Je peux t'accompagner si tu veux.

   C. J'ai laissé mon livre au parc, je dois aller le chercher

   D. Il n'y a personne au parc.

9. **(Personne A)** Mes enfants aiment que je leur raconte une histoire avant de dormir. Tes enfants aussi?
(personne B)

   A. Mes enfants aiment aussi les histoires.

   B. Les livres pour enfants sont chers dans cette librairie.

   C. Ma fille aime colorier.

   D. Je m'endors souvent avant mes enfants lorsque je leur raconte des histoires.

French

10. *(Personne A)* **Je dois acheter un cadeau à ma mère pour son anniversaire. As-tu des idées?** *(personne B)*

   A. J'ai acheté une montre à ma mère.

   B. Je n'aime pas acheter des cadeaux.

   C. J'ai reçu un bon cadeau hier.

   D. Tu peux peut être lui demander ce dont elle a besoin.

Answer Key

1. A
2. C
3. C
4. A
5. B
6. C
7. C
8. B
9. A
10. D

Please note that this is a sample portion of the CLEP French examination. A complete practice test is available for purchase at Amazon.com and Barnesandnoble.com as an ebook. ISBN 9781607875123

German

Description of the Examination

The German Language examination is designed to measure knowledge and ability equivalent to that of students who have completed two to four semesters of college German language study. It focuses on skills typically achieved from the end of the first year through the second year of college study; material taught during both years is incorporated into a single examination. The examination is administered in three separately timed sections:

- Sections I and II: Listening
- Section III: Reading

The examination contains approximately 120 questions to be answered in 90 minutes. The three sections are weighted so that each question contributes equally to the total score. Any time candidates spend on tutorials or providing personal information is in addition to the actual testing time. Most colleges that award credit for the German Language examination award either two or four semesters of credit, depending on the candidate's score on the exam.

Knowledge and Skills Required

Questions on the German Language examination require candidates to demonstrate the abilities listed in each section below. The percentages indicate the approximate percentage of exam questions focused on each ability.

40% **Sections I and II: Listening**

- 15% Rejoinders
  Ability to understand spoken language through short stimuli or everyday situations
- 25% Dialogues and Narratives
  Ability to understand the language as spoken by native speakers in longer dialogues and narratives

60% **Section III: Reading**

- 16% Part A: Discrete sentences: Mastery of vocabulary and structure in the context of sentences
- 20% Part B: Short cloze passages: Mastery of vocabulary and structure in the context of paragraphs
- 24% Part C: Reading comprehension: Ability to read and understand texts representative of various styles and levels of difficulty (e.g., passages of about 200 words; shorter pieces such as advertisements, signs, etc.)

German

SECTION I

Listening: Rejoinders

> **Directions:** You will hear short conversations or parts of conversations. You will then hear four responses, designated (A), (B), (C), and (D). After you hear the four responses, select the response that most logically continues or completes the conversation. Write your answer choice on your answer sheet. Neither the answer choices nor the conversations will be printed in your test booklet, so you must listen very carefully. You will have 10 seconds to choose your response before the next conversation begins.

1. **Man A:** Nächste Woche werden meine Eltern nach Spanien fliegen, weil sie dort Urlaub machen möchten.

   Woman: Was tun die Eltern nächste Woche?

   Man B:
   A. Sie werden zum Flughafen fahren.
   B. Sie reisen nach Italien.
   C. Sie werden sehr fleißig arbeiten.
   D. Sie werden zu Hause bleiben.

2. **Woman A:** Kennst Du den Film „Lola Rennt"? Den fand ich ganz toll! Du solltest ihn auch mal sehen.

   Man: Was passiert hier?

   Woman B:
   A. Die Frau erzält von einem Film, den sie schrecklich fand.
   B. Die Frau empfiehlt einen Film, der ihr gut gefallen hat.
   C. Die Frau hat den Film schon dreimal gesehen.
   D. Die Frau freut sich darauf, einen ihr unbekannten Film zu sehen.

3. **Man A:** Vorgestern bin ich in die Stadt gefahren und habe Milch, Apfelsaft, Brot, Eier und Käse gekauft.

   Woman: Was ist passiert vorgestern?

   Man B:
   A. Der Mann ist im Supermakt einkaufen gegangen.
   B. Der Mann ist in der Polizeistation einkaufen gegangen.
   C. Der Mann ist bei der Post einkaufen gegangen.
   D. Der Mann ist in der Bibliothek einkaufen gegangen.

4. **Woman A:** Wollen wir am Samstag oder Sonntag wandern gehen?
   Woman B: Was für eine tolle Idee! Wenn es nicht regnet, gehen wir bestimmt.

   Man A: Was beschließen die zwei Frauen?

   Man B: A. So lange das Wetter gut sein wird, werden sie auf eine einwöchige Wanderung gehen.
   B. Wenn es regnet, gehen sie am Wochenende wandern.
   C. Am Samstag oder Sonntag wird das Wetter schlecht sein.
   D. So lange das Wetter gut sein wird, werden sie am Wochenende Wandern gehen.

5. **Man A:** Wenn ich in die Kneipe gehe, trinke ich am liebsten Bier. Du auch, oder?
   Man B: Nein, eigentlich nicht. Mir gefällt am besten Rotwein.

   Woman A: Worüber sprechen die zwei Männer?

   Woman B: A. Wo sie zur Zeit etwas Alkohol trinken wollen
   B. Getränke, die ihnen am wenigsten gefallen
   C. Ihren gemeinsamen Geschmack in Alkohol
   D. Ihren unterschiedlichen Geschmack in Alkohol

6. **Woman A:** Michael, hast Du Julia schon angerufen und zum Abendessen eingeladen?
   Man A: Nein, ich wollte sie beim Arbeiten nicht stören. Ich werde sie etwas später anrufen.

   Woman B: Was tut Michael?

   Man B: A. Er wird Julia in ein paar Stunden anrufen.
   B. Er wird Julia sofort anrufen.
   C. Er wird Julia nicht anrufen.
   D. Er hat Julia schon angerufen.

7. **Man A:** Wie wollen wir dorthin? Zu Fuß oder mit einem Taxi?
   Woman A: Eine Taxifahrt wäre viel zu teuer.

   Woman B: Was wurde hier beschlossen?

   Man B: A. Dorthin fahren sie nicht mit einem Taxi.
   B. Dorthin fahren sie überhaupt nicht.
   C. Dorthin fahren sie nicht mit dem Bus.
   D. Dorthin fahren sie doch lieber mit einem Taxi.

German

8. **Man A:** Meine Schwester studiert Rechtswissenschaft an der Universität.

Woman: Was möchte sie danach wohl werden?

Man B:
A. Automechanikerin
B. Tierärztin
C. Rechtsanwältin
D. Physikerin

9. **Woman A:** Seit drei Jahren isst Elke kein Fleisch mehr.

Man: Was bedeutet das?

Woman B:
A. Seit drei Jahren isst sie Fleisch besonders gern.
B. Sie trinkt auch keine Milch mehr.
C. Seit drei Jahren isst sie nur Obst.
D. Sie ist Vegetarierin geworden.

10. **Man A:** Ich habe Lust auf ein Eis, also werde ich mir bald eins holen.

Woman: Welches Geschmack isst Du am Liebsten?

Man A:
A. Blau
B. Schokolade
C. Rot
D. Heiß

Answer Key

1. A	6. A
2. B	7. A
3. A	8. C
4. D	9. D
5. D	10. B

Please note that this is a sample portion of the CLEP German examination. A complete practice test is available for purchase at Amazon.com and Barnesandnoble.com as an ebook.
ISBN 9781607875369

Spanish

Description of the Examination

The Spanish Language examination is designed to measure knowledge and ability equivalent to that of students who have completed two to four semesters of college Spanish language study. The exam focuses on skills typically achieved from the end of the first year through the second year of college study; material taught during both years is incorporated into a single exam.

The examination contains approximately 120 questions to be answered in approximately 90 minutes. Some of these are pretest questions that will not be scored. There are three separately timed sections. The three sections are weighted so that each question contributes equally to the total score. Any time candidates spend on tutorials or providing personal information is in addition to the actual testing time.

There are two Listening sections and one Reading section. Each section has its own timing requirements.
- The two Listening sections together are approximately 30 minutes in length. The amount of time candidates have to answer a question varies according to the section and does not include the time they spend listening to the test material.
- The Reading section is 60 minutes in length.

Most colleges that award credit for the Spanish Language exam award either two or four semesters of credit, depending on the candidate's test scores.

Knowledge and Skills Required

Questions on the Spanish Language examination require candidates to comprehend written and spoken Spanish. The subject matter is drawn from the following abilities. The percentages next to the main topics indicate the approximate percentage of exam questions on that ability.

60% **Section III: Reading**
- 16% Part A: Discrete sentences (vocabulary and structure)
- 20% Part B: Short cloze passages (vocabulary and structure)
- 24% Part C: Reading passages and authentic stimulus materials (reading comprehension)

15% **Section I:**
- Listening: Rejoinders
- Listening comprehension through short oral exchanges

25% **Section II:**
- Listening: Dialogues and Narratives
- Listening comprehension through longer spoken selections

Spanish

SECTION I

Listening: Rejoinders

Directions: You will hear short conversations or parts of conversations. You will then hear four responses, designated (A), (B), (C), and (D). After you hear the four responses, select the response that most logically continues or completes the conversation. Fill in the corresponding oval on your answer sheet. Neither the answer choices nor the conversations will be printed in your test booklet, so you must listen very carefully. You will have 10 seconds to choose your response before the next conversation begins.

Número 1.   **HOMBRE:** Si fuera millonario como tú, compraría una casa en Miami.
                MUJER:
                A. Yo voy para los Estados Unidos en agosto.
                B. Gracias a la venta de lotería, se sostiene la salud del país.
                C. Creo que es un gasto inoficioso.
                D. Mis abuelos viven en Miami.

Número 2.   **HOMBRE:** ¿Qué horas son?
                MUJER:
                A. 3 de Septiembre.
                B. Las 10 en punto.
                C. Son las 15 más 60.
                D. 1998.

Número 3.   **MUJER:** Hola Andrés, ¿Cómo se llama tu abuela?
                HOMBRE: A. Pedro.
                B. Raúl.
                C. Andrés.
                D. María.

Número 4.   **MUJER:** ¿Has visto la nueva película de comedia?
                HOMBRE: A. No la he visto.
                B. No lo he visto.
                C. Ya lo vi.
                D. Ya las vi.

Número 5.   **HOMBRE:** ¿Has estado alguna vez en Bogotá?
                MUJER: A. No fue.
                B. Si, estuvo.
                C. El año pasado.
                D. Si, hemos estado una vez.

Número 6.   **HOMBRE:** ¿Vamos al cine esta noche?
                MUJER: A. Voy de vacaciones en Diciembre.
                B. Comencé la universidad hace una semana.
                C. Me fui para la casa.
                D. Debo estudiar para un examen que tendré mañana.

Número 7.   **HOMBRE:** ¿Qué programa estudias en la universidad?
                  MUJER: A. Lenguas modernas.
                                B. Un ejercicio de matemáticas.
                                C. Para una prueba de español.
                                D. El programa de televisión, «Los Vaqueros».

Número 8.   **HOMBRE:** ¿Por qué la despidieron del trabajo?
                  MUJER: A. Porque siempre daba lo mejor de ella para realizar cualquier tarea de su trabajo.
                                B. Porque la reconocieron por su buen trabajo.
                                C. Porque era la mejor trabajadora.
                                D. Porque siempre llegaba tarde.

Número 9.   **HOMBRE:** Estuve viajando todo el día.
                  MUJER: A. ¿Qué lugares conociste?
                                B. ¿Qué cenaste?
                                C. ¿Cómo se llama tú mascota?
                                D. ¿Cómo es la luna?

Número 10.   **HOMBRE:** Viajaré a México el próximo mes.
                  MUJER: A. ¿Qué hiciste en navidad?
                                B. ¿Comprarás un avión?
                                C. ¿Visitarás a Claudia?
                                D. No sabía que te gustaba Manizales.

Número 11.   **HOMBRE:** El médico me prohibió el licor.
                  MUJER: A. ¿Qué coctel quieres?
                                B. ¿Te invito a tomar whisky?
                                C. ¿Cuál es tu licor favorito?
                                D. ¿Por cuánto tiempo?

Número 12.   **MUJER:**   ¿Vives en una casa o un apartamento?
                  HOMBRE: A. Mi madre vive en una casa.
                                B. ¡Adivina!, en un edificio.
                                C. Mi hermana vive en un apartamento.
                                D. La universidad es muy grande.

Número 13.   **MUJER:**   ¿Cuál es tu nacionalidad?
                  HOMBRE: A. Perú.
                                B. Colombiano.
                                C. Argentina.
                                D. Brasilia.

Número 14. **MUJER:** ¿Qué vehículo tienes?
HOMBRE: A. Un carro y una motocicleta.
B. Una casa en la playa.
C. Un perro pequeño.
D. Una piscina privada.

Número 15. **MUJER:** ¿Tocas algún instrumento?
HOMBRE: A. Mi padre toca la batería.
B. Toco la puerta de mi casa.
C. Guitarra y además canto.
D. Mi hija está estudiando piano.

Número 16. **MUJER:** ¿Te gustan los animales?
HOMBRE: A. Me gustan todos.
B. Mi abuela tiene dos perros.
C. A mi tía le encantan los pájaros.
D. Mi novia tiene cuatro gatos.

Número 17. **MUJER:** ¿Tienes hijos?
HOMBRE: A. Tenemos dos niñas.
B. Ella está embarazada.
C. Se llama Luciana.
D. Un bebé.

Número 18. **MUJER:** ¿Tu novia habla español?
HOMBRE: A. Sí, hablo español.
B. Sí, hablo cuatro idiomas.
C. Sí, es su lengua materna.
D. No, ella es de Argentina.

Spanish

SECTION II
Listening: Dialogues and Narratives

Directions: You will hear a series of dialogues, news reports, narratives, and announcements. Listen carefully, because each selection will be stated only once. One or more questions with four possible answers are printed in your test booklet. They will not be stated. After each selection has been read, choose the best answer choice for each question and fill in the corresponding oval in your answer sheet. You will be given 12 seconds to answer each question.

Selección número 1: **Dos amigos en el aeropuerto**

MÓNICA: Entonces, Andrés, ¿Cómo va tu trabajo nuevo?
ANDRÉS: Muy bien. Inicié hace seis meses y es genial.
MÓNICA: Y hasta el momento ¿A qué países has ido?
ANDRÉS: Principalmente a los de Europa. ¡Me encantan!
MÓNICA: ¿Y pudiste conocer los Países Bajos, porque son un gran atractivo turístico?
ANDRES: Lastimosamente no, porque después de cada vuelo terminé muy cansado y sólo tuve tiempo para irme a descansar a mi cuarto de hotel.
MÓNICA: Bueno, yo sé que tú sirves bebidas y comidas. ¿Qué otras funciones tienes?
ANDRES: A ver, ayudamos a los pasajeros nerviosos o enfermos. También nos cercioramos de que la gente obedezca y cumpla con las reglas de seguridad.
MÓNICA: ¡Vaya! Tu trabajo es fantástico, quisiera uno de esos.
ANDRES: Si es bastante bueno, sin embargo, algunas veces los horarios son muy extensos y no tengo tiempo para compartir con mi familia.

NARRADOR: Ahora contesta las preguntas 19, 20, y 21.

19. ¿Qué países conoce Andrés?

    A. Italia, Francia, y España.

    B. Casi toda Europa con excepto de los países Bajos.

    C. Los Países Bajos.

    D. Alemania, Inglaterra, y Suecia.

20. ¿A qué se dedica Mónica?

    A. A servir bebidas y comidas

    B. Es compañera de trabajo de Andrés.

    C. Ella no menciona su actividad.

    D. Es amiga de Andrés.

21. Además de servir bebidas y comidas, ¿qué otros servicio se prestan en los vuelos?

    A. Aconsejan a los pasajeros acerca del uso del baño.

    B. Dar recomendaciones sobre el comportamiento de los pasajeros durante el vuelo.

    C. Verificar los boletos de vuelo de los pasajeros.

    D. No se presta ningún servicio adicional.

Spanish

Selección número 2: **¿Dónde está el dentista?**

LAURA: Buenos días, Señor Vigilante, tengo un dolor muy fuerte en mi muela y quisiera que me atendieran lo más pronto posible para sanar mi dolor.
VIGILANTE: Buenos días, chica. Debes esperar un momento mientras atienden a los pacientes que han llegado antes de ti, ¿Puedes darme tu nombre y número de identificación?
LAURA: Si, es Laura Colorado y mi número es 10465741.
VIGILANTE: Puedes sentarte en las sillas que se encuentran en el pasillo.
LAURA: Muchas gracias, Señor Vigilante
DOCTORA LINA: Laura puedes seguir. ¿Cuéntame--que te pasa?
LAURA: Buenas noches, Doctora. Me está doliendo mucho mi muela y quisiera que me recetaras algún medicamento.
DOCTORA LINA: Primero debo examinarte para saber exactamente qué es lo que te sucede.
LAURA: Hum, ¡Está bien!
DOCTORA LINA: Laura, lamento decirte que debo extraerte la muela porque el problema está afectando tu nervio.
LAURA: A pesar de que suena muy doloroso, lo permitiré. Muchas gracias, Doctora.

NARRADOR: Ahora contesta las preguntas de 22, 23, y 24.

22. **¿Qué desea Laura al ingresar al Centro Médico?**

    A. Que el vigilante le saque la muela.

    B. Que le presten el servicio de inmediato.

    C. Que la afilien al sistema de salud.

    D. Que atiendan a su madre urgentemente.

23. **¿Qué le solicita el vigilante a Laura?**

    A. Sus datos personales.

    B. La dirección de ella.

    C. Los datos personales de su madre.

    D. Su nombre y número telefónico.

24. **¿Quién se sienta en las sillas del pasillo?**

    A. La madre de Laura.

    B. La doctora.

    C. Laura y su madre.

    D. La paciente.

Selección número 3: En la Universidad

ADRIANA: Hola querida amiga, ¿cómo estás?

LORENA: Hola amiga, un poco preocupada porque ya se acerca el final del último corte y no entiendo el tema del examen de Física II.

ADRIANA: ¿Y qué tal es tu profesor?

LORENA: Es difícil porque los temas que él dicta son muy abstractos y no sabe explicarlos muy bien.

ADRIANA: ¿Y cuál es el tema que no entiendes?

LORENA: El tema de Ley de Gauss.

ADRIANA: ¡Ah!, ¡Interesante! No te preocupes amiga. Yo te puedo ayudar con eso.

LORENA: Que buena noticia, me volvió el alma al cuerpo. ¿Cuándo me puedes explicar?

ADRIANA: Hoy mismo, y sé que te va a ir muy bien con mi ayuda.

LORENA: Muchas gracias amiga. Te debo este favor.

NARRADOR: Ahora contesta las preguntas 25, 26, y 27.

25. ¿Qué son las dos mujeres del diálogo?

    A. Primas.

    B. Hermanas.

    C. Compañeras.

    D. Familiares.

26. ¿Por qué está preocupada una de las mujeres?

    A. Porque no ha tenido tiempo de estudiar.

    B. Porque no entiende el tema de la prueba.

    C. Porque perdió el examen.

    D. Porque su profesor diseña exámenes muy difíciles de pasar.

27. Mencione las razones por lo que el tema es difícil:

    A. Tiene muchos temas de matemática y física.

    B. Son inconcretos y ella no le entiende a su profesor.

    C. Ella no entiende el idioma del profesor.

    D. Ella ha faltado en asistir a varias clases.

Selección número 4: **Dos compañeros de trabajo**

FELIPE: Hola Claudia, ¿sabes cuál es la última noticia?
CLAUDIA: No sé, ¿Me puedes compartir esa información?
FELIPE: Parece que las ventas están muy bajas y la competencia de la industria de las golosinas está muy fuerte.
CLAUDIA: ¿Pero, esto nos afecta?
FELIPE: Por supuesto, de hecho esta mañana el gerente en una reunión corporativa anunció algunos cierres de unas sucursales que funcionan en nuestro país--y habrán despidos.
CLAUDIA: Es bastante alarmante, pero también escuché que las personas que van a continuar trabajando son las que llevan más de dos años en la compañía.
FELIPE: ¡Uf! entonces tú y yo seguiremos ya que somos también excelentes, no te preocupes
CLAUDIA: Esperemos que sí, porque el día de mañana será la decisión definitiva
FELIPE: Perfecto, Claudia. Pronto nos volvemos a ver y ojalá sea en esta misma compañía.
CLAUDIA: Listo querido Felipe. Estaremos en contacto.

NARRADOR: Ahora contesta las preguntas 28, 29, y 30.

28. ¿Qué le va a compartir Felipe a Claudia?

    A. Unas golosinas muy exquisitas.

    B. Las nuevas estrategias que tiene la Compañía.

    C. Le va a decir que la empresa tiene clientes nuevos.

    D. Una información muy importante.

29. Lo que le dice Felipe a Claudia tiene que ver con:

    A. Las ventas altas y el dinamismo de la competencia.

    B. Las ventas bajas y la intensidad de la competencia.

    C. Las ventas y la competencia fuerte.

    D. Las ventas y la competencia.

30. ¿Afectaría a los empleados de la empresa el anuncio que dio el gerente?

    A. No, porque el cierre de sucursales no afectará a los empleados.

    B. No, porque la sucursales nuevas generarán más empleos.

    C. Sí, porque el cierre de las sucursales provocará despidos.

    D. Sí, porque el cierre de las sucursales generará caos.

Selección número 5: Viaje

LUCIANA: Ven, ¿cuéntame cómo te fue en el viaje?
JACOBO: Estuvo genial, lástima que no fuiste, ¿Qué te paso?
LUCIANA: ¡Que rabia! Tenía que cumplir con un informe de trabajo y desafortunadamente coincidieron las fechas, ¿Y qué tal Venecia?
JACOBO: ¡Es encantadora, sus canales, sus hoteles, su gastronomía y sus paisajes son fantásticos!
LUCIANA: Ojalá hubiera podido ir, pero mi esposo también estaba muy indispuesto y lo único que quería hacer era visitar al doctor. Por lo tanto fue difícil acompañarte.
JACOBO: Para una próxima ocasión, planeamos un viaje incluso mejor que éste.
LUCIANA: Si, me parece muy buena idea.

NARRADOR: Ahora contesta las preguntas 31, 32, y 33.

31. ¿Cómo le fue en el viaje a Jacobo?

    A. Tuvo muchos inconvenientes.

    B. Le fue muy bien pero no le gusto la ciudad a su esposa.

    C. Le dio mucha rabia porque le fue mal.

    D. Muy bien, pero le dio tristeza porque su amiga no fue.

32. ¿Por qué no fue Luciana al viaje?

    A. Porque su esposo estaba muy indispuesto.

    B. Porque el esposo debía ir al doctor y ella debía presentar informes.

    C. Porque no tenía dinero.

    D. Porque al pagar las deudas no le quedo dinero.

33. ¿En qué se destaca Venecia?

    A. En sus paisajes, hoteles, canales, y gastronomía.

    B. En sus canales, hoteles, y gastronomía.

    C. En su gastronomía, paisajes, y canales.

    D. Por su laguna adriática.

Selección número 6: **La aplicación número 1 de los teléfonos móviles**

En la actualidad, *WhatsApp* ha revolucionado las comunicaciones en el mundo entero pero está perjudicando a las Compañías que ofrecen mensajería instantánea y llamada de voz. *WhatsApp*, como es conocida, funciona con datos, como 3G, 2G o Wi-Fi. Esta aplicación se destaca por ofrecer servicios de calidad sin precio alguno; al igual que sus competidores actuales como *Tango, Viber, Line*, etcétera sin embargo, ésta aplicación marca la diferencia por sus cerca de 500 mil usuarios activos en el 2015, y porque cuenta con muchas características que son llamativas para los usuarios entre las que sobresalen; la actualización de los contactos a través de la agenda del teléfono móvil, la gratuidad para los distintos sistemas operativos como: *iOS, Android, Windows Phone, BlackBerry*, y la comunicación en tiempo real.

NARRADOR: Ahora contesta las preguntas 34, 35, y 36.

34. ¿Qué beneficios le ha traído WhatsApp a las empresas de comunicaciones?

    A. Los usuarios se pueden comunicar en tiempo real.

    B. Ha generado más empleo dentro de las compañías.

    C. Al contrario, WhatsApp las está afectando.

    D. Ha obligado a hacer alianzas entre las compañías.

35. ¿Por qué medio de conexión funciona WhatsApp?

    A. Wifi, 2G, 3G.

    B. 2G, 1G, 4G.

    C. Wifi, 3G ,4G.

    D. Wifi, 2G,4G.

36. ¿En la actualidad cuántos usuarios activos tiene WhatsApp?

    A. Medio millón de usuarios.

    B. Mil quinientos millones de usuarios.

    C. Quinientos millones de usuarios.

    D. Un millón de usuarios.

Selección número 7: **El ejercicio físico: Un buen aliado**

No cabe duda que el ejercicio es bueno para el cuerpo y la mente y una adecuada práctica de éste aumenta los niveles de energía e incluso ayuda a equilibrar las emociones. Los expertos recomiendan hacer ejercicio por una hora cada día, sin embargo, sólo el 15 por ciento lo practican, el resto de la población lo abandona por falta de interés, y se dedica mejor al sedentarismo, siendo éste último el causante de las enfermedades que aquejan a las personas en la actualidad. El ejercicio es sinónimo de prevención, si se practica con regularidad. Lo más probable es que los trastornos, las dolencias, y los desequilibrios emocionales sean temas del pasado.

NARRADOR: Ahora contesta las preguntas 37, 38, y 39.

37. ¿Qué produce el ejercicio?

    A. Una mente y un cuerpo sano, y contribuye al equilibrio de las emociones.

    B. Oxigena el cerebro y quema calorías.

    C. Aumenta los niveles de energía y ayuda a la concentración.

    D. Mejora la capacidad mental para desarrollar las actividades cotidianas efectivamente.

38. ¿Qué recomiendan los expertos?

    A. Caminar durante 60 minutos cada día.

    B. Hacer 70 minutos de ejercicio cada día.

    C. Trotar media hora y caminar otra media hora.

    D. Hacer una hora de ejercicio cada día.

39. Según la narración, ¿cuántas son las personas que están practicando ejercicio?:

    A. El 75 por ciento de la población lo practica.

    B. La cuarta parte de la población lo practica.

    C. La mitad de la población lo practica dos veces al día.

    D. El 50 por ciento de la población lo practica.

Selección número 8: La realidad del cambio climático

Es indiscutible--el cambio climático es evidente y está sucediendo. Ese es gracias al descontrol del ser humano en el uso desmesurado de herramientas modernas y otros elementos para hacer la vida más fácil y cómoda a la humanidad y que ha afectado el planeta. Se está generando un efecto devastador que está terminando con la vida de la fauna y la flora del planeta tierra. El calentamiento global debería empezar a disminuir, pero al contrario, la actividad de los seres humanos lo está aumentando más cada día. Los estudios demuestran que los últimos 11 años han sido los más calurosos, incrementado la temperatura global promedio en 0.74°C durante el Siglo XXI, y a esto se suma el dióxido de carbono que ha dominado el comportamiento de este cambio climático.

NARRADOR: Ahora contesta las preguntas 40, 41, y 42.

40. ¿Cómo perjudica el humano al planeta tierra?

    A. Con los desperdicios que emiten las empresas.

    B. Con el uso de trenes.

    C. Con la utilización de tecnologías.

    D. Con el arrojo de basuras a los ríos.

41. ¿Cuáles especies se están extinguiendo debido al cambio climático?

    A. Los jaguares.

    B. La flora y fauna amazónica.

    C. Todas las especies del África.

    D. La fauna y flora de todos los continentes.

42. ¿Está disminuyendo el calentamiento global?

    A. Sí, porque el humano se ha concientizado para cuidar el planeta.

    B. No, porque los humanos lo aumentan con sus actividades.

    C. Sí, porque la contaminación lo disminuye cada día.

    D. No, al contrario los humanos están derrumbando los bosques.

Selección número 9: La religión en un mundo complejo

Las religiones están viviendo uno de sus mejores momentos. El hecho reside es que por primera vez en muchos años se puede diferenciar claramente entre las creencias y la estructura social moderna. Pues en los últimos años ante tantos problemas que enfrenta el mundo actual, se están generando vivencias negativas para muchas personas como: la depresión, la baja autoestima, etcétera--lo que están aprovechando para dar a conocer la palabra de salvación al dar absolución a los pecados. Sin embargo, según un informe hecho por una universidad Colombiana a los participantes, sólo la mitad de las propuestas establecidas por la religión han sido exitosas en Latinoamérica, por consiguiente los líderes religiosos deben ser constantes con la expansión de las iglesias y templos, para ir en búsqueda de una religión sólida que prometa y cumpla cada palabra.

NARRADOR: *Ahora contesta las preguntas 43, 44, y 45*

43. ¿Qué religiones se mencionan en el texto?

    A. El Hinduismo.

    B. El Cristianismo.

    C. El Budismo.

    D. Todas las religiones.

44. ¿Por qué las religiones están en su mejor momento?

    A. Porque debido a la violencia, las religiones juegan un papel de liderazgo en la generación de paz.

    B. Porque la fe es la tendencia actual.

    C. Porque hay más construcciones de templos e iglesias.

    D. Porque debido a las enfermedades emocionales del Siglo XXI, las personas buscan en que tener fe.

45. ¿De qué manera están inculcando las religiones la fe en las personas?

    A. Guiando al hombre hacia la paz.

    B. Enseñando el camino de lo divino a través de la redención.

    C. Mostrando testimonios de personas que han conseguido la felicidad.

    D. Dando herramientas para aprender a orar o meditar.

Selección número 10: Comprar o no comprar

Un comprador compulsivo difícilmente puede controlarse. No es grave cuando compra para satisfacer sus necesidades, pero si lo es cuando decide comprar cosas que no necesita. Muchos expertos afirman que las personas que se comportan de esta manera, están ligados a diversos trastornos psicológicos que además están afectando su círculo social. La depresión y la ansiedad son las causas principales por la que las personas con esta enfermedad deciden comprar exageradamente. La personalidad típica del comprador compulsivo es una mujer o un hombre, no importa que clase social, que ha desarrollado una costumbre que fuerza a comprar ropa, zapatos, joyas, productos de belleza, aparatos tecnológicos, y otras herramientas para el hogar. Sobre este tema se deben modificar estos comportamientos, porque se debe entender que comprar no los hace feliz. Al final termina consumiendo a las personas y quizás con el dolor de haber gastado un dinero que se necesitaba para otras cosas más importantes realmente.

NARRADOR: *Ahora contesta las preguntas de la 46, 47, y 48.*

46. Una persona que va de compras constantemente es:

   A. Un comprador generoso.

   B. Feliz.

   C. Satisface todas sus necesidades.

   D. Padece de un trastorno psicológico.

47. ¿Cuál es la causa por la que una persona se convierte en un comprador compulsivo?

   A. La falta de gastarse el dinero.

   B. El pensamiento consumista.

   C. Estados del comprador compulsivo después de ir de compras.

   D. Trastornos emocionales.

48. ¿Cuál es la verdadera problemática que refleja la narración?

   A. Los daños que puede causar comprar exageradamente.

   B. Los trastornos emocionales.

   C. Cómo debemos invertir nuestro dinero.

   D. Qué lugares debemos visitar para hacer compras.

SECTION III

Reading Part A: Discreet Sentences

Directions: The following statements are incomplete, followed by four suggested completions. Select the one that best completes the sentence.

49. Aquellos libros son _____ Juan Carlos.

    A. de

    B. para

    C. dentro

    D. por

50. Mi abuela se _____ de cólera hace dos años.

    A. enferma

    B. enfermera

    C. enfermó

    D. enfermaron

51. Maud Wagner es la _____ tatuadora reconocida en los Estados Unidos.

    A. primeras

    B. primero

    C. primera

    D. primeros

52. La Tierra _____ alrededor del Sol todos los días.

    A. giró

    B. girar

    C. giraba

    D. gira

53. Julieta es capaz de memorizar datos _____.

    A. fácilmente.

    B. facilidad.

    C. facílmente.

    D. fácil.

54. Ernesto y Ramón _____ estado hablando sobre política durante toda la reunión.

    A. a

    B. ha

    C. han

    D. hemos

55. La _____ aun y cuando no sea metálica, puede llegar a ser pesada. De ahí su nombre, que proviene de la palabra griega *baros*. Tiene diversos usos en la industria automotriz y médica.

   A. varita

   B. varitas

   C. barita

   D. baritas

56. ¿Quiénes se _____ al vecindario la semana pasada?

   A. viene

   B. trae

   C. están

   D. mudaron

57. Yo estaba _____ la ropa sucia mientras tú cocinabas.

   A. lavar

   B. planchando

   C. lavando

   D. habiendo planchado

58. A mí me gusta escuchar _____ radio _____ enterarme de las noticias Internacionales.

   A. el, por

   B. la, para

   C. el, debido a

   D. el, para

59. Marcelo _____ Hilda se conocen _____ que tenían cinco años de edad.

   A. e, desde

   B. y, desde

   C. e, por

   D. y, durante

60. Aun y cuando no _____ limpiar la casa, lo tienen que hacer.

   A. quieres

   B. quiera

   C. querer

   D. quieran

61. _____ papá quiere verte enseguida.

   A. tu

   B. Tú

   C. Tu

   D. tús

62. Los aviones son _____

  A. guapas.

  B. metálicas.

  C. perezosos.

  D. rápidos.

63. _____ no sabía que yo había ganado el concurso, cuando Tomás me dio la noticia.

  A. Todavía

  B. Ellos

  C. María y Juan

  D. Para

64. _____ tuvieron una _____ discusión sobre política.

  A. María y Juan, débil

  B. Antonella y Mario, fuerte

  C. Carlos y Brenda, apoderada

  D. María y Juan, sencilla

65. ¿Cuál es el predicado en la siguiente oración?

  <u>Ana María y sus hermanas son las hijas del dueño de la hacienda.</u>

  A. Ana María y sus hermanas son

  B. Ana María

  C. son las hijas del dueño de la hacienda

  D. las hijas de dueño de la hacienda

66. Todos me dijeron que en el festival bailé <u>estupendamente.</u>
La palabra subrayada es:

  A. adjetivo.

  B. adverbio.

  C. complemento circunstancial de modo.

  D. B y C.

67. _____ niño tiene gripe.

  A. La

  B. Los

  C. Las

  D. El

Spanish

SECTION III
Reading Part B: Short Cloze Passages

Directions: In each of the following paragraphs, there are blanks indicating that words or phrases have been omitted. For each blank, choose the completion that is most appropriate, given the context of the entire paragraph.

I. ____68____ Dálmata es una ____69____ de perros originarios de la histórica región de Dalmacia. ____70____ característica principal es el ____71____ blanco con manchas negras.

68. A. Un	69. A. raza	70. A. Una	71. A. pelos
B. Los	B. rasa	B. Sus	B. pelaje
C. El	C. razo	C. Unos	C. cabello
D. La	D. raso	D. Su	D. cabellera

II. A mi ____72____ materna le dio ____73____. La cual, es una enfermedad causada por un virus, altamente mortal. Quienes la padecen se quejan de un agudo dolor en la ____74____. Dicha enfermedad se detectó por primera vez en 1976 y desde entonces no se ha podido erradicar al ____75____ porciento.

72. A. abuelas	73. A. abuelas	74. A. cienes	75. A. cienes
B. abuela	B. abuela	B. sien	B. sien
C. ebola	C. ebola	C. cien	C. cien
D. ébola	D. ébola	D. sienes	D. sienes

III. *El ingenioso hidalgo Don Quijote de La Mancha* es la novela más publicada y ____76____ de la historia después de La Biblia. La ____77____ Miguel de Cervantes Saavedra. La segunda parte ____78____ en 1615 y desde entonces ha influenciado la ____79____.

76. A. traducción	77. A. escribió	78. A. apareció	79. A. economía
B. traducida	B. escrita	B. escribió	B. literatura
C. traduje	C. escritura	C. mostró	C. publicidad
D. tradujeron	D. han escrito	D. se perdió	D. mercadotecnia

IV. Una pregunta frecuente en la medicina es ¿____80____ dan comezón las cicatrices? Se cree que es ____81____ la piel se está regenerando y deshaciéndose del tejido muerto, generando comezón. Quienes pasan por esta situación se preocupan ____82____ la cicatriz pueda infectarse. Información a fondo sobre el ____83____ de dicho malestar puede ser encontrada en línea y libros referentes al tema.

80. A. porque	81. A. porque	82. A. porque	83. A. porque
B. por que	B. por que	B. por que	B. por que
C. Por qué	C. Por qué	C. Por qué	C. Por qué
D. porqué	D. porqué	D. porqué	D. porqué

Spanish

V. Leonor y yo ____84____ conocemos desde la primaria. Ella vivía ____85____ mi vecindario. Todos los días caminábamos juntas hacia la escuela. A veces la ____86____ a jugar a ____87____ casa.

84. A. nos
B. se
C. las
D. te

85. A. por
B. para
C. entre
D. de

86. A. mandaba
B. manchaba
C. invitaba
D. invité

87. A. tu
B. mi
C. mí
D. tú

VI. Hay ___88___ edificios históricos en esta calle. La biblioteca es la primera. __89__ museo está a la izquierda de la biblioteca. ____90____ del museo está el teatro. El teatro es mi edificio favorito, porque es el más ____91____ de todos, datando desde la época colonial.

88. A. dos
B. cuatro
C. tres
D. uno

89. A. Un
B. El
C. Allá
D. Ahí

90. A. Encima
B. Sobre
C. Debajo
D. Detrás

91. A. antiguo
B. descuidado
C. nuevo
D. sucio

Spanish

SECTION III

Reading Part C: Reading Passages & Authentic Stimulus Material

Directions: Read each of the passages below. Each passage is followed by questions or incomplete statements. Choose the best answer according to the text and mark in the corresponding answer.

Archivo Parroquial de la Catedral de Santiago del Saltillo, Fondo Colonial. (1742). El Obispo Regaña a los Tlaxcaltecas. [La Gazeta del Saltillo Antiguo]. Libro de Gobierno No. 1, c5. F2. Source: http://www.archivomunicipaldesaltillo.info

92. ¿Qué objeto sostiene la mano?

    A. una cuchara.

    B. una vela.

    C. una pelota.

    D. un tenedor.

De León, J. (2014). Uso y desuso de las cosas. [Newspaper]. Source http://www.archivomunicipaldesaltillo.info

93. ¿Qué se observa en la imagen?

    A. teteras.

    B. una estufa.

    C. utensilios de cocina.

    D. comida.

Limón, N. (2014). Estrategias de autorrepresentación fotográfica, el caso de Frida Kahlo. UC3M

94. ¿Qué tiene en la cabeza la mujer?

A. una diadema.

B. un sombrero.

C. un tocado de flores.

D. un moño.

Vanguardia Liberal. (2015). Falleció el Fotógrafo Nereo López. [Newspaper]. Source: http://www.vanguardia.com

95. ¿Cuál es el lugar de origen del sujeto?

A. Nueva York.

B. Cartagena.

C. Barranquilla.

D. Ciudad de México

96. ¿Cuál era la profesión de Nereo López Meza?

A. Reportero.

B. Trotamundos.

C. Modelo.

D. Vendedor de sombreros.

La Florida, que en 1819 había sido anexada a la gran federación americana, fue erigida en estado algunos años más tarde. Por esta anexión, el territorio estadounidense aumentó en una extensión de 67,000 millas cuadradas. En resumen, la Florida se presenta como un país aparte y hasta extraño, con sus habitantes mitad españoles, mitad americanos y sus indios seminolas, muy diferentes a sus congéneres del «Far West»'
~ *Julio Verne, 1887; «Norte contra Sur»*

97. ¿Cuál es el tema principal del párrafo?

   A. La guerra civil de los Estados Unidos.

   B. Los habitantes de Norteamérica.

   C. La anexión de la Florida a los Estados Unidos.

   D. La extensión territorial de los Estados Unidos.

Europa conocía a Asia desde la antigüedad, pero fue sólo después del descubrimiento de rutas comerciales nuevas en el Siglo XVI que los contactos entre los dos continentes se intensificaron. Como consecuencia de los relatos de los navegantes, de los exploradores y de los mercaderes que habían visitado aquellas tierras, surgió en Europa una gran curiosidad hacia los pueblos orientales. Fueron sobre todo los misioneros católicos quienes sirvieron de puente entre la civilización de China y del mundo europeo.

98. ¿Quiénes eran la conexión entre Asia y Europa?

   A. Los chinos.

   B. Los navegantes.

   C. Los misioneros católicos.

   D. Los comerciantes.

El artista neerlandés, Maurits C. Escher, nació en Leeuwarden el 17 de junio de 1898. Su padre George, era ingeniero civil y estaba casado en segundas nupcias. Su madre, Sarah, era hija de un ministro. Movido por su deseo de ser arquitecto, Escher se matriculó en la Escuela de Arquitectura y Artes Decorativas de Haarlem. Él es conocido mundialmente por sus grabados y obras gráficas expresas de efectos espaciales enigmáticos.

99. ¿Cuál era la profesión de Escher?

   A. Artista.

   B. Ministro.

   C. Arquitecto.

   D. Ingeniero Civil.

Al analizar el progreso de la mujer a través de variables cuantitativas, la Fundación Clinton lanzó un reporte extensivo sobre las regulaciones nupciales de cada país, donde se reveló – para sorpresa de muchos – que ciertos estereotipos sobre las naciones ricas y pobres no son necesariamente aplicables. Países como Rusia, China, y Etiopía prohíben el matrimonio antes de los 18 años, mientras que en gran parte de América esto es permitido «con el consentimiento de los padres».

100. ¿Qué se puede deducir del párrafo?

A. En China y Rusia hay muchas bodas.

B. El párrafo sugiere que continúan las bodas infantiles aún en el Siglo XXI, sorpresivamente tanto en países establecidos, así como en naciones emergentes.

C. La Fundación Clinton es una organización importante dedicada al cuidado y bienestar de las niñas alrededor del mundo.

D. El matrimonio antes de los 18 años limita el potencial máximo de las niñas, afectando la salud, educación y seguridad.

Se cree que el tenedor llegó a Occidente procedente de Constantinopla en el siglo XI. Cuando Teodora, hija del emperador Constantino X Ducas, contrajo nupcias con el Dux Doménico Selvo. Sin embargo, Teodora, era señalada como escandalosa e incoherente debido a esta y otras costumbres por lo que autoridades eclesiásticas, llamaron a dicho utensilio «instrumentum diaboli», que en Español significa «instrumento diabólico».

101. ¿A qué se refiere la palabra «utensilio» en la quinta línea?

A. A Constantinopla.

B. Al tenedor.

C. A *instrumentum diaboli*.

D. A las costumbres.

CONTRATO AL QUE SE DEBERÁ DE SUJETAR LA MAESTRA (1923)

No casarse. Este contrato quedará automáticamente anulado y sin efecto si la maestra se casa. 2.- No andar en compañía de hombres. 3.- Estar en su casa entre las 8:00 de la noche y las 6:00 de la mañana a menos que sea para atender alguna función escolar. 4.- No pasearse por las heladerías del centro de la ciudad. 5.- No abandonar la ciudad bajo ningún concepto sin permiso del presidente del Consejo de Delegados. 6.- No fumar. Este contrato quedará automáticamente anulado y sin efecto si se encontrara a la maestra fumando. 7.- No beber cerveza ni vino ni whisky. Este contrato quedará automáticamente anulado y sin efecto si se encontrara a la maestra bebiendo cerveza o vino o whisky. 8.- No viajar en coche o en automóvil con ningún hombre con excepto de su hermano o su padre. 9.- No usar ropa de color brillante. 10.- No teñirse el cabello. 11.- No usar polvos faciales ni pintarse los labios.
~Saltillo de Coahuila de Zaragoza, 1923.

102. ¿Qué tipo de documento se infiere que es?

A. Una carta de amor.

B. Un contrato del año de 1923.

C. Un anuncio de publicidad de 1923.

D. Un contrato de bomberos.

103. ¿Cuál de las siguientes opciones es motivo para anular tal contrato?

A. Maquillarse.

B. Ejercitarse.

C. Cantar.

D. Bailar.

₁La Isla de Pascua, localizada en la Polinesia en medio del océano Pacífico, es la isla chilena más grande.

Actualmente, cuenta con una población de 5035 habitantes, todos ellos concentrados en la ciudad de Hanga Roa. La característica principal de este poblado son las esculturas misteriosas conocidas como «Moáis». Se conocen más de 900, mismas que se cree, fueron esculpidas por los «rapa nui», los habitantes aborígenes del lugar. Labradas en «toba» volcánica, algunas de ellas no terminadas, su significado es aún incierto. El nombre completo de las estatuas en su idioma original es «Moai Aringa Ora» que significa «rostro vivo de los ancestros». Lo que sugiere que fueron esculpidas para ₁₀representar a Gobernantes y antepasados importantes. Los reyes poseían este poder de manera innata; otros podían adquirirlo realizando una serie de hazañas extraordinarias que involucraban principalmente, la resistencia física. Dichas esculturas fueron esculpidas en distintos tamaños y con características distintas. Éstas eran esculpidas sobre la roca volcánica en el cráter mismo, después cinceladas por la espalda ₁₅para desprenderlas de sus nichos para posteriormente ser transportadas hasta el lugar que les pertenecía. La mayoría de ellas, de espaldas al mar. Es, sin duda, un lugar lleno de misterio y riqueza cultural, siendo uno de los atractivos turísticos principales del mundo.

104. ¿Cómo se les llama a los aborígenes de La Isla de Pascua?

A. Moáis.

B. Hanga Roas.

C. Rapa Nui.

D. Pascuenses.

105. ¿Qué significa la palabra *«innata»* en la octava línea?

A. Del lugar.

B. Aborígenes.

C. De nacimiento.

D. Cultural.

106. ¿De qué material están hechas las esculturas?

A. De oro.

B. Piedra volcánica.

C. De plata.

D. De arcilla.

Cuando los marcianos no hablan
₁Uno de los desafíos más grandes para los hombres es interpretar correctamente y apoyar a una mujer cuando habla de sus sentimientos. El mayor desafío para las mujeres es interpretar correctamente y apoyar a un hombre cuando no habla. El silencio resulta muy fácilmente malinterpretado por las mujeres. Hombres y mujeres piensan y procesan ₅información

en forma muy diferente. Las mujeres piensan en voz alta compartiendo su proceso de descubrimiento interior con un oyente interesado. Aún hoy, una mujer a menudo descubre qué quiere decir a través del proceso verbal simple. Este proceso de dejar simplemente que los pensamientos fluyan en libertad y expresarlos en voz alta, la ayuda en obtener provecho de su intuición. Este proceso es perfectamente normal y a veces especialmente necesario.

Pero los hombres procesan la información en forma muy diferente. Antes de hablar o responder, «meditan» o piensan en lo que escucharon o experimentaron. Interna y silenciosamente imaginan la respuesta más correcta y útil. Primero la formulan en su interior y luego la expresan. Este proceso podría tomar minutos u horas y para confundir aún más a las mujeres, si no tienen suficiente información para procesar una respuesta, pueden llegar a no responder.

Las mujeres necesitan entender que cuando él está en silencio, está diciendo: «Todavía no sé qué decir, pero estoy pensando en ello». En lugar de eso, ellas escuchan: «No te estoy respondiendo porque tú no me importas y yo voy a ignorarte. Lo que me has dicho no es importante y por lo tanto no responderé».
~John Gray, *Los hombres son de Marte y las mujeres son de Venus, 1995.*

107. ¿Cuál es el tema principal del texto?

   A. Los marcianos.

   B. Los extraterrestres.

   C. Los procesos mentales.

   D. Las mujeres.

108. Según el texto ¿Cómo procesan la información los hombres?

   A. Diferente.

   B. «Meditan».

   C. Rápido.

   D. Muy rápidamente.

109. ¿Cuál es el mayor desafío para las mujeres?

   A. Interpretar y apoyar correctamente a un hombre cuando habla de sus sentimientos.

   B. Interpretar y apoyar correctamente a un hombre cuando medita.

   C. Interpretar y apoyar correctamente a un hombre cuando no habla.

   D. Interpretar y apoyar correctamente a un hombre en la toma de decisiones.

110. ¿Qué sucede cuando los hombres se mantienen en silencio?

   A. Están formulando una pregunta para expresarla.

   B. Las mujeres lo malinterpretan y se enojan.

   C. Están formulando una respuesta para expresarla.

   D. Las mujeres están formulando una respuesta para expresarla.

111. ¿A qué se refiere la frase «piensan en voz alta» en la línea 5?

    A. Son ruidosas.

    B. Externan sus sentimientos y sus pensamientos.

    C. Hablan mucho.

    D. Piensan más rápido que los demás.

112. ¿Cuánto dura el procesamiento de pensamientos en el género masculino?

    A. Una hora.

    B. Minutos y horas.

    C. 30 minutos.

    D. Un minuto.

113. ¿Cómo traducen las mujeres el silencio en los hombres?

    A. Como falta de interés de los hombres por los sentimientos y pensamientos de las mujeres.

    B. Como ignorancia y miedo a responder acertadamente a los sentimientos de las mujeres.

    C. Saben que los hombres necesitan tiempo para meditar y procesar la información.

    D. Saben que los hombres tienen problemas para interpretar los sentimientos correctamente.

₁El pensamiento es esa pérdida de tiempo que tiene lugar entre el momento en que percibimos algo y el momento en que sabemos cómo manejarnos con respecto a lo percibido. Es un espacio de tiempo ocupado por la serie de ideas que se van sucediendo, una a partir de la otra, cuando intentamos elaborar la situación que nos resulta desconocida hasta transformarla en algo conocido que sabemos cómo enfrentar. Más ₅tarde, el hombre aprende a recrearse jugando con las ideas por el placer de hacerlo. Pero la finalidad biológica fundamental del pensamiento consiste en capacitar al organismo vivo para sobrevivir, procurándose todo aquello que necesita y alejándose de lo que le representa un peligro. De lo que se trata es de saber cómo reaccionar ante una situación: ¿Será conveniente abalanzarse con avidez o retroceder con recelo?
₁₀Tres son los pensamientos básicos que utilizan los seres vivos a fin de conocer las cosas lo bastante como para reaccionar ante ellas en forma apropiada.

1. *Instinto:* Es una reacción fija, integrada de tal modo que el organismo, ante una situación determinada, producirá automáticamente una respuesta determinada. Es directa, es automática, es inmutable como la iluminación de un ambiente 15cuando encendemos la luz. No se requiere ningún aprendizaje.

2. *Aprendizaje:* Existen dos tipos de aprendizaje: De primera mano y de segunda mano. El aprendizaje de primera mano es un proceso lento por medio del cual un organismo encuentra la respuesta conveniente a una situación mediante ensayo y error. Así un secretario descubre cómo es que su patrón prefiere que las cartas 20a los clientes sean escritas. El gato aprende a regresar al hogar y el jugador de tenis a sacar la pelota. Por otra parte, el aprendizaje de segunda mano es una

especie de instinto artificial. Conlleva respuestas inmediatas para situaciones, sin necesidad de pasar por el proceso lento de prueba y error. Es un tipo de aprendizaje transmitido, proviene de la televisión, y de la escuela.

3. *25Comprensión: ¿Qué sucede cuando lo que se nos presenta una situación desconocida, nueva totalmente para nuestra mente para la cual no tenemos respuesta? La comprensión es el proceso por el cual transformamos una situación desconocida en una situación conocida, para saber así cómo reaccionar ante ella. Proceso mediante el cual, se pasa de una idea a otra, con tal de afianzarla en la 30psique. El pasar de ideas es el pensamiento. Y comprender es pensar.*

114. **¿Cuáles son los tres pensamientos básicos que utilizan los seres vivos para reaccionar?**

    A. Pensar, aprender, y comprender.

    B. Pensar, actuar, e iluminar.

    C. Responder, comprender, y aprender.

    D. Aprender, comprender, e intuir.

115. **Según la lectura, ¿Qué es el pensamiento?**

    A. Una pérdida de tiempo.

    B. El momento entre percibir y actuar con respecto a lo percibido.

    C. Es un espacio de tiempo ocupado por cosas que suceden alrededor.

    D. Las situaciones que suceden una detrás de la otra.

116. **¿A qué se refiere la frase, «como la iluminación de un ambiente cuando encendemos la luz»?**

    A. La energía eléctrica es rápida y costosa.

    B. Es una manera de relacionar a, y explicar el concepto mediante la metáfora.

    C. Los ambientes con iluminación son automáticos y dinámicos.

    D. El pensamiento en general es tan rápido como la luz.

117. ¿Cómo se describe el aprendizaje de segunda mano?

   A. Se aprende por medio de la televisión y de la escuela.

   B. Los gatos aprenden a llegar a su hogar de segunda mano.

   C. Es un tipo de inteligencia artificial que se encuentra en la mente de los humanos.

   D. Es un tipo de aprendizaje transmitido y se efectúa por medio de respuestas inmediatas.

118. ¿Con cuál de las siguientes opciones se asemeja la palabra, «totalmente» en la línea 28?

   A. Absoluto.

   B. Suma.

   C. Resultado.

   D. Todo.

119. ¿Cuál es el tipo de pensamiento para el cual no se requiere aprendizaje?

   A. Instinto.

   B. Pensamiento.

   C. Comprensión.

   D. Aprendizaje.

120. ¿A qué se refiere la palabra, «psique» en la última línea?

   A. A la alma.

   B. Al cerebro.

   C. A la mente.

   D. Al pensamiento.

Spanish

ANSWER KEY

Question Number	Correct Answer	Your Answer	Question Number	Correct Answer	Your Answer	Question Number	Correct Answer	Your Answer
1	C		41	D		81	A	
2	B		42	B		82	A	
3	D		43	D		83	D	
4	A		44	D		84	A	
5	C		45	B		85	A	
6	D		46	D		86	C	
7	A		47	D		87	B	
8	D		48	A		88	C	
9	A		49	B		89	B	
10	C		50	C		90	D	
11	D		51	C		91	A	
12	B		52	D		92	A	
13	B		53	A		93	C	
14	A		54	C		94	D	
15	C		55	C		95	A	
16	A		56	D		96	B	
17	D		57	C		97	C	
18	C		58	B		98	C	
19	B		59	A		99	A	
20	D		60	D		100	B	
21	B		61	C		101	B	
22	B		62	D		102	B	
23	A		63	B		103	A	
24	D		64	B		104	C	
25	C		65	C		105	C	
26	B		66	B		106	B	
27	B		67	D		107	C	
28	D		68	C		108	B	
29	B		69	A		109	C	
30	C		70	D		110	B	
31	D		71	B		111	B	
32	B		72	B		112	B	
33	A		73	D		113	A	
34	C		74	B		114	A	
35	A		75	C		115	B	
36	A		76	B		116	B	
37	A		77	D		117	C	
38	D		78	B		118	C	
39	B		79	C		119	A	
40	C		80	C		120	C	

American Government

Description of the Examination

The American Government examination covers material that is usually taught in a one-semester introductory course in American government and politics at the college level. The scope and emphasis of the exam reflect what is most commonly taught in introductory American government and politics courses in political science departments around the United States. These courses go beyond a general understanding of civics to incorporate political processes and behavior. The exam covers topics such as the institutions and policy processes of the federal government, the federal courts and civil liberties, political parties and interest groups, political beliefs and behavior, and the content and history of the Constitution.

The examination contains approximately 100 questions to be answered in 90 minutes. Some of these are pretest questions that will not be scored. Any time candidates spend on tutorials and providing personal information is in addition to the actual testing time.

Knowledge and Skills Required

Questions on the American Government examination require candidates to demonstrate one or more of the following abilities in the approximate proportions indicated.

- Knowledge of American government and politics (about 55%–60% of the exam)
- Understanding of typical patterns of political processes and behavior (including the components of the behavioral situation of a political actor), the principles used to explain or justify various governmental structures and procedures (about 30%–35% of the exam)
- Analysis and interpretation of simple data that are relevant to American government and politics (10%–15% of the exam)

The subject matter of the American Government examination is drawn from the following topics. The percentages next to the main topics indicate the approximate percentage of exam questions on that topic.

30%–35% Institutions and Policy Processes: Presidency, Bureaucracy, and Congress
- The major formal and informal institutional arrangements and powers
- Structure, policy processes, and outputs
- Relationships among these three institutions and links between them and political parties, interest groups, the media, and public opinion

15%–20% Federal Courts, Civil Liberties, and Civil Rights
- Structure and processes of the judicial system with emphasis on the role and influence of the Supreme Court
- The development of civil rights and civil liberties by judicial interpretation
- The Bill of Rights
- Incorporation of the Bill of Rights
- Equal protection and due process

15%–20% **Political Parties and Interest Groups**
- Political parties (including their function, organization, mobilization, historical development, and effects on the political process)
- Interest groups (including the variety of activities they typically undertake and their effects on the political process)
- Elections (including the electoral process)

10%–15% **Political Beliefs and Behavior**
- Processes by which citizens learn about politics
- Political participation (including voting behavior)
- Public opinion
- Beliefs that citizens hold about their government and its leaders
- Political culture (the variety of factors that predispose citizens to differ from one another in terms of their political perceptions, values, attitudes, and activities)
- The influence of public opinion on political leaders

American Government

SAMPLE TEST

DIRECTIONS: Read each item and select the best response.

1. **The term that best describes how the Supreme Court can block laws that may be unconstitutional from being enacted is:**

   A. Jurisprudence

   B. Judicial review

   C. Exclusionary rule

   D. Right of petition

   E. The blocking right

2. **On the spectrum of American politics, the label that most accurately describes voters "to the right of center" is:**

   A. Moderates

   B. Liberals

   C. Conservatives

   D. Socialists

   E. Independents

3. **The branch of government responsible for developing the federal budget is:**

   A. The legislative branch

   B. The judicial branch

   C. The executive branch

   D. The Congress

   E. Each of the 50 states

4. **The United States legislature is bicameral. This means:**

   A. It consists of several houses

   B. It consists of two houses

   C. It meets twice a year

   D. The vice president is in charge of the legislature when in session.

   E. It has an upper house and a lower house

5. **What Supreme Court ruling established the principal of judicial review?**

   A. *Jefferson v. Madison*

   B. *Lincoln v. Douglas*

   C. *Marbury v. Madison*

   D. *Marbury v. Jefferson*

   E. *Lincoln v. Davis*

American Government

6. **To be eligible to be elected president, one must:**

   A. Be a U.S. citizen for at least five years

   B. Be a U.S. citizen for seven years

   C. Have been born a U.S. citizen

   D. Be a naturalized U.S. citizen

   E. Have been born to a U.S. citizen

7. **The international organization established to work for world peace at the end of Second World War is the:**

   A. League of Nations

   B. Union of Nations

   C. United Federation of Nations

   D. United Nations

   E. United World League

8. **In the United States, the right to declare war is a power of:**

   A. The president

   B. Congress

   C. The executive branch

   D. The Supreme Court

   E. The states

9. **Which of the following is an example of a direct democracy?**

   A. Elected representatives

   B. Greek city–states

   C. The United States Senate

   D. The United States House of Representatives

   E. State legislatures

10. **To plead the Fifth Amendment means to:**

    A. Refuse to speak so one does not incriminate oneself

    B. Plead "no contest" in court

    C. Ask for freedom of speech

    D. Ask to appear before a judge when charged with a crime

    E. Petition for self-defense

11. **The political document that was the first to try to organize the newly *independent* American colonies was the:**

    A. Declaration of Independence

    B. Articles of Confederation

    C. Constitution

    D. Confederate States

    E. Magna Carta

12. In 1792, Alexis de Tocqueville came to America to study the:

    A. Economic system
    B. Congress
    C. Prison system
    D. Election process
    E. Constitution

13. The first ten amendments to the Constitution are called:

    A. Bill of petition
    B. Petition of Rights
    C. Rights of Man
    D. Constitutional rights
    E. Bill of Rights

14. Socialists believe that the government should have a _____ role in the economy.

    A. minimal
    B. controlling
    C. equal to business'
    D. less than the individual's
    E. nonexistent

15. One difference between *totalitarianism* and *authoritarianism* is that totalitarianism believes in:

    A. Total control over all aspects of society
    B. Minimum government control
    C. There is no difference
    D. The difference is unknown
    E. Authoritative control over government

16. The constitution is called a "living document" because:

    A. It has the ability to change with different times
    B. It was created by people
    C. It is a static document
    D. Excessive reliance on the Constitution will kill it
    E. Anyone can change it

17. In the feudal system, who has the most power?

    A. The peasant or serf
    B. The noble or lord
    C. The worker
    D. The merchant
    E. The soldier

18. **The idea that the European powers should stay out of the affairs of the American hemisphere is known as:**

    A. Containment policy

    B. The Eisenhower Doctrine

    C. Neo-isolationism

    D. The Truman Doctrine

    E. The Monroe Doctrine

19. **The Exclusionary Rule prevents:**

    A. Illegally seized evidence from being used in court

    B. Persons from incriminating themselves in court

    C. Police from entering a private home for any reason

    D. Evidence, however gathered, from being used in court if one side in a court case objects to it

    E. Evidence, regardless of how it is collected, from being excluded

20. **The idea that "the government is best that governs least" is most closely associated with:**

    A. The Soviet communist system

    B. The American free enterprise system

    C. British conservatism

    D. Mussolini's corporate state

    E. A dictatorship

21. **In the United States Constitution, political parties are:**

    A. Never mentioned

    B. Called "a necessary part of the political process"

    C. Most effective if there are only two major ones

    D. Called harmful to the political process

    E. Required to have at least 100 members

22. **Civil suits deal mostly, but not exclusively, with:**

    A. Money

    B. Violent crime

    C. The government

    D. Political fundraising

    E. Mental illness

23. **"Common law" refers mostly to:**

    A. The precedents and traditions that have gone before in society and have become accepted norms

    B. The laws dealing with the "common people"

    C. Law that is written and codified

    D. The House of Commons in Great Britain

    E. Law that is common among different countries

American Government

24. **Anarchists believe in:**

    A. Strong government

    B. Corporate state system

    C. Weak, mild government

    D. Populist government

    E. No government

25. **The U.S. government's federal system consists of:**

    A. Three parts: the executive, the legislative, and the judiciary

    B. Three parts: the legislative, the Congress, and the presidency

    C. Four parts: the executive, the judiciary, the courts, and the legislative

    D. Two parts: the government, and the governed

    E. Two parts: the president and state governors

26. **One difference between a presidential and a parliamentary system is that in a parliamentary system:**

    A. The prime minister is head of government, while a president or monarch is head of state

    B. The president is head of government, and the vice president is head of state

    C. The president pro tempore of the Senate is head of state, while the prime minister is head of government

    D. The president appoints the head of state

    E. The prime minister is elected

27. **The American concept of Manifest Destiny means:**

    A. America had a right to spread across the American continent from coast to coast

    B. The United States should respect the right of native peoples it encounters in its push westward

    C. The rest of the world powers should stay out of North America

    D. America should strive to be the dominant world power

    E. America belonged to the native people of the region

American Government

28. In an <u>indirect</u> democracy:

    A. All the people together decide on issues

    B. People elect representatives to act for them

    C. Democracy can never really work

    D. Government is less efficient than in a direct democracy

    E. People directly elect their representatives

29. In a communist system, _____ controls the means of production.

    A. A professional managerial class

    B. The owners of business and industry

    C. The workers

    D. The parliament

    E. The state

30. Congress can override a president's veto with a _____ vote.

    A. One-half

    B. Two-thirds

    C. Six-tenths

    D. Three-fourths

    E. Four-fifths

31. To become a citizen, an individual generally must have lived in the United States for at least:

    A. Six years

    B. Five years

    C. One year

    D. Ten years

    E. Fifteen years

32. Give the correct order of the following: the Constitution, the Declaration of Independence, and the Articles of Confederation.

    A. The Constitution, the Declaration of Independence, the Articles of Confederation

    B. The Declaration of Independence, the Constitution, the Articles of Confederation

    C. The Declaration of Independence, the Articles of Confederation, the Constitution

    D. The Articles of Confederation, the Declaration of Independence, the Constitution.

    E. The Constitution, the Articles of Confederation, the Declaration of Independence

American Government

33. **The ability of the president to veto an act of Congress is an example of:**

    A. Separation of powers

    B. Checks and balances

    C. Judicial review

    D. Presidential prerogative

    E. Executive order

34. **To impeach an elected official means to:**

    A. Bring charges against the official

    B. Remove the official from office

    C. Reelect the official

    D. Override the official's veto

    E. Arrest the official

35. **An obligation identified with citizenship is:**

    A. Belonging to a political party

    B. Educating oneself

    C. Running for political office

    D. Donating to a political party

    E. Voting

36. **The doctrine that sought to keep communism from spreading was:**

    A. The Cold War

    B. Rollback

    C. Containment

    D. Détente

    E. Mutually assured destruction

37. **The power to declare war, establish a postal system, and coin money rests with which branch of the government?**

    A. Presidential

    B. Judicial

    C. Legislative

    D. Executive

    E. State governments

38. **If a president neither signs nor vetoes a bill for ten days, the bill becomes:**

    A. A pocket veto

    B. A refused law

    C. Unconstitutional

    D. A presidential veto

    E. A passed law

American Government

39. What was George Washington's advice to Americans about foreign policy?

    A. America should have strong alliances

    B. America should avoid alliances

    C. Foreign policy should take precedence over domestic policy

    D. Domestic policy should take precedence over foreign policy

    E. American should build a big military

40. The belief that government should stay out of economic affairs is called:

    A. Mercantilism

    B. Laissez-faire

    C. Democratic socialism

    D. Corporatism

    E. Socialism

41. The term that describes the division of government function is:

    A. Free enterprise

    B. Constitutional prerogative

    C. Checks and balances

    D. Divisive government

    E. Separation of powers

42. Which of the following is an important idea expressed in the Declaration of Independence?

    A. People have the right to change their government

    B. People should obey the government authority

    C. A monarchy is a bad thing

    D. Indirect democracy is best

    E. People should disobey authority

43. Oligarchy refers to:

    A. Rule of a single leader

    B. Rule of a single political party

    C. Rule by a select few

    D. Rule by many

    E. Rule by a family

44. The Judiciary Act of 1789 established the:

    A. Supreme Court

    B. Principle of judicial review

    C. State court system

    D. Federal and circuit court system

    E. The number of justices on the Supreme Court

American Government

45. The international organization established to work for world peace at the end of the First World War was the:

    A. United Earth League
    B. Confederate States
    C. United Nations
    D. League of Nations
    E. Allied Foundation

46. Which statement closely resembles the political philosophy of John Hobbes?

    A. Citizens should give unquestioning obedience to the state authority so long as it can maintain public order
    B. Citizens have a right to rise against the state whenever they choose
    C. All state authority is basically evil and should be eliminated
    D. People are generally good and cooperative if given a chance
    E. People should not be trusted

47. In the United States, the right to declare war is a power of:

    A. The president
    B. Congress
    C. The executive
    D. The states
    E. The Supreme Court

48. A tort is:

    A. A private or civil action brought into court
    B. A type of confection
    C. A penal offense
    D. One who solicits
    E. A case without any award

49. A boycott is:

    A. The refusal to buy goods or services
    B. An imbalance of trade
    C. The refusal to speak in court
    D. A writ of assistance
    E. An agreement to trade

50. In the United States, checks and balances refers to:

    A. The ability of each branch of government to "check," or limit, the actions of the other branches
    B. Balance of payments
    C. International law
    D. The federal deficit
    E. Setting the federal budget

51. **An amendment is:**

    A. A change or addition to the United States Constitution

    B. The right of a state to secede from the Union

    C. The addition of a state to the Union

    D. The right of the Supreme Court to check actions of Congress and the president

    E. Changing congressional bills

52. **The executive branch refers to:**

    A. The Senate

    B. The legislature

    C. Congress

    D. The president and vice president

    E. The CEOs in the United States

53. **An ex post facto law is:**

    A. A law made against an act after it has been committed

    B. A law proclaimed unconstitutional by the Supreme Court

    C. An executive order

    D. A law relating to the postal system

    E. A law without basis

54. **The judiciary refers to:**

    A. The president

    B. Congress

    C. The legal system

    D. The system of states' rights

    E. A judge

55. **A tariff is:**

    A. A law passed by the Congress and vetoed by the president

    B. An appointed official mandated to preserve public order

    C. A tax a government places on internationally traded goods, usually goods entering a country

    D. A tax a government places on goods produced for domestic use, also known as a sales tax

    E. A tax a government places on all exported goods

56. **In a parliamentary system, the person who becomes prime minister is usually:**

    A. The leader of the majority party in the legislature

    B. Elected by a direct national vote

    C. Chosen by the president of the country

    D. Chosen by the cabinet

    E. The leader of the minority party

57. **The Declaration of Independence owes much to the philosophy of:**

    A. Vladimir Lenin

    B. Karl Marx

    C. Thomas Hobbes

    D. Alexander Hamilton

    E. John Locke

58. **The highest appellate court in the United States is the:**

    A. Federal judiciary

    B. Circuit court

    C. Supreme Court

    D. Court of appeals

    E. District court

59. **The Bill of Rights was mostly written by:**

    A. Thomas Jefferson

    B. James Madison

    C. George Washington

    D. Alexander Hamilton

    E. John Adams

60. **The U.S. Constitution was ratified by the required number of states in:**

    A. August 1861

    B. July 1776

    C. June 1788

    D. September 1848

    E. July 1864

61. **To be a naturalized citizen means:**

    A. To have been refused citizenship

    B. To have dual citizenship

    C. To be a native-born citizen

    D. To renounce one's citizenship

    E. To acquire citizenship

62. **George Washington's opinion of the United States having trade with other nations was:**

    A. Approval in only some instances

    B. Disapproval

    C. Approval

    D. Unsure

    E. Anger

63. "Walk softly and carry a big stick" is a statement associated with:

    A. Franklin Roosevelt

    B. Theodore Roosevelt

    C. George Washington

    D. Thomas Hobbes

    E. Ronald Reagan

64. The Bill of Rights says that any rights it does not mention are:

    A. Reserved to the federal government

    B. Not important

    C. Judged by the Supreme Court

    D. Not legal rights

    E. Reserved to the states or to the people

65. The process of the state taking over industries and businesses is called:

    A. Industrialization

    B. Nationalization

    C. Redistribution

    D. Amalgamation

    E. Reclamation

66. The first election in which political parties played a role was in:

    A. 1787

    B. 1776

    C. 1888

    D. 1796

    E. 1725

67. The vast land area west of the Mississippi River that the United States bought from France was:

    A. California and New Mexico

    B. The State of Florida

    C. The Louisiana Purchase

    D. The Gadsden Purchase

    E. The Monroe Claim

68. The War of 1812 involved the United States and:

    A. Russia

    B. Great Britain

    C. France

    D. Spain

    E. Germany

American Government

69. **The term *suffrage* means:**

    A. The right to vote

    B. The power of the court

    C. A Supreme Court ruling

    D. Legislative action

    E. To suffer silently

70. **What was Seward's Folly?**

    A. The purchase of Alaska

    B. The purchase of Louisiana

    C. The Mexican–American War

    D. The annexation of Texas

    E. The settlement of California

71. **Those who wanted the United States to stay out of world affairs are called:**

    A. Neo-conservatives

    B. Isolationists

    C. Non-interventionists

    D. Nationalists

    E. Independents

72. **Early civilizations developed systems of government:**

    A. To provide for defense against attack

    B. To regulate trade

    C. To regulate and direct the economic activities of the people as they worked together in groups

    D. To decide on the boundaries of the different fields during planting seasons

    E. To create jobs

73. **The most common type of local government in the United States at present is:**

    A. Commission–Manager

    B. President–Legislature

    C. Council–Manager

    D. Mayor–Council

    E. Mayor–People

74. **The first political parties in the United States were:**

    A. Democratic-Republicans and Nationalists

    B. Progressives and Populists

    C. Democratic-Republicans and Federalists

    D. Democrats and Republicans

    E. Social Democrats and Populists

American Government

75. To become a citizen, one must be at least _____ old.

A. 25 years

B. 18 years

C. 21 years

D. 19 years

E. 16 years

76. The Spanish–American War started in:

A. 1889

B. 1914

C. 1927

D. 1898

E. 1900

77. A major feature of many multiparty political systems is:

A. Separation of powers

B. Inability to represent sectional interests

C. Coalition government

D. Strong centralized government

E. Weak executive branch

78. Which of the following statements about American history is an opinion rather than a fact?

A. The doctrine of Manifest Destiny can be said to have been an excuse for the expansionism of the United States on the American continent

B. America's wealth, power, and influence increased with its size

C. America's expansion was justified by its superior political and economic system

D. The expansion of the United States was generally detrimental to the interests of native peoples

E. America entered the two World Wars because American interests were attacked.

79. Which is a shared power of the federal and state governments?

A. The power to declare war

B. The power to build roads

C. The power to coin money

D. The power to regulate interstate trade

E. The power to educate

80. The foreign policy known as the Good Neighbor Policy was associated with the administration of:

   A. James Madison
   B. Franklin Roosevelt
   C. Woodrow Wilson
   D. Theodore Roosevelt
   E. John F. Kennedy

81. Direct democracy was a feature of:

   A. Greek city–states
   B. Ancient Rome
   C. Medieval Europe
   D. Sumerian theocracy
   E. The Indus Valley civilizations

82. In a constitutional monarchy, like that of Great Britain, that has a parliamentary system of government, the sovereign takes the place of the:

   A. Prime minister
   B. President
   C. Premier
   D. Speaker of Parliament
   E. Vice president

83. The type of city administration that is supposed to eliminate political patronage and fiscal waste is:

   A. Commission–Council
   B. Mayor–Council
   C. Council–Manager
   D. Metropolitan–Manager
   E. City Manager–Council

84. Which of the following statements about the Supreme Court is true?

   A. The Supreme Court has only an appellate jurisdiction in all matters
   B. The Supreme Court shall have original jurisdiction in all areas involving foreign officials, public officials, and cases in which a state is a party
   C. The Supreme Court shall exercise original jurisdiction only over those cases involving the chief executive
   D. The Supreme Court shall have original jurisdiction over appellate matters only
   E. The Supreme Court shall have jurisdiction over all matters, regardless of jurisdiction

85. **What happens if the president vetoes a bill?**

    A. It goes back to Congress, which can override the veto with a two-thirds vote

    B. It goes back to the congressional committees

    C. It goes back to Congress, which can override it with a three-fourths vote

    D. It still becomes a law

    E. It goes back to Congress, which can override it with a simple majority

86. **The Truman Doctrine was an attempt to prevent the spread of:**

    A. German expansionism

    B. Imperialism

    C. Communism

    D. Fascism

    E. Democracy

87. **To impeach a president:**

    A. The charges are brought by the House of Representatives and tried in the Senate

    B. The charges are brought by the Senate and tried in the House of Representatives

    C. The charges are brought by the states and tried in Congress

    D. The charges are brought by Congress and tried before the Supreme Court

    E. The charges are brought by the vice president and tried in the Senate

88. **In the United States, the legal voting age is:**

    A. 19

    B. 18

    C. 21

    D. 25

    E. 16

American Government

89. **In the United States' electoral system, who is allowed to vote in primary elections?**

    A. Generally, only registered party members are allowed to vote for their candidates in the party

    B. Any registered voters may vote for candidates in either party primary

    C. Only voters actively engaged in party affairs may vote in a primary

    D. Generally, the United States does not engage in primary elections, though there are exceptions

    E. Nonregistered individuals are allowed to vote in primary elections

90. **A important *direct* consequence of the First World War was:**

    A. The end of European colonialism

    B. The Great Depression

    C. The rise of communism

    D. The end of fascism

    E. The socialist state

91. **In journalism, the term *muckraking* refers to:**

    A. An attempt to uncover alleged corruption of public officials

    B. The attempt to cover up the alleged corruption of public officials

    C. The process of buying up various media outlets

    D. The investigation of government inefficiency and waste

    E. Dragging a person's reputation through the mud

92. **The Voting Rights Act of 1965 sought to:**

    A. Extend the franchise to minorities

    B. Undo the last remaining features of unequal suffrage in the United States

    C. Establish the party primary

    D. Give women the right to vote

    E. Take away the voting rights of prisoners

93. **The United States is a(n):**

    A. Direct democracy

    B. Quasi-democracy

    C. Semi-democracy

    D. Indirect democracy

    E. Non-democracy

American Government

94. The United States is presently comprised of:

A. Fifty-two states, the District of Columbia, and various overseas territories

B. Forty-eight states, the District of Columbia, and various overseas territories

C. Fifty states, the District of Columbia, and various overseas territories

D. Fifty states and the District of Columbia

E. Fifty-six states and two territories

95. Powers concurrent to both the federal and state governments are:

A. To tax, to raise an army, to establish courts, to provide for the general welfare, and to fix the standards for weights and measures

B. To tax, to charter banks, to borrow money, to make and enforce laws, and to provide for the general welfare

C. To tax, to borrow money, to establish courts, to regulate international trade, and to make and enforce laws

D. To ratify amendments, to tax, to make and enforce laws, to provide for the general welfare, and to raise a militia

E. To tax, to regulate trade, to charter schools, and to make laws

96. The term *welfare capitalism* or *the welfare state* is used most often to describe:

A. The former Soviet Union

B. The interval between mercantilism and capitalism

C. The United States and various European countries

D. The Chinese experiments with communism

E. The Middle East

97. A poll tax is associated with:

A. Tariffs on internationally traded goods

B. Voting rights

C. Government construction

D. The income tax structure in a given state

E. A tax imposed during an election

98. Who of the following wrote about modern economic problems?

A. John Locke

B. Thomas Hobbes

C. John Maynard Keynes

D. Alexander Hamilton

E. Alexis de Tocqueville

American Government

99. *Gerrymandering* is:

A. The consolidation of various voting districts into larger, more efficient entities

B. The adjustment of voting districts to achieve some goal, usually to promote greater political representation of a given demographic of voters

C. The removal of certain inefficient political departments

D. The fixing of the economic infrastructure

E. The process of endless debate in the Senate

100. Interest groups form to influence:

A. Government funding

B. State funding

C. Government policy

D. State policy

E. All of the above

American Government

ANSWER KEY

Question Number	Correct Answer	Your Answer
1	B	
2	C	
3	C	
4	B	
5	C	
6	C	
7	D	
8	B	
9	B	
10	A	
11	B	
12	C	
13	E	
14	B	
15	A	
16	A	
17	B	
18	E	
19	A	
20	B	
21	A	
22	A	
23	A	
24	E	
25	A	
26	A	
27	A	
28	B	
29	E	
30	B	
31	B	
32	C	
33	B	
34	A	

Question Number	Correct Answer	Your Answer
35	E	
36	C	
37	C	
38	A	
39	B	
40	B	
41	E	
42	A	
43	C	
44	D	
45	D	
46	A	
47	B	
48	A	
49	A	
50	A	
51	A	
52	D	
53	A	
54	C	
55	C	
56	A	
57	E	
58	C	
59	B	
60	C	
61	E	
62	C	
63	B	
64	E	
65	B	
66	D	
67	C	
68	B	

Question Number	Correct Answer	Your Answer
69	A	
70	A	
71	B	
72	C	
73	D	
74	C	
75	B	
76	D	
77	C	
78	C	
79	B	
80	D	
81	A	
82	B	
83	C	
84	B	
85	A	
86	C	
87	A	
88	B	
89	A	
90	C	
91	A	
92	B	
93	D	
94	C	
95	B	
96	C	
97	B	
98	C	
99	B	
100	E	

History of the United States I

Description of the Examination

The History of the United States I: Early Colonization to 1877 examination covers material that is usually taught in the first semester of a two-semester course in United States history. The examination covers the period of United States history from early European colonization to the end of Reconstruction, with the majority of the questions on the period of 1790-1877. In the part covering the seventeenth and eighteenth centuries, emphasis is placed on the English colonies.

The examination contains approximately 120 questions to be answered in 90 minutes. Some of these are pretest questions that will not be scored. Any time candidates spend on tutorials and providing personal information is in addition to the actual testing time.

Knowledge and Skills Required

Questions on the History of the United States I examination require candidates to demonstrate one or more of the following abilities.

- Identification and description of historical phenomena
- Analysis and interpretation of historical phenomena
- Comparison and contrast of historical phenomena

The subject matter of the History of the United States I examination is drawn from the following topics. The percentages next to the main topics indicate the approximate percentage of exam questions on that topic.

Topical Specifications

- 35% Political institutions, political developments, behavior, and public policy
- 25% Social developments
- 10% Economic developments
- 15% Cultural and intellectual developments
- 15% Diplomacy and international relations

Chronological Specifications

- 30% 1500–1789
- 70% 1790–1877

The following themes are reflected in a comprehensive introductory survey course:

- The impact of European discovery and colonization upon indigenous societies
- The nature of indigenous societies in North America
- The origins and nature of slavery and resistance
- Immigration and the history of ethnic minorities
- Major movements and individual figures in the history of women and the family
- The development and character of colonial societies
- British relations with the Atlantic colonies of North America
- The changing role of religion in American society
- The content of the Constitution and its amendments, and their interpretation by the Supreme Court
- The development and expansion of participatory democracy
- The growth of and changes in political parties
- The changing role of government in American life
- The intellectual and political expressions of nationalism

History of the United States I

- Major movements and individual figures in the history of American literature, art, and popular culture
- Abolitionism and reform movements
- Long term democratic trends (immigration and internal migration)
- The motivations for and character of American expansionism
- The process of economic growth and development
- The causes and impacts of major wars in United States history

History of the United States I

SAMPLE TEST

1. **Which of the following is a way that ancient civilizations did NOT contribute to the government of the United States?**

   A. Direct democracy

   B. Philosophy of government

   C. Indirect democracy

   D. Checks and balances

   E. Welfare

2. **The Atlantic slave trade lasted approximately how many years?**

   A. Four hundred

   B. Three hundred

   C. Two hundred

   D. One hundred

   E. Six hundred

3. **The belief that the United States should control all of North America was called:**

   A. Westward Expansion

   B. Pan Americanism

   C. Manifest Destiny

   D. Nationalism

   E. American Sovereignty

4. **Early French settlement gave the French control over which two rivers?**

   A. The Missouri and Mississippi

   B. The St. Lawrence and the Hudson

   C. The Hudson and Missouri

   D. The Mississippi and the St. Lawrence

   E. The Missouri and the St. Lawrence

5. **How did the Treaty of Paris of 1783 affect the Native Americans?**

   A. It did not

   B. It set aside areas for them to live

   C. Native American land was ceded to the United States

   D. Native American land was ceded to French Canada

   E. It ceded French Canadian land to Native Americans

History of the United States I

6. **Geographically, how were the New England and Middle colonies different?**

   A. New England had an abundance of good soil but the Middle colonies did not

   B. New England's farms produced a large supply of food but Middle colonies imported most of their foodstuffs

   C. The Middle colonies had a rocky shoreline and the New England colonies had large seaports

   D. The Middle colonies had a less severe climate than the New England colonies

   E. The Middle colonies had shorter growing seasons than the New England colonies

7. **In what ways are the Mayflower Compact and Fundamental Orders of Connecticut similar?**

   A. They both pledged loyalty to the king of England

   B. They were joint resolutions of various communities

   C. They were expressions of views and forms of government

   D. They were both peace treaties

   E. They were created in the late 1700s before statehood

8. **In what way did spatial exchange influence the development of colonial society?**

   A. Population was diffused throughout the colonies

   B. It affected the settlement of inland colonies

   C. It was the reason colonists settled the Midwest

   D. Population focused on its importance in forming towns

   E. It caused an increased population density along the Atlantic coast

9. **What effect did the passage of acts such as the Sugar Act, the Stamp Act, and the Townshend Acts have on colonial America?**

   A. The acts polarized the colonists

   B. The acts were accepted with dignity

   C. The colonists tolerated the acts

   D. The colonists resisted the acts

   E. The acts spurred economic growth in colonial America

10. **Why did King George III repeal the Stamp Act?**

    A. He feared rebellion

    B. He no longer needed funds

    C. Parliament recommended repeal

    D. Parliament amended the act

    E. England was losing money

11. **How did England benefit from the Navigation Acts?**

    A. The acts were revenue producing

    B. The acts assured England's economic supremacy

    C. The acts required the use of English ships

    D. The acts monitored colonial commerce

    E. The acts made it easier for other nations to trade with the colonies, strengthening ties between Britain and other colonial powers

12. **All of the following are reasons why the government under the Articles of Confederation was not retained EXCEPT**

    A. It did not provide for a strong chief executive

    B. It lacked the ability to regulate finances

    C. It lacked power to enforce legislation

    D. It lacked the power to enforce treaties

    E. It allowed each state to issue its own money

13. **The Federalists:**

    A. supported states' rights

    B. desired a weak central government

    C. favored a strong central government

    D. were also called Loyalist

    E. opposed protective tariffs

14. **Generally, _____ favored low tariffs.**

    A. Democratic-Republicans

    B. the Supreme Court

    C. Federalists

    D. Congress

    E. the executive branch

15. What event sparked a great migration of people from all over the world to California during the mid-1800s?

    A. The birth of labor unions

    B. Manifest Destiny

    C. The invention of the automobile

    D. The Gold Rush

    E. The Dust Bowl

16. After the settlers inhabited _____, they believed they were destined to settle the North American continent.

    A. the Louisiana Territory

    B. the Northwest Territory

    C. the Piedmont of Virginia

    D. Texas

    E. the Florida panhandle

17. Which area was acquired last by the United States?

    A. Annexation of Texas

    B. Acquisition of Oregon

    C. The Louisiana Purchase

    D. Indian Stream Territory

    E. The Gadsden Purchase

18. Why did Northerners first oppose the admission of Texas to statehood?

    A. Texas was controlled by Mexico

    B. Texas did not have the required population

    C. Texas wanted to allow slavery

    D. Texas owed debts to the U.S. government

    E. Texas had a weak economy

19. Which was not an issue that caused sectionalism?

    A. Mechanization of farming

    B. Tariffs

    C. Slavery

    D. Land speculation

    E. Immigrant populations

20. The principle of "popular sovereignty" that allowed people in any territory to make their own decisions concerning the slavery issue was first stated by:

    A. Henry Clay

    B. Daniel Webster

    C. John C. Calhoun

    D. Stephen A. Douglas

    E. Andrew Johnson

21. **Who was a Confederate commander?**

    A. Ambrose Burnside

    B. George McClellan

    C. J. E. B. Stuart

    D. Irvin McDowell

    E. Ulysses Grant

22. **Which statement is true about the Radical Republicans?**

    A. They favored Andrew Johnson's plan of Reconstruction

    B. They favored harsh measures of Reconstruction

    C. They established the Freedmen's Bureau

    D. They opposed "black codes"

    E. They opposed the Wade-Davis Bill

23. **Why were Alfred Mahan's theories important in shaping U.S. foreign policy?**

    A. He believed America should "speak softly and carry a big stick"

    B. He believed a strong army would avoid confrontations

    C. He believed the use of the atomic bomb would end war

    D. He believed a strong navy showed a strong foreign policy

    E. He wanted the U.S. to have a stronger presence in Central America

24. **Which of the following is not an example of an advancement of transportation that took place during the post-Civil War period?**

    A. Rail passenger service

    B. Completion of the transcontinental railroad

    C. Jet planes

    D. Automobile

    E. Establishment of interstate highways

25. Which political philosophy is concerned with the commonsense needs of the average person?

    A. Popular sovereignty

    B. Populism

    C. Progressivism

    D. Protectionism

    E. Proletarianism

26. All of the following are causes of the Industrial Revolution EXCEPT

    A. immigrants from southeast Europe

    B. inventions

    C. machines

    D. extensive rail service

    E. The Embargo Act of 1807

27. Which Native American tribes moved west of the Mississippi in the early nineteenth century?

    A. The Wichitas, Comanches, and Caddoes

    B. The Coahuiltecans, Lipans, and Kiowas

    C. The Cherokee, Choctaw, and Shawnee

    D. The Tonkawas, Wichitas, and Caddoes

    E. The Cherokee, Seneca, Witchitas, and Lakota

28. What was the cause of friction between the United States and Spain after the Louisiana Purchase in 1803?

    A. Spain resented American involvement in the Cuban War of Independence

    B. Mexico wanted to buy the Louisiana Territory from France

    C. Spain angered the United States by sinking the American battleship The Maine

    D. Both nations disputed the boundary between Texas and Louisiana

    E. Spain still used and occupied parts of territory from the Louisiana Purchase

29. Why did missionaries abandon east Texas in 1693?

    A. The Mexican War of Independence forced abandonment

    B. They moved their mission into the sunny beaches of Spanish Florida

    C. American citizens began to settle in the region

    D. The climate was too harsh

    E. Tensions with Native Americans over a smallpox outbreak scared them away

30. Who was the first American allowed to obtain a colonial grant to settle in Texas?

    A. Stephen F. Austin

    B. Agustin de Iturbide

    C. Moses Austin

    D. Fray Damián Massanet

    E. Brigham Young

31. What was one of the causes of the Mexican War of Independence?

    A. Taxation of the thirteen colonies

    B. Abdication of Napoleon

    C. Debt from the War of 1812

    D. The assassination of the Catholic priest Miguel Hidalgo

    E. Confiscation of church property

32. What was the final battle of the Texas Revolution?

    A. Battle of the Alamo

    B. Battle of San Jacinto

    C. Battle of Gonzales

    D. Battle of Gettysburg

    E. Battle of Little Big Horn

33. What early Texas pioneer documented daily life during the Republic of Texas and early statehood?

    A. Sam Houston

    B. Stephen F. Austin

    C. Mary Maverick

    D. Joshua Houston

    E. Warren Dallas

34. Which event motivated Texas to hold a secessionist vote in 1861?

    A. Battle of Palmito Ridge

    B. Battle of Galveston

    C. Texas Revolution

    D. South Carolina's secession from the Union

    E. Georgia's secession from the Union

35. _____ is the fundamental law of the U.S. republic.

    A. Separation of powers

    B. Checks and balances

    C. Federalism

    D. The Constitution

    E. The Declaration of Independence

36. **Federal taxation legislation must originate in:**

    A. the House of Representatives.

    B. the Senate

    C. either the House or the Senate

    D. both the House and Senate simultaneously

    E. both the House and Supreme Court

37. **The Thirteenth, Fourteenth, and Fifteenth Amendments were called the "Civil War" amendments because they:**

    A. abolished slavery, gave voting rights to former slaves, and provided for equal protection

    B. provided due process, direct election of U.S. senators, and voting rights regardless of race, color, or previous condition of servitude

    C. provided equal protection, prohibited the poll tax, and abolished slavery

    D. prohibited the poll tax, provided for direct election of U.S. Senators, and provided due process

    E. provided due process and universal suffrage to veterans of the Civil War

38. **The American governmental system is a federal system because:**

    A. the national and state governments share powers

    B. state governments have three branches of government

    C. there are fifty states and one national government

    D. the federal government has administrative agencies

    E. each state has its own federal government

39. **How did the federal government demonstrate that education was important in the westward expansion movement?**

    A. Congress required students to attend school until the age of 15

    B. Congress provided funds for agricultural colleges

    C. Congress required each township to establish a school

    D. Congress established teacher-training colleges

    E. Congress penalized underperforming townships

40. **The temperance movement resulted in:**

    A. women gaining the right to vote

    B. the increased manufacture of alcohol

    C. enactment of the Prohibition Amendment

    D. reduction of abuses of drunkenness

    E. a decrease in birth rate

41. **The Mayflower Compact is an example of:**

    A. a resistance to illegitimate government

    B. the law of nature

    C. a divine right theory document

    D. a foreign peace treaty

    E. a social contract theory document

42. **In which type of government system are coalition parties common?**

    A. Monarchy

    B. Dictatorship

    C. Federalist

    D. Parliamentary system

    E. Oligarchy

43. **Adam Smith believed that:**

    A. labor was a value-determining factor

    B. free markets should exist without government interference

    C. aggregate spending determined the level of economic activity

    D. collective ownership and administration of goods was necessary

    E. government needed to influence free mark1ets

44. **All of the following are reasons why Europeans came to the New World EXCEPT**

    A. To provide protection for indigenous populations

    B. To increase the monarch's power

    C. To find natural resources for manufacturing

    D. To spread their nation's religious views

    E. To spread out and develop their nation's population

45. **The Department of Treasury:**

    A. handles federal investigations by making them into business activities

    B. assures fair and free competition between businesses

    C. runs the Government Accounting Office

    D. advises the president on fiscal policy

    E. monitors the development of local businesses

46. **Which publishers' newspapers included modern features such as comics, puzzles, illustrations, columnists, and sports?**

    A. William Randolph Hearst

    B. Edward W. Scripps

    C. Charles A. Dana

    D. Alfred Nobel

    E. Joseph Pulitzer

47. **All of the following are reasons why the United States went to war with Britain in 1812 EXCEPT**

    A. Spain's resentment over the sale, exploration, and settlement of the Louisiana Territory

    B. The westward expansion of settlers

    C. The agitation of Native Americans by fur traders

    D. The continued seizure of American ships on British seas

    E. The need for more land

48. There is no doubt the U.S. Constitution was a vast improvement over the weak Articles of Confederation. Which one of the five statements below is not a description of the document?

    A. The establishment of a strong central government in no way lessened or weakened the individual states.

    B. Individual rights were protected and secured.

    C. The Constitution demands unquestioned respect and subservience to the federal government by all states and citizens.

    D. Its flexibility and adaptation to change gives it a sense of timelessness

    E. The constitution requires ¾ of all states to agree on ratifying an amendment as opposed to requiring all states to agree.

49. From about 1870 to 1900 the settlement for America's "last frontier", in the west was made possible by:

    A. construction of major highways

    B. the building of the railroad

    C. The invention of the automobile

    D. The signing of the Treaty of Holston with the Cherokee

    E. The popularization of the steamboat

50. Who wrote the famous line "these are the times that try men's souls" in the 16 part pamphlet *The American Crisis*?

    A. Thomas Hobbes

    B. Henry Clay

    C. Thomas Paine

    D. John Locke

    E. Benjamin Franklin

51. Which country first sent explorers to the New World during the "Age of Exploration"?

    A. Portugal

    B. Denmark

    C. England

    D. Spain

    E. France

52. Which of the following is not a responsibility of U.S. political parties?

   A. Obtaining funds needed for elections

   B. Choosing candidates to run for office

   C. Raising voters' awareness of political issues

   D. Writing platforms for candidates to state their positions

   E. Holding elections

53. Who is considered to be the father of modern economics?

   A. John Stuart Mill

   B. John Maynard Keynes

   C. Thomas Malthus

   D. Adam Smith

   E. John Locke

54. Immediately after the American Revolution, which nation owned the most land in the Americas?

   A. The United States of America

   B. Great Britain

   C. France

   D. Spain

   E. Portugal

55. Constitutionalism is a political system in which:

   A. it is run by a head of state, the elected or self-appointed president

   B. laws and traditions put limits on the power of government

   C. a strong, centralized national government holds together the nation

   D. a group of representatives are led by a prime minister

   E. a monarch has only limited legal and ceremonial powers

56. What was the political significance of Marbury v. Madison (1803)?

   A. It established judicial review

   B. It made popular sovereignty possible in the U.S.

   C. It relied on the notion of supreme law of the land

   D. The elastic clause of the Constitution was a major influence on the decision

   E. It established universal suffrage

57. **Who was the first European explorer to land in Florida?**

    A. John Cabot

    B. Christopher Columbus

    C. Panfilo de Navarez

    D. Juan Marco Valdez

    E. Ponce de Leon

58. **Which Revolutionary battle was the main factor in the establishment of the Franco-American Alliance of 1777?**

    A. The Battle of Gettysburg

    B. Battle of Monmouth

    C. The Battle of Saratoga

    D. The Battle of Bunker Hill

    E. The Siege of Yorktown

59. **During the Treaty of Paris in 1763, Britain received _____ from Spain:**

    A. the land west of Florida (Alabama, Louisiana)

    B. Florida

    C. Texas

    D. the Great Lake States

    E. Missouri and Kansas

60. **Impeaching the President of the United States means:**

    A. removing the president from office

    B. bringing formal charges against the president

    C. reelecting the president for a second term

    D. fining the president for disagreeing with Congress

    E. overriding the president's veto

61. **_____ was established in 1789 by Article 3 of the Constitution.**

    A. The state court system

    B. The Supreme Court

    C. Judicial review

    D. The Federal circuit court system

    E. The concept of checks and balances

62. **The Bill of Rights, and most of the Constitution, were written by:**

    A. George Washington

    B. Thomas Jefferson

    C. Alexander Hamilton

    D. Andrew Jackson

    E. James Madison

63. **The United States Constitution was ratified by the required nine states on which month and year?**

   A. July, 1776

   B. August, 1861

   C. June, 1788

   D. January, 1848

   E. February, 1815

64. **Which statement is true about colonization of North America in the 1600s?**

   A. The Portuguese built a plantation society in South America

   B. The Spanish controlled much of Central America

   C. The French controlled much of the Great Lakes area

   D. The French controlled what is present-day Florida

   E. The English controlled the Mississippi River fur trade

65. **Which colonial region became known as the "breadbasket" of the New World?**

   A. New England

   B. Middle colonies

   C. Virginia

   D. The Great Lakes area

   E. West

66. **The "Trail of Tears" refers to:**

   A. Native American removal

   B. the treatment of slaves

   C. retreat of the Confederate army from Gettysburg

   D. Civil War defeats

   E. French losses in the Midwest

67. **Nullification means:**

   A. the state government had the right to decide whether a federal law was unconstitutional

   B. the state government had the right to require the state to follow federal law

   C. the federal government could nullify an act of Congress

   D. state government had the right to nullify Supreme Court decisions made in cases of a given state

   E. Congress could declare state legislation null

68. The Compromise of 1850 did all of the following EXCEPT

   A. addressed the issue of slavery

   B. abolished the slave trade in Washington D.C.

   C. changed the borders of Texas to its present day borders

   D. admitted California as a slave state

   E. permitted runaway slaves to be returned to their owner

69. What was an advantage the South had as it entered the Civil War?

   A. Confidence

   B. Population

   C. Transportation facilities

   D. Military leadership

   E. Natural resources

70. Ulysses S. Grant was victorious at _____ and severed the western Confederacy from the eastern Confederacy.

   A. Saratoga

   B. Chickamauga

   C. Gettysburg

   D. Bull Run

   E. Vicksburg

71. An example of a way to avoid the conditions of the Fifteenth Amendment was:

   A. Sit-ins

   B. Poll taxes

   C. Litigation

   D. Bus boycotts

   E. Freedom rides

72. Which political party first raised the women's suffrage issue?

   A. Democratic

   B. Republican

   C. Radical-Republicans

   D. Liberty

   E. Whig

73. Which of the following developments changed the lifestyles of all Native Americans in Texas?

   A. The widespread acceptance of agriculture

   B. The utilization of the mixed economy

   C. The introduction of the horse

   D. The introduction of the matrilineal society

   E. The development of a rudimentary jail system

74. **What were the main causes of the Mexican-American War?**

    A. Land disputes

    B. Treaty of Annexation

    C. Santa Fe Expedition

    D. Both A and B

    E. Both A and C

75. **Why did the U.S. government name Quanah Parker as chief of the Comanches?**

    A. He was well-respected by the Comanches

    B. He was a great military leader

    C. He transitioned quickly to reservation life

    D. He received the most votes in Congress

    E. He advocated renewing hostility with American settlers

76. **What was an effect of the abolition movement?**

    A. It solidified the nation

    B. It eliminated divisiveness

    C. It created unity

    D. It split the country

    E. It destroyed international trade in the Americas

77. **In what way was John Locke's political philosophy expressed in the Declaration of Independence?**

    A. People have the right to resist arbitrary action of a ruler

    B. Kings should not have a divine right to rule

    C. Government is a social contract

    D. Government should serve to protect the welfare of the people

    E. Government should not interfere in business

78. **Why did Federalists, such as Alexander Hamilton, want a national bank?**

    A. Because it represented states' rights

    B. Because the U.S. experienced severe inflation, surplus levels of counterfeiting, and had difficulty in financing military operations

    C. Because the U.S. population and revenue was increasing so fast that state banks could not keep up with the amount of gold species coming in

    D. Because there were to many regulations on individual state banks

    E. Because the governmental insurance was spending too much on states banks to protect deposits in case of a bank failure

79. **What did the Democrat-Republicans, such as Andrew Jackson, believe in during the early nineteenth century?**

    A. Nationalism, Centralism, Modernization, and Monetarism

    B. Pro-immigration, Pro-taxation, and Pro-trade

    C. Pro-commerce, Pro-social improvements, and Pro-manufacturing

    D. Manifest Destiney, Agriculturalism, States Rights, and Populism

    E. Anti-Masonry, Protectionism, and Social Conservatism

80. **Who drafted the Virginia Statute for Religious Freedom in 1777?**

    A. George Washington

    B. Thomas Jefferson

    C. James Madison

    D. John Dickenson

    E. Benjamin Franklin

81. **What did the Statue of Liberty symbolize for the United States in 1886?**

    A. It was a sign of friendship between France and the United States

    B. Freedom

    C. A welcoming sight for immigrants coming from boats

    D. Progress

    E. All of the above

82. **What were the men and women called who remained loyal to the British Crown in the American Revolution?**

    A. Parliament's men

    B. Tories

    C. King's army

    D. Georgenites

    E. True colonists

83. What was one of the causes of the French and Indian War in 1754?

   A. Land expansion conflict between the British colonists in Virginia and the French colonists east of the Great Lakes

   B. The French disagreed with how Native Americans traded

   C. France invaded Prussia

   D. The French massacred British in Uniontown, Pennsylvania near Fort Duquesne

   E. Indians raided Saratoga, New York

84. Which Native American tribe was one of the only tribes to ally with the British during the French and Indian War?

   A. Algonquian allies

   B. Sioux

   C. Delawares

   D. Shawnees

   E. The Iroquois League

85. Why did Native American groups make an alliance with the British during the French and Indian War?

   A. French animosity

   B. British colonists forced them to

   C. Strong friendship with colonists

   D. British patriotism

   E. Animosity towards other tribes and hope for British favor after the war

86. What was the Whig parties' ideology?

   A. The people hold popular sovereignty, rather than the people being subjects to a monarchy

   B. That one person holds sovereignty

   C. A belief that government should control the economy

   D. To maintain the existing or traditional order

   E. They believed in removing some powers from the states and giving more powers to the national government

87. **The British system of mercantilism was opposed by many American colonists because it:**

    A. discouraged the export of raw materials to England

    B. placed restrictions on trading

    C. encouraged British manufacturing

    D. benefited Native Americans

    E. placed quotas on immigration

88. **The main reason Great Britain established the Proclamation Line of 1763 was to:**

    A. avoid conflicts between American colonists and Native American Indians

    B. make a profit by selling the land west of the Appalachian Mountain

    C. prevent American industrial development in the Ohio River valley

    D. allow Canada to control the Great Lakes region

    E. to keep a monopoly on the trade market with Native Americans

89. **Which act coined the famous saying "No Taxation without Representation?"**

    A. Currency Act, 1764

    B. The Mayflower Compact

    C. The Tea Act, 1765

    D. The Stamp Act, 1765

    E. Boston Compromise, 1764

90. **The 1494 Treaty of Tordesillas, allowed what two nations to divide the entire non-European world into two areas of exploration and colonization?**

    A. England and France

    B. The Dutch Republic and Spain

    C. Spain and Portugal

    D. England and the Dutch Republic

    E. France and Portugal

91. **In which battle was General Stonewall Jackson killed?**

    A. The Battle of Chancellorsville

    B. The Battle of Gettysburg

    C. The Battle of Shiloh

    D. The Peninsular Campaign

    E. The First Battle of Battle Run

History of the United States I

92. **What did the Homestead Act of 1862 claim?**

    A. Those of age had to enlist in the Union army

    B. Anyone who had never taken up arms against the United States could claim ownership of land, up to 160 acres, at little or no cost

    C. Anything west of the Mississippi could be claimed by white male land owners

    D. Those of age had to enlist in the Confederate army

    E. None of these

93. **Which president enforced the Homestead Act of 1862?**

    A. Jefferson Davis

    B. Alexander H. Stephens

    C. Abraham Lincoln

    D. Ulysses S. Grant

    E. Andrew Johnson

94. **What did the Federalists, led by Alexander Hamilton in the early eighteenth and late nineteenth centuries, believe in?**

    A. A fiscally sound and strong nationalistic government

    B. A weak federal government and strong states government

    C. No government

    D. Monarchy

    E. Anti-affiliation with British affairs

95. **Which of the following pairings most accurately links the presidential candidate with what he advocated or embodied?**

    A. John C. Calhoun-western expansion

    B. Jon Quincy Adams-opposition to an activist government

    C. Henry Clay-states' rights

    D. Andrew Jackson-nationalist pride

    E. Martin Van Buren-large government

96. In the 1830s and 1840s, the major difference between Whigs and the Democrats was that:

   A. the Democrats favored an activist role for the federal government to help the economy while the Whigs opposed such an expansion of federal power

   B. the Whigs favored the abolition of slavery while the Democrats said that it was not a federal concern

   C. the Whigs believed in an activist federal government, while the Democrats favored a federal government with conscribed powers

   D. the Democrats power stemmed from an alliance of Northern and Southern monetary interests while farmers supported the Whigs

   E. the Whigs opposed westward expansion and the Democrats favored it

97. Indian removal was an example of President Jackson's endorsement of:

   A. protectionism

   B. nullification

   C. states' rights

   D. internal improvements

   E. a strong federal judiciary

98. Which FORMER president's wife preformed her First Lady duties for her husband and for President Thomas Jefferson?

   A. Abigail Adams

   B. Dolley Madison

   C. Sarah York Jackson

   D. Elizabeth Monroe

   E. Martha Jefferson Randolph

99. What was the main difference in weaponry used in the Civil War compared to wars fought earlier in the nineteenth century?

   A. Prior wars involved rudimentary weapons which lent themselves to hand-to-hand combat and close range fighting

   B. There was no difference

   C. All of the weapons used in the Civil War were completely different

   D. Weaponry in prior wars was less accurate but more deadly

   E. Weaponry in prior wars was more accurate but not as deadly

100. From 1790 until the early nineteenth century women were largely thought to be what characteristic?

   A. Virtuous

   B. Courageous

   C. Intelligent

   D. Prosperous

   E. Strong

101. Which answer describes the First Amendment?

   A. Protection from quartering of troops

   B. Freedom of speech, press, religion, peaceable assembly, and to petition the government

   C. Right for the people to keep and bear arms, as well as to maintain a militia

   D. Civil trial by jury

   E. Due process, double jeopardy, self-incrimination, private property

102. What was the major type of economic production in the South?

   A. Textile

   B. Factory

   C. Transportation

   D. Agriculture

   E. Iron/Steel

103. Harriet Beecher Stowe's "Uncle Tom's Cabin" aroused northern outrage over the implications of the

   A. Missouri Compromise

   B. Virginia Run Away Slave Act

   C. Fugitive Slave Act

   D. Kansas-Nebraska Act

   E. Dred Scott decision

104. What was the main provision of the Fugitive Slave Law?

   A. Slaves were free if they got to the North

   B. The Underground Railroad was legalized

   C. Blacks found without proper litigation could be enslaved

   D. Southerners could not pursue escaped slaves

   E. Aiding runaway slaves was a crime

105. The United States refused to annex Texas in 1836 because:

A. Most of Texas's inhabitants were native Mexicans

B. Texans did not want to be annexed to the United States

C. The American government was opposed to armed rebellions against established governments

D. There weren't enough inhabitants for it to become a state

E. Of fear that it would provoke war with Mexico

106. Which of the following people organized the first women's rights convention at Seneca Falls?

A. Dorthea Dix and Susan B. Anthony

B. Dorthea Dix and Lucretia Mott

C. Lucretia Mott and Elizabeth Cady Stanton

D. Susan B. Anthony and Elizabeth Cady Stanton

E. Horace Mann and Noah Webster

107. What did the Neutrality Proclamation on 1793 mean for the United States?

A. That Congress could declare war and neutrality

B. That the President could declare war and neutrality

C. That the President could declare neutrality but not war

D. That Congress could not declare war or neutrality

E. None of the above

108. What effect did railroads play in westward expansion?

A. Quicker transportation and it increased national revenue

B. Allowed slaves to escape easier

C. Decreased the overall population

D. Increased the national debt

E. Decreased agricultural economy and implanted it with manufacturers

109. **The Indian Removal Act of 1830 removed southeastern tribes to Indian Territory. In what present day state was this territory located?**

    A. Nebraska

    B. Oklahoma

    C. Kansas

    D. Texas

    E. Indiana

110. **What was one factor that influenced the creation of the National Market Economy?**

    A. Revolution in transportation

    B. Public policy at state and national levels to promote enterprise

    C. Nationalism of the Republican Party (aka Jefferson Party)

    D. Judicial nationalism, creation of legal requirements for a national market

    E. All of the above

111. **Why was the "penny press" or the Daily News Papers (1835) a technological advancement in mass media?**

    A. Only the rich could afford it, therefore, they held common knowledge over citizens of less income, Native Americans, or slaves

    B. It was an affordable and economically savvy way to spread information, political views and agendas

    C. It was the first newspaper

    D. It was the first time the nation could become unified over any mass media advancement

    E. None of the above

112. **What was the fastest growing social class during the Antebellum Era?**

    A. Low-class

    B. Slave

    C. Middle-class

    D. Upper-class

    E. Immigrants

113. **The second Great Awakening of the first half of the nineteenth century had what effect on life in America?**

    A. It increased concern over slavery

    B. Promoted a greater focus on democratic ideals that coincided with the Age of Jacksonian ideology- "the common man"

    C. Created a desire for control and order

    D. Bars, brothels, and jails closed down

    E. All of the above

114. **Mormonism in the Antebellum Period reflected:**

    A. a strong antislavery bias

    B. a celebration of individual liberty

    C. a desire to improve the status of women

    D. a strong desire to isolate believers from general society

    E. a belief in human perfectibility

115. **The creation of "asylums" for social deviants was an effort to:**

    A. punish the inmates

    B. get the deviants out of society

    C. reform and rehabilitate the inmates

    D. cut down the cost of crime and punishment

    E. All answers are correct

116. **What group of people had the largest population in the South during the early to mid-nineteenth century:**

    A. yeoman farmers

    B. merchants

    C. slaves

    D. planters

    E. seafaring merchants

117. **What effect did the Slave Trade Act of 1807 have on the United States?**

   A. That slavery was abolished

   B. That one could buy slaves in all states, despite state laws

   C. That no one could import international slaves

   D. That 1/3 of every slave bought internationally would be taxed higher than slaves bought within the nation

   E. That only white landowners could buy international slaves

118. **A major difference between Northern and Southern societies prior to the Civil War is illustrated by the role women played in the:**

   A. establishment of educational institutions in the South

   B. growth of the Northern factory system

   C. emergence of a Southern literary tradition

   D. explosion of religious revivalism in the North

   E. political spheres

119. **The U.S. Naturalization Law of March 26, 1790 included only:**

   A. free white persons

   B. Asians

   C. Native Americans

   D. free blacks

   E. indentured whites

120. **What document contains a list of individual rights and liberties that limit the United States federal government?**

   A. The Declaration of Independence

   B. Magna Carta

   C. Liberty Bill

   D. Bill of Rights

   E. Petition of Rights

History of the United States II

ANSWER KEY

Question Number	Correct Answer	Your Answer	Question Number	Correct Answer	Your Answer	Question Number	Correct Answer	Your Answer
1	D		41	E		81	E	
2	A		42	D		82	B	
3	C		43	B		83	A	
4	D		44	A		84	E	
5	C		45	D		85	E	
6	D		46	E		86	A	
7	E		47	A		87	B	
8	B		48	C		88	A	
9	D		49	B		89	D	
10	A		50	C		90	C	
11	D		51	A		91	A	
12	C		52	E		92	B	
13	C		53	D		93	C	
14	A		54	D		94	A	
15	D		55	B		95	D	
16	A		56	A		96	C	
17	E		57	E		97	C	
18	C		58	C		98	B	
19	A		59	A		99	A	
20	D		60	B		100	A	
21	C		61	B		101	B	
22	B		62	E		102	D	
23	D		63	C		103	C	
24	B		64	E		104	E	
25	B		65	B		105	E	
26	A		66	A		106	C	
27	C		67	A		107	C	
28	D		68	D		108	A	
29	E		69	A		109	B	
30	C		70	E		110	E	
31	E		71	B		111	B	
32	B		72	D		112	C	
33	C		73	C		113	E	
34	D		74	D		114	E	
35	D		75	C		115	C	
36	C		76	D		116	C	
37	A		77	A		117	C	
38	C		78	B		118	B	
39	B		79	D		119	A	
40	C		80	B		120	D	

History of the United States II

Description of the Examination

The History of the United States II: 1865 to the Present examination covers material that is usually taught in the second semester of what is often a two-semester course in United States history. The examination covers the period of United States history from the end of the Civil War to the present, with the majority of the questions being on the twentieth century.

The examination contains approximately 120 questions to be answered in 90 minutes. Some of these are pretest questions that will not be scored. Any time candidates spend on tutorials and providing personal information is in addition to the actual testing time.

Knowledge and Skills Required

Questions on the History of the United States II examination require candidates to demonstrate one or more of the following abilities.
* Identification and description of historical phenomena
* Analysis and interpretation of historical phenomena
* Comparison and contrast of historical phenomena

The subject matter of the History of the United States II examination is drawn from the following topics. The percentages next to the main topics indicate the approximate percentage of exam questions on that topic.

Topical Specifications

35% Political institutions, behavior, and public policy
25% Social developments
10% Economic developments
15% Cultural and intellectual developments
15% Diplomacy and international relations

Chronological Specifications

30% 1865–1914
70% 1915–present

The following are among the specific topics tested:
- The impact of the Civil War and Reconstruction upon the South
- The motivations and character of American expansionism
- The content of constitutional amendments and their interpretations by the Supreme Court
- The changing nature of agricultural life
- The development of American political parties
- The emergence of regulatory and welfare-state legislation
- The intellectual and political expressions of liberalism, conservatism, and other such movements
- Long-term demographic trends
- The process of economic growth and development
- The changing occupational structure, nature of work, and labor organization
- Immigration and the history of racial and ethnic minorities
- Urbanization and industrialization
- The causes and impacts of major wars in American history
- Major movements and individual figures in the history of American arts and letters
- Trends in the history of women and the family

History of the United States II

SAMPLE TEST

DIRECTIONS: Read each item and select the best response.

1. **What law was passed that finally abolished slavery in December of 1865?**

   A. The Appomattox Treaty

   B. The Thirteenth Amendment

   C. The Fourteenth Amendment

   D. Emancipation Proclamation

   E. Black Codes

2. **What treaty ended the Civil War on April 9, 1865?**

   A. The Appomattox Treaty

   B. The Thirteenth Amendment

   C. Reconstruction Treaty

   D. Force Act

   E. There was no treaty

3. **Which era, started in 1863 and ended in 1877, covers the complete history of the entire country following the Civil War and focuses on the transformation of the Southern United States?**

   A. Civil Rights

   B. Civil War era

   C. Reconstruction era

   D. Antebellum era

   E. Gilded Age

4. **What is a practice that was defended by Ulysses S. Grant in 1872 in which a political party, after winning an election, gives government jobs to its supporters, friends and relatives as a reward for working toward victory, and as an incentive to keep working for the party?**

   A. The Spoil System

   B. Enfranchisement

   C. Merit System

   D. The Jacksonian System

   E. Republicanism

5. The _____ Act of 1887 allowed the United States to divide Indian Territories for Native Americans who wanted their own land, individually. Those that did were allowed American citizenship.

    A. Dawes

    B. Medill

    C. Roosevelt

    D. Separation

    E. Indian

6. What organization in the United States encouraged families to band together to promote the economic and political well-being of the community and agriculture? This organization was responsible for implementing the Granger Laws, which helped raise fare prices of railroad and grain elevator companies.

    A. Agrarian party

    B. Agricultural movement

    C. The Green party

    D. The Grange movement

    E. Kelly's agrarian movement

7. As modernism and the industrial revolution swept over America what movement advocated for social justice and environmentalism?

    A. Suffragette movement

    B. Conservationist movement

    C. Anti-Communist movement

    D. The Democratic movement

    E. The Progressive movement

8. Which event symbolizes the idea of the "Wild West" in 1890?

    A. Johnson County War

    B. Dead Man's Tree

    C. Castellammaarese War

    D. Oxnard Strike

    E. Hay–Bunau-Varilla Treaty

9. **What did the landmark case Lochner vs New York ensue?**

   A. New York could regulate the hours of bakers (They were not permitted to work above 60 hours a week).

   B. New York's regulation of the working hours of bakers was not a justifiable restriction (they could work over 60 hours a week) on the right to contract freely under the 14th Amendment's guarantee of liberty.

   C. Facilities for blacks and whites are constitutional under the doctrine of separate but equal, which holds for close to 60 years.

   D. With only a few narrow exceptions, every person born in the United States acquires United States citizenship at birth via the Citizenship Clause of the Fourteenth Amendment.

   E. The Constitution grants to the states the power to prosecute individuals for wrongful interference with the right to travel.

10. **What was the informal agreement between the United States and the Empire of Japan in which the United States of America would not impose restriction on Japanese immigration, and Japan would not allow further emigration to the U.S. called?**

    A. Gentlemen's Agreement of 1907

    B. Japanese-American Agreement

    C. The Immigration Act

    D. The Emigration Act

    E. Treaty of Mutual Cooperation and Security

11. **What was the name of an union that formed an international, radical labor union, consisting of anarchist and socialist movements, 1905? The union combines general unionism with industrial unionism.**

    A. Communist Party

    B. International Association of Bridge and Structural Iron Workers

    C. Amalgamated Clothing Workers

    D. Industrial Workers of the World

    E. Teamsters

12. What act sought to prevent anticompetitive practices in their incipiency?

    A. Congressional Review Act

    B. Clayton Antitrust Act

    C. Federal Reserve Act

    D. Pure food and Drug Act

    E. Dawes Severely Act

13. How did the American public feel about entering World War One in 1914?

    A. They wanted to remain neutral

    B. They wanted to remain Neutral, even though they supported Germany.

    C. They immediately entered the war on the side of the Allies.

    D. They immediately entered the war on the side of the Central powers.

    E. After the sinking of sinking of the passenger liner RMS Lusitania, the US entered the conflict.

14. What opened in 1914 that opened trade to the Far East?

    A. Panama Canal

    B. American Frontier

    C. Cuba

    D. Bohemian Canal

    E. Mexican Straight

15. In the 1920s what was prohibited to manufacture and sell by an amendment by the constitution, but later ratified?

    A. Marijuana

    B. Firearms

    C. Cocaine

    D. Alcohol

    E. Coke a cola

16. The United States (as well as other Allie nations) imposed what treaty on Germany, which demanded unrealistic demands and became a key factor in the rise of the Nazi party?

    A. Versailles

    B. Grenoble

    C. Berlin

    D. Normandy

    E. Allies

17. **What era was named after the great economic prosperity, festive (namely jazz) music, excessive style, and embrace of modernity?**

    A. Prosperity Years

    B. The Modern Era

    C. Roaring Twenties

    D. Gilded Age

    E. Counter Culture

18. **What hate organization reached up to four million members in the 1920s, claiming membership of President Harding, and sympathies of President Wilson?**

    A. Aryan Nation

    B. The KKK

    C. American Nazi Party

    D. Communist Party

    E. Extreme Democrats

19. **What event officially ended the Great Depression?**

    A. The New Deal

    B. Keynesian Theory

    C. The election of Franklin Roosevelt

    D. Social Security

    E. The admission into War World II

20. **What is the New Deal?**

    A. President Franklin D. Roosevelt and Democrats different efforts to end the Great Depression and reform the American economy, principally by enlarging the United States government and its spending.

    B. A time period when President Harry S. Truman enlarged local governments and minimalized the federal government in order to bring more power back to the states.

    C. A series of events which eventually caused the Great Depression.

    D. President Harry S. Truman and Republican different efforts to end the Great Depression and reform the American economy, principally by enlarging the United States government and its spending.

    E. A time period when President Franklin D. Roosevelt enlarged local governments and minimalized the federal government in order to bring more power back to the states.

21. What event caused the United States of America to enter World War II?

    A. Zimmerman Note

    B. The bombing of Pearl Harbor

    C. The invasion of France

    D. The invasion of Poland

    E. The Holocaust

22. What is the line called that separated the US, Britain, and France from the Soviet Union?

    A. The Berlin Wall

    B. Soviet Union Border

    C. Satellite Border

    D. The Iron Curtain

    E. The Bronze Wall

23. What was the fundamental theoretical problem that divided the US and the Soviet Union that caused the Cold War?

    A. capitalism with liberal democracy vs totalitarian communism

    B. capitalism with conservative democracy vs totalitarian communism

    C. liberal democracy vs communism

    D. capitalism with liberal democracy vs mass communism

    E. capitalism with liberal democracy vs Trotskyite communism

24. What general successfully won at the Battle of Inchon, turning the Korean War around; eventually leading to an invasion of North Korea?

    A. Robert A. Parson

    B. Dwight D. Eisenhower

    C. Douglas MacArthur

    D. Colin Powell

    E. Daniel McDaniel

25. What was the policy in which Americans fought communist expansion where ever it occurred?

    A. Control Policy

    B. Anti-Communist Strategy

    C. Increase Liberty

    D. Containment Policy

    E. Pro- Capitalism Strategy

26. What did the outcome of the court case Roe v. Wade legalize in 1973?

    A. Abortion

    B. Communism

    C. Alcohol consumption

    D. Women's right to vote

    E. Integrated school systems

History of the United States II

27. **What was the Civil Rights Act of 1964?**

    A. Prohibited individual citizens from carrying firearms

    B. A civil rights act that provided private solutions.

    C. Prohibited individuals to purchase or loiter in private sectors (super markets, bars, etc.) if unwanted.

    D. Outlawed discrimination based on race, color, religion, and national origin, but not sex.

    E. Outlawed discrimination based on race, color, religion, sex, or national origin.

28. **Which three were famous African American Civil Rights activists that were assonated in the 1960s?**

    A. Bull Connor, Nathan B. Forest, and Medgar Evans

    B. Bull Connor, Martin Luther King, and Medgar Evers

    C. Rev. George Lee, Martin Luther King, and Medgar Evers

    D. William Lewis Moore, Martin Luther King, and Medgar Evers

    E. Nathan B. Forest, Martin Luther King, and Medgar Evers

29. **What program was a result of Lyndon B Johnson's "Great Societies" War on Poverty"?**

    A. Medicare

    B. Obama Care

    C. Johnson care

    D. Social Security

    E. Department of Education

30. **What was the multi-billion dollar research project for a missile defense system that could shoot down incoming Soviet missiles and eliminate the need for mutually assured destruction?**

    A. Missile Defense Program

    B. Star Wars (Strategic Defense Initiative)

    C. US Nuclear Program

    D. US Missile Security

    E. None of the above

31. **What Landmark Supreme Court decision declared that racial segregation in schools is unconstitutional?**

    A. Black v. Department of Education

    B. Rice v. Board of Education

    C. Sweatt v. Painter

    D. Brown v. Board of Education

    E. Roe v. Wade

32. The Twenty-Sixth Amendment lowered the voting age from ___ to ____ in 1971?

    A. 21 to 18

    B. 24 to 21

    C. 20 to 18

    D. 30 to 18

    E. The Twenty-Sixth Amendment had nothing to do with the voting age.

33. McCarthyism in the 1950's was similar to the Palmer Raids (Red Scare) in the 1920s in what way?

    American citizen's liberties were breached

    B. Immigrants were suspicious of white communists

    C. Anarchists were the biggest conspirators

    D. The Ku Klux Klan led the assault against "Anti-Americans"

    E. No immigrants entered the country during these time periods.

34. How did president Nixon Presidency end?

    A. Impeachment

    B. Resignation

    C. Death

    D. Illness

    E. Like every other president, he was president for four years. However, he was not voted in again because of the Watergate scandal.

35. What hurt economic growth the most during the 1970s through the 1980s?

    A. Decrease in manual labor

    B. Inflation on unique metals

    C. Increase in oil prices

    D. Lack of technology innovation

    E. Increase in water prices

36. What island(s) in the Caribbean did the US invade in 1983 in order to stop a small Marxist faction with holding power?

    A. Cuba

    B. Grenada

    C. Portugal

    D. Bermuda

    E. Virgin Islands

37. **Who was sworn in as the first woman Supreme court Justice?**

    A. Sandra Day O'Connor

    B. Ruth Bader Ginsberg

    C. Sonia Sotomayor

    D. Elena Kagan

    E. Condoleezza Rice

38. **What were the economic policies of the former US president Ronald Reagan called that associated especially with the reduction of taxes and the promotion of unrestricted free-market activity?**

    A. Reaganomics

    B. Keynesian Economics

    C. Command Economics

    D. Traditional Economics

    E. Conservative Economics

39. **Under what era did the United States have its longest time frame of economic prosperity?**

    A. Roaring Twenties

    B. Progressive Years

    C. Antebellum

    D. Reconstruction

    E. 1990s (Information Age)

40. **What was Truman Doctrine?**

    A. It was an American foreign policy during President Harry S. Truman's term to stop Soviet imperialism during the Cold War.

    B. President Harry S. Truman plan to give American citizens universal healthcare.

    C. President Franklin D. Roosevelts great depression bailout plan, though up by vice president Harry S. Truman.

    D. A set of rules brought to the U.N. by President Harry S. Truman to hinder fascist leaders from gaining power in former axis powers lands.

    E. A set of pro-Soviet laws enforced during President Harry S. Truman's candidacy.

41. **What landmark piece of federal legislation was in 1964 in the United States lead by Lyndon B. Johnson prohibits racial discrimination in voting such as requiring some states (mostly in the south) that want to change its districts have to go through the department of justice?**

    A. Public Law

    B. Help America Vote Act

    C. Voting Rights Act

    D. Patriot Act

    E. 15th Amendment

42. **What was the initial reason of the First Persian Gulf War?**

    A. U.N. need for oil

    B. American need for oil

    C. Saddam Hussein's genocide of northern Iraqis

    D. Iran's invasion of Iran

    E. Iraq's invasion of Kuwait

43. **Which administration used the term "War on Terrorism" first when referring to terrorist?**

    A. George H. W. Bush

    B. George W. Bush

    C. Ronald Reagan

    D. Bill Clinton

    E. Lyndon B. Johnson

44. **What agreement in 1994 tried to eliminate barriers to trade and investment between the U.S., Canada and Mexico?**

    A. North American Nationality Organization (NANO)

    B. Western Alliance, Sect II

    C. The North American Triple Alliance (NTATA)

    D. North American Free Trade Agreement (NAFTA)

    E. Canada–United States Free Trade Agreement

45. **What is the traditional view of why the United States "won" the Cold War?**

    A. During the Carter and Reagan Administrations the United States upped military spending. The USSR tried to keep up, however, could not afford it and eventually collapsed.

    B. During the Bush and Clinton Administrations the United States upped military spending. The USSR tried to keep up, however, could not afford it and eventually collapsed.

    C. The Soviet Union eastern satellite nations won independence, severing the USSR economy.

    D. The USSR could not evoke desire in its citizens to work, therefore the economy eventually collapsed.

    E. Covert successful CIA mission missions in Afghanistan against Soviets led to a total breakdown of Soviet military and then later economy.

46. What was the label President John F Kennedy's give the 1960s with its unknown opportunities and perils such as uncharted areas of science and space, unsolved problems of peace and war, unconquered problems of ignorance and prejudice, unanswered questions of poverty and surplus?

    A. The Beat Generation

    B. The Lost Generation

    C. The New Age

    D. The Peace Age

    E. The New Frontier

47. The New Left in the 1960s and 70s sympathized with what school of thought?

    A. Frankfurt School of Critical Theory

    B. Taoism

    C. Functionalism

    D. Classic Liberalism

    E. Republicanism

48. What was the plans that was enacted in 1947 that goals were to rebuild war-devastated regions, remove trade barriers, modernize industry, make Europe prosperous again, and prevent the spread of communism called?

    A. Dawes Plan

    B. Marshall Plan

    C. Truman Plan

    D. Morganthau Plan

    E. Versailles Compromise

History of the United States II

49. **What was the difference between First New Deal and Second New Deal?**

    A. The First New Deal regulated the private sector of society, however, the Second New Deal focused on regulating the corporate sector.

    B. The First New Deal focused more or the war effort, whereas the Second New Deal was more about poverty.

    C. The First New Deal was an effort to reshape the American electoral. landscape whereas the Second New Deal focused on ending poverty.

    D. At first it was just trying to find an immediate stop the depression. Relief, Recovery and Reform. The second was to have government regulate labor, housing, and farms.

    E. There really was no difference except Franklin D. Roosevelt changed the name in order to invoke more votes because of the popularity of the first deal.

50. **Before ratification of the 22nd amendment in 1951, most presidents served no more than two terms because of**

    A. Tradition

    B. Federal law

    C. Supreme Court Decision

    D. The Eight Year Clause

    E. Anti-tyranny laws

51. **The 15th Amendment allowed former African American slaves to _____.**

    A. buy land

    B. vote

    C. acquire ownership of a public facility

    D. return back to Africa for free

    E. be compensated for free labor

History of the United States II

52. **What were Jim Crow Laws?**

    A. State and local laws enforcing racial segregation predominantly in the South. Enacted after the Reconstruction period, these laws continued in force until 1965.

    B. Racist laws enforced by Alabama Governor Jim Crow. Northerner politicians coined the universal racist laws in the South after him.

    C. Laws that supported black rights during the Reconstruction period.

    D. Laws enforced by the national government to restrict African. Americans directly after the Civil War.

    E. Racist laws enforced by South Carolina Governor Jim Crow. Northerner politicians coined the universal racist laws in the South after him.

53. **What was a key device for the removal of ex-Confederates from the political arena during the Reconstruction of the United States in the 1860s, requiring every white male to swear they had never borne arms against the Union or supported the Confederacy (in the Wade–Davis Bill)?**

    A. Reconstruction Plan

    B. Fourteenth Amendment

    C. Ten-Percent Plan

    D. Ironclad Oath

    E. Republican Circle

54. **What was the series of acts of Congress that promoted the construction of a "transcontinental railroad" through authorizing the issuance of government bonds and granting Native American, private, and government lands to railroad companies?**

    A. Pacific Railroad Acts

    B. Transcendental Acts

    C. Johnson Acts

    D. West Acts

    E. The Gilead Acts

55. **Congress passed ten-year restrictions on _____ immigration in 1882 and 1892 and a permanent exclusion act in 1902.**

    A. German

    B. Irish

    C. Japanese

    D. Italian

    E. Chinese

56. What was the idea called, led by William Graham Sumner, that argued the best equipped to win the struggle for survival was the American businessman, and concluded that taxes and regulations serve as dangers to his survival?

    A. Marxism

    B. Social Darwinism

    C. Capitalism

    D. Laissez Faire

    E. Imperialism

57. What was the name given to the cultural, social, and artistic explosion that took place in Harlem between the end of World War I and the middle of the 1930s?

    A. Civil Rights Movement

    B. Black Lives Matter

    C. Reconstruction Era

    D. African American Rights

    E. Harlem Renaissance

58. What genre of dancing was famous from 1900 to 1918, beginning in African American communities?

    A. The Waltz

    B. Swing Dance

    C. Ragtime

    D. Modern Dance

    E. Balboa

59. What was the process in which people moved (or migrated) toward the city in the early twentieth century in order to work in the booming industrial era?

    A. Urbanization

    B. Modernization

    C. Counterurbanization

    D. Reconstruction

    E. City Overhaul

60. During the Progressive era what was supported in order to bring about a more "purer" vote to the American elections?

    A. Prohibition laws

    B. African American rights

    C. Woman Suffrage

    D. Anti-Immigration laws

    E. Immigration laws

61. **What did President Wilson's "New Freedom" campaign seek to reform?**

    A. Tariff, Business, and Banking

    B. Tariff, Race, and State Rights

    C. Business, Race, and Banking

    D. Race, Tariff, and Banking

    E. Federal Rights, State Rights, and Tariff

62. **Before War World War, what was the general reaction towards external conflicts by American citizens?**

    A. Interventionism

    B. Indirect Interference

    C. Interference

    D. Isolationism

    E. Reactionary

63. **What was one reason the US entered World War One?**

    A. Invasion of Poland

    B. The sinking of the Lusitania

    C. Pearl Harbor

    D. Invasion of Austria

    E. Attacks on Britain

64. **Two Senators and fifty Representatives voted against the war resolution, including the first female ever to sit in Congress, _____ of Montana.**

    A. Joni Ernst

    B. Hattie Caraway

    C. Rebecca Felton

    D. Jeannette Rankin

    E. Ruth Elandor

65. **What authorized the federal government to raise a national army for the American entry into World War I through the compulsory enlistment of people?**

    A. Draft

    B. Selective Service Act

    C. Draft Lottery

    D. Conscription Act

    E. There was no draft during WWI

History of the United States II

66. The widespread use of what technological advancement in the 1920s revolutionized dating, education, change in work patters as well as an increase in recreational time?

    A. Radio

    B. Train

    C. Automobile

    D. Airplane

    E. Bicycle

67. The American Mafia, an Italian-American organized-crime network with operations in cities across the United States, particularly New York and Chicago, rose to power through its success in the illicit _____ during the 1920s Prohibition era.

    A. Illicit narcotic drug trade

    B. Alcohol trade

    C. Firearms trade

    D. Assignations of corporate leaders

    E. Burglary

68. What was the series of raids in 1919-1920 called that focused on eastern Europeans and sympathizers of communist and anarchist ideology?

    A. Second Red Scare

    B. McCarthyism

    C. Anti-Communism

    D. Swift Raids

    E. Palmer Raids

69. What was one result of the Great depression?

    A. Increase in divorce rates

    B. Crime rates dropped

    C. Recreations activities dropped such as watching movies in a cinema.

    D. Migration from rural areas to urban

    E. Individuals in rural areas stayed stationary (cities were expensive and the transportation procedure was too expensive)

70. Prodded by Eleanor Roosevelt, FDR created women's auxiliary forces for?

    A. Transportation system

    B. Conservation

    C. Agriculture

    D. Universities

    E. Military

71. What attributed to the rise in suburbia in the 1950s?

    A. Increase in revenue

    B. Outburst of population from rural areas

    C. Overpopulation

    D. Racial fears, affordable living, avoidance of the "dirtiness" of the city

    E. Growth of conservative citizens that could not stand the normally progressive stance held by cities

72. What groups of individuals, led by writers such as Jack Kerouac and Alan Ginsberg, were specifically known for their refusal to conform to social norms?

    A. Renaissance Era

    B. Post-Moderns

    C. Baby Boomers

    D. Beat Generation

    E. Lost Generation

73. What Supreme Court decision overruled the Plessy v. Ferguson case and declared that in the field of public education the doctrine of separate but equal' has no place. Separate educational facilities are inherently unequal.

    A. Plessy v. Ferguson II

    B. Brown v. Board of Education

    C. Shelley v. Kraemer

    D. Powell v. Anderson

    E. Powell v. Alabama

74. The Maoist tenet "Political power comes through the barrel of a gun" was adopted by which group?

    A. Nation of Yahweh

    B. Black Back To Africa

    C. Black Panther

    D. NAACP

    E. United Nuwaubian Nation of Moors

75. What war started because France was determined to reclaim all its territories after World War II? This war was unique because American tradition dictated sympathy for the revolutionaries over any colonial power. However, supporting the Marxist in this given circumstance was unthinkable, given the new strategy of containing communism.

    A. Korean War

    B. Afghanistan

    C. Vietnam War

    D. Geneva Island

    E. Chile Civil War

76. Who was the first US President to visit China after the communist takeover?

    A. Franklin D. Roosevelt

    B. Dwight D. Eisenhower

    C. Harry Truman

    D. Lyndon B. Johnson

    E. Richard Nixon

77. What was one aspect that feminists such as Margret Sanger fought for in the early 1960s?

    A. The use of contraceptives

    B. The right to vote

    C. The enforcement of prohibition laws

    D. Improved childcare laws

    E. Free Trade

78. What did the New Right consist of?

    A. Extremist immigrants groups

    B. Extremist political groups, conservative Christians, and CEO's of corporations

    C. Fringe political groups, Christian evangelicals, and higher ups of corporations

    D. Extreme Libertarians

    E. Followers of Reagan

79. With the growing economy, many middle-class Americans rushed to invest in the stock market and to flaunt their newly acquired wealth. What group of people supplanted the hippies of the former generation?

    A. Young Urban Professionals

    B. Rockers

    C. Punk rockers

    D. Society of X's

    E. Baby Boomers

80. What was the historic time called throughout 1997–2000 during which stock markets in industrialized nations saw their equity value rise rapidly from growth in the Internet sector and related fields (especially with the invention of the World Wide Web)?

    A. The Information Age

    B. Dot-Com Bubble

    C. Great Moderation

    D. Golden Age of Capitalism

    E. World Wide Consumerism

81. The rapid expansion of _____ led to real wage growth of 60% between 1860 and 1890.

    A. Agriculture

    B. Racial equality

    C. Industrialization

    D. Emigration

    E. Progressive ideals

82. In 1869, the First Transcontinental Railroad opened new areas of opportunity in _____.

    A. Far-west mining and ranching regions

    B. South American mining

    C. African American mobility

    D. Oil Revenue

    E. Exotic fur trade

83. The Reconstruction era brought many changes to the very poor and broken South such as _____.

    A. Higher Education

    B. Equality

    C. Republicanism

    D. Mercantilism

    E. Sharecropping

84. What was the US financial crisis called that took place over a three-week period starting in mid-October, when the New York Stock Exchange fell almost 50% from its peak the previous year? Panic occurred, and eventually spread throughout the nation when many state and local banks and businesses entered bankruptcy.

   A. Depression of 1910

   B. Great Depression

   C. Panic of 1907

   D. The End of the Industrial Age

   E. The Second Great Depression

85. The Federal road building program ended in 1818, 98 year gap, leaving states to build roads until the _____.

   A. Car and Road Act 1916

   B. Autobahn

   C. Dwight D. Eisenhower National System of Interstate and Defense Highways

   D. Federal Road Act of 1916

   E. Highway act of 1916

86. In order to deal with the crisis in banking at the time of his inauguration, President Franklin D Roosevelt.

   A. Closed the banking system for four days giving them a "banking holiday."

   B. Enlarged the Federal Bank.

   C. Prohibited for more than 1000 USD to be taking from any accounts that were to be used for recreational purposes.

   D. Fired all the Federal Bank board members and replaced them with Keynesian theorists

   E. President Roosevelt did nothing, he thought the bank would come out of its cycle if left alone.

87. What was the policy adopted by the United States in 1939 to preserve neutrality while aiding the Allies? Britain and France could buy goods from the United States if they paid in full and transported them.

   A. Isolation act

   B. Cash and Carry

   C. Prohibition Act

   D. Debt Default Act

   E. New Deal

88. **What is one reason the US has had a dramatic increase in economic since the 1950s?**

    A. The end of the Korean War

    B. The end of the Vietnam War

    C. Oil prices have decreased

    D. More of a focus is agriculture

    E. Baby Boomers

89. **What policy did the Office of Economic Opportunity originate from?**

    A. Personal Responsibility and Work Opportunity Act

    B. War on Poverty

    C. VISTA

    D. New Deal

    E. None of the Above

90. **The 1973 Oil Crisis began when**

    A. OAPEC proclaimed an oil embargo- raising the price of oil to four times as much.

    B. OPEC proclaimed and oil embargo- raising the price of oil to four times as much.

    C. large Oil fields caught on fire in Saudi Arabia, causing global oil prices to rise.

    D. the United States congress voted against drilling in Alaska and Texas, raising oil prices to three times as much.

    E. There was no Oil crisis in 1973.

91. **What was one term used to define President Reagan's economic policy to cut both federal spending and taxes to release private revenue for future investments?**

    A. Supply-side

    B. Reagan Conservatism

    C. Laissez-faire

    D. New Conservative Economics

    E. Capitalism

History of the United States II

92. What was reason for the longest and largest economic boom in the 1990s?

    A. Cost of living decreased

    B. Lower taxes

    C. The ending of the food tax

    D. The creation of the World Wide Web

    E. Invasion of Iraq

93. What organization formed after the ending of the Civil War in 1865, later became known as the largest hate organization known in the United States?

    A. White Aryan Resistance

    B. Southern Democrats

    C. Ku Klux Klan

    D. Anti-Defense League

    E. White Supremists

94. The idea (that originated in the 1880s by farmers and their associates) that the government was being made up of industrialists and bankers was called?

    A. Progressivism

    B. Populism

    C. Conservatism

    D. True Liberalism

    E. Free Republicanism

95. Many of the middle class in the beginning of the 20th century believed that unfair election systems, exploitation of workers, women and children, corruption in the business class and the legal system all meant that there was an unfair political system. These people were called?

    A. Progressivism

    B. Populism

    C. Conservatism

    D. True Liberalism

    E. Free Republicanism

96. What was the genre of writing called that appeared after the Civil War and had great effect on the American populist all the wat into the Twentieth Century? The style of writing derived from the presentation of the features and peculiarities of a particular locality and its inhabitants.

    A. Beat Generation

    B. Transcendentalism

    C. Realism

    D. Local Colour

    E. Expressionism

97. What did Jeffries V. Johnson boxing fright prove to the United States populace?

   A. The United States was the strongest nation

   B. Anyone can fulfil the American dream

   C. Whites were more intelligent

   D. Blacks were equals

   E. That blacks were not meant to live in cities

98. The NAACP was developed in order to?

   A. Fight radical black activism.

   B. Defend Jim Crow laws.

   C. To fight for equality on a national front.

   D. Support Ku Klux Klan

   E. Support Progressive politicians

99. Conscription policies in the First and Second World Wars differed significantly in that in the First World War

   A. The draft began before the US entered

   B. Blacks were enlisted

   C. German skepticism

   D. Airplanes were not used

   E. Automatic weapons were not used

100. What were the northern, urban, single, young, middle-class women from the 1920s called who enjoyed dancing to jazz music, wearing dresses at their knees, wearing short hair, and participating in night life?

   A. Revolutionists

   B. Hippies

   C. Valley girls

   D. Flappers

   E. Victorians

101. What was the third largest political party in 1920?

   A. Republicans

   B. Democrats

   C. Socialist

   D. Communists

   E. Whig

102. In 1925 Tennessee passed what law that prohibited the teaching of Darwin's theory of evolution in schools?

    A. Bryan Laws

    B. Religious Freedom Law

    C. Creationism act

    D. Separate but Equal act

    E. Butler Law

103. What is the term for the practice of making accusations of subversion or treason without proper regard for evidence originating from the Second Red Scare, characterized by heightened political repression against communists?

    A. Anti-Soviet

    B. McCarthyism

    C. Palmerizing

    D. False allegations

    E. Anti-American

104. What was the Indian Termination Policy?

    A. President Franklin Roosevelts plan to destroy all Native American ancestry in the US

    B. President Dwight Eisenhower's policy to shape a series of laws and policies with the intent of assimilating Native Americans into mainstream American society fairly quickly (ending reservations and Native American sovereignty)

    C. President Franklin Roosevelts policy to shape a series of laws and policies with the intent of assimilating Native Americans into mainstream American society fairly quickly (ending reservations and Native American sovereignty)

    D. President Franklin Roosevelts plant to end Americans plans to destroy Native American plans by creating suburbs on Native American reservations.

    E. President Harry Truman's plan to end Native American ancestry in the US

History of the United States II

105. **What was the anti-establishment cultural phenomenon in the 1950s and 1960s called?**

    A. The Counter-Culture

    B. Brights Movement

    C. Ecofeminism

    D. Cultural Movement

    E. Human Rights Movement

106. **What is one difference in first and second wave feminism?**

    A. First wave feminism pursued the right to vote while second wave feminism sought equality in the workforce

    B. First wave feminism was much more radical than its counterparts

    C. Second wave feminism was more focused on woman outside the United States

    D. First wave feminism pursued the equality in the work place, second wave feminism focused on solely education

    E. Second wave feminism was more ideological

107. **Why did (/do) the majority of African American women not participate in all three feminist movements?**

    A. They did not like white people

    B. The majority of the movement was made up of middle class white women. Blacks felt they could not relate with the white experience.

    C. All three movements did not admit African Americans.

    D. Black women were not educated enough.

    E. Question is incorrect, the majority of the feminist movement was black.

108. **What started the Montgomery Bus Boycott and was one reason that sparked the Civil Rights movement?**

    A. Rosa Parks' refusal to move on a Montgomery bus.

    B. Martin Luther King's organization of the Montgomery Bus riots.

    C. The assignation of Rosa Parks.

    D. Ralph Abernathy, King formed the Southern Christian Leadership Conference (SCLC), which invoked African Americans to riot, including bus riots.

    E. Malcom X refusal to get off a Montgomery all white bus

109. From the beginning of the decade until the end of the 90s, new forms of entertainment, commerce, research, work, and communication became commonplace in the United States. The driving force behind much of this change was an innovation popularly known as the Internet. This age is known as the _____?

   A. Information age

   B. Modernity

   C. Education age

   D. Consumer age

   E. Baby Boomers

110. What was the term for the 1970s decade when many young people were focused on themselves, rather than the world at large?

   A. Me Decade

   B. The Counter Culture

   C. Hippies

   D. Civil Rights

   E. Rockers

111. _____ was one of the most significant restrictions on free immigration in US history, prohibiting all immigration of Chinese laborers.

   A. Anti-Chinese Act

   B. Chinese Exclusion Act

   C. Civil Rights Act

   D. Magnuson Act

   E. Immigration and Nationality Act

112. What was the policy proposed in 1899 to keep China open to trade with all countries on an equal basis?

   A. Immigration Act

   B. Mutual Security Act

   C. Foreign Assistance Act

   D. Open Door Policy

   E. Act for International Development

113. **What did the Roosevelt Corollary mean for the US international position?**

    A. It allowed the United States to intervene in Russian affairs.

    B. It allowed the United States to intervene in the Middle East.

    C. Being an addition to the Monroe doctrine, it allowed the United States to interfere in Europe and South American countries.

    D. It ended a hundred year suppression on Native American lands.

    E. It allowed the ending of colonization in South America.

114. **Why is the Alaska Purchase sometimes called "Seward folly"?**

    A. Because he had to pay Russia and then he had to pay Siberia for it.

    B. Secretary of State William Seward bought Alaska on behalf of the US and died in Alaska when trying to relocate the territories capital.

    C. The purchase threatened British colonies in the Pacific west, causing Britain to put tariffs on Western United States goods.

    D. People were critical of the deal and thought Secretary State William Seward payed too much for a piece of land that was mostly unexplored.

    E. Secretary of State William Seward killed thousands of local tribes trying to inhabit the newly purchased land.

115. **What did the United States Congress in the 1930s, do in response to the growing turmoil in Europe and Asia that eventually led to World War II?**

    A. Ludlow Amendments

    B. McGovern–Hatfield Amendment

    C. World War II Acts

    D. Spot Resolutions

    E. Neutrality Acts of the 1930s

116. What was the first international difficulty the U.S. had with the U.S.S.R.?

   A. Yugoslavia revolt

   B. Cuban Missile Crisis

   C. Bay of Pigs

   D. Berlin Blockade

   E. War in Vietnam

117. How did the U.S. help stop communism in Afghanistan form 1979-1989?

   A. Created sanctions against the Soviet Union.

   B. Fought Soviet Union directly in Afghanistan.

   C. Assonated rebel leader Zulfikar Ali Bhutto

   D. Practiced the doctrine of containment by giving military aid to Afghanistan rebels.

   E. All are incorrect. The U.S. stayed neutral in this particular situation.

118. What example would best describe Reagan doctrine?

   A. Giving covert aid to anti-communist militia

   B. Creating an isolationist society

   C. Creating open trade diplomacy with the USSR

   D. Creating open trade with every country except the USSR

   E. Fight the Soviet Union with a direct military offensive.

119. What was the largest military operation after Vietnam War in the United States?

   A. Persian Gulf War

   B. Somalia

   C. Yugoslavia

   D. Grenada

   E. India-Pakistan War

120. Journalist organization, WikiLeaks, released a United States cable leak describing

 A. classified receipts of illegal transactions of military weapons sent from the U.S. government.

 B. classified information about the Iraq War

 C. classified cables that had been sent to the U.S. State Department by 274 of its consulates, embassies, and diplomatic missions around the world.

 D. classified information about the U.S military presence in eastern European countries.

 E. falsified information that supposedly exposed U.S. senate members of embezzling money.

History of the United States II

ANSWER KEY

Question Number	Correct Answer	Your Answer	Question Number	Correct Answer	Your Answer	Question Number	Correct Answer	Your Answer
1	B		41	C		81	C	
2	E		42	E		82	A	
3	C		43	C		83	E	
4	A		44	D		84	C	
5	A		45	A		85	D	
6	D		46	E		86	A	
7	E		47	A		87	B	
8	A		48	B		88	E	
9	B		49	D		89	B	
10	A		50	A		90	A	
11	D		51	B		91	A	
12	B		52	A		92	D	
13	A		53	D		93	C	
14	A		54	A		94	B	
15	D		55	E		95	A	
16	A		56	B		96	D	
17	C		57	E		97	D	
18	B		58	C		98	C	
19	E		59	A		99	A	
20	A		60	C		100	D	
21	B		61	A		101	C	
22	D		62	D		102	E	
23	A		63	B		103	B	
24	C		64	D		104	B	
25	D		65	B		105	A	
26	A		66	C		106	A	
27	E		67	B		107	B	
28	C		68	E		108	A	
29	A		69	D		109	A	
30	B		70	E		110	A	
31	D		71	D		111	B	
32	A		72	D		112	D	
33	A		73	B		113	C	
34	B		74	C		114	D	
35	C		75	C		115	E	
36	B		76	E		116	D	
37	A		77	A		117	D	
38	A		78	C		118	A	
39	E		79	A		119	A	
40	A		80	B		120	C	

Human Growth and Development

Description of the Examination

The Human Growth and Development examination (Infancy, Childhood, Adolescence, Adulthood, and Aging) covers material that is generally taught in a one-semester introductory course in developmental psychology or human development. An understanding of the major theories and research related to the broad categories of physical development, cognitive development, and social development is required, as is the ability to apply this knowledge.

The examination contains approximately 90 questions to be answered in 90 minutes. Some of them are pretest questions that will not be scored. Any time candidates spend on tutorials and providing personal information is in addition to the actual testing time.

Knowledge and Skills Required

Questions on the Human Growth and Development examination require candidates to demonstrate one or more of the following abilities.
- Knowledge of basic facts and terminology
- Understanding of generally accepted concepts and principles
- Understanding of theories and recurrent developmental issues
- Applications of knowledge to particular problems or situations

The subject matter of the Human Growth and Development examination is drawn from the following categories. For each category, several key words and phrases identify topics with which candidates should be familiar. The percentages next to the main categories indicate the approximate percentage of exam questions on that topic.

10% Theoretical Perspectives
- Cognitive developmental
- Evolutionary
- Learning
- Psychodynamic
- Social cognitive
- Sociocultural

5% Research Strategies and Methodology
- Case study
- Correlational
- Cross-sectional
- Cross sequential
- Experimental
- Longitudinal
- Observational

10% Biological Development Throughout the Life Span
- Development of the brain and nervous system
- Heredity, genetics, and genetic testing
- Hormonal influences
- Influences of drugs
- Motor development
- Nutritional influences
- Perinatal influences
- Physical growth and maturation, aging
- Prenatal influences
- Sexual maturation
- Teratogens

7% Perceptual Development Throughout the Life Span
- Sensitive periods
- Sensorimotor activities
- Sensory acuity
- Sensory deprivation

12% Cognitive Development Throughout the Life Span
- Attention
- Environmental influences

- Executive function
- Expertise
- Information processing
- Memory
- Piaget, Jean
- Play
- Problem solving and planning
- Thinking
- Vygotsky, Lev
- Wisdom

8% Language Development
- Bilingualism
- Development of syntax
- Environmental, cultural, and genetic influences
- Language and thought
- Pragmatics
- Semantic development
- Vocalization and sound

4% Intelligence Throughout the Life Span
- Concepts of intelligence and creativity
- Developmental stability and change
- Heredity and environment

10% Social Development Throughout the Life Span
- Aggression
- Attachment
- Gender
- Interpersonal relationships
- Moral development
- Prosocial behavior
- Risk and resilience
- Self
- Social cognition
- Wellness

8% Family, Home, and Society Throughout the Life Span
- Abuse and neglect
- Bronfenbrenner, Urie
- Death and dying
- Family relationships
- Family structures
- Media and technology
- Multicultural perspectives
- Parenting styles
- Social and class influences

8% Personality and Emotion
- Attribution styles
- Development of emotions
- Emotional expression and regulation
- Emotional intelligence
- Erikson, Erik
- Freud, Sigmund
- Stability and change
- Temperament

8% Learning
- Classical conditioning
- Discrimination and generalization
- Habituation
- Operant conditioning
- Social learning and modeling

5% Schooling, Work, and Interventions
- Applications of developmental principles
- Facilitation of role transitions
- Intervention programs and services
- Learning styles
- Occupational development
- Preschool care, day care, and elder care
- Retirement

5% Atypical Development
- Antisocial behavior
- Asocial behavior, fears, phobias, and obsessions
- Attention-deficit/hyperactivity disorder

- Autism spectrum disorders
- Chronic illnesses and physical disabilities
- Cognitive disorders, including dementia
- Genetic disorders
- Giftedness
- Learning disabilities
- Intellectual Disability
- Mood disorders
- Trauma-based syndromes

Human Growth and Development

SAMPLE TEST

1. Among the choices below, what is the earliest sign that infants are engaging an adult in a mutually reinforcing social interaction?

   A. Displaying a social smile to an adult

   B. Crying if left in an unfamiliar place by an adult

   C. Playing peek-a-boo with an adult

   D. Trusting an adult stranger to hold them

   E. Expressing disgust after tasting an unpalatable food offering from an adult

2. Parents decides to ignore the recently occurring and frequent tantrums their two-year-old boy throws whenever they attempt to put on the child's shoes. After about a week the child no longer throws a tantrum when a parent puts on his shoes. According to the theory of operant conditioning, this scenario is a demonstration of

   A. Sensory deprivation

   B. Negative reinforcement

   C. Extinction

   D. A conditioned response

   E. habituation

3. What is an indication that a child is not ready for toilet training?

   A. child has an automatic "no" response to every request

   B. child does not have regular bowel movements at night

   C. child has habitual finger-sucking behavior

   D. child has an older sibling who is not toilet trained

   E. child is less than 26 months of age

4. What finding in a child warrants an immediate medical evaluation for autism?

   A. No babbling or baby talk by 12 months of age

   B. No use of toys in creative ways by 24 months of age

   C. Refuses to be held at 24 months of age

   D. Screams when spoken to after 12 months of age

   E. Engages in back-and-forth gestures such as pointing or waving after 9 months of age

5. Katy is a 4th grade student who has received excellent grades in all of her classes except for math. She does well on homework assignments and claims she understands the course material well. She reports that she has trouble sleeping the night before a math test and has" butterflies" before the exam. She has trouble concentrating during the exam. Her math test grades this year are all "Cs". Her overall non-math GPA is 3.7 for this year and the past three years. Which of the statements below is most likely true for Kati?

   A. her performance is not likely to improve without individual math tutoring

   B. she would perform better if she had an older brother who was a good math student

   C. she would perform better if her math instructors were female

   D. she probably feels the same before any test, but does not realize this

   E. she would perform better on math tests if immediately before the test, she wrote a paragraph or two about her feelings

6. The concrete operational stage is described in which theory of cognitive development?

   A. Robbie Case's theory

   B. Piaget's theory

   C. Vygotsky's theory

   D. Information processing theory

   E. Kurt Fisher's theory

7. Studies have shown that vocabulary knowledge in children

   A. Improves with increased socioeconomic status

   B. Is independent of the number of words per hour heard at home

   C. Improves with increasing birth order

   D. Does not correlate with school failure rates in boys

   E. Correlates most strongly with parental ethnicity

Human Growth and Development

8. **Which of the choices below is an example of a cross-sectional study?**

   A. A study analyses data from a single standardized test administered on the same day to all 3rd graders in a school district

   B. A study compares average standardized test scores for students in each grade level of a K-6 elementary school for a specific school year with another specific school year

   C. A study collects and analyzes IQ scores of a group of students throughout their elementary school careers

   D. A study compares percentile distribution scores for all high school students in a single school district taking the ACT in a specific year to percentile distribution scores of all students taking the SAT in the same year and in the same school district.

   E. A study compares the GPAs of all 5th grade white children to the GPAs of all 5th grade non-white children in a school district over the past ten years.

9. **Children go through age-specific time ranges where they most easily acquire knowledge in a specific fashion. What is the term for these ranges of time?**

   A. Transformation ranges

   B. Encoding stages

   C. Metacognitive timeframes

   D. Sensitive periods

   E. Phoneme acquisition stages

10. **In psychoanalytic theory, what is the only personality structure component or stage that is present at birth?**

    A. Sensorimotor stage

    B. Concrete operational stage

    C. The id

    D. Preoperational stage

    E. The ego

11. A teacher institutes the principles of operant conditioning to change a student's undesirable behavior to a new and more desirable behavior. Which of the positive reinforcement schedules shown below is most likely to result in a permanent change in the undesired behavior to the desired behavior?

   A. Immediately reward the behavior every time it occurs

   B. Immediately reward the behavior every third time it occurs

   C. Immediately but variably reward the behavior on an average of every fifth time it occurs

   D. Reward the behavior every time it occurs after a brief waiting period

   E. Reward the behavior every third time it occurs after a brief waiting period

12. Harry Harlow's experiments with wire mesh and cloth-clad surrogate mothers for infant monkeys showed that infant monkeys spent a greater amount of time with

   A. Wire mesh surrogates that provided a source of nourishment over any cloth-clad surrogates that did not provide a source of nourishment

   B. Surrogates that provided an electrical source of heat over any other surrogates

   C. Any cloth-clad surrogates over any wire mesh surrogates

   D. Any surrogate that provided both nourishment and warmth over any surrogate that provide neither nourishment nor warmth

   E. Wire mesh surrogates that provided both nourishment and warmth over cloth-clad surrogates that provide nourishment only

13. **Which of the following is a description of the Moro reflex?**

    A. A newborn infant flexes his big toe upward when the lateral side of the foot is rubbed with a blunt instrument

    B. A newborn infant automatically turns its face towards anything that strokes its cheek or mouth

    C. A 4-month-old infant responds to a sudden loss of physical support by first throwing its arms out, then bringing her arms back to her body and then begins to cry.

    D. A 3-month-old infant swings its head and torso toward a stroke along one side of its back

    E. A newborn infant flexes his big toe downward when the lateral side of the foot is rubbed with a blunt instrument

14. **What type of problem is represented by this riddle? Three men need to cross from one side of a river to the other. Two of the men weigh 100 lbs. each and one man weighs 200 lbs. The boat they use to cross can carry no more than 200 lbs. at one time. How do the men all cross to the other side of the river?**

    A. Analogy

    B. Experimental

    C. Classification

    D. Heuristic

    E. transformation

15. **Which of the following statements is true regarding an autosomal dominant trait?**

    A. Children with the trait always have at least one parent with the trait

    B. Children with the trait may have both parents who do not have the trait

    C. If both parents have the trait there is a 50% chance their children will have the trait

    D. If at least one parent has the trait, all of the children will have the trait

    E. If both parents have the trait, all of the children will have the trait

16. **The memory process of encoding**

    A. Is the first step in memory retrieval

    B. Occurs primarily during REM stage sleep

    C. Allows conversion of verbal memories into visual imagery

    D. Begins with a sensory perception

    E. Is the last step in memory consolidation

17. A decrease in the production of what hormone begins the process of menopause in women?

   A. Aldosterone

   B. Progesterone

   C. Estrogen

   D. cortisol

   E. testosterone

18. Which stage of development is not included in Jean Piaget's theory of cognitive development?

   A. Postformal thought

   B. Formal operations

   C. Concrete operations

   D. Sensorimotor

   E. Pre-operational

19. Teresa is a 31-year-old woman who is seeing a psychoanalytic therapist. The therapy sessions are currently focusing on Teresa's tendency to choose intimate male partners who possess traits that she finds similarity to those of her father. The therapist would most likely explain this tendency in terms of

   A. Anaclitic object choice

   B. Erotogenicity

   C. Transference

   D. Counter-transference

   E. Ego cathexis

20. In cognitive psychology, what is the term applied to the proposed mechanism of language acquisition where children are able to generate a new hypothesis based on even one single exposure to a unit of information?

   A. Referent selection

   B. Associative proposal

   C. Whole-object bias

   D. Cross situational learning

   E. Fast mapping

Human Growth and Development

21. **In James Marcia's identity status theory, which statement below represents the adolescent stage of identity foreclosure?**

    A. "I am going to be a fireman because my father was a fireman."

    B. "I believe in God, but I am going to investigate a wide range of religions to determine which feels right for me"

    C. "I don't really fit in with any of the social cliques at my high school, and that's fine with me"

    D. "I refuse to change who I am regardless of anyone else's opinion"

    E. "I sometimes wonder if I really have any identity at all"

22. **Theorist Lev Vygotsky proposes that social interactions**

    A. Require higher-level cognitive functionality

    B. Occur in children only after they attain identity stability

    C. Play a fundamental role is the development of human cognition

    D. Are based on behavioral tendencies that are present at birth

    E. Interfere with objective awareness of existential threats

23. **A retrospective study on residents in a Japanese fishing village showed that severe neurological damage occurred in many villagers during a specific time span. Researchers were able to use the study data to identify the agent that caused the neurological damage, an organic form of the heavy metal mercury. Study data also showed a direct, strong correlation between the level of severity of neurological damage in subjects of the study and the total amount of fish consumed from the bay of the village during a critical time span by subjects of the study. In this study, the level of neurological damage was the**

    A. Cohort

    B. Dependent variable

    C. Independent variable

    D. Controlled variable

    E. correlation coefficient

24. A researcher conducted a study of a population of South Pacific Islanders and concluded, based on structured interviews, that the islanders, as a single ethnic group, had a much higher rate of acceptance of promiscuity and infidelity compared to other ethnic groups. Researchers later discovered that the islanders actually view promiscuity and infidelity at least as unfavorably as other ethnic groups, and that they, as a group, had conspired to provide the opposite impression to the original researcher as an elaborate practical joke. The erroneous conclusion in the original study represents

    A. An inadequate methodology

    B. A cultural bias of the researcher

    C. A failure to provide a control group

    D. A failure to replicate the original study before reaching a conclusion

    E. A selection bias

25. Some females are born with condition called mosaic Turner syndrome, where some of their cells have only one X chromosome and the other cells have two X chromosomes. If 50% of a female's cells have only one X chromosome. At what stage of prenatal development did the chromosomal abnormality likely first occur?

    A. Before ovulation

    B. During ovulation

    C. After ovulation and before fertilization

    D. At the zygote stage

    E. After the zygote stage but before the fetal stage

26. The Tanner scale is used to evaluate which of the following?

    A. External primary and secondary sex characteristics

    B. Stages of formal operations

    C. Emotional levels of maturity

    D. Levels of memory impairment

    E. Maturity levels of motor functioning

27. A toddler is about to probe an electrical wall socket with a metal fork. As he moves the fork forward, he glances back at his mother and observes the mother displaying facial expression of extreme fear and disapproval. In response, the toddler withdraws the fork and looks for other forms of entertainment. The toddler during this scenario is demonstrating

   A. Social modeling
   B. An unconditioned response
   C. Social referencing
   D. Self-preservation
   E. Mirroring

28. A 39-year-old woman is in her 12th week of pregnancy. Her obstetrician has recommended that she undergo chorionic villus sampling. What is the purpose of this test?

   A. To test for chromosomal or genetic abnormalities of the fetus
   B. To determine if the fetus is at a normal developmental stage
   C. To determine if the mother has a different Rh blood type than the fetus
   D. To determine if the fetus has an adequate umbilical blood supply
   E. To test for abnormalities in the amniotic fluid surrounding the fetus.

29. In studies comparing the shared expression of traits between monozygotic twins raised in the same household vs. those raised in separate households, which trait should show the least environmental influence on its expression?

   A. Eye color
   B. Male pattern baldness
   C. Adult height
   D. Intelligence
   E. Skin tone

30. Researchers have demonstrated that infants are capable of integrating information acquired simultaneously through at least two different senses. This ability to transfer learning from one sense to another is referred to as

   A. Sensory indexing
   B. Synesthesia
   C. Immediate consciousness
   D. Intermodal perception
   E. Multitasking

31. Jennifer is a college senior. She has a few friends and a pleasant though somewhat distant relationship with her close family members. She enjoys spending time with her new boyfriend Jeff. For the first time she has someone she feels comfortable discussing very personal issues with. Jennifer now thinks she knows what qualities she is looking for in a potential husband, and she is discovering that Jeff possesses many of these qualities. Jennifer is most likely in the Erik Erikson's stage of

    A. initiative vs. guilt

    B. industry vs. inferiority

    C. trust vs. mistrust

    D. identity vs. identity confusion

    E. Intimacy vs. isolation

32. Brian is a 50-year-old man who was recently demoted by his work supervisor to a position of significantly lesser authority and monetary compensation. Brian adopts an attitude of "well, things could be worse, I'll get by." According to Hopson's model of transitions, Brian is engaging in

    A. Role blurring

    B. Minimization

    C. Internalization

    D. Derealization

    E. Optimization

33. According to the principles of Social Learning Theory, vicarious reinforcement is occurring in which of the following situations?

    A. A baseball pitcher learns to throw a curveball by watching other pitchers throw curveballs

    B. An actor visualizes an Oscar nomination resulting from successfully reproducing subtle attributes he imagines for a character he is portraying in a film

    C. A student overcomes fear of public speaking by speaking first in front of friends, than to gradually less familiar audiences

    D. A singer increases her vocal range by receiving praise from her voice coach each time she is able to reproduce a note with a pitch slightly outside of her previous range.

    E. A Basketball player modifies his ball-handling style based on spectator reactions to other player's ball-handling styles

34. Erin is a 25-year-old woman who is changing a flat tire for the first time. She is in an extremely hazardous location and must move her vehicle at least one mile uphill to remove herself from this life-threatening situation. The tire has four lug nuts. As Erin mounts a replacement tire, the four lug nuts fall down a steep embankment and are irretrievable. Erin devises a temporary solution for her dilemma by removing one lug nut from each of the other three tires and using the three lug nuts to satisfactorily mount the replacement tire. According to Robert Sternberg's theory, Erin's thought process demonstrates

    A. Risk and resilience

    B. Pragmatism

    C. Prosocial behavior

    D. Role transitioning

    E. High Intelligence

35. Which of the following is an example of an occurrence of semantic under extension?

    A. A child refers to all four-legged creatures as "cats"

    B. A child refers to the family cats as cats but does not refer to other cats as cats

    C. A child refers to a gardener as a "plant-man."

    D. A child assumes the family dog, named Fido, is a "Fido" and refers to all other dogs are "Fidos."

    E. A child states: "I home," meaning "I am at home."

36. In terms of age-normal visual ability, an 8-month-old infant

    A. Cannot focus on objects between eight and 15 inches away

    B. Cannot focus on objects greater than 3 feet away

    C. Cannot discriminate between basic colors

    D. Has limited depth perception

    E. Has normal adult vision

37. B.F. Skinner's theory of language acquisition proposes that

    A. Language acquisition occurs by reinforcement.

    B. Children are born with an innate universal grammar ability

    C. Children have an highly refined ability to recognize patterns in language

    D. Children are born with an ability to recognize any phoneme in any language

    E. Acquisition of language occurs by a gradual pattern learning process based on the concept of "morphemes."

38. An 8-year-old boy has been classified as having a moderate intellectual disability. Based on this classification, which of the following statements is true regarding the child?

    A. He can learn up to a normal sixth grade level

    B. He has poor social awareness

    C. He has poor motor coordination

    D. He has an IQ between 70 and 90

    E. He has extremely limited cognition

39. Research has shown that older people tend to have lower IQ scores than younger people. The Flynn effect states that this age related difference in IQ scores is

    A. Evidence that intelligence decreases with age

    B. Due to a worldwide increase in IQ scores at a rate of 3 points per decade

    C. A consequence of lower motivation to test well in older persons rather than an actual lower average IQ in older persons

    D. A result of a strong correlation between increasing IQ and mortality in World War II.

    E. A statistical failure to renormalize IQ scoring resulting in an IQ score of 110 today being equivalent to an IQ score of 100 in 1940.

40. Each of the choices below describes a reaction by a young child to the presence of a stranger. Choose the reaction that indicates the highest level of anxiety in the child.

    A. running to a caregiver

    B. grabbing the caregiver's legs

    C. silence and wariness combined with a fearful facial expression

    D. demanding to be picked up by a caregiver

    E. refusing to look into the eyes of a stranger

41. In Kohlberg's theory of Cognitive development, modeling the behavior of members of the same sex occurs

    A. After the realization that the gender of a person does not change

    B. Before the age of three

    C. Only after a child has developed the mental construct of a gender association schema

    D. With a delayed onset in single parent households where the parent is of the opposite sex

    E. As early as the first month of life

42. Choose the correct order when infants begin to demonstrate the following motor skills from the earliest to the latest age:

    I. Rolls from back to side
    II. Holds head up when sitting
    III. Bears weight on forearms

    A. I, II, III

    B. III, I, II

    C. II, III, I

    D. I, III, II

    E. III, II, I

43. In Pavlov's experiments, dogs learned to salivate in response to an auditory cue. In later experiments these dogs began to salivate in response to a different but similar auditory cue. What is the term for this type of new response?

    A. Operant conditioning

    B. Unconditioned

    C. Discrimination

    D. Sensitization

    E. Generalization

44. Research has shown children are more likely to have higher IQs on average if they are

    A. An only child

    B. Female and have an older brother

    C. The second born of three siblings

    D. The second born and have no other siblings

    E. Male and have an at least one older brother

45. **In psychology, what is a general principle that is shared by stage theory and non-stage models of information processing in humans?**

    A. Multiple neuro-anatomical locations of information storage

    B. Two-way flow of information

    C. Serial, discontinuous information processing

    D. Different levels of elaboration during information processing

    E. Lack of a biological predisposition to process information

46. Among the choices below, which is the recommended method of discouraging undesirable behavior in children based on the principles of operant conditioning?

    A. Distracting the child while the behavior is occurring

    B. Punishing the behavior on a frequent but unpredictable schedule

    C. Punishing the behavior every time it occurs

    D. Rewarding the child for not engaging in the behavior for a specified period of time

    E. Rewarding the child every time the behavior is voluntarily terminated upon request

47. Which type of theory proposes that a person can learn to start a fire using only naturally occurring forest resources without first practicing any of the techniques required to achieve this task?

    A. Social cognitive

    B. Sociocultural

    C. Psychodynamic

    D. Evolutionary

    E. Behavioral

Human Growth and Development

48. A 3-year-old child has been scratched by several different cats. After investigating the family cat's paws, he discovers they contain sharp claws. The child concludes all cats can probably scratch him. What cognitive ability did the child use to reach this conclusion?

    A. Deductive reasoning

    B. Inductive reasoning

    C. Abductive reasoning

    D. Conjectural reasoning

    E. Suppositional reasoning

49. According to John Holland's theory, which personality type prefers physical jobs that involve skill strength and coordination?

    A. Enterprising

    B. Social

    C. Realistic

    D. Conventional

    E. Artistic

50. What field of knowledge addresses the ambiguity in the statement "I saw the room with a telescope?"

    A. Etymology

    B. Symbolics

    C. Semantics

    D. Pragmatics

    E. Lexicology

51. Severe, progressive memory loss is most characteristic of which of the following conditions?

    A. Down's syndrome (trisomy 13)

    B. Autism

    C. Parkinson's disease

    D. Lou Gehrig's disease (ALS)

    E. Alzheimer's disease

52. According to Elisabeth Kübler-Ross' theory, adults who erroneously believe that they could have taken actions to directly prevent the recent death of a loved one are in which stage of grief?

    A. Retrospective

    B. Denial

    C. Imaginary

    D. Bargaining

    E. Depression

53. **What is one of the major criticisms of Piaget's principles in his theory of learning?**

    A. Very young children are markedly involved in egocentric speech

    B. Research studies have shown that children can learn particular concepts before they reach prerequisite stages

    C. Other cultures have a high regard for scientific thinking

    D. Children can understand the conservation of weight and the conservation of number at the same operational stage

    E. On average, boys are able to learn particular concepts at a younger age than girls

54. **Which theorist describes the concept of the "zone of proximal development"?**

    A. Erik Erikson

    B. Jean Piaget

    C. John Holland

    D. Lev Vygotsky

    E. Robert Sternberg

55. **In behaviorist theory, habituation is occurring in which of the following scenarios?**

    A. A wife experiences increasingly strong desires for alcohol intake each succeeding night that her husband arrives home late from work

    B. Over a several month period, a child takes less time to finish a particular chore in response to his mother's constant nagging.

    C. Over time a man is able to fall asleep more easily despite the continuous nightly barking of a neighbor's dog just outside the man's bedroom window

    D. When an attractive girl smiles at a boy every time he rubs his nose, over time the boy begins to rub his nose each time the girl smiles at him

    E. A drug addict experiences increased cravings for a drug even though he is increasing the frequency that he uses the drug.

56. In terms of age, from earliest to latest, in what order do children typically acquire the grammatical morphemes?

   I. Regular plural – s (dog – dogs)
   II. Possessive – s (Mom – Mom's)
   III. Present progressive – ing (walk – walking)

   A. I, II, III
   B. II, I, III
   C. III, II, I
   D. I, III, II
   E. III, I, II

57. Robert Sternberg's triangle theory describes three components of

   A. Language acquisition
   B. Moral development
   C. Adult love
   D. Faith development
   E. Object relations

58. Stavros is a United States born, 35-year-old son of ethnic Greek immigrant parents. He is successful and happily married. He began to identify himself as ethnically Greek in his early teenage years. Today his ethnic heritage is a source of pride and this ethnic image of himself plays a major role in most aspects of his life. According to social theory, Stavros' ethnic identity

   A. May have replaced an earlier negative ethnic self-image
   B. Probably includes an exaggerated sense of importance of Greek culture within the overall culture of the United States
   C. Represents an internalization of his ethnicity
   D. Probably serves to mask significant insecurity issues related to his ethnic minority status
   E. Is very likely to play a diminishing role in his choice of social activities as he gets older

59. In what age range is the initial diagnosis of schizophrenia most common?

   A. Between 10 and 24 years
   B. Between 16 and 30 years
   C. Between 25 and 40 years
   D. Between 45 and 59 years
   E. After age 60 years

60. A research study follows 100 children with a history of lead exposure for a 10-year period. They each are administered three separate standardized tests each year. The results are compared to score distribution curves for the tests results of all children of the same age nationwide who took the tests in the same years. What is the cohort in this study?

   A. Lead exposure

   B. The group of 100 children

   C. The three standardized tests

   D. The 10-year period

   E. The nationwide test score distribution curves

61. A young child who is using telegraphic speech is

   A. Using one word to function as a full sentence

   B. Compressing a grammatically correct statement into a two-word statement lacking conjunctions or articles

   C. Speaking with an exaggerated tone and rhythm

   D. Speaking softly in a manner not directed at or intended for others to hear

   E. Verbally conveying a thought that is intelligible and grammatically correct

62. Which researcher's work has shown that newborns younger than 8 months appear to have an innate ability to universally distinguish all fundamentally unique speech sounds, and that this ability is not present in adults who are learning a new language?

   A. Noam Chomsky

   B. Anne Fernald

   C. Jenny Saffran

   D. Richard Montague

   E. Janet Werker

63. According to Lawrence Kolberg's theory, a teenage that arrives at a moral judgment of an act by considering the social consequences of the act is in what stage of moral development?

   A. Pre-conventional

   B. conventional

   C. post-conventional

   D. empirical

   E. transcendental

64. Researchers using data collected from a study find there is a linear relationship between two variables. If the correlation coefficient (r) is calculated from a graph plot of the data, which of the correlation coefficient values shown below would indicate the strongest relationship between the two variables?

   A. 0.2

   B. -0.9

   C. 0.5

   D. -0.1

   E. 0.0

65. Mildred Parten's theory and classification of play participation in children describes activities that are interactive but lacking in formal rules or organization as

   A. Parallel play

   B. Independent play

   C. Associative play

   D. Immature play

   E. Chaotic play

66. According to psychological theories of cognitive development, which of the following tasks requires the highest level of executive function?

   A. Selecting the most qualified persons to fill management positions in a company

   B. Accurately predicting trends in emerging markets

   C. Developing strong interpersonal relationships with important business clients

   D. Providing persuasive testimony in support of desirable regulatory legislation

   E. Devising novel, focused adaptations to a complex, rapidly changing business environment

67. What is a valid evolutionary explanation for the relative success of societies that place a high value on the contributions of their elderly citizens to the well-being of the society?

   A. There is a very small percentage of elderly persons in such societies

   B. Insufficient time has passed for evolutionary process to have selected out these societies

   C. Such societies are geographically isolated from other societies.

   D. The elderly in these societies provide information and services that increase the likelihood that children will survive and produce viable offspring

   E. An individual's longevity is correlated with high reproductive success during the individual's fertile years.

68. Research has shown that the divorce rate in the United States is

   A. Lower for couples who both have a 4-year college degree compared to those with only a high school degree

   B. Lower for second marriages compared to first marriages

   C. Lower for Black couples than Hispanic couples

   D. Lower in couples who cohabitate before marriage compared to couples who do not cohabitate before marriage

   E. Lower for couples who marry at a young age compared to couples who marry later in life

69. In infants who are exclusively breast-fed beyond the age of six months, which nutrient is not provided is sufficient amounts?

   A. Vitamin A

   B. Protein

   C. Riboflavin

   D. Vitamin B-12

   E. Iron

70. Which of the following cognitive skills does not normally decline in an individual as a result of aging?

    A. Fluid intelligence

    B. Recall of recent events

    C. Divided attention

    D. Vocabulary

    E. Word retrieval

71. Miranda is an 18-year-old woman who has an overwhelming fear of spiders. A clinical psychologist has recommended that Amanda undergo a course of aversion therapy in order to overcome this abnormal level of fear. What is the theoretical basis for this form of therapy?

    A. Operant conditioning

    B. Classical conditioning

    C. Principles of psychoanalysis

    D. Principles of social cognition

    E. Principles of Socratic methodology

72. Ingrid is a young woman who has completed a Big Five standardized personality inventory questionnaire. She scores highly in one of the five personality dimensions indicating she strongly prefers planned behaviors over spontaneous behaviors. What personality dimension is this?

    A. Openness to experience

    B. Conscientiousness

    C. Extraversion

    D. Agreeableness

    E. Neuroticism

73. Deborah is a private tutor for a 5th grade student, Rick, who is having difficulty with the task of determining the slope of a line from a graph. Deborah's teaching method begins with choosing an interesting graphing task and then guiding Rick in a step by step fashion through the process of plotting data on a graph and then obtaining the slope of the resulting line. Successive lessons involve less input by Deborah until Rick is able to determine the slope of a line without Deborah's assistance. What is the term for this learning process?

    A. Cognitive guidance

    B. Instructional scaffolding

    C. Semiotic instruction

    D. Pedagogy

    E. Inquiry learning

74. Peyton is a 17-year-old girl who has never had a menstrual period. A physical examination the previous year showed no physical abnormalities. Among the choices below what is an important possible explanation for Peyton's delayed menarche?

A. Undiagnosed herpes simplex infection

B. Excessive dietary iron intake

C. Food allergies

D. Pregnancy

E. Lack of physical exercise

75. Bevan is a 15-year-old boy who emigrated to the United States with his biological parents 12 years ago. Bevan has maintained a 4.0 grade point average throughout his elementary and high school career. His teachers all agree that Bevan has always been exceptionally motivated to perform well in school. Among the choices below, which is most likely to account for Bevan's high motivation to achieve academic success?

A. Both parents have high IQs

B. A higher socioeconomic status compared to most other student's households.

C. High resiliency due to exposure to significant but manageable environmental stress at a young age.

D. A compensatory response to perceived ethno-cultural prejudice

E. A cultural background that emphasizes the importance of academic achievement

76. Vertigo that is not caused by an abnormality occurring inside the brain is most likely to be caused by

   A. Abnormal functioning of the semicircular canals

   B. Damage to the retina

   C. Abnormal hormone levels

   D. Damage to a large peripheral motor nerve

   E. Small nerve damage in patients with diabetes

77. Paul, a 10-year-old boy, has observed that another student at school, Tim, is the object of ridicule by a clique of peers that Paul considers to be "the cool kids". Paul decides to punch Tim in the face. If Paul's decision was motivated by the fact that the "in crowd "clique was sure to witness his assault on Tim, Paul's behavior is most likely an example of

   A. Passive-aggressive behavior

   B. Instrumental aggression

   C. Scapegoating

   D. Dehumanization

   E. Subservience

78. A young boy observes that his father always mows the lawn and that his mother always does the laundry. From these observations and others in the outside world he has concluded that men are physically strong and women are comparatively physically weak. Over time the boy develops a mental catalogue of this and other gender related connections. In gender schema theory, this mental framework

   A. Is required to allow the boy to assign himself a gender

   B. Leads to the recognition that gender is constant throughout life

   C. Provides a mechanism to evaluate discrepancies observed in gender based behavior in other individuals

   D. Influences judgments about behavior and promotes gender stereotyping

   E. Is an example of generalized behavior pattern seen in most mammals that live in herds or other extended groups

79. **What theorist proposed an explanation of personality based on conscious forces and unconscious desires and beliefs?**

    A. Sigmund Freud

    B. Jean Piaget

    C. Hans Jürgen Eysenck

    D. Raymond Cattell

    E. Urie Bronfenbrenner

80. **Beginning around the age of three to four months, what is most likely to elicit laughter from a child?**

    A. Actions that involve another child close to their own age

    B. Interactions with a household pet

    C. Interactions with caregivers that deviate from normal interactions

    D. Actions that result in laughter from a caregiver

    E. Interactions that occur in a group activity of three or more persons including the child

81. **Akihiro's native language is Japanese. He is twenty-five years old and began learning English five years ago. He has achieved professional working fluency in English, but tests conducted by a linguistic audiologist confirms he is unable to detect the difference between the English "L" and "R" sounds. For example, the words "lent" and "rent" sound the same to him. This is an example of**

    A. Aphonia

    B. Echolalia

    C. Categorical perception

    D. Dyslexia

    E. Atonic dissonance

82. Sarah is an 8-year-old girl who was born with a group of characteristic abnormal facial features. Her development of many gross and fine motor skills occurred at a significantly later age than normal. She suffers from mental retardation, impaired language development and seizures. During Sarah's prenatal development, which of the factors described below is the most likely explanation for her condition?

    A. Inadequate thiamine intake by the mother

    B. Heavy alcohol use by the mother

    C. Heavy marijuana use by the mother

    D. Undiagnosed diabetes in the mother

    E. Heavy cigarette smoking by the mother

83. Margaret is a 40-year-old independent consultant who was recently hired by a large company because of Margaret's track record of utilizing multiple highly effective strategies to provide solutions to companies who were experiencing serious, complex and unexpected problems. Margaret's value to her clients, in psychological terms, is her

    A. Altruism

    B. Pragmatism

    C. Wisdom

    D. Expertise

    E. Resilience

Human Growth and Development

84. In Psychology, risk and resiliency theories would most likely propose a mechanism to explain which of the following observations?

    A. In a controlled situation, a driver demonstrates lower than expected impairment of driving skills while under the influence of alcohol

    B. Some employees are able to perform tasks exceptionally well in a rapidly changing work environment

    C. Teenagers sharing certain types of interpersonal relationships are less likely to engage in drug use

    D. An undesirable behavior continues to recur despite repeated application of negative reinforcement schedules

    E. A religious practice among a group persists despite decades of repression by a government

85. A 50-year-old woman has end-stage pancreatic cancer. Her physicians have recommended her transfer to a facility that will provide care and treatment that provide comfort but no further treatment that is designed to alter the course of her disease. In the United States, what is the term for this type of care?

    A. Custodial

    B. Minimal

    C. Euthanasia

    D. supportive

    E. Hospice

86. In substance abuse and compulsive behavior intervention programs, which of the following encourage the subject of the intervention to adopt a set of guiding principles?

    A. Twelve-step programs

    B. Paradoxical intervention programs

    C. Primal therapy programs

    D. Transference interpretation programs

    E. Behavioral therapy intervention programs

Human Growth and Development

87. Critics of evolutionary theories of social behavior claim certain prosocial behaviors cannot be explained based on the principles of evolution. Which of the following is an example of this type of prosocial behavior?

    A. Altruism

    B. Nepotism

    C. Cooperativism

    D. Commensalism

    E. hedonism

88. Jerry is a 30-year-old man who is interviewing for a job. During the interview, Jerry engages in subconscious behavior to build rapport with the interviewer. Jerry is most likely

    A. Misdirecting

    B. patronizing

    C. Mirroring

    D. Supplicating

    E. Soliciting

89. Douglas is a 26-year-old man who is widely regarded by his family and friends as a person with a very optimistic attitude. Whenever Doug experiences a negative event in his life he is more likely to attribute the cause of the event to

    A. Random chance instead of a specific cause

    B. An error on his part instead of someone else's

    C. A spiritual rather than a naturalistic cause

    D. A temporary set of external circumstances rather than a permanent external condition

    E. Unavoidable external rather than avoidable external circumstances

90. Martin is a normal, healthy 5-year-old boy who has always been in the 60th percentile of height and weight for boys his age. Assuming Martin has a typical childhood environment and upbringing, with no significant health or psychiatric issues, what would be his least likely height vs. weight percentiles at age 18?

   A. 60th percentile for height vs. 60th percentile for weight

   B. 60th percentile for height vs. 50th percentile for weight

   C. 70th percentile for height vs. 70th percentile for weight

   D. 70th percentile for height vs. 50th percentile for weight

   E. 80th percentile for height vs. 70th percentile for weight.

Human Growth and Development

ANSWER KEY

Question Number	Correct Answer	Your Answer	Question Number	Correct Answer	Your Answer	Question Number	Correct Answer	Your Answer
1	A		31	E		61	B	
2	C		32	B		62	E	
3	B		33	E		63	B	
4	A		34	E		64	B	
5	E		35	B		65	C	
6	B		36	D		66	E	
7	A		37	A		67	D	
8	A		38	B		68	A	
9	D		39	B		69	E	
10	C		40	C		70	D	
11	C		41	A		71	B	
12	C		42	B		72	C	
13	C		43	E		73	B	
14	E		44	A		74	D	
15	A		45	C		75	E	
16	D		46	C		76	A	
17	C		47	A		77	B	
18	A		48	B		78	D	
19	A		49	C		79	A	
20	E		50	D		80	C	
21	A		51	E		81	C	
22	C		52	D		82	B	
23	B		53	B		83	D	
24	A		54	D		84	C	
25	E		55	C		85	E	
26	A		56	E		86	A	
27	C		57	C		87	A	
28	A		58	A		88	C	
29	A		59	B		89	D	
30	D		60	B		90	D	

Introduction to Educational Psychology

Description of the Examination

The Introduction to Educational Psychology examination covers material that is usually taught in a one-semester undergraduate course in this subject. Emphasis is placed on principles of learning and cognition, teaching methods and classroom management, child growth and development, and evaluation and assessment of learning.

The examination contains approximately 100 questions to be answered in 90 minutes. Some of these are pretest questions that will not be scored. Any time candidates spend on tutorials and providing personal information is in addition to the actual testing time.

Knowledge and Skills Required

Questions on the Introduction to Educational Psychology examination require candidates to demonstrate one or more of the following abilities.

* Knowledge and comprehension of basic facts, concepts, and principles
* Association of ideas with given theoretical positions
* Awareness of important influences on learning and instruction
* Familiarity with research and statistical concepts and procedures
* Ability to apply various concepts and theories as they apply to particular teaching situations and problems

The subject matter of the Introduction to Educational Psychology examination is drawn from the following topics. The percentages next to the main topics indicate the approximate percentage of exam questions on that topic.

5% **Educational Aims and Philosophies**
- Lifelong learning
- Moral/character development
- Preparation for careers
- Preparation for responsible citizenship
- Socialization

15% **Cognitive Perspective**
- Attention and perception
- Memory
- Complex cognitive processes (e.g., problem solving, transfer, conceptual change)
- Applications of cognitive theory

11% **Behavioral Perspective**
- Classical conditioning
- Operant conditioning
- Schedules of reinforcement
- Applications of behavioral perspectives

15% **Development**
- Cognitive
- Social
- Moral
- Gender identity/sex roles

10% **Motivation**
- Social-cognitive theories of motivation (e.g., attribution theory, expectancy-value theory, goal orientation theory, intrinsic and extrinsic motivation, self-efficacy, self-determination theory)
- Learned helplessness
- Teacher expectations/Pygmalion effect
- Anxiety/stress
- Applications of motivational theories

17%	**Individual Differences**
- Intelligence
- Genetic and environmental influences
- Exceptionalities in learning (e.g., giftedness, learning disabilities, behavior disorders)
- Ability grouping and tracking
12%	**Testing**
- Classroom assessment (e.g., formative and summative evaluation, grading procedures)
- Norm- and criterion-referenced tests
- Test reliability and validity
- Bias in testing
- High-stakes assessment
- Interpretation of test results (e.g., descriptive statistics, scaled scores)
- Use and misuse of tests
10%	**Pedagogy**
- Planning instruction for effective learning
- Social constructivist pedagogy (e.g., scaffolding)
- Cooperative/collaborative learning
- Classroom management
5%	**Research Design and Analysis**
- Research design (e.g., longitudinal, experimental, case study, quasi-experimental)
- Research methods (e.g., survey, observation, interview)
- Interpretation of research (e.g., correlation versus causation, descriptive statistics

Introduction to Educational Psychology

SAMPLE TEST

1. **Erik Erikson is known for his theory of:**

   A. Operant versus classical conditioning

   B. Eight stages of psychosocial development

   C. The zone of proximal development

   D. Emotional intelligence

   E. Multiple intelligences

2. **"A response that is given a satisfactory outcome will be repeated, while a response that incurs a negative outcome will be less likely to happen again in the future."**

   This is the definition of which theory?

   A. Operant conditioning

   B. Classical conditioning

   C. Law of effect

   D. Behaviorism

   E. Humanism

3. **Henry loves ocean life. He has categorized all sea life as fish. Henry's teacher tells him that a whale is not a fish, but actually is a mammal. Henry does not understand how this could be true.**

   This is an example of:

   A. Classical conditioning

   B. Law of effect

   C. Cognitive dissonance

   D. Attribution

   E. Operant conditioning

4. **Which type of conditioning is based on involuntary behaviors?**

   A. Classical conditioning

   B. Operant conditioning

   C. Attributive conditioning

   D. A & B

   E. None of the above

5. **Lucy raises her hand to answer a question, and the teacher responds by saying, "Great job raising your hand!"**

   This response is an example of:

   A. Operant conditioning

   B. Classical conditioning

   C. Attributive conditioning

   D. A & B

   E. None of the above

6. **Negative Reinforcement is best described as:**

   A. A stimulus decreases problem behaviors.

   B. The removal of an aversive stimulus is likely to increase a problem behavior.

   C. Negative and positive stimuli cancel one another out.

   D. Stimuli increases the probability of problem behaviors recurring.

   E. Stimuli decreases the probability of problem behaviors returning.

7. **Positive Reinforcement is best described as:**

   A. A conditioning technique where an individual receives a desirable result for a positive behavior that subsequently increases the probability of that behavior reoccurring A parable, warning of the dangers inherent in nature.

   B. Negative and positive stimuli cancel one another out.

   C. Stimuli increases the probability of problem behaviors recurring.

   D. Stimuli decreases the probability of problem behaviors returning.

   E. A stimulus decreases problem behaviors.

8. **Limitations of teaching large groups include all of the following except:**

   A. There is pressure to accept group values without analyzing them

   B. The teacher has to deal with a diverse population

   C. People sometimes function poorly in groups

   D. Individuals in the group can justify their present status by reinforcement from the group

   E. People are less likely to be engaged in large groups

Introduction to Educational Psychology

9. **The role the teacher can take in assisting participants in the behavioral support process includes:**

    A. Demonstration of classroom behavior management techniques

    B. Describing the nature of the problem

    C. Teaching specific skills

    D. Helping devise strategies to change behaviors

    E. Switching to a different teacher

10. **The process of an active organism exhibiting controlled behavior is called:**

    A. Operant Conditioning

    B. Modeling

    C. Counterconditioning

    D. Transference

    E. Hippy culture

Answer Key

1. B
2. C
3. C
4. A
5. A
6. B
7. A
8. B
9. A
10. A

Please note that this is a sample portion of the CLEP Introduction to Educational Psychology examination. A complete practice test is available for purchase at Amazon.com and Barnesandnoble.com. ISBN 9781607875451

Principles of Macroeconomics

Description of the Examination

The Principles of Macroeconomics examination covers material that is usually taught in a one-semester undergraduate course in this subject. This aspect of economics deals with principles of economics that apply to an economy as a whole, particularly the general price level, output and income, and interrelations among sectors of the economy. The test places particular emphasis on the determinants of aggregate demand and aggregate supply, and on monetary and fiscal policy tools that can be used to achieve particular policy objectives. Within this context, candidates are expected to understand basic economic concepts such as scarcity and comparative advantage and measurement concepts such as gross domestic product, consumption, investment, unemployment and inflation. Candidates are also expected to demonstrate knowledge of the institutional structure of the Federal Reserve Bank and the monetary policy tools it uses to stabilize economic fluctuations and promote long-term economic growth, as well as the tools of fiscal policy and their impacts on income, employment, price level, deficits, and interest rate. Basic understanding of foreign exchange markets, balance of payments, and effects of currency appreciation and depreciation on a country's imports and exports is also expected.

The examination contains approximately 80 questions to be answered in 90 minutes. Some of these are pretest questions that will not be scored. Any time candidates spend on tutorials and providing personal information is in addition to the actual testing time.

Knowledge and Skills Required

Questions on the Principles of Macroeconomics examination require candidates to demonstrate one or more of the following abilities.

- Understanding of important economic terms and concepts
- Interpretation and manipulation of economic graphs
- Interpretation and evaluation of economic data
- Application of simple economic models

The subject matter of the Principles of Macroeconomics examination is drawn from the following topics. The percentages next to the main topics indicate the approximate percentage of exam questions on that topic.

8-12% **Basic Economic Concepts**
- Scarcity, Choice, and Opportunity Cost
- Production Possibilities Curve
- Comparative Advantage, Specialization, and Exchange
- Demand, Supply, and Market Equilibrium

12-16% **Measurement of Economic Performance**
- National Income Accounts
  - Circular Flow
  - Gross Domestic Product
  - Components of Gross Domestic Product
  - Real vs. Nominal Gross Domestic Product

Principles of Macroeconomics

- Inflation Measurement and Adjustment
  - Price Indices
  - Nominal and Real Values
  - Demand-Pull vs. Cost-Push Inflation
  - Costs of Inflation
- Unemployment
  - Definition and Measurement
  - Types of Unemployment
  - Natural Rate of Unemployment

15–20% **National Income and Price Determination**
- Aggregate Demand
  - Determinants of Aggregate Demand
  - Multiplier and Crowding-Out Effects
- Aggregate Supply
  - Short-Run vs. Long-Run Analysis
  - Sticky vs. Flexible Prices and Wages
  - Determinants of Aggregate Supply
- Macroeconomic Equilibrium
  - Real Output and Price Level
  - Short and Long Run
  - Actual vs. Full-Employment Output
  - Business Cycle and Economic Fluctuations

15-20% **Financial Sector**
- Money Banking and Financial Markets
  - Definition of Financial Assets: Money, Stocks, and Bonds
  - Time Value of Money (Present and Future Value)
  - Measures of Money Supply
  - Banks and Creation of Money
  - Money Demand
  - Money Market
  - Loanable Funds Market
- Central Bank and Control of the Money Supply
  - Tools of Central Bank Policy
  - Quantity Theory of Money
  - Real vs. Nominal Interest Rates

20-25% **Inflation, Unemployment, and Stabilization Policies**
- Fiscal and Monetary Policies
  - Demand-Side Effects
  - Supply-Side Effects
  - Policy Mix
  - Government Deficits and Debt
- Inflation and Unemployment
  - The Phillips Curve: Short-Run vs Long-Run
  - Role of Expectations

5-10% **Economic Growth and Productivity**
- Investment in Human Capital
- Investment in Physical Capital
- Research and Development, and Technological Progress
- Growth Policy

9-13% **Open Economy: International Trade and Finance**
- Balance of Payments Accounts
  - Balance of Trade
  - Current Account
  - Financial Account

- Foreign Exchange Market
    - Demand for and Supply of Financial Exchange
    - Exchange Rate Determination
    - Currency Appreciation and Depreciation
    - Exchange Rate Policies
- Inflows, Outflows and Restrictions
    - Net Exports and Capital Flows
    - Links to Financial and Goods Markets
    - Tariffs and Quotas

Principles of Macroeconomics

SAMPLE TEST

1. A decrease in _____ is likely to shrink a nation's production possibilities curve:

   A. Inflation

   B. Labor forces

   C. Taxes

   D. GDP

   E. Interest rates

2. _____ causes a rightward shift in the short-run aggregate supply curve:

   A. Increased prices

   B. Decreased fiscal spending

   C. Improved technology

   D. Decreased investing

   E. Decreased savings

3. Ceteris paribus, a $100 million increase in GDP can be accomplished through an _____ injection, with MPC of 75%:

   A. $75 million

   B. $100 million

   C. $25 million

   D. Government can't increase GDP

   E. $200 million

4. _____ causes real interest rates to increase:

   A. Decreased investing

   B. Decreased savings

   C. Decreased consumption

   D. Decreased production

   E. Decreased inflation

5. _____ will ease deflationary pressure during a period of economic recession:

   A. Increasing taxation

   B. Increasing interest rates

   C. Increasing money supply

   D. Decreasing money supply

   E. Stopping new currency production

6. _____ decreases long-run economic growth:

   A. Decreasing expenditures on corporate subsidies

   B. Increasing privatization

   C. Decreasing expenditures in education/training

   D. Increasing taxation

   E. Increasing government spending

7. ____ results from appreciating a nation's currency in the forex market:

   A. No change in imports or exports

   B. Decreased imports, increased exports

   C. Decreased imports, decreased exports

   D. Increased imports, decreased exports

   E. Increased imports, increased exports

8. Tariffs are not used to _____:

   A. Increase tax revenues

   B. Decrease import prices

   C. Increase import prices

   D. Mitigate the impact of dumping

   E. Impose sanctions

9. **Federal Reserve Open Market Operations means:**

   A. Changing federal reserve ratio

   B. Buying and selling of federal debt to manage money supply and interest rates

   C. Printing money to cause inflation

   D. Changing tax rates

   E. Increasing government spending

10. ____ will not cause an increase to a nation's current account :

    A. Federal debt purchased by a foreign nation

    B. Exporting consumer goods

    C. Foreign tourists visiting

    D. Food aid from foreign nations

    E. Exporting agricultural goods

11. ___ will not cause an increase to the capital account:

    A. Foreign investment in corporate bonds

    B. Direct investment into foreign nations

    C. Foreign investment in government bonds

    D. Importing consumer goods

    E. Importing agricultural goods

12. **According to the International Fisher Effect, a 1% appreciation in nation A's currency relative to Nation B will result from:**

    A. A 1% increase in real interest rates relative to Nation B

    B. A 1% higher nominal interest to nation B

    C. A 1% lower nominal interest rate relative to Nation B

    D. A 1% increase in inflation relative to Nation B

    E. A 1% increase in exports to Nation B

13. **The light-hearted measurement of purchasing power parity is called:**

    A. Fast Food Index

    B. White Castle Index

    C. Burger Index

    D. Whopper Index

    E. Big Mac Index

14. **A currency with PPP of 1 and exchange rate of 1/2 is considered:**

    A. Undervalued

    B. Overvalued

    C. Appreciated

    D. Depreciated

    E. In equilibrium

15. **A tax on imported cars that begins after the first 5,000 is an example of:**

    A. Tariff-rate quota

    B. Quota by unit

    C. Quota by weight

    D. Tariff

    E. Embargo

16. **A fiat currency is:**

    A. Any item whose value is derived from its ability to be used as a measurement of value

    B. Any pegged currency

    C. Any currency subject to inflation

    D. Any floating currency

    E. Any currency currently in print

17. **A currency with PPP of 1 and exchange rate of 3/1 is considered:**

    A. Overvalued

    B. Undervalued

    C. In equilibrium

    D. Appreciated

    E. Depreciated

18. Nation B's currency is pegged to Nation A; if Nation A's currency strengthens 10% more than Nation B, then to maintain stability Nation B must:

    A. End the peg

    B. Appreciate

    C. Depreciate

    D. Revalue

    E. Devalue

19. The AK model is a simple example of:

    A. Endogenous growth model

    B. Solow-Swan model

    C. Harrod-Domar model

    D. Exogenous growth model

    E. Unified growth model

20. "Output is a function of capital" is indicative of:

    A. Solow-Swan model

    B. Harrod-Domar model

    C. Endogenous growth model

    D. Exogenous growth model

    E. Unified growth model

21. "Growth is a function of capital and labor" is indicative of:

    A. Solow-Swan model

    B. Harrod-Domar model

    C. Endogeous growth model

    D. Exogenous growth model

    E. Unified growth model

22. "Growth is a function of capital and technology" is indicative of:

    A. AK model

    B. Exogenous growth model

    C. Solow-Swan model

    D. Harrod-Domar model

    E. Unified growth model

23. An increase in supply without an increase in demand will:

    A. Increase unemployment until surplus inventories and capacity are absorbed

    B. Increase unemployment in the short-run

    C. Decrease unemployment in the long-run

    D. Decrease unemployment in the short-run

    E. Increase unemployment until inflation slows

24. **Technological progress**

    A. Replaces human capital

    B. Shifts the production possibilities curve left

    C. Decreases employment

    D. Increases employment

    E. Increases per capita production potential

25. **Knowledge Spillover is:**

    A. Increased production potential resulting from shared information between non-competitors

    B. Leaked industry secrets

    C. Unemployment from surplus human capital

    D. The result of investing in technology too quickly

    E. Gains from increased competition resulting from expired patents

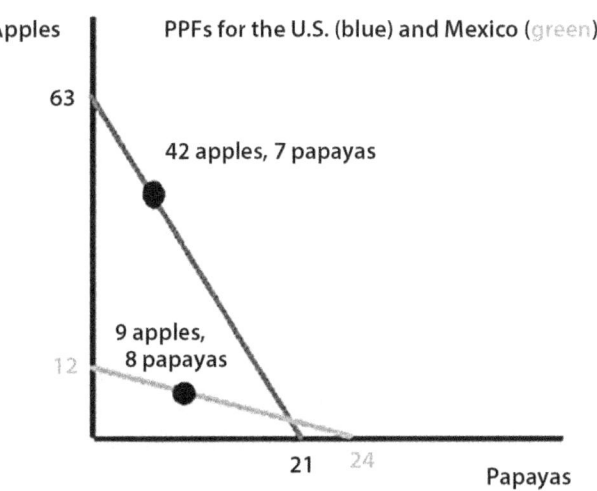

26. **Which nation has an absolute advantage:**

    A. US

    B. Mexico

    C. US in apples

    D. Mexico in papayas

    E. Mexico in apples

Principles of Macroeconomics

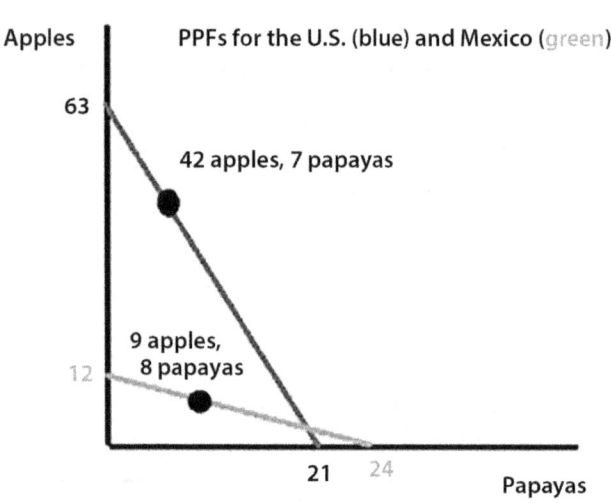

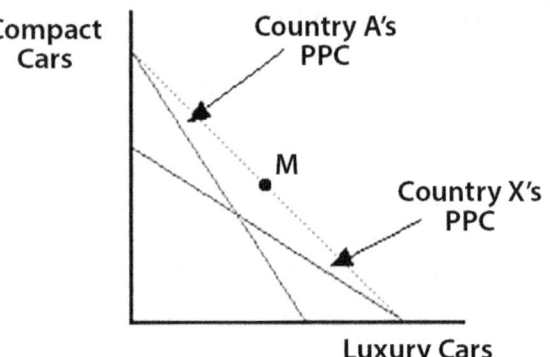

27. **What is Mexico's opportunity cost per papaya:**

    A. 0.5

    B. 2

    C. 12

    D. 24

    E. 0.33

28. **What is US's opportunity cost per papaya:**

    A. 0.33

    B. 3

    C. 63

    D. 21

    E. 2

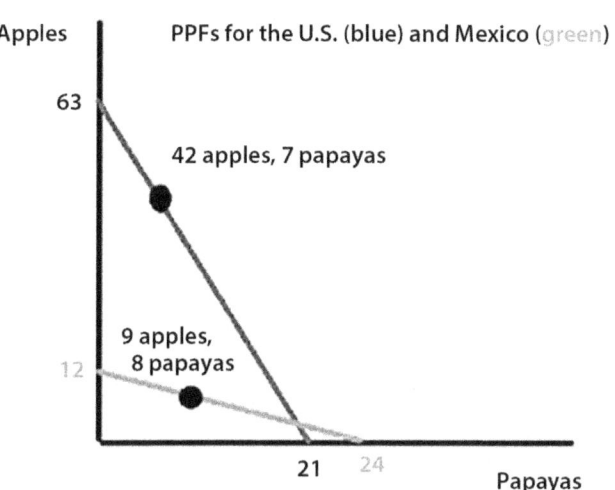
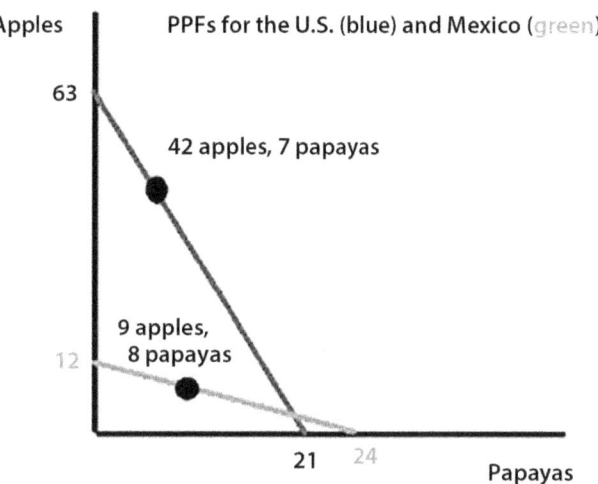

29. What is the maximum combined production without trade:

   A. 90
   B. 24
   C. 63
   D. 49
   E. 66

30. What is the maximum combined production with trade:

   A. 24
   B. 90
   C. 63
   D. 66
   E. 49

31. _____ would cause a demand curve to shift right:

   A. Drought
   B. Increased median income
   C. Increased unemployment
   D. Inflation
   E. Overproduction

32. _____ would cause a supply curve to shift right:

    A. Increased producer price index

    B. Shortages of raw materials

    C. Technological advancement

    D. Consumer demand

    E. Nothing

33. **Long-run aggregate supply is:**

    A. Increasing with price

    B. The same at all price levels

    C. Decreasing with price

    D. Drops to 0 at any price other than equilibrium

    E. The same as short-run aggregate supply

34. **A linear aggregate supply curve which starts at 0 and with point [$40 for 80 units] has a marginal price of:**

    A. $0.5

    B. $2

    C. $40

    D. $80

    E. $0

35. **Economics only matters because of:**

    A. Banks

    B. Government

    C. Trade

    D. Money

    E. Scarcity

36. **It is true that:**

    A. Investment creates its own supply

    B. Supply creates its own demand

    C. Demand creates its own supply

    D. Supply creates its own investment

    E. Supply creates its own savings

37. **The New Deal was created to:**

    A. End the Great Depression through conscripted labor

    B. End the Great Depression by increasing aggregate supply

    C. End the Great Depression by stimulating consumption through social investment

    D. Stimulate competition by providing companies with funds to invest

    E. Stimulate competition by breaking-up large companies called trusts

38. **Lower consumption levels will:**

    A. Decrease company revenues, discouraging investment

    B. Increase savings, making more loanable funds available

    C. Create surplus supply, causing an immediate reduction in price

    D. Force investing in new innovations that people will want

    E. Be common during times of economic success

39. **The Square Deal was created to:**

    A. End the Great Depression

    B. Stimulate competition by breaking-up large companies called trusts

    C. Reduce taxation

    D. Reduce the federal deficit

    E. Fund infrastructure development

40. **Increased inflation will:**

    A. Decrease exports

    B. Increase exports

    C. Increase imports

    D. Slow trade

    E. Slow economic growth

41. **Decreased unemployment will:**

    A. Have no influence on inflation

    B. Decrease inflation

    C. Increase inflation

    D. Decrease the amount of inflationary pressure

    E. Increase the amount of inflationary pressure

42. **____ is an example of cost-push inflation:**

    A. Drought making agricultural production more expensive

    B. Production of new consumer products at higher prices

    C. Increased income driving demand higher

    D. Increased money supply driving money value down

    E. High interest rates reducing demand for money

43. **____ can cause demand-pull inflation:**

    A. High interest rates

    B. Birth of a natural monopoly

    C. Population boom

    D. Increased taxation

    E. Increased money supply

44. _____ can cause monetary inflation:

A. Increased demand

B. Birth of a natural monopoly

C. Decreased money supply

D. Reduction in federal reserve ratio

E. Decreased taxation

45. _____ causes structural unemployment:

A. Low levels of inflation

B. Wages below equilibrium

C. AS>AD

D. Mismatch of labor demand and skills

E. People changing jobs

46. _____ causes frictional unemployment:

A. People changing jobs

B. AS>AD

C. Mismatch of labor demand and skills

D. Wages below equilibrium

E. Low inflation

47. _____ causes cyclical unemployment:

A. Wages below equilibrium

B. AD<AS

C. Mismatch of labor demand and skills

D. Low inflation

E. People changing jobs

48. Phillips Curve states that:

A. Unemployment and inflation are direct opposites

B. High unemployment increases inflation

C. High inflation increases unemployment

D. Unemployment and inflation put inverse pressure on each other but are not direct opposites

E. There is no relationship between inflation and unemployment

49. **NAIRU states that:**

    A. In the long-run, the labor markets will adjust to any rate of inflation to return to the natural rate of unemployment

    B. Inflation will accelerate at unemployment levels above natural

    C. Full employment will be reached at 0% inflation

    D. Unemployment and inflation are inversely related

    E. Unemployment and inflation are directly related

50. **Stagflation is:**

    A. A state of high unemployment and high inflation

    B. A state of high unemployment and low inflation

    C. A state of low unemployment and high inflation

    D. A state of low unemployment and low inflation

    E. Inflation in the market for stag pelts

51. ____ and ____ unemployment are still seen during full employment:

    A. Structural, frictional

    B. Structural, cyclical

    C. Frictional, cyclical

    D. Cyclical, full

    E. No unemployment exists at full unemployment

52. **Full employment is:**

    A. 2% unemployment

    B. A state wherein the entire labor for is actively employed

    C. A state wherein the entire population is actively employed

    D. A state wherein the entire labor force is actively employed or engaged in changing employment

    E. 0% unemployment

Principles of Macroeconomics

53. **The multiplier effect:**

    A. The amount of final income created from a stimulus package

    B. The number of times the same money changes hands, contributing to economic growth, within a time period

    C. The amount by which GDP multiplies in response to policy

    D. The amount that employment increases in response to increased spending resulting from initial employment stimulus

    E. The increase in monetary velocity created by monetary inflation

54. **Monetary velocity is:**

    A. The speed with which money is created

    B. The amount of final income created from a stimulus package

    C. The number of times the same money changes hands, contributing to economic growth, within a time period

    D. Volume of foreign exchange transactions

    E. The rate of inflation created by monetary policy

55. **Long-term NAIRU stabilization is possible due to:**

    A. Policies developed to reduce unemployment

    B. Policies developed to reduce inflation

    C. Expectations of inflation allowing a return to the natural rate of unemployment

    D. AS = AD

    E. Price stickiness

56. **Which tariff gives domestic companies an unfair advantage:**

    A. Domestic Price: $150
       Foreign Price: $125
       Tariff: 21%

    B. Domestic Price: $75
       Foreign Price: $45
       Tariff: 60%

    C. Domestic Price: $125
       Foreign Price: $100
       Tariff: 24%

    D. Domestic Price: $100
       Foreign Price: $90
       Tariff: 10%

    E. Domestic Price: $100
       Foreign Price: $80
       Tariff: 20%

Principles of Macroeconomics

57. **A $100,000 economic stimulus package with a multiplier of 5 shows a MPC of _____:**

    A. 8

    B. 2

    C. 0.5

    D. 0.2

    E. 0.8

58. **What is the relationship between federal deficit and federal debt:**

    A. Federal deficit reduces the federal debt

    B. Federal debt causes an increase in the federal deficit

    C. Federal debt is used to fund deficit spending

    D. Federal deficit causes an increase in the federal debt

    E. There is no relationship

59. **A deficit of $100,000 funded with 20-year bonds at 1% will have a total nominal cost of _____ for taxpayers:**

    A. $100,000

    B. $120,000

    C. $1,000

    D. $20,000

    E. $250,000

60. **Who is included as a part of the national labor force:**

    A. People who were seriously injured on the job

    B. People who have given-up seeking employment

    C. People unemployed but seeking employment

    D. Children

    E. All of the above

61. **Which is not a measurement of inflation:**

    A. Purchasing power parity

    B. Foreign exchange rates

    C. Producer Price Index

    D. Consumer Price Index

    E. GDP growth

62. **A $10 tax return to an employee has a quarterly monetary velocity of 1.8, calculate how much economic growth it creates in 1 year:**

    A. $18

    B. $10

    C. $72

    D. $40

    E. $22

Principles of Macroeconomics

63. The components of GDP by expenditure are:

A. Y+P+R

B. C+I+G+(X-M)

C. GNP+NNI

D. C+I+G+(M-X)

E. C+I+G+(X+M)

64. Market shocks result from:

A. Monetary mismanagement

B. Volatility which lowers investor expectations

C. Small, frequent change making production volume predictions difficult

D. Fiscal mismanagement

E. Sudden, large changes which impacts the economy more quickly than it can respond to those changes

65. The process of the state taking over industries and businesses is called:

A. Industrialization

B. Nationalization

C. Redistribution

D. Amalgamation

E. Reclamation

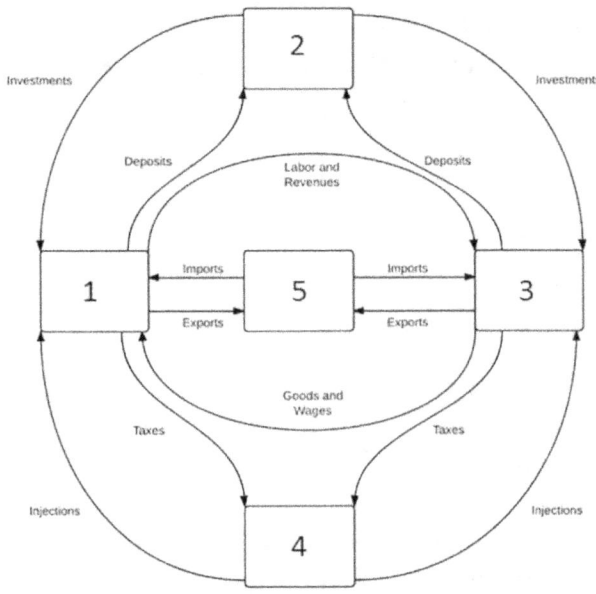

66. Sector 1 is:

A. Financial

B. Government

C. Foreign

D. Households

E. Companies

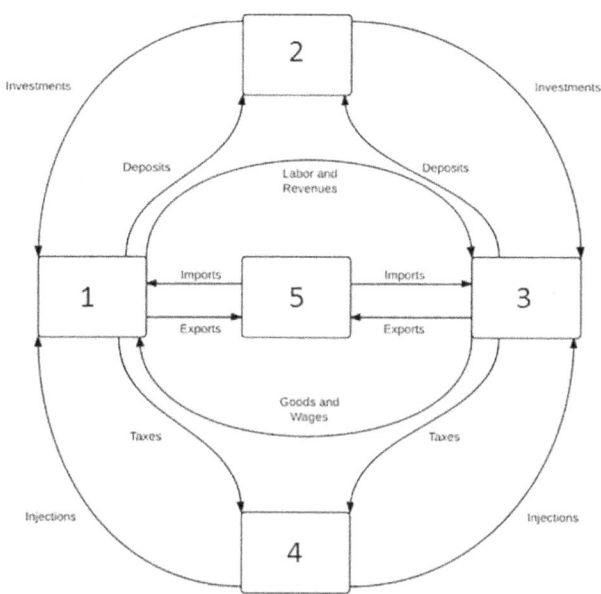
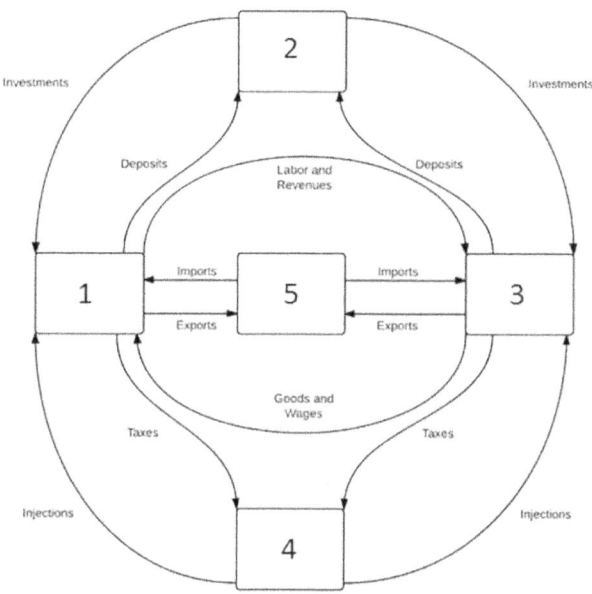

67. **Sector 2 is:**

   A. Households

   B. Foreign

   C. Financial

   D. Government

   E. Companies

68. **Sector 3 is:**

   A. Households

   B. Companies

   C. Financial

   D. Foreign

   E. Government

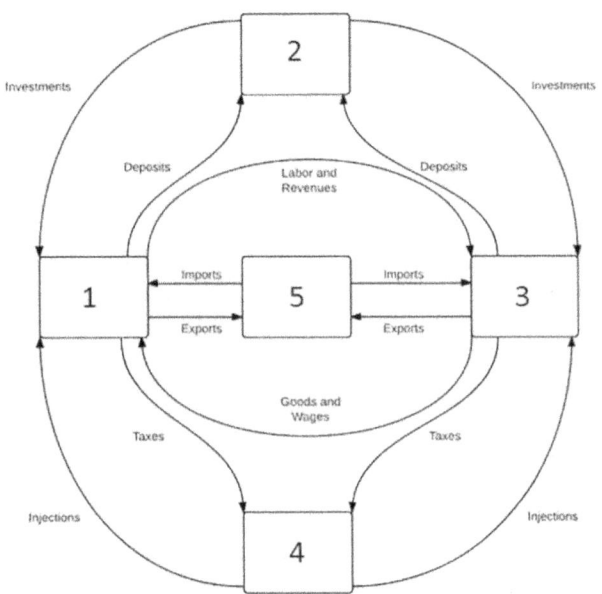
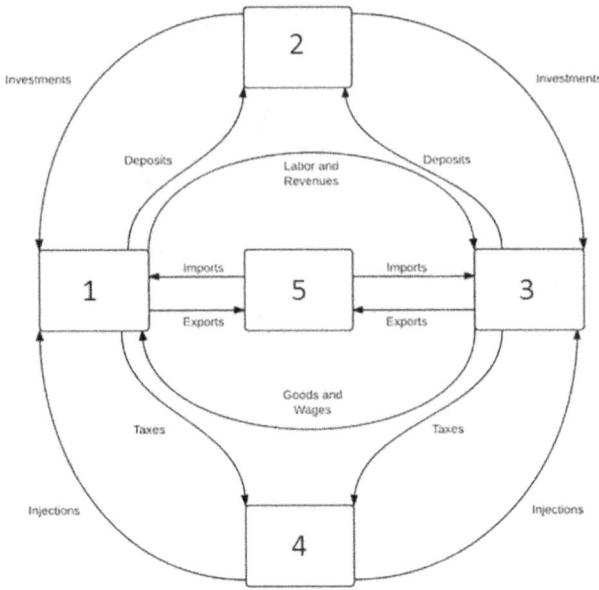

69. Sector 4 is:

    A. Government

    B. Financial

    C. Foreign

    D. Companies

    E. Households

70. Sector 5 is:

    A. Foreign

    B. Financial

    C. Government

    D. Households

    E. Companies

71. Any period of time in which the economy cannot fully respond to a change, typically determined by the replacement of large capital, is:

    A. Long-term

    B. Short-term

    C. Medium-term

    D. Time value

    E. Business cycle

Principles of Macroeconomics

72. **A recession is formally defined as:**

    A. Any period in which unemployment exceeds 5%

    B. Any period in which unemployment exceeds 7%

    C. Two consecutive quarters of negative GDP growth

    D. Any period greater than one quarter in which AS>AD

    E. Any period in which gross wages drop more than 5% for greater than one quarter

73. **When government spending or investment impose-upon or hinder private spending or investment, it is:**

    A. Multiplier

    B. Privatization

    C. Nationalization

    D. Crowding out

    E. Municipalization

74. **Aggregate demand, national income, and gross domestic product all share the same:**

    A. Income-based approach

    B. Consumption-based approach

    C. Mathematical formula

    D. Production-based approach

    E. Graphical model

75. **A grouping of large numbers of unlike things for the sake of measuring trends between them:**

    A. Macro

    B. Aggregate

    C. Statistic

    D. Bundle

    E. Economy

76. **Nominal rate = 5%, Inflation = 2% Calculate real interest rate:**

    A. 2%

    B. 2.5%

    C. 10%

    D. 3%

    E. 7%

77. **Principle = $100,000
    Rate = 0.005
    Time = 10 years
    Calculate the balance using simple interest:**

    A. $5,000,000

    B. $5,000

    C. $105,000

    D. $150,000

    E. $50,000

78. **Principle = $100,000
Rate = 0.005
Time = 10 years
Calculate the balance using continuously compounding interest:**

   A. $150,000

   B. $105,000

   C. $105,127

   D. $150,127

   E. $105,126

79. **Future value = $100,000
Rate = 0.005
Time = 10 years
Calculate present value:**

   A. $95,140

   B. $95,135

   C. $95,130

   D. $105,000

   E. $100,000

80. **NPV is calculated by:**

   A. Subtracting the sum of present values from the initial outlay

   B. Subtracting total returns from initial outlay

   C. Adding together all the cash flows on an investment

   D. Adding together all the present values on an investment

   E. Subtracting the sum of cash flows from the initial outlay

81. **Monetary policy includes managing the ____ and ____ of money:**

   A. Supply and price

   B. Supply and velocity

   C. Price and multiplier

   D. Velocity and multiplier

   E. Price and velocity

82. **Fiscal policy is managed by ____ and monetary policy by ____:**

   A. Federal Reserve, Congress

   B. Congress, Federal Reserve

   C. President, Federal Reserve

   D. Federal Reserve, President

   E. Congress, President

Principles of Macroeconomics

83. **The Gold Standard:**

    A. Was highly successful

    B. Relied on the intrinsic value of gold to define the US economy

    C. Used gold as a fiat currency to which the dollar was pegged

    D. Did not create limitations on monetary policy

    E. Resolved the currency war between European and North American countries

84. **The value of money is derived from:**

    A. The amount of hard assets owned by a country

    B. The ability to purchase things, backed by the production which is measured using that currency

    C. Supply and demand of currency markets

    D. Government promises of debt repayment

    E. Nowhere – it is valueless

85. **With money supply of $100,000 at equilibrium with production, a $10,000 nominal increase in production with no change in money supply will result in:**

    A. Deflation of 10%

    B. Inflation of 10%

    C. No inflation

    D. Inflation of 90%

    E. Deflation of 5%

86. **Government debt that matures in 1 year or less is:**

    A. Treasury Bond

    B. Treasury Note

    C. Treasury Bill

    D. Corporate Bond

    E. Stock

87. **Aggregate supply, production possibilities curve, and economic growth all share the same:**

    A. Factors

    B. Equation

    C. Usage

    D. Graphs

    E. Model

Principles of Macroeconomics

88. The market efficiency hypothesis fails as a result of:

    A. Sticky prices and wages

    B. Imperfect information

    C. Fixed nature of large capital

    D. A, B, and C

    E. Nothing, the market is efficient

89. Delayed response to sudden price changes by companies using LIFO inventory management is an example of:

    A. Price stickiness

    B. Price Rigidity

    C. Price flexibility

    D. Imperfect information

    E. Cost stickiness

90. ____ is a common method for slowing unsustainable rates of economic growth:

    A. Increasing fiscal spending

    B. Decreasing interest rates

    C. Increasing bank reserve ratios

    D. Issuing a tax refund

    E. Depreciating foreign exchange rate

91. A corporation with 10 million shares outstanding with share price of $2 has a total market capitalization of:

    A. $20 million

    B. $10 million

    C. $5 million

    D. $200,000

    E. $15 million

92. Banks earn the majority of their revenues by:

    A. Charging fees and fines

    B. Borrowing money from deposits and then lending it to borrowers at a higher interest rate

    C. Buying investments and then reselling them through brokerage accounts

    D. Government benefits

    E. Laundering illegal funds earned through front-businesses

93. The Federal Reserve lends money to ____ at the _____ rate:

    A. Anyone, discount

    B. Corporations, federal funds

    C. Individuals, federal funds

    D. Banks, federal funds

    E. Banks, discount

Principles of Macroeconomics

94. Long-Run Aggregate Supply is:

A. The same vertical line as NAIRU

B. The curve showing how much a nation can produce at a given price level at some point in time

C. The maximum production potential of a nation at any price level

D. Perfectly price elastic

E. Representative of actual production rather than full-employment production

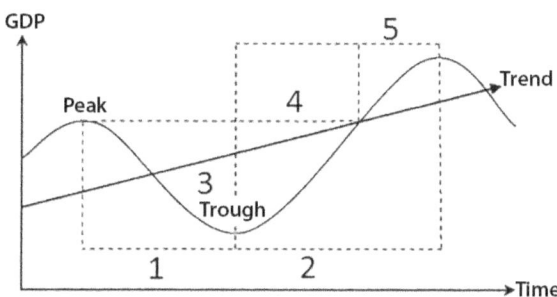

95. A period of _____ is shown at 1:

A. Expansion

B. Contraction

C. Recession

D. Recovery

E. Boom

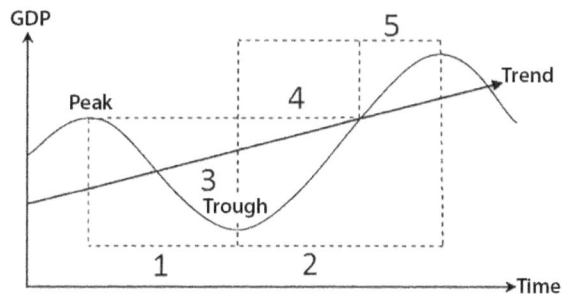

96. A period of _____ is shown at 2:

A. Contraction

B. Recession

C. Expansion

D. Boom

E. Recovery

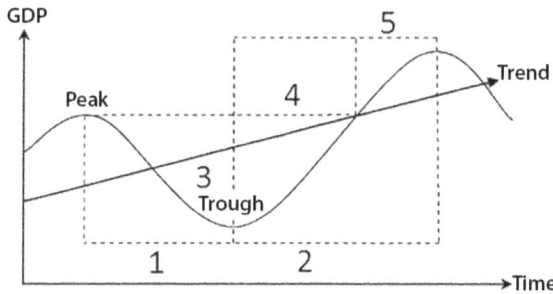

97. A _____ has been reached at 3:

A. Contraction

B. Recession

C. Expansion

D. Recovery

E. Boom

332

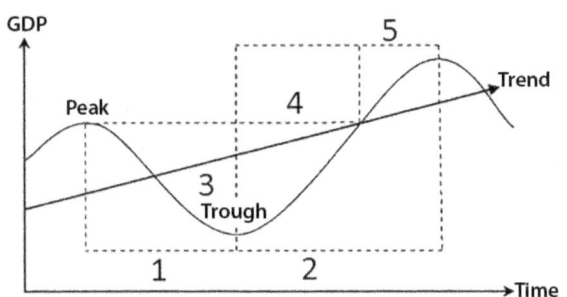

98. At 4, the economy is in _____ :

A. Boom

B. Expansion

C. Recovery

D. Contraction

E. Recession

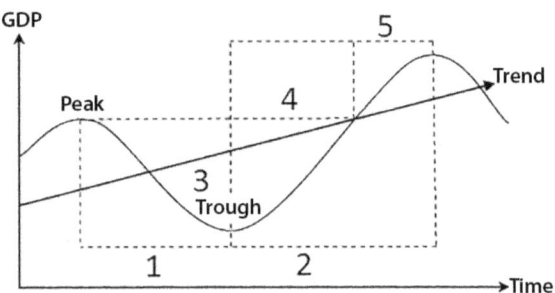

99. At 5, the economy is in a ____ :

A. Recession

B. Boom

C. Contraction

D. Recovery

E. Expansion

100. Economic terms include _____ and _____

A. Socialism, capitalism

B. Communism, capitalism

C. Socialism, communism

D. Capitalism, individualism

E. Free market economy, planned economy

Principles of Macroeconomics

RATIONALES

Question Number	Correct Answer	Your Answer	Question Number	Correct Answer	Your Answer	Question Number	Correct Answer	Your Answer
1	B		35	E		69	A	
2	C		36	C		70	A	
3	C		37	C		71	B	
4	B		38	A		72	C	
5	C		39	B		73	D	
6	C		40	B		74	C	
7	D		41	E		75	B	
8	B		42	A		76	D	
9	B		43	C		77	C	
10	A		44	D		78	C	
11	B		45	D		79	B	
12	C		46	A		80	D	
13	E		47	B		81	A	
14	B		48	A		82	B	
15	A		49	A		83	C	
16	A		50	A		84	B	
17	B		51	A		85	A	
18	E		52	D		86	C	
19	A		53	A		87	A	
20	B		54	C		88	D	
21	A		55	C		89	A	
22	A		56	A		90	C	
23	A		57	E		91	A	
24	E		58	C		92	B	
25	A		59	B		93	D	
26	A		60	C		94	C	
27	A		61	E		95	B	
28	B		62	C		96	C	
29	E		63	B		97	B	
30	B		64	E		98	C	
31	B		65	B		99	B	
32	C		66	D		100	E	
33	B		67	C				
34	A		68	B				

Principles of Microeconomics

Description of the Examination

The Principles of Microeconomics examination covers material that is usually taught in a one-semester undergraduate course in introductory microeconomics. This aspect of economics deals with the principles of economics that apply to the analysis of the behavior of individual consumers and businesses in the economy. Questions on this exam require candidates to apply analytical techniques to hypothetical as well as real-world situations and to analyze and evaluate economic decisions. Candidates are expected to demonstrate an understanding of how free markets work and allocate resources efficiently. They should understand how individual consumers make economic decisions to maximize utility, and how individual firms make decisions to maximize profits. Candidates must be able to identify the characteristics of the different market structures and analyze the behavior of firms in terms of price and output decisions. They should also be able to evaluate the outcome in each market structure with respect to economic efficiency, identify cases in which private markets fail to allocate resources efficiently, and explain how government intervention fixes or fails to fix the resource allocation problem. It is also important to understand the determination of wages and other input prices in factor markets, and analyze and evaluate the distribution of income.

The examination contains approximately 80 questions to be answered in 90 minutes. Some of these are pretest questions that will not be scored. Any time candidates spend on tutorials and providing personal information is in addition to the actual testing time.

Knowledge and Skills Required

Questions on the Principles of Microeconomics examination require candidates to demonstrate one or more of the following abilities.

- Understanding of important economic terms and concepts
- Interpretation and manipulation of economic graphs
- Interpretation and evaluation of economic data
- Application of simple economic models

The subject matter of the Principles of Microeconomics examination is drawn from the following topics. The percentages next to the main topics indicate the approximate percentage of exam questions on that topic.

8-14%   **Basic Economic Concepts**
- Scarcity, Choice, and Opportunity Cost
- Production Possibilities Curve
- Comparative Advantage, Specialization, and Trade
- Economic Systems
- Property Rights and the Role of Incentives
- Marginal Analysis

55-70%   **The Nature and Functions of Product Markets**

15-20%   **Supply and Demand**
- Market Equilibrium
- Determinants of Supply and Demand
- Price and Quantity Controls
- Elasticity
  - Price, Income, and Cross Elasticity of Demand
  - Price Elasticity of Supply
- Consumer Surplus, Product Surplus, and Market Efficiency

Principles of Microeconomics

- Tax Incidence and Deadweight Loss

5-10% **Theory of Consumer Choice**
- Total and Marginal Utility
- Utility Maximization and Equalizing Marginal Utility Per Dollar
- Individual and Market Demand Curves
- Income and Substitution Effects

10-15% **Production and Costs**
- Production Functions: Short- and Long-Run
- Marginal Product and Diminishing Returns
- Short-Run Costs
- Long-Run Costs and Economies of Scale
- Cost Minimizing Input Combination

15-20% **Firm Behavior and Market Structure**
- Profit
  - Accounting vs Economic Profit
  - Normal Profit
  - Profit Maximization: MR=MC Rule
- Perfect Competition
  - Perfect Competition
  - Short-Run Supply and Shut-Down Decision
  - Firm and Market Behaviors in Short-Run and Long-Run Equilibria
  - Efficiency and Perfect Competition
- Monopoly
  - Sources of Market Power
  - Profit Maximization
  - Inefficiency of Monopoly
  - Price Discrimination
- Oligopoly
  - Interdependence, Collusions and Cartels
  - Game Theory and Strategic Behavior
- Monopolistic Competition
  - Product Differentiation and Role of Advertising
  - Profit Maximization
  - Short-Run and Long-Run Equilibrium
  - Excess Capacity and Inefficiency

8-14% **Factor Markets**
- Derived Factor Demand
- Marginal Revenue Product
- Labor Market and Firms' Hiring of Labor
- Market Distribution of Income

10-16% **Market Failure and the Role of Government**

Externalities
- Marginal Social Benefit and Cost
- Positive Externalities
- Negative Externalities
- Remedies

Public Goods
- Public vs Private Goods
- Provision of Public Goods

Public Policy to Promote Competition
- Antitrust Policy
- Regulation

Income Distribution
- Equity
- Sources of Income Inequality

Principles of Microeconomics

SAMPLE TEST

DIRECTIONS: Read each item and select the best response.

1. **The law of increasing opportunity cost results from:**

    A. Increasing price elasticity of supply

    B. Increasing allocation of resources which are better suited to other production

    C. Missed investments and the time value of money

    D. Scarcity of resources

    E. The marginal rate of substitution

2. **A price in decrease for Coke will cause demand do _____ and will force Pepsi to _____ their price:**

	Coke	Pepsi
A.	Increase	Increase
B.	Increase	Decrease
C.	Decrease	Decrease
D.	No Change	Increase
E.	Increase	No Change

3. **When a peoples' income increases, they will have greater demand for the price/volume of goods as a result of:**

    A. The substitution effect

    B. Income elasticity

    C. The income effect

    D. Demand elasticity

    E. Supply elasticity

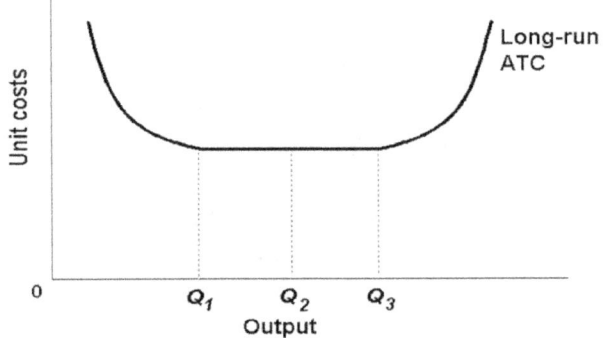

4. **The long-run average total cost curve above shows:**

    A. Decreasing returns to scale from 0 - Q1

    B. Constant returns to scale from Q1 - Q3

    C. Increasing returns to scale from 0 - Q1

    D. Constant returns to scale after Q3

    E. Decreasing returns to scale after Q3

5. ____ is the shut-down point for a profit-maximizing company:

   A. R<AFC

   B. AVC<ATC

   C. P<AVC

   D. ATC<AVC

   E. AVC<P

6. **In perfect competition, the marginal cost of labor:**

   A. Increases more quickly than in oligopoly

   B. Increases more quickly than in monopolistic competition

   C. Remains constant at any volume

   D. Increases with higher demand for labor

   E. Decreases with higher demand for labor

7. **A positive externality results in:**

   A. Overproduction from a disproportionately high price relative to the benefits

   B. Overproduction from a disproportionately low price relative to the benefits

   C. Underproduction from a disproportionately high price relative to the benefits

   D. Underproduction from a disproportionately low price relative to the benefits

   E. Efficient production and price

8. **Antitrust laws were passed by Teddy Roosevelt as part of "The Square Deal" in order to:**

   A. Protect the rights of large companies

   B. Facilitate market competition

   C. Formally recognize organized labor

   D. Privatize utilities

   E. Reform subsidies spending

9. Person A is in an ambulance with a serious injury and will be taken directly to the nearest hospital. The market has failed as a result of:

   A. Positive externalities

   B. Elimination of consumer choice and competition

   C. Price collusion in an oligopoly

   D. Overpayment to insurance companies

   E. Negative externalities

10. Military is a market failure as a result of:

    A. Nonexcludability

    B. Public goods

    C. Negative externalities

    D. National income misallocation

    E. Off-balance sheet expenses

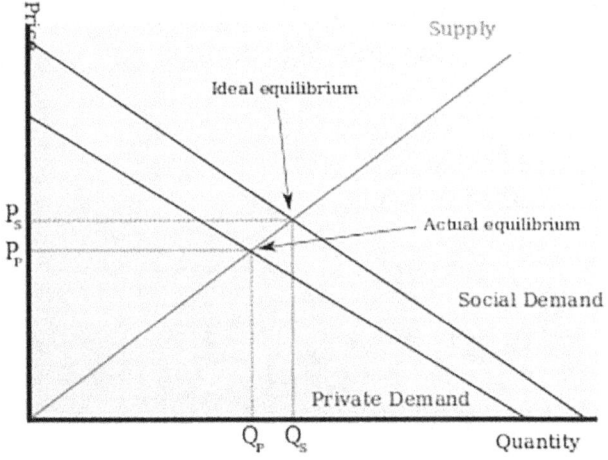

11. This graph illustrates:

    A. Negative externality

    B. Positive externality

    C. Increased demand

    D. Increased price

    E. Decreased price

12. The economy is currently at a rate of static-state consumption. What must happen for the economy to grow without entering degradation levels of consumption:

    A. Decreased consumption of resources through lower production

    B. Decreased efficiency of the resources consumed

    C. Increased efficiency of the resources consumed

    D. Restoration levels of consumption

    E. Decreased efficiency of the resources produced

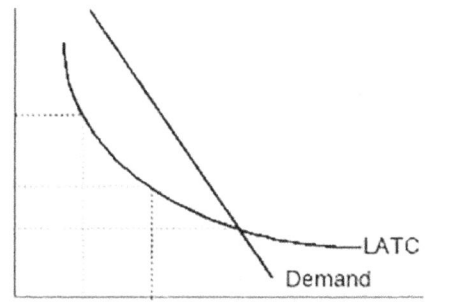

13. **This graph illustrates:**

    A. Natural Monopoly

    B. Negative externalities

    C. Positive externalities

    D. Competitive monopoly

    E. Public goods

14. **MPC elasticity of income resulting in investment differentials in a non-regulated market naturally causes:**

    A. Decreasing income inequality

    B. Increasing income inequality

    C. Higher economic growth

    D. Lower savings rates

    E. Monopolies

15. **A loss of market influence in the supply and demand of labor for individual workers results from:**

    A. Income dependence and market competition

    B. Collective bargaining

    C. Income inequality

    D. Public goods

    E. Positive externalities

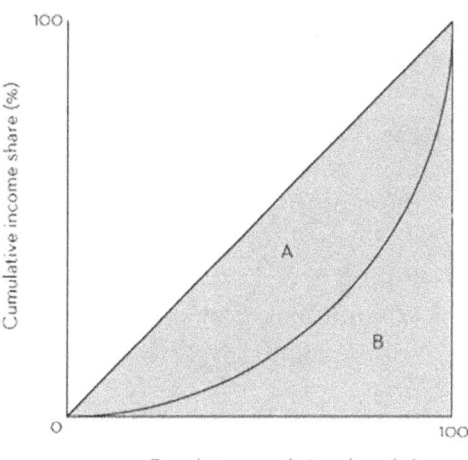

16. **The Gini Coefficient measuring national income inequality is calculated as:**

    A. A/B

    B. B/A

    C. B-A

    D. 2A+B

    E. A+2B

Principles of Microeconomics

17. A Lorenz Curve with a Gini Coefficient of 0 with have a slope of:

    A. 0
    B. 1
    C. 1/2
    D. 2/1
    E. 1/3

18. Free-riding of public goods causes constantly increasing air and water pollution in an unregulated market because:

    A. Public goods cannot be freely consumed, so only those who use them must pay for their cost
    B. Public goods are controlled by the government, preventing the market from reaching equilibrium
    C. Public goods are sold to producers
    D. Public goods can be consumed without paying directly for their cost, placing the burden on taxpayers
    E. Public goods are natural monopolies

19. A linear demand curve with m=1/2 has point [q=500, p=$500], what will demand be at p=$1,000:

    A. $750
    B. $1,000
    C. $1,500
    D. $2,500
    E. $500

20. Ceteris paribus, a firm operating at PED = -1/2 will benefit most from a _____ strategy:

    A. Revenue maximization
    B. Profit maximization
    C. Price competition
    D. Cost reduction
    E. Niche

21. Ceteris paribus, a firm operating at PED = -3/1 will benefit most from a _____ strategy:

    A. Revenue maximization
    B. Profit maximization
    C. Cost reduction
    D. Second-mover
    E. Niche

Principles of Microeconomics

22. **Company A has CED = 2/1 relative to Company B, what is Company A likely to do to their price relative to Company B, ceteris paribus:**

    A. Decrease price because Company B will lose customers faster than Company A lowers price

    B. Increase price because Company A will increase profitability faster than Company B will gain customers

    C. Increase price because Company A will increase profitability faster than Company B will lose customers

    D. Decrease price because Company B will lose customers faster than Company A raises price

    E. Decrease price because Company B will increase costs faster than Company A will lose customers

23. **A linear supply curve with points [q=10, p=$20] and [q=20, p=$50], what is PES:**

    A. 1/3

    B. -1/3

    C. 3/1

    D. -3/1

    E. 1/2

24. **A linear demand curve for a superior good will be ____ and for an inferior good it will be ____:**

    A. Positive, Positive

    B. Positive, Negative

    C. Negative, Negative

    D. Negative, Positive

    E. None of these

25. **Which of these companies is most likely to thrive during a deep recession:**

    A. Dollar Tree

    B. Maserati

    C. Gucci

    D. Rolex

    E. Louis Vuitton

Principles of Microeconomics

26. An increase in minimum wage will cause:

A. A short-run reduction in producer surplus, and long-run cost-push inflationary pressure

B. A short-run shortage of jobs, and long-run cost-push inflationary pressure

C. A short-run reduction in producer surplus, and long-run shortage of jobs

D. A short-run reduction in producer surplus, and long-run increase in deadweight loss

E. A long-run reduction in consumer surplus, and a short run increase in producer surplus

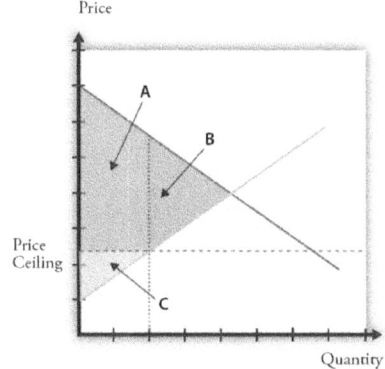

27. Area A is:

A. Consumer surplus

B. Deadweight loss

C. Producer surplus

D. Shortage quantity

E. Price ceiling

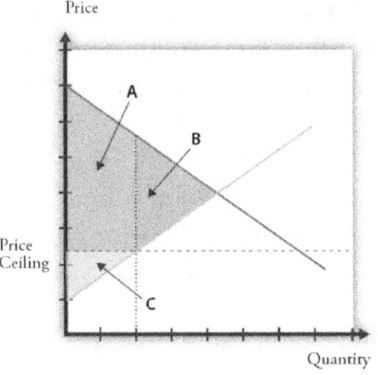

28. Area B is:

A. Consumer surplus

B. Deadweight loss

C. Producer surplus

D. Surplus quantity

E. Price floor

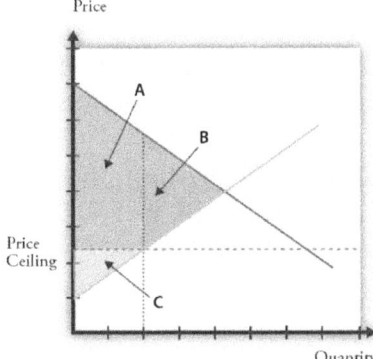

29. Area C is:

A. Consumer surplus

B. Deadweight loss

C. Producer surplus

D. Equilibrium

E. Minimum wage

30. **Subsidies contribute most to:**

    A. Price reductions

    B. Recipient profitability

    C. Decreased consumer surplus

    D. Increased deadweight loss

    E. Decreased costs

31. **Company A sells 50 units for $10 each, and their competitor Company B sells 55 units for $8. If they have a CED of 1/2, how will a 10% tax change their relative positions, ceteris paribus:**

    A. Company A will gain customers

    B. Company B will gain customers

    C. Both companies will gain customers

    D. No effect

    E. Company A will lose customers

32. **A consumer tax refund increases short-term demand 5%. This is an example of:**

    A. Income elasticity of supply

    B. The substitution effect

    C. The income effect

    D. Deadweight loss

    E. Price elasticity of supply

33. **Two economists are walking down the street when they see $100 on the ground. One stops to pick it up, and the other replies "Don't bother. If it was real someone would have picked it up already". This is a criticism of:**

    A. Market equilibrium

    B. Efficient market hypothesis

    C. Imperfect information

    D. Price control

    E. Arbitrage

34. **Which is not a determinant of supply:**

    A. Capital gains tax

    B. Equity markets

    C. Bond prices

    D. Quantity demanded

    E. Degree of trade barriers

35. **Which is not a determinant of demand:**

    A. Income

    B. Population

    C. Employment

    D. Profitability

    E. Consumer preference

Principles of Microeconomics

36. Money = $25
    $5 Pizza = 10U-2n
    $5 Beer = 20U-5n
    Maximize total U:

    A. 50
    B. 55
    C. 60
    D. 100
    E. 120

37. ____ is not an example of the law of diminishing marginal utility:

    A. Getting sick after too many beers
    B. Decreased labor efficiency after scheduling too many people
    C. Increased productivity through specialization of labor
    D. Increasing interest rates with increased borrowing
    E. Increasing risk with higher equity market prices

38. Increased demand as a result of changes in consumer preferences after repeated exposure through advertising is an example of:

    A. Mere-exposure effect
    B. Substitution effect
    C. Income effect
    D. Marginal utility optimization
    E. Marketing effect

39. The implications of the income effect on an individual company can be calculated by:

    A. $\Delta D/\Delta P$
    B. $\Delta D/\Delta Y$
    C. $\Delta S/\Delta P$
    D. $\Delta I/\Delta D$
    E. $\Delta D/\Delta I$

40. $\Delta U/\Delta Q$ calculates:

    A. The rate of increase in nominal utility
    B. The rate of decrease in marginal utility
    C. The rate of decrease in quantity demanded with price increases
    D. The rate of increase in quantity supplied with price decreases
    E. The rate of increase in utility resulting from increasing quantity

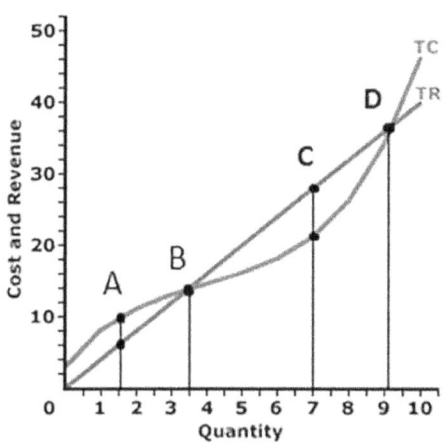

41. Revenue is maximized at:

A. A
B. B
C. C
D. D
E. 0

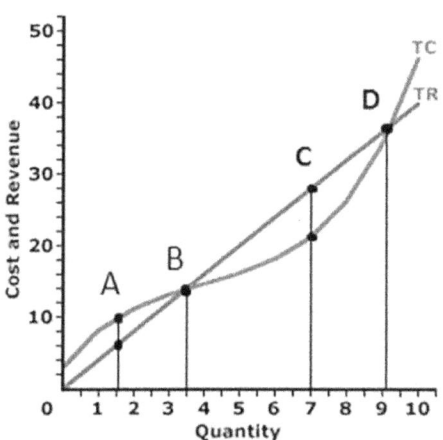

42. The breakeven point is at:

A. A
B. B
C. C
D. D
E. 0

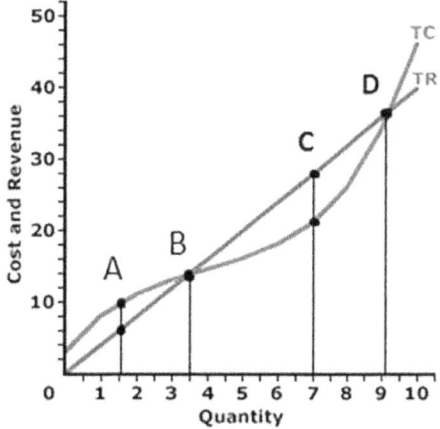

43. Profit is maximized at:

A. A
B. B
C. C
D. D
E. 0

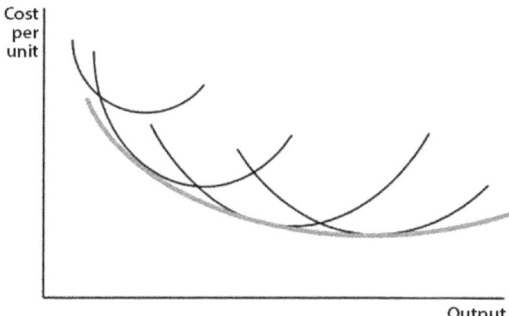

44. The black curves are:

A. LRAC with changes in capital potential
B. SRAC with changes in capital potential
C. LRAC using current capital
D. SRAC using current capital
E. LRAC using SRAC

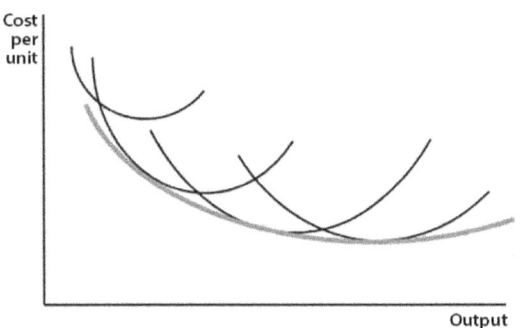

45. The red curve is:

A. LRAC with current capital

B. SRAC with current capital

C. SRAC with changes in capital potential

D. LRAC with changes in capital potential

E. LRAC using SRAC

46. Why do SRAC and LRAC decrease:

A. Increases in current capital productivity decrease AFC until capacity then more productive capital is purchased

B. Decreases in current capital productivity increase AFC until capacity then more productive capital is purchased

C. Increases in current capital productivity increase SRAC until capacity then more productive capital is purchased

D. Decreases in current capital productivity decrease SRAC until capacity then more productive capital is purchased

E. Economies of scale only cause average costs to increase

**47. FC=$100,000
VC = $100
1,000 unit AC =:**

A. $1,000

B. $1,100

C. $100

D. $110,000

E. $110

48. **Decreased costs resulting from being in close proximity to suppliers, partners, and customers is called:**

    A. Economies of agglomeration

    B. Economies of scale

    C. Diseconomies of agglomeration

    D. Diseconomies of scale

    E. Economies of proximity

49. **Basic cost minimization combination is modeled as:**

    A. $MP_L/w = MP_K/r$

    B. $MP_L/r = MP_K/w$

    C. $MP_L-w = MP_K-r$

    D. $MP_L-r = MP_K-w$

    E. $MP_r-L = MP_w-k$

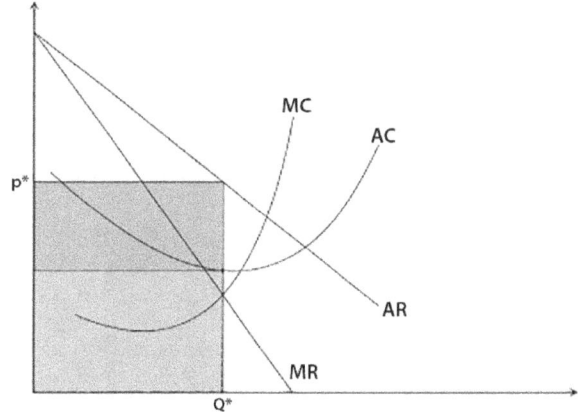

50. **Monopolistic profits are maximized at the point:**

    A. $MR = MC$

    B. $AR = Q$

    C. $MC = AR$

    D. $AC = AR$

    E. $MC > MR$

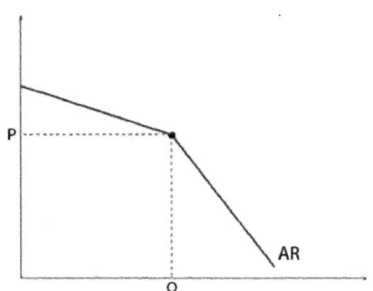

51. The kink in this curve occurs because:

A. A decrease in price is more elastic than an increase, leading to collusion

B. An increase in price is more elastic than a decrease, leading to competition

C. A decrease in price is less elastic than an increase, leading to collusion

D. It's supposed to be curvilinear but differential calculus is too hard

E. The kink doesn't occur at all

52.

	Price 1	Price 2
Price 1	50, 50	75, 25
Price 2	25, 75	25, 25

This game is typical of:

A. Differentiation in monopolistic competition

B. Price elasticity of demand in perfect competition

C. Monopolistic profit maximization

D. Oligopoly market collusion incentive

E. Prisoner's dilemma

53. In perfect competition, producers are _____ and consumers are _____:

A. Price makers, price takers

B. Price takers, price makers

C. Price takers, price takers

D. Price makers, price makers

E. Consumers, producers

Principles of Microeconomics

54. **In oligopoly, producers are ____ and consumers are ____:**

    A. Price takers, price takers

    B. Price takers, price makers

    C. Price makers, price takers

    D. Price makers, price makers

    E. Consumers, producers

55. **In perfect competition there are ____ producers with ____:**

    A. Few, high

    B. Many, low

    C. Infinite, none

    D. One, full

    E. One, none

56. **Monopolistic competition relies on ____ firms with ____ products:**

    A. Many, differentiated

    B. Many, homogeneous

    C. Few, differentiated

    D. Few, homogeneous

    E. One, differentiated

57. **Can monopolistic profits be sustained indefinitely:**

    A. Yes because MR=MC

    B. Yes because a monopoly has no competition

    C. No because competitors will take customers

    D. No because of the threat of new entrants

    E. No because MR=MC

58. **Shutdown occurs at:**

    A. MR<FC

    B. MR<MC

    C. MR<AVC

    D. MR<ATC

    E. AVC<MR

59. **Market exit occurs at:**

    A. MR<LRAC

    B. P<LRAC

    C. MR<SRAC

    D. P<SRAC

    E. LRAC<P

60. Does ATC decrease until MC>ATC:

A. No because decreasing AFC will always lower MC with higher quantity

B. Yes because AFC increases with higher quantity

C. Yes because each unit with MC>ATC will raise ATC

D. No because ATC will always be the lowest as FC is distributed over higher quantity

E. No because each unit with ATC>MC will raise ATC

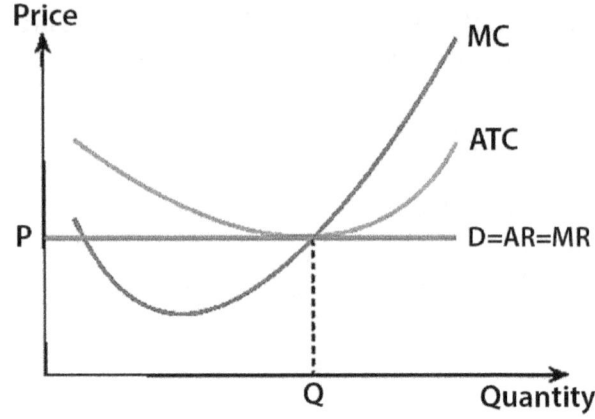

61. Firms in perfect competition will produce at MC=ATC=MR because:

A. Producers are price takers

B. Firms must continue to MR=MC to break-even

C. Marginal profits are maximized when ATC is at its lowest point

D. Q>MC would create per unit losses and market efficiency prevents greater profits by limiting Q.

E. MC>Q would create per unit losses and market efficiency prevents greater profits

62. **Abnormal profits can be earned in monopolistic competition?**

A. Only in the short-run due threats from competitors

B. Only in the long-run after the years to break-even

C. In both the short- and long-run due to continuous development of new differentiations

D. In neither the short- or long-run because firms of price takers

E. In both the short- and long-run due to new entrants

63. **Monopsony markets are not found in:**

A. Defense

B. Utilities

C. Labor

D. Agriculture

E. Infrastructure

64. **Monopsony and monopsonistic competition contribute to:**

A. Greater output per capita through lower employment levels

B. Greater innovation through intense labor competition

C. Lower levels of unemployment as a single company hires everyone

D. Higher income disparity through lower competitive strength by workers in labor markets

E. Lower levels of inflation

65. **Lower wages do not lead to higher employment because:**

A. Fewer people are willing to work at a given price level despite their need to survive

B. Companies will never hire more people than they need to meet production demand, regardless of wage level

C. Lower wages cause greater per-person output

D. Higher employment requires higher price levels to increase supply

E. Unions prevent labor negotiations

Principles of Microeconomics

66. **Leader and follower competitive games are indicative of:**

    A. Nash equilibrium

    B. Bertrand competition

    C. Cournot competition

    D. Stackelberg competition

    E. Perfect competition

67. **Suppliers that set price and consumers that set quantity are indicative of:**

    A. Cournot competition

    B. Stackelberg competition

    C. Bertrand competition

    D. Nash equilibrium

    E. Perfect competition

68. **Coercive monopolies use all of these methods to prevent new entrants, except:**

    A. Predatory pricing

    B. Competitive wages

    C. Expensive lawsuits

    D. Acquisitions

    E. Intellectual property rights

69. **Anti-trust laws do everything except:**

    A. Limit the power of unions

    B. Increase free market competition by breaking-up monopolies

    C. Protect against bid rigging

    D. Prevent collusion in oligopolies

    E. Protect against price gouging

70. **Antitrust laws were established by Teddy Roosevelt as part of the ____ Deal:**

    A. Square

    B. New

    C. Good

    D. Slick

    E. Hot

71. **Intellectual property rights give incentive to _____ but _____ prices:**

    A. Hire, increases

    B. Innovate, increases

    C. Increase supply, decreases

    D. Invest, decreases

    E. Invest, increases

Principles of Microeconomics

72. **Money facilitates transactions due to the trait of:**

    A. Spendability

    B. Convertibility

    C. Transferability

    D. Exchangeability

    E. Flexibility

73. **"It is not from the benevolence of the butcher, the brewer, or the baker that we expect our dinner, but from their regard to _____":**

    A. Demonstrate superior morals

    B. Earn receivables

    C. Develop social capital

    D. Their own interest

    E. Government regulations

74. **A person who makes pins can make 1 million per day, but if they also tried to smelt their own metal that number would drop to 100 per day. This is a result of:**

    A. Transfer pricing in multi-step production

    B. Longer production cycles

    C. Trade between specialists in the division of labor

    D. Labor burnout

    E. Overtime

75. **The factors of production do not include:**

    A. Labor

    B. Producers

    C. Land

    D. Entrepreneurship

    E. None of these

76. **An entrepreneur is deciding on a venture to purchase. Which do they choose:**

    A. P=1 million, r=.16, t=3

    B. P=$2 million, r=.05, t=10

    C. P=$500,000, r=.17, t=7

    D. P=$1 million, r=.15, t=5

    E. P=$2 million, r=.15, t=5

77. **A competitive advantage requires an activity to be everything except:**

    A. Rare

    B. Unsubstitutable

    C. Imitable

    D. Valuable

    E. Inimitable

Principles of Microeconomics

78. A company whose competitive advantage is innovation would benefit most from a ____ strategy:

    A. Price leader

    B. Differentiation

    C. First mover

    D. Niche

    E. Second mover

79. A company whose competitive advantage is in managing supply chain will benefit most from a ___ strategy:

    A. First mover

    B. Price leader

    C. Niche

    D. Differentiation

    E. Second mover

80. The PED of emergency healthcare is:

    A. -1/2

    B. 1

    C. 0

    D. ∞

    E. Undefined

81. Profit = $1 million
    Cost = $125,000
    The ROI is:

    A. 7

    B. 10

    C. 8

    D. 5

    E. 6

82. MR=MC is:

    A. Productive efficiency

    B. Allocative efficiency

    C. Pareto efficiency

    D. Kaldor-Hicks efficiency

    E. Market efficiency

83. The point at which it is impossible to allocate resources to one activity without taking them away from another is called:

    A. Productive efficiency

    B. Allocative efficiency

    C. Pareto efficiency

    D. Kaldor-Hicks efficiency

    E. Market efficiency

84. **That we put more value on the things we own than the exact same things owned by others is a result of:**

    A. Disposition effect

    B. Endowment effect

    C. Substitution effect

    D. Observation effect

    E. Income Effect

85. **The marginal rate of substitution calculates:**

    A. The changing amount of one product it requires to equal the utility of a substitute product

    B. The rate at which PED changes along a demand curve

    C. The rate at which labor is substituted for capital over time

    D. The rate of production required of workers to remain competitive against improving technological capital

    E. The substitution effect

86. **The relationship between the marginal rate of substitution and the law of decreasing marginal utility is:**

    A. They are competing measures of consumer utility

    B. Diminishing utility means it takes marginally less of Product A to create the same utility as 1 unit of Product B

    C. Diminishing utility means it takes marginally more of Product A to create the same utility as 1 unit of Product B

    D. There is no relationship

    E. Marginal rate of substitution measures the law of decreasing marginal utility

87. **If Company A acquires a competitor, it is an example of _____ integration:**

    A. Horizontal

    B. Vertical

    C. Diagonal

    D. Orthogonal

    E. Inverse

Principles of Microeconomics

88. If Company A acquires a supplier, it is an example of _____ integration:

    A. Diagnoal

    B. Horizontal

    C. Orthogonal

    D. Vertical

    E. Inverse

89. Pat builds a website which requires $10,000 worth of construction. Pat will do $6,000 of it, but needs someone to build $4,000 of economic models for the back-end. What is the derived factor demand:

    A. $4,000

    B. $6,000

    C. $10,000

    D. $2,000

    E. $3,000

90. Cost = $10,000
    Revenue = $20,000
    Revenue from 2nd Choice = $15,000
    The accounting profit is ____ and the economic profit is _____:

    A. $10,000, $25,000

    B. $5,000, $10,000

    C. $10,000, $5,000

    D. $10,000, -$5,000

    E. -$10,000, -$5,000

91. At L=100, R=$10,000
    At L=500, R=$100,000
    MRP is:

    A. 2

    B. 10

    C. 5

    D. ½

    E. 1

92. A labor supply curve will sometimes bend backwards at higher wage rates due to the following possibilities except:

    A. Unreasonably long work hours

    B. Lack of skill level required at that wage

    C. Forgoing other benefits for higher wages

    D. Unsafe types of work

    E. Undesirable types of work

93. Cost = $10,000
    Revenue = $20,000
    Revenue from 2nd Choice = $15,000
    The opportunity cost is:

    A. $20,000

    B. $35,000

    C. $10,000

    D. $15,000

    E. $5,000

94. **The principle of scarcity states that:**

    A. In times of shortage, price increases

    B. There are not enough resources for everyone to have a comfortable life

    C. It is not possible to produce enough to meet the wants and needs of everyone

    D. There are not enough resources for everyone to survive

    E. We will eventually run-out of resources

95. **For a person or firm to contribute to supply or demand, they must have:**

    A. Willingness but not ability

    B. Willingness and ability

    C. Ability but not willingness

    D. Already participated in an exchange

    E. Income

96. **"Firms" include everything except:**

    A. Households

    B. Businesses

    C. Industries

    D. Governments

    E. Non-profits

97. **That a firm is a collection of resources and the activities which utilize those resources comes from:**

    A. Knowledge-based view of the firm

    B. Resource-based view of the firm

    C. Factor-based view of the firm

    D. Asset-based view of the firm

    E. Capital-based view of the firm

98. **That a firm is a collection of ideas, policies, knowledge, and expertise comes from:**

    A. Resource-based view of the firm

    B. Factor-based view of the firm

    C. Knowledge-based view of the firm

    D. Asset-based view of the firm

    E. Ideal-based view of the firm

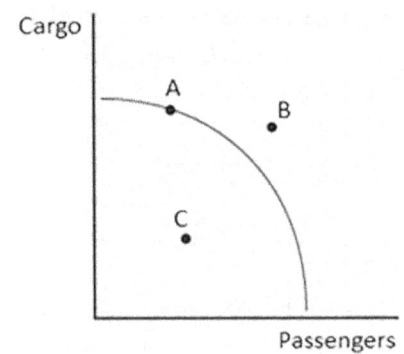

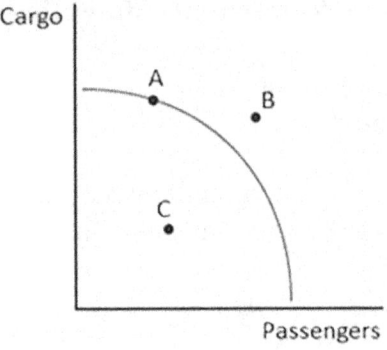

99. The efficient frontier is:

A. B

B. A

C. C

D. Min cargo or min passengers

E. 0

100. Production is possible at:

A. B and C

B. A, B, and C

C. A and B

D. A and C

E. None of these

Principles of Microeconomics

ANSWER KEY

Question Number	Correct Answer	Your Answer
1	B	
2	C	
3	C	
4	B	
5	C	
6	C	
7	D	
8	B	
9	B	
10	A	
11	B	
12	C	
13	A	
14	B	
15	A	
16	A	
17	B	
18	D	
19	A	
20	B	
21	A	
22	A	
23	A	
24	D	
25	A	
26	A	
27	A	
28	B	
29	C	
30	B	
31	D	
32	C	
33	B	
34	A	

Question Number	Correct Answer	Your Answer
35	D	
36	C	
37	C	
38	A	
39	B	
40	B	
41	D	
42	B	
43	C	
44	D	
45	D	
46	A	
47	B	
48	A	
49	A	
50	A	
51	A	
52	D	
53	A	
54	C	
55	C	
56	A	
57	D	
58	C	
59	B	
60	C	
61	D	
62	C	
63	B	
64	D	
65	B	
66	D	
67	C	
68	B	

Question Number	Correct Answer	Your Answer
69	A	
70	A	
71	B	
72	C	
73	D	
74	C	
75	B	
76	D	
77	C	
78	C	
79	B	
80	D	
81	A	
82	B	
83	C	
84	B	
85	A	
86	C	
87	A	
88	D	
89	A	
90	C	
91	A	
92	B	
93	D	
94	C	
95	B	
96	C	
97	B	
98	C	
99	B	
100	D	

Introductory Psychology

Description of the Examination

The Introductory Psychology examination covers material that is usually taught in a one-semester undergraduate course in introductory psychology. It stresses basic facts, concepts and generally accepted principles in thirteen areas listed in the following section.

The examination contains approximately 95 questions to be answered in 90 minutes. Some of these are pretest questions that will not be scored. Any time candidates spend on tutorials and providing personal information is in addition to the actual testing time.

Please note that the questions on the CLEP Introductory Psychology exam will continue to adhere to the terminology, criteria and classifications referred to in the fourth edition of the *Diagnostic and Statistical Manual of Mental Disorders* (DSM-IV-TR) until further notice.

Knowledge and Skills Required

Questions on the Introductory Psychology examination require candidates to demonstrate one or more of the following abilities.
- Knowledge of terminology, principles and theory
- Ability to comprehend, evaluate and analyze problem situations
- Ability to apply knowledge to new situations

The subject matter of the Introductory Psychology examination is drawn from the following topics. The percentages next to the main topics indicate the approximate percentage of exam questions on that topic.

8%-9% **History, Approaches, Methods**
- History of psychology
- Approaches: biological, behavioral, cognitive, humanistic, psychodynamic
- Research methods: experimental, clinical, correlations
- Ethics in research

8%-9% **Biological Bases of Behavior**
- Endocrine system
- Etiology
- Functional organization of the nervous system
- Genetics
- Neuroanatomy
- Physiological techniques

7%-8% **Sensation and Perception**
- Attention
- Other senses: somesthesis, olfaction, gustation, vestibular system
- Perceptual development
- Perceptual process
- Receptor processes: vision, audition
- Sensory mechanisms: thresholds, adaptation

5%-6% **States of Consciousness**
- Hypnosis and meditation
- Psychoactive drug effects
- Sleep and dreaming

10%-11% **Learning**
- Biological bases
- Classical conditioning
- Cognitive process in learning
- Observational learning
- Operant conditioning

8%-9%	**Cognition** - Intelligence and creativity - Language - Memory - Thinking and problem solving		- Theories of psychopathology
7%-8%	**Motivation and Emotion** - Biological bases - Hunger, thirst, sex, pain - Social motivation - Theories of emotion - Theories of motivation	7%-8%	**Treatment of Psychological Disorders** - Behavioral therapies - Biological and drug therapies - Cognitive therapies - Community and preventive approaches - Insight therapies: psychodynamic and humanistic approaches
8%-9%	**Developmental Psychology** - Dimensions of development: physical, cognitive, social, moral - Gender identity and sex roles - Heredity-environment issues - Research methods: longitudinal, cross-sectional - Theories of development	7%-8%	**Social Psychology** - Aggression/antisocial behavior - Attitudes and attitude change - Attribution processes - Conformity, compliance, obedience - Group dynamics - Interpersonal perception
7%-8%	**Personality** - Assessment techniques - Growth and adjustment - Personality theories and approaches - Research methods: idiographic, nomothetic - Self-concept, self-esteem	3%-4%	**Statistics, Tests and Measurement** - Descriptive statistics - Inferential statistics - Measurement of intelligence - Mental handicapping conditions - Reliability and validity - Samples, populations, norms - Types of tests
8%-9%	**Psychological Disorders and Health** - Affective disorders - Anxiety disorders - Dissociative disorders - Health, stress and coping - Personality disorders - Psychoses - Somatoform disorders		

Introductory Psychology

SAMPLE TEST

1. Which of the following describes an expression of favor or disfavor for a person, place, thing, or event?

   A. Attitude

   B. Belief

   C. Cognition

   D. Drive

   E. Behavior

2. Which of the following is a theory by Ajzen and Fishbein that outlines a model for the prediction of behavioral intention?

   A. Cognitive Dissonance Theory

   B. Social Judgment Theory

   C. Theory of Reasoned Action

   D. Information Integration Theory

   E. Congruity Theory

3. According to Petty and Cacioppo's Elaboration Likelihood Model, when a person is persuaded by the likeability of a speaker, he or she is using which processing route?

   A. Central

   B. Heuristic

   C. Peripheral

   D. Systemic

   E. None of the above

4. Which of the following psychologists coined the term *group dynamics* to describe the positive and negative forces within groups of people?

   A. Maslow

   B. Lewin

   C. Freud

   D. Pavlov

   E. Skinner

5. Which of the following "deals with how the social perceiver uses information to arrive at causal explanations for events?"

   A. Cognitive Dissonance Theory

   B. Classical conditioning

   C. Psychoanalysis

   D. Attribution Theory

   E. Frequency Theory

6. **Which of the following describes obedience?**

   A. The act of changing one's beliefs and attitudes to match those of other members of a social group

   B. The act of following orders without question because they come from a legitimate authority

   C. The act of adapting one's actions to another's wishes or rules

   D. The act of influencing another's attitudes, beliefs, or behaviors

   E. The act of establishing credibility and authority

7. **Paul is driving to work when another driver cuts him off in traffic. Paul begins shouting and pounding on the steering wheel. Paul is exhibiting _____.**

   A. passive aggression

   B. passivity

   C. instrumental aggression

   D. dissociative rage

   E. impulsive aggression

8. **According to Maslow's Hierarchy of Needs, humans must satisfy their physiological needs before they will desire to satisfy which other category of needs?**

   A. Safety

   B. Belonging

   C. Esteem

   D. Self-actualization

   E. All of the above

9. **Which of the following is considered a prosocial emotion?**

   A. Anger

   B. Sadness

   C. Shame

   D. Happiness

   E. Awe

10. **Which of the following statements is true of long-term memory?**

    A. Long-term memory has nearly infinite storage capacity.

    B. Long-term memory is also known as working memory.

    C. Long-term memory allows people to temporarily store and manipulate visual images.

    D. Long-term memory has a shorter duration than working memory.

    E. None of the above statements are true of long-term memory.

11. **The term *chunking* refers to**

    A. transferring memories from short-term to long-term

    B. combining small bits of information into larger, familiar pieces

    C. sensory memory

    D. repeating information over and over to increase the duration of time in which it stays in short-term memory

    E. an organizational process for cataloguing memories

12. **The smallest units of speech are called**

    A. vowels

    B. syllables

    C. phonemes

    D. semantic

    E. syntax

13. **Which of the following terms describes the process by which memories fade over time?**

    A. Memory loss

    B. Memory fade

    C. Memory decay

    D. Memory delay

    E. Memory recall

14. **The study of psychology began in _____ and was established by _____.**

    A. The United States; Freud

    B. Germany; Freud

    C. Germany; Ebbinghaus

    D. The United States; Skinner

    E. France; Piaget

15. **Conduction aphasia is caused by which of the following?**

    A. Disruptions in the connection between the Wernicke's and Broca's areas

    B. Disruptions in the ability to consolidate information at a neural level

    C. Short-term memory loss due to retrograde amnesia

    D. Blockage of neural circuits in working memory

    E. Damage to the cerebellum

16. **An experiment that produces identical results each time is considered which of the following?**

    A. Valid, but not reliable

    B. Reliable, but not valid

    C. Valid and reliable

    D. Reliable with questionable validity

    E. Valid with questionable reliability

17. **The assumption that maladaptive thought patterns and behaviors are learned is associated with which of the following?**

    A. Behavioral therapy

    B. Cognitive therapy

    C. Psychoanalytic therapy

    D. Rogerian therapy

    E. Group therapy

18. **You have conducted two experiments in which you failed to get the same result although the conditions under which both experiments are identical. It is clear that the measurement lacks which of the following?**

    A. Face validity

    B. Construct validity

    C. Inter-rater reliability

    D. Reliability

    E. Internal validity

19. **When is punishment most effective is changing or suppressing behavior?**

    A. Punishment is most effective when it is delayed, inconsistent, and mild.

    B. Punishment is most effective when it is immediate, consistent, and intense.

    C. Punishment is most effective when it is explained.

    D. Punishment is most effective when it is immediate, consistent, and mild.

    E. Punishment is most effective when it is vague.

20. **A psychologist administers the same IQ test three times to the same subject and receives identical or similar results each time. However, many scholars argue that IQ tests do not measure intelligence, but rather measure one's test-taking ability. This suggests that IQ tests are which of the following?**

    A. Valid but not reliable

    B. Both valid and reliable

    C. Neither valid nor reliable

    D. Reliable but not valid

    E. Lacking internal reliability

21. **Which of the following attempts to establish an unpleasant response to the object that produces an undesired behavior?**

    A. Systematic desensitization

    B. Implosion therapy

    C. Aversive classical conditioning

    D. Punishment

    E. Unconditioned stimulus

22. **The ability to imitate the behavior of others and perform the same behavior under the same or similar conditions describes which of the following?**

    A. Modeling

    B. Shaping

    C. Imitation

    D. Reinforcement

    E. Play

23. **Which approach to psychology suggests that people are controlled by their environments?**

    A. Humanism

    B. Behaviorism

    C. Psychodynamic

    D. Cognitive

    E. Biological

24. Which of the following statements best describes the evolutionary perspective of psychology?

    A. The evolutionary approach explains human behavior in terms of classical and operational conditioning.

    B. The evolutionary approach studies the effects of genes on human behavior.

    C. The evolutionary approach seeks to understand the function of different mental processes.

    D. The evolutionary approach explains human behavior in terms of the selective pressures that shape behavior.

    E. The evolutionary approach seeks to study the whole person.

25. Which of the following psychologist founded the psychodynamic perspective of psychology?

    A. Sigmund Freud

    B. Ivan Pavlov

    C. B. F. Skinner

    D. Abraham Maslow

    E. Carl Rogers

26. Jane's experiment did not produce significant results and she is afraid that her paper will not get published. She decides to change some of the numbers in her data to get the outcome she desired. Jane has violated which general principle of ethics, according to the APA?

    A. Beneficence

    B. Fidelity

    C. Responsibility

    D. Justice

    E. Integrity

27. With which of the following research methods does the observer have direct contact with the group he or she is observing?

    A. Field experiment

    B. Participant observation

    C. Laboratory experiment

    D. Natural observation

    E. Controlled observation

28. The requirement that researchers explain to potential participants the purpose and nature of a study, as well as any possible risks associated with participation, is known as

   A. informed consent

   B. integrity

   C. researcher responsibility

   D. liability

   E. confidentiality

29. Which of the following topics do cognitive psychologists study?

   A. Behavior

   B. Emotion

   C. Self-actualization

   D. Memory and learning

   E. Genes and DNA

30. Which of the following psychologists can be categorized as a humanist?

   A. Sigmund Freud

   B. Ivan Pavlov

   C. B. F. Skinner

   D. Abraham Maslow

   E. Wilhelm Wundt

31. Which of the following prevents a person from moving while experiencing dreams?

   A. REM atonia

   B. NREM sleep

   C. Muscle relaxers

   D. Beta waves

   E. Alpha waves

32. During the beginning of sleep, when a person is still relatively awake, the brain produces

   A. Rapid Eye Movement

   B. Beta Waves

   C. Alpha waves

   D. Hallucinations

   E. None of the above

33. Dreaming most often occurs during which phase of sleep?

   A. Stage 1 (theta waves)

   B. Stage 2 (sleep spindles)

   C. Stage 3 (delta waves)

   D. Stage 4 (REM)

   E. Dreaming occurs in all of the above stages

34. Which of the following is NOT considered a benefit of meditation?

    A. Greater capacity for empathy

    B. Decreased stress

    C. Increased anxiety

    D. Increased gray matter in the brain

    E. Improved sleep

35. Research on sleep provides evidence to support the ideas that

    A. sleep is not necessary in the production of brain proteins

    B. all individuals require at least 8 hours of sleep each night for optimal functioning

    C. low-quality sleep and sleep deprivation negatively impact mood

    D. sleep does not impact learning

    E. sleep is not essential to well-being

36. A dog learns that when it rings a bell, its owner will let it outside. This is an example of which kind of learning?

    A. Modeling

    B. Classical conditioning

    C. Instrumental conditioning

    D. Stimulus control

    E. Operant conditioning

37. Which of the following types of learning involves reinforcement and punishment?

    A. Operant conditioning

    B. Classical conditioning

    C. Habituation

    D. Instrumental conditioning

    E. Modeling

38. Which of the following types of learning involves a stimulus and response?

    A. Operant conditioning

    B. Classical conditioning

    C. Habituation

    D. Instrumental conditioning

    E. Modeling

39. Which of the following depicts Freud's stages of psychosexual development in the correct order?

    A. Oral, phallic, anal, latent, genital

    B. Genital, phallic, anal, latent, oral

    C. Phallic, oral, anal, genital, latent

    D. Oral, anal, phallic, latent, genital

    E. Anal, oral, latent, phallic, genital

40. According to Piaget, the sensorimotor stage occurs between which ages?

    A. 0-2 years

    B. 2-7 years

    C. 7-11 years

    D. 11-15 years

    E. 15+ years

41. Piaget's theory of cognitive development is concerned with which population?

    A. Newborn babies

    B. Children of all ages

    C. Young adults

    D. Mature adults

    E. Elderly adults

42. Which theory explains how parent-child relationships emerge and influence subsequent development?

    A. Psychoanalytic theory

    B. Social learning theory

    C. Cognitive development

    D. Attachment theory

    E. None of the above

43. Developmental psychologists often prefer which type of research design?

    A. Experimental

    B. Participant observation

    C. Case study

    D. Cross-sectional

    E. Longitudinal

44. On which level of Kohlberg's moral stages is a child whose morality is based on rules and punishments?

    A. Level I. Pre-conventional/premoral

    B. Level II: Conventional/Role conformity

    C. Level III: Post-conventional/Self-accepted moral principles

    D. Level IV: Fully moral

    E. None of the above

45. Which of the following disorders is characterized by hallucinations and delusions such as hearing voices?

    A. Depression

    B. Obsessive compulsive disorder

    C. Bipolar disorder

    D. Schizophrenia

    E. Mania

46. Which of the following drugs has stimulant and hallucinogenic effects?

    A. Molly

    B. Adderall

    C. Marijuana

    D. Cocaine

    E. Pain killers

47. Jimmy is experiencing recurring negative thoughts, a loss of interest in activities that used to excite him, trouble sleeping, and a loss of appetite. From which of the following disorders is Jimmy most likely suffering?

    A. Depression

    B. Obsessive compulsive disorder

    C. Bipolar disorder

    D. Schizophrenia

    E. Mania

48. Which of the following anxiety disorders is characterized by a fear of losing control, being trapped, or panicking in public places?

    A. Acrophrobia

    B. Agoraphobia

    C. Generalized anxiety disorder

    D. Post-traumatic stress disorder

    E. General panic attack

49. Antidepressants are often associated with which of the following side effects?

    A. Insomnia

    B. Dry mouth

    C. An increase in suicidal thoughts

    D. Decreased sexual drive and function

    E. All of the above

50. Which of the following types of disorders is characterized by real physical symptoms that cannot be fully explained by a medical condition, the effects of a drug, or another mental disorder?

    A. Personality disorders

    B. Anxiety disorders

    C. Somatoform disorders

    D. Affective disorders

    E. Dissociative disorders

51. Which of the following personality disorders is characterized by an exaggerate sense of self-importance, a strong desire to be admired, and a lack of empathy?

    A. Borderline personality disorder
    B. Histrionic personality disorder
    C. Avoidant personality disorder
    D. Narcissistic personality disorder
    E. Antisocial personality disorder

52. People with which of the following personality disorders often lack empathy and remorse, and exhibit aggressive, impulsive, reckless, or irresponsible behavior?

    A. Borderline personality disorder
    B. Histrionic personality disorder
    C. Avoidant personality disorder
    D. Narcissistic personality disorder
    E. Antisocial personality disorder

53. A person who experiences depressive and manic episodes may have which of the following disorders?

    A. Depression
    B. Obsessive compulsive disorder
    C. Bipolar disorder
    D. Schizophrenia
    E. Mania

54. Hypochondria is an example of which of the following types of disorders?

    A. Personality disorders
    B. Anxiety disorders
    C. Somatoform disorders
    D. Affective disorders
    E. Dissociative disorders

55. The _____ nervous system prepares the body for action, while the _____ nervous system keeps the body still.

    A. Sympathetic, parasympathetic
    B. Autonomic, sympathetic
    C. Parasympathetic, autonomic
    D. Sympathetic, autonomic
    E. Parasympathetic, sympathetic

56. Which of the following theories of emotion suggests that people experience emotions because they perceive physiological changes in their bodies?

    A. Cognitive appraisal
    B. Schachter and Singer's Two-Factor Theory
    C. Evolutionary Theory
    D. James-Lange Theory
    E. Cannon-Bard Theory

57. Which of the following terms describes a theoretical construct that is used to explain the reasons for people's actions, desires, and needs?

   A. Emotion

   B. Empathy

   C. Motivation

   D. Hunger

   E. Thirst

58. Which of the following is an example of intrinsic motivation?

   A. Money

   B. Receiving an award

   C. Feeling a sense of accomplishment

   D. Winning a prize

   E. A cheering crowd

59. Which of the following drugs is commonly abused by college students because its stimulant effects can aid in studying?

   A. Cocaine

   B. Marijuana

   C. Adderall

   D. Alcohol

   E. All of the above

60. Which of the following theories suggests that we are motivated to take action based on our biological needs?

   A. Drive reduction theory

   B. Arousal theory

   C. Instinct theory

   D. Maslow's Hierarchy of Needs

   E. Goal-setting theory

61. Which of the following theories of emotion argues that one's experience of emotion depends on their physiological arousal and cognitive interpretation of that arousal?

   A. Cognitive appraisal

   B. Schachter and Singer's Two-Factor Theory

   C. Evolutionary Theory

   D. James-Lange Theory

   E. Cannon-Bard Theory

62. Which of the following is the correct term for vision that comes from the side of the eye?

   A. Peripheral vision

   B. Tunnel vision

   C. Perceptive vision

   D. Sensation

   E. Detection

63. Which of the following correctly lists Piaget's stages of cognitive development?

    A. Sensorimotor, concrete operational, preoperational, formal operational

    B. Preoperational, formal operational, concrete operational. sensorimotor

    C. Formal operational, concrete operational, preoperational, sensorimotor

    D. Concrete operational, preoperational, sensorimotor, formal operational

    E. Sensorimotor, preoperational, concrete operational, formal operational

64. Which of the following therapies is considered a last resort method of treating depression when all other therapies have failed?

    A. Antidepressant medication

    B. Psychoanalytic therapy

    C. Cognitive-behavioral therapy

    D. Electroconvulsive shock therapy

    E. Group therapy

65. Which of the following best describes a cross-sectional study?

    A. A researcher follows the same participants over a period of time.

    B. A researcher examines different groups of people who share one or more similar characteristics.

    C. A researcher brings people into a lab and has them complete a task.

    D. A researcher observes people in their homes.

    E. A researcher surveys observes people in public.

66. Psychology researchers use which of the following terms to describe thinking, reasoning, and solving problems?

    A. Emotion

    B. Intuition

    C. Perception

    D. Sensation

    E. Cognition

67. Lawrence Kohlberg is known for his research in the area of _____ development.

    A. Cognitive
    B. Moral
    C. Personality
    D. Emotional
    E. Physical

68. Which of the following statements about antidepressants do most psychology researchers and practitioners consider true?

    A. Antidepressants are helpful in treating some forms of depression.
    B. For many patients, antidepressants are less helpful than individual therapy in treating depression.
    C. Antidepressants alone are not enough to successfully treat depression in many patients.
    D. All of the above
    E. None of the above

69. Which of the following therapies helps people work through problems by interacting with one or more therapists as well as other individuals experiencing similar struggles?

    A. Individual therapy
    B. Drug therapy
    C. Group therapy
    D. Psychoanalytic therapy
    E. Social-Emotional therapy

70. According to Kübler-Ross, the correct order of the stages of grief are:

    A. denial, anger, bargaining, depression, acceptance.
    B. anger, denial, depression, bargaining, acceptance.
    C. denial, depression, anger, acceptance, bargaining.
    D. depression, denial, anger, bargaining, acceptance.
    E. acceptance, denial, anger, bargaining, depression.

71. Which of the following correctly describes the difference between depression and grief?

    A. Grief often entails a sense of worthlessness whereas depression does not.

    B. Grief involves excessive guilt and depression does not.

    C. Grief lasts longer than major depression.

    D. Grief subsides after a period of time whereas depression often persists for extended periods of time.

    E. Grief is a clinical condition whereas depression is a normal, healthy emotion.

72. Cara describes herself as outgoing, funny and friendly. These characteristics are part of her

    A. self-esteem.

    B. motivation.

    C. self-concept.

    D. group identity.

    E. physique.

73. In personality research, which of the following describes personal characteristics that are biologically determined?

    A. Nature

    B. Environment

    C. State

    D. Trait

    E. Ego

74. Which of the following is not a standard method used to assess personality?

    A. Self-reports

    B. Observer-reports

    C. Test data

    D. Projective measures

    E. Laboratory study

75. **The Big Five personality traits are:**

    A. Humor, openness, extraversion, agreeableness, neuroticism.

    B. Extraversion, agreeableness, enlightenment, openness, neuroticism

    C. Openness, conscientiousness, extraversion, agreeableness, neuroticism.

    D. Extraversion, introversion, humor, neuroticism, openness

    E. Happiness, neuroticism, shyness, openness, extraversion

76. **_____ refers to the pattern of thoughts, feelings, social adjustments and behaviors consistently exhibited over time.**

    A. Preferences

    B. Self-esteem

    C. Construct

    D. Personality

    E. Extraversion

77. **Conscientiousness refers to one's**

    A. tendency to be creative, curious, and open to new ideas.

    B. tendency to be organized and self-disciplined.

    C. tendency to experience unpleasant emotions easily.

    D. tendency to be compassionate and cooperative towards others.

    E. tendency to exhibit to seek stimulation in the company of others.

78. **Which of the following types of psychologists believe that one's personality consists of learned patterns**

    A. Emotional psychologists

    B. Humanists

    C. Behavioral psychologists

    D. Psychoanalytic theorists

    E. Cognitive psychologists

79. Kim lives in Alaska and says that a 60-degree day is warm. Steve lives in Arizona and thinks 60-degree weather is cold. Their perceptions differ because of

    A. their frame of reference
    B. where they place their attention
    C. perceptual constancy
    D. their personalities
    E. their top-down processing

80. Which of the following terms explains why roads appear to converge in the distance?

    A. Light and shadow
    B. Continuing patterns
    C. Texture gradient
    D. Linear perspective
    E. None of the above

81. Anything that can be perceived with one of the five senses is considered _____ stimulus, whereas _____ stimulus refers to the specific object upon which one is focused.

    A. Attended, environmental
    B. Image, recognition
    C. Environmental, attended
    D. Neural, retinal
    E. Neural, image

82. An image on the retina of the eye is transformed into electrical signals in a process known as which of the following?

    A. Transcendence
    B. Abduction
    C. Transformation
    D. Intensification
    E. Transduction

83. Which of the following is true of secondary reinforcers?

    A. They are learned.
    B. They are ineffective.
    C. They are more effective than primary reinforcers.
    D. They are innate.
    E. They are natural.

84. The analysis of information starting with features and building into a complete perception is known as which of the following?

    A. Perceptual constancy
    B. Top-down processing
    C. Bottom-up processing
    D. Chunking
    E. Linking

85. Which of the following allows humans to perceive the world in three dimensions?

    A. Depth perception
    B. Sensation
    C. Disparity
    D. Convergence
    E. Accommodation

86. Neurons are made up of which of the following?

    A. Anterior cell, posterior cell, axon
    B. Dendrite, soma, axon
    C. Cell body, cell wall, nucleus
    D. Myelin, dendrite, cell wall
    E. None of the above

87. Which of the following describes the main function of myelin?

    A. Myelin forms a protective coating over nerve axons.
    B. Myelin decreases the speed with which information travels from nerve cell to nerve cell.
    C. Myelin blocks reception of acetylcholine.
    D. Myelin slows down nerve degeneration.
    E. Myelin aids in the transference of neurotransmitters.

88. Neurotransmitters are released at which part of a cell?

    A. Dendrite
    B. Axon terminal
    C. Nucleus
    D. Soma
    E. Myelin

89. Communication within a neuron is a(n) _____ process, while communication between neurons is a(n) _____ process.

    A. Chemical; mechanical
    B. Electrical; mechanical
    C. Chemical; electrical
    D. Electrical; chemical
    E. Mechanical; electrical

90. Human behavior is influenced by genetic processes as well their environments and experiences. In psychology, this is known as which of the following?

    A. Genes versus experience
    B. Heredity versus environment
    C. Climate versus science
    D. Nature versus nurture
    E. Genes versus personality

Introductory Psychology

91. Which of the following is the main link between the brain and the glandular system in the human body?

    A. Hypothalamus

    B. Prefrontal cortex

    C. Central nervous system

    D. Sympathetic nervous system

    E. Parasympathetic nervous system

92. The endocrine system is responsible for which of the following functions?

    A. It pumps blood throughout the body.

    B. It brings oxygen into the body.

    C. It secretes hormones into the blood stream for communication between cells.

    D. It processes sensory information from the eyes and ears.

    E. None of the above.

93. An EEG records which of the following?

    A. The electrical rhythm of the heart.

    B. Electrical impulses from the brain.

    C. Hormone secretion in the bloodstream.

    C. Electrical currents in the body.

    E. The number of neurons in the brain.

94. In Pavlov's famous experiment, the dog's salivation over food was considered which of the following?

    A. Conditioned response

    B. Conditioned stimulus

    C. Automatic stimulus

    D. Unconditioned response

    E. Unconditioned stimulus

95. Which of the following scientists is known for studying operant conditioning?

    A. Pavlov

    B. Freud

    C. Maslow

    D. Piaget

    E. Skinner

Introductory Psychology

RATIONALES

Question Number	Correct Answer	Your Answer
1	A	
2	C	
3	C	
4	B	
5	D	
6	B	
7	E	
8	E	
9	C	
10	A	
11	B	
12	C	
13	C	
14	C	
15	A	
16	D	
17	A	
18	D	
19	B	
20	D	
21	C	
22	A	
23	B	
24	D	
25	A	
26	E	
27	B	
28	A	
29	D	
30	D	
31	A	
32	B	

Question Number	Correct Answer	Your Answer
33	D	
34	C	
35	C	
36	E	
37	A	
38	B	
39	D	
40	A	
41	B	
42	D	
43	E	
44	A	
45	D	
46	A	
47	A	
48	B	
49	E	
50	A	
51	D	
52	E	
53	C	
54	C	
55	A	
56	D	
57	C	
58	C	
59	C	
60	A	
61	B	
62	A	
63	E	
64	D	

Question Number	Correct Answer	Your Answer
65	B	
66	E	
67	B	
68	D	
69	C	
70	A	
71	D	
72	C	
73	D	
74	E	
75	C	
76	D	
77	B	
78	C	
79	A	
80	D	
81	C	
82	E	
83	A	
84	C	
85	A	
86	B	
87	A	
88	B	
89	D	
90	D	
91	A	
92	C	
93	B	
94	D	
95	E	

Introductory Sociology

Description of the Examination

The Introductory Sociology examination is designed to assess an individual's knowledge of the material typically presented in a one-semester introductory sociology course at most colleges and universities. The examination emphasizes basic facts and concepts as well as general theoretical approaches used by sociologists. Highly specialized knowledge of the subject and the methodology of the discipline is not required or measured by the test content.

The examination contains approximately 100 questions to be answered in 90 minutes. Some of these are pretest questions that will not be scored. Any time candidates spend on tutorials and providing personal information is in addition to the actual testing time.

Knowledge and Skills Required

Questions on the Introductory Sociology examination require candidates to demonstrate one or more of the following abilities. Some questions may require more than one of these abilities.

- Identification of specific names, facts, and concepts from sociological literature
- Understanding of relationships between concepts, empirical generalizations, and theoretical propositions of sociology
- Understanding the methods by which sociological relationships are established
- Application of concepts, propositions, and methods to hypothetical situations
- Interpretation of tables and charts

The subject matter of the Introductory Sociology examination is drawn from the following topics. The percentages next to the main topics indicate the approximate percentage of exam questions on that topic.

20% **Institutions**
- Economic
- Educational
- Family
- Medical
- Political
- Religious

10% **Social Patterns**
- Community
- Demography
- Human ecology
- Rural/urban patterns

25% **Social Processes**
- Collective behavior and social movements
- Culture
- Deviance and social control
- Social change
- Social interaction
- Socialization

25% **Social Stratification**
- Aging
- Power and inequality
- Professions and occupations
- Sex and gender roles
- Social class
- Social mobility

20% **The Sociological Perspective**
- History of sociology
- Methods
- Sociological Theory

Introductory Sociology

SAMPLE TEST

DIRECTIONS: Read each item and select the best response

1. **Karl Marx is considered the founder of:**

   A. Structural Functionalism

   B. Rational Choice Theory

   C. Conflict Theory

   D. Racial Formation Theory

   E. Symbolic Interactionism

2. **A process where affluent people (often white) move into urban areas and displace the original lower-income residents (often people of color) is known as:**

   A. Gentrification

   B. Urban decay

   C. White flight

   D. Environmental racism

   E. Steering

3. **The practice of placing students in higher and lower-level curriculum groups based on test scores, grades, and/ or teacher discretion is known as:**

   A. The hidden curriculum

   B. Accomplishment of natural growth

   C. Stereotype threat

   D. Tracking

   E. The hidden threat

4. **Sociologists often use samples to make inferences about a population. The most important quality of a sample is that it is:**

   A. It is easy to conduct

   B. It is inexpensive

   C. It is large

   D. It includes people who do not wish to participate

   E. It is representative of the population

5. In the United States, it is usually considered rude not to make direct eye contact when talking to another person. Making eye contact is therefore an example of a:

   A. Right
   B. Taboo
   C. Norm
   D. Value
   E. Law

6. The process by which we learn how to become members of social and cultural groups is:

   A. Learning
   B. Socialization
   C. Gendering
   D. Societization
   E. Culturalization

7. Failing to cover your mouth when you sneeze is a violation of a:

   A. Taboo
   B. More
   C. Health code
   D. Law
   E. Folkway

8. Sarah is a sociologist studying roller derbies. To collect data she joins a roller derby team. Sarah is conducting a(n):

   A. Survey
   B. Experiment
   C. Content analysis
   D. Ethnography
   E. Natural experiment

9. The theory that views society as an organism in which all parts work together to promote stability is:

   A. Structural Functionalism
   B. Conflict Theory
   C. Symbolic Interactionism
   D. Structuralism
   E. Social Bonding Theory

10. Imagine you wanted to use the sociological imagination to understand depression. To do so, you might consider how an individual's likelihood of experiencing depression is related to:

    A. Personality
    B. Family income
    C. Use of anti-depressants
    D. Genetics
    E. Psychological history

11. When a group of people share a language, values, and a history they are referred to as a(n):

    A. Racial group

    B. Subculture

    C. Family

    D. Tribe

    E. Ethnic group

12. Social mobility happens most frequently in a:

    A. Social class system

    B. Caste system

    C. Feudal system

    D. Slavery system

    E. Royal system

13. Which of the following is NOT a dimension of social class?

    A. Wealth

    B. Income

    C. Race

    D. Educational Attainment

    E. Prestige

14. Which of the following is NOT an example of a social movement?

    A. The Civil Rights Movement

    B. The Gay Rights Movement

    C. Feminism

    D. Roe v. Wade

    E. The Pro-Life Movement

15. Women often do not reach the upper ranks of corporations due to an invisible barrier known as:

    A. The glass escalator

    B. The glass ceiling

    C. Sexism

    D. Discrimination

    E. Racism

16. Most women in the United States take their husband's last name when they marry. This is evidence that the United States is:

    A. Matrilineal

    B. Patrilineal

    C. Patriarchal

    D. Matriarchal

    E. Egalitarian

17. Which of the following terms refers to the belief that an individual's successes and failures in life are solely a result of effort, intelligence, and ability?

    A. Stratification

    B. Class privilege

    C. Ideology

    D. The myth of meritocracy

    E. Color-blind racism

18. "I am never asked to speak for all the people of my racial group" is an example of:

    A. White privilege

    B. Class privilege

    C. Male privilege

    D. Structural inequality

    E. Color-blind racism

19. Who claimed that society is composed of two opposing social classes – the bourgeoisie and the proletariat?

    A. C. Wright Mills

    B. Karl Marx

    C. Max Weber

    D. Emile Durkheim

    E. Auguste Comte

20. Who is considered the founder of sociology?

    A. C. Wright Mills

    B. Karl Marx

    C. Max Weber

    D. Emile Durkheim

    E. Auguste Comte

21. According to Emile Durkheim's famous study on suicide, suicide rates are higher among the unmarried compared to the married. Durkheim argued that this was became unmarried people _____.

    A. Are less happy than married people

    B. Are less likely to be prevented from committing suicide by a spouse

    C. Have weaker social ties

    D. Are less likely to have access to mental health care

    E. Are more likely to be Protestant

22. Teenagers who participate in abstinence-only sex education programs have higher rates of teen pregnancy than teenagers who do not participant in these programs. According to Merton, a famous structural-functionalist, this is an example of a(n) _____.

   A. Manifest function

   B. Latent function

   C. Accidental function

   D. Structural function

   E. Unexpected function

23. Which of the following theories posits that individuals act in ways that are based on meanings formed through social interaction with others?

   A. Structural Functionalism

   B. Rational Choice Theory

   C. Conflict Theory

   D. Racial Formation Theory

   E. Symbolic Interactionism

24. Ricardo tells a joke at a party and everyone stares blankly at him. He interprets their reactions to mean that he is not funny and in turn, worries that he is not a funny person. Ricardo's experience is an example of _____.

   A. The looking glass self

   B. Differentiation of the self

   C. Embarrassment

   D. Imitating others

   E. Taking the role of the other

25. An Asian American woman with a college degree whose parents are doctors is likely to marry an Asian American man with a college degree and whose parents are professionals. This pattern is an example of _____.

   A. Exogamy

   B. Monogamy

   C. Homogamy

   D. Patriarchy

   E. Propinquity

26. Emile Durkheim developed a term to refer to a mismatch between personal standards and larger social standards. This term is _____.

    A. Rebellion

    B. Socialization

    C. Group think

    D. Anomie

    E. Deviance

27. When sociologists conduct experiments, they are attempting to isolate and measure the effect produced by a(n) _____.

    A. Independent variable

    B. Dependent variable

    C. Confounding variable

    D. Mediating variable

    E. Moderating variable

28. A positive correlation or association refers to when _____.

    A. Variables stay the same

    B. Something good happens

    C. One variable goes up and another goes down

    D. Two variables move in opposite directions

    E. Two variables move in the same direction

29. Rowan examined advertisements in magazines in order to understand the different ways that men and women are portrayed in advertisements. This is an example of a(n) _____.

    A. Survey

    B. Experiment

    C. Content analysis

    D. Ethnography

    E. Natural experiment

30. After the passage of Brown v. Board of Education of Topeka, there was a mass exodus of whites from racially-diverse urban areas to racially-homogenous suburbs. This process is: _____.

    A. Gentrification

    B. Urban decay

    C. White flight

    D. Environmental racism

    E. Steering

31. Rates of poverty in the United States are highest for which of the following groups?

    A. The elderly

    B. Children under 18

    C. Unmarried men

    D. Married couple households

    E. Individuals who live in urban areas

32. The fact that environmentally hazardous materials (e.g., toxic waste, pollution) are more likely to be located in low-income or minority communities is referred to as _____.

    A. Gentrification

    B. Urban decay

    C. White flight

    D. Environmental racism

    E. Environmental injustice

33. The fact that, on average, non-white children go to schools with fewer resources compared to white children is an example of _____.

    A. Overt racism

    B. Covert racism

    C. Institutional racism

    D. Prejudice

    E. Segregation

34. Which group has the lowest marriage rates in the United States?

    A. White men

    B. Black men

    C. Hispanic men

    D. Hispanic women

    E. Black women

35. According to Merton's strain theory, which type of deviance occurs when an individual accepts cultural goals (e.g., getting rich) but rejects the socially acceptable means of achieving them (e.g., by stealing)?

    A. Innovation

    B. Conformity

    C. Ritualism

    D. Retreatism

    E. Rebellion

36. Sociologists believe that sex is _____ whereas gender is _____.

    A. Socially constructed; biological

    B. Biological; socially constructed

    C. Relevant; irrelevant

    D. Irrelevant; relevant

    E. Mutable; immutable

37. Over the past several decades, the U.S. economy has shifted from one based on _____ to one based on _____.

    A. Services; manufacturing

    B. Manufacturing; goods

    C. Goods; manufacturing

    D. Manufacturing; services

    E. Finances; goods

38. Which of the following statements about social mobility in the U.S. is false?

    A. Anyone who works hard enough will achieve upward mobility

    B. Most social mobility happens within the middle class (e.g., from lower middle class to upper middle class)

    C. Most people remain in the same social class as their family of origin

    D. Educational attainment matters for social mobility

    E. Social mobility is usually related to societal-level factors, not individual ones

39. If a new employee starts working at a faster pace than the other workers, this an example of _____.

    A. Efficiency

    B. Division of labor

    C. Rate busting

    D. Loafing

    E. Rate setting

40. We are just beginning to witness which of the following large-scale demographic shifts?

    A. An increase in the divorce rate

    B. An increase in age at first marriage

    C. An increase in age at first birth

    D. An increase in the percentage of the population that is 65 and older

    E. An increase in stay-at-home mothers

41. Which of the following demographic trends did NOT occur in the 20th century?

    A. An increase in life expectancy

    B. Migration from urban to rural areas

    C. An increase in female-headed households

    D. An increase in the divorce rate

    E. An increase in the number of women in the labor force

42. **Urban ethnographic sociology emerged from:**

    A. The Chicago school

    B. The New York school

    C. The Harvard school

    D. The Emory school

    E. The Yale school

43. **Which famous sociologist argued that capitalism was a result of the Protestant ethic?**

    A. C. Wright Mills

    B. Karl Marx

    C. Max Weber

    D. Emile Durkheim

    E. Auguste Comte

44. **Which famous sociologist wrote about the power elite?**

    A. C. Wright Mills

    B. Karl Marx

    C. Max Weber

    D. Emile Durkheim

    E. Auguste Comte

45. **Which famous sociologist is considered the first academic sociologist?**

    A. C. Wright Mills

    B. Karl Marx

    C. Max Weber

    D. Emile Durkheim

    E. Auguste Comte

46. **Food deserts refer to:**

    A. Desert communities where there is too much food

    B. Desert communities with unhealthy foods

    C. Desert communities with not enough food

    D. Communities that lack access to fresh, healthy foods

    E. Communities without any restaurants

47. **Which sociological theory maintains that reality is based on culturally agreed upon meanings?**

    A. Rational choice theory

    B. Social constructionism

    C. Positivism

    D. Structural functionalism

    E. Conflict theory

48. **Which statement best describes trends in the economy since the 1970s?**

    A. Declining levels of income inequality

    B. Declining levels of wealth inequality

    C. Declining levels of income and wealth inequality

    D. Increasing levels of income inequality

    E. Increasing levels of income and wealth inequality

49. **What is the term used to describe a process by which human conditions become defined and treated as medical conditions?**

    A. Medicalization

    B. Mentalization

    C. Healthism

    D. Pathologism

    E. Deviation

50. **Which famous sociologist wrote extensively about bureaucracy?**

    A. C. Wright Mills

    B. Karl Marx

    C. Max Weber

    D. Emile Durkheim

    E. Auguste Comte

51. **The McDonaldization of society refers to:**

    A. The spread of McDonald's chains all over the globe

    B. A process by which cultural products become homogenous and predictable

    C. An increase in the number of fast food restaurants

    D. The rise in obesity rates

    E. The rise in the number of foods with preservatives

52. **Research that uses both qualitative and quantitative methods is known as:**

    A. Ethnography

    B. Participant observation

    C. Action research

    D. Experiments

    E. Mixed methods

Introductory Sociology

53. **Quantitative methods are best for:**

    A. Exploratory research

    B. Collecting non-numerical data

    C. Confirming a hypothesis

    D. Generating a new theory

    E. Small sample sizes

54. **Research that attempts to understand the past is referred to as:**

    A. Experimental

    B. Survey research

    C. Ethnography

    D. Historical research

    E. Mixed methods

55. **Brianna moves from a small rural town in Pennsylvania to New York City. She is overwhelmed by the fast pace of life in New York. The term that best describes her experience is _____.**

    A. Culture shock

    B. Socialization

    C. The looking glass self

    D. Deviance

    E. Social control

56. **Which of the following is an example of a counterculture?**

    A. Catholics

    B. The Amish

    C. Nurses

    D. Athletes

    E. Latinos

57. **Which of the following is an example of an occupation in the secondary labor market?**

    A. Physician

    B. Professor

    C. Fast food worker

    D. Lawyer

    E. Plumber

58. **Which of the following statements about stratification is true?**

    A. All societies have equal levels of stratification

    B. All societies have some form of stratification

    C. Capitalist societies have less inequality than socialist ones

    D. Levels of stratification have not changed over time in the U.S.

    E. Social mobility is not possible in class-based societies

59. Behaviors that violate social norms are referred to as _____.

    A. Culture shock
    B. Socialization
    C. The looking glass self
    D. Deviance
    E. Social control

60. Which institution is primarily responsible for reproducing members of society?

    A. The family
    B. The economy
    C. Religion
    D. Education
    E. Politics

61. What explanation does NOT explain why women are paid less than men?

    A. Discrimination
    B. Men and women tend to have different occupations
    C. Men and women tend to have different specialties within occupations
    D. Women have primarily responsibility for childcare
    E. Women are less concerned with income

62. The practice of women taking two or more husbands at a time is known as:

    A. Monogamy
    B. Polygyny
    C. Polyandry
    D. Bigamy
    E. Bisexuality

63. Policies and practices that push schoolchildren (particularly low-income minorities) out of classrooms and into the criminal justice systems is referred to as:

    A. Out of place policing
    B. Steering
    C. Institutional racism
    D. The hidden curriculum
    E. The school-to-prison pipeline

64. Schools in the U.S. have dramatically different levels of resources, in part, because school funding at the local level comes primarily from:

    A. Income taxes
    B. Property taxes
    C. Sales taxes
    D. Donations
    E. Tax credits

Introductory Sociology

65. **Which group is NOT under-represented in the U.S. Congress?**

    A. Women

    B. Latinos

    C. Whites

    D. African Americans

    E. Asian Americans

66. **The process by which existing social roles and norms are altered or replaced by new ones is known as:**

    A. Culture shock

    B. Socialization

    C. The looking glass self

    D. Resocialization

    E. Social control

67. **A type of social movement that advocates for the restoration of a previous social arrangement (e.g., for the repeal of Roe v. Wade) is known as a _____ social movement.**

    A. Reactionary

    B. Reformist

    C. Revolutionary

    D. Personal transformation

    E. Civil Rights

68. **A process by which collective delusions of threats to society spread rapidly through a social group is known as _____.**

    A. Social control

    B. Deviance

    C. Mass hysteria

    D. The bystander effect

    E. The looking glass self

69. **A process by which individuals attempt to influence the perceptions of others is referred to as _____.**

    A. Social control

    B. Deviance

    C. The bystander effect

    D. The looking glass self

    E. Impression management

70. **The process by which individuals do not offer assistance to victims when other people are present is referred to as _____.**

    A. Social control

    B. Deviance

    C. Mass hysteria

    D. The bystander effect

    E. The looking glass self

Introductory Sociology

71. The Hispanic paradox is the name given to describe the fact that despite having lower average incomes than whites, Hispanics in the U.S. have _____ compared to whites.

    A. Higher levels of educational attainment

    B. Better health outcomes

    C. Larger families

    D. Higher marriage rates

    E. Fewer children

72. A medical sociologist would study all of the following topics EXCEPT:

    A. Mortality patterns

    B. Marriage and health

    C. Erectile dysfunction

    D. Cesarean sections

    E. Political candidates

73. Which of the following sociological terms refers to the capacity for individuals to make their own free choices?

    A. Agency

    B. Social control

    C. Structure

    D. Socialization

    E. Resocialization

74. A demographer would study all of the following topics EXCEPT:

    A. Fertility rates

    B. Infant mortality rates

    C. Migration patterns

    D. Reproductive rates

    E. Cultural meanings of in-vitro fertilization

75. In sociological models of social change, what both shapes and limits an individual's agency?

    A. Autonomy

    B. The social structure

    C. The looking glass self

    D. Deviance

    E. Impression management

76. What is the term used to describe discrimination on the basis of age?

    A. Heterosexism

    B. Prejudice

    C. Racism

    D. Ageism

    E. Sexism

77. What is the primary vehicle for upward social mobility in the United States?

   A. Winning the lottery

   B. Inheritance

   C. Education

   D. Hard work

   E. Marriage

78. The term for norms, values, and beliefs that are conveyed indirectly in schools is:

   A. Out of place policing

   B. Steering

   C. Institutional racism

   D. The hidden curriculum

   E. The school-to-prison pipeline

79. Sociologists use the term _____ to describe a decline in the cultural and social significance of religion.

   A. Atheism

   B. Anti-religious

   C. Modernization

   D. Secularization

   E. Rationalization

80. Which sociological theory would argue that because some jobs are important to society, they should be more highly rewarded?

   A. Structural Functionalism

   B. Rational Choice Theory

   C. Conflict Theory

   D. Racial Formation Theory

   E. Symbolic Interactionism

81. What discredited theory maintains that poverty is perpetuated by the cultural deficiencies and behaviors of the poor?

   A. Rational choice theory

   B. Culture of poverty theory

   C. Reproduction of poverty theory

   D. Conflict theory

   E. Racial formation theory

82. A conflict theorist would make which of the following claims about deviance?

   A. Deviance is functional for society

   B. Deviant behaviors only exist among the poor

   C. Deviant behavior is medicalized

   D. Deviant behaviors only exist among the rich

   E. Powerful groups label behaviors that do not benefit them as deviant

83. The way that the federal poverty line is calculated is frequently criticized by sociologists because:

    A. It is subject to interpretation

    B. It overestimates poverty in the U.S.

    C. It treats people as a number

    D. It excludes elder poverty

    E. It underestimates poverty because thresholds were developed in the 1960s and have not been revised to reflect rising costs of housing and healthcare

84. What do sociologists call the process through which we learn what is appropriate for each gender?

    A. Social Learning Theory

    B. Social structure

    C. Socialization

    D. Resocialization

    E. Social control

85. The study of aging is _____.

    A. Demography

    B. Gerontology

    C. Social structure

    D. Socialization

    E. Social control

86. What is the term given for social change that is initiated by individuals or groups with little or no formal institutional power?

    A. Bottom-up social change

    B. Top-down social change

    C. Minion social change

    D. Reactionary social change

    E. Revolutionary social change

87. What term is used to describe a group of people who experienced the same event within the same time period?

    A. Life course

    B. Gerontology

    C. Cohort

    D. Elderly

    E. Baby boomers

88. Residential communities that are within commuting distance to a larger city are known as _____.

    A. Rural areas

    B. Exurbs

    C. Urban areas

    D. Suburbs

    E. Gentrified cities

89. A population shift from rural to urban areas is called _____.

    A. Gentrification
    B. Urbanization
    C. Suburbanization
    D. Exurbanization
    E. Urban renewal

90. What theory maintains that political power is distributed among many groups?

    A. Pluralism
    B. Marxism
    C. Social Learning Theory
    D. Rational Choice Theory
    E. Multiple Group Theory

91. What is the term used in political sociology to describe legitimate or socially approved uses of power?

    A. Bureaucracy
    B. Social control
    C. Deviance
    D. Authority
    E. Rationality

92. What is the term used to describe a process whereby urban areas are revitalized?

    A. Urbanization
    B. Urban renewal
    C. Gentrification
    D. Suburbanization
    E. Exurbanization

93. Efforts to prevent or control deviant behavior is called _____.

    A. Social change
    B. Socialization
    C. Impression management
    D. Rationalization
    E. Social control

94. Which of the following statements about socialization is true?

    A. Socialization begins at birth
    B. Socialization begins when children enter kindergarten
    C. All cultures use the same socialization techniques
    D. Socialization stops in adolescence
    E. Resocialization is not possible

95. Who wrote that religion is the "opium of the people"?

    A. C. Wright Mills

    B. Karl Marx

    C. Max Weber

    D. Emile Durkheim

    E. Auguste Comte

96. Which large-scale economic trend happened in the U.S. in the 1970s?

    A. The number of manufacturing jobs increased

    B. The number of women in the workforce declined

    C. The number of the women in workforce increased

    D. Life expectancy declined

    E. Wages increased for the average worker

97. Which of the following jobs would be considered part of the primary labor market?

    A. A retail employee at a small boutique store

    B. A retail employee at a large discount store

    C. A bus driver

    D. An accountant

    E. A nanny

98. Who believed that culture and ideas were the driving force of social change?

    A. C. Wright Mills

    B. Karl Marx

    C. Max Weber

    D. Emile Durkheim

    E. Auguste Comte

99. The primary source of strain in the typical one-parent household is:

    A. The lack of a male role model

    B. Emotional stress caused by divorce

    C. That the children are being raised by only one parent

    D. Violence

    E. Poverty because most one-parent households are headed by women

100. Examining the linkages between early and later life events is known as _____.

    A. A life course approach

    B. Social Learning Theory

    C. An eco-cycle approach

    D. Resocialization

    E. Rational Choice theory

Introductory Sociology

Answer Key

Question Number	Correct Answer	Your Answer
1	C	
2	A	
3	D	
4	E	
5	C	
6	B	
7	E	
8	D	
9	A	
10	B	
11	E	
12	A	
13	C	
14	D	
15	B	
16	C	
17	D	
18	A	
19	B	
20	E	
21	C	
22	B	
23	E	
24	A	
25	C	
26	D	
27	A	
28	E	
29	C	
30	C	
31	B	
32	D	
33	C	

Question Number	Correct Answer	Your Answer
34	E	
35	A	
36	B	
37	D	
38	A	
39	C	
40	D	
41	B	
42	A	
43	C	
44	A	
45	D	
46	D	
47	B	
48	E	
49	A	
50	C	
51	B	
52	E	
53	C	
54	D	
55	A	
56	B	
57	C	
58	B	
59	D	
60	A	
61	E	
62	C	
63	E	
64	B	
65	C	
66	D	

Question Number	Correct Answer	Your Answer
67	A	
68	C	
69	E	
70	D	
71	B	
72	E	
73	A	
74	E	
75	B	
76	D	
77	C	
78	D	
79	D	
80	A	
81	B	
82	E	
83	E	
84	C	
85	B	
86	A	
87	C	
88	D	
89	B	
90	A	
91	D	
92	B	
93	E	
94	A	
95	B	
96	C	
97	D	
98	C	
99	E	
100	A	

Social Sciences and History

Description of the Examination

The Social Sciences and History examination covers a wide range of topics from the social sciences and history disciplines. While the exam is based on no specific course, its content is drawn from introductory college courses that cover United States history, Western civilization, world history, government/political science, geography, sociology, economics, psychology, and anthropology.

The primary objective of the exam is to give candidates the opportunity to demonstrate that they possess the level of knowledge and understanding expected of college students who meet a distribution or general education requirement in the social sciences/history areas.

The Social Sciences and History examination contains approximately 120 questions to be answered in 90 minutes. Some of them are pretest questions that will not be scored. Any time candidates spend on tutorials and providing personal information is in addition to the actual testing time.

Note: This examination uses the chronological designations b.c.e. (before the common era) and c.e. (common era). These labels correspond to b.c. (before Christ) and a.d. (anno Domini), which are used in some textbooks.

Knowledge and Skills Required

The Social Sciences and History examination requires candidates to demonstrate one or more of the following abilities.
- Familiarity with terminology, facts, conventions, methodology, concepts, principles, generalizations, and theories
- Ability to understand, interpret, and analyze graphic, pictorial, and written material
- Ability to apply abstractions to particulars and to apply hypotheses, concepts, theories, and principles to given data

The content of the exam is drawn from the following disciplines. The percentages next to the main disciplines indicate the approximate percentage of exam questions on that topic.

40% History

Requires general knowledge and understanding of time- and place-specific human experiences. Topics covered include political, diplomatic, social, economic, intellectual, and cultural material.

17% United States History

Covers the colonial period, the American Revolution, the early republic, the Civil War and Reconstruction, industrialization, the Progressive Era, the First World War, the 1920s, the Great Depression and the New Deal, the Second World War, the 1950s, the Cold War, social conflict-the 1960s and 1970s, the late twentieth century

15% Western Civilization

Covers ancient Western Asia, Egypt, Greece, and Rome as well as medieval Europe and modern Europe, including its expansion and outposts in other parts of the world

8% World History

Covers Africa, Asia, Australia, Europe, North America, and South America from prehistory to the present, including global themes and interactions

Social Sciences and History

13% Government/Political Science, including
- Comparative politics
- International relations
- Methods
- United States institutions
- Voting and political behavior

11% Geography, including
- Cartographic methods
- Cultural geography
- Physical geography
- Population
- Regional geography
- Spatial interaction

10% Economics, including
- Economic measurements
- International trade
- Major theorists and schools
- Monetary and fiscal policy
- Product markets
- Resource markets
- Scarcity, choice, and cost

10% Psychology, including
- Aggression
- Biopsychology
- Conformity
- Group process
- Major theorists and schools
- Methods
- Performance
- Personality
- Socialization

10% Sociology, including
- Demography
- Deviance
- Family
- Interaction
- Major theorists and schools
- Methods
- Social change
- Social organization
- Social stratification
- Social theory

6% Anthropology, including
- Cultural anthropology
- Ethnography
- Major theorists and schools
- Methods
- Paleoanthropology

SAMPLE TEST

1. The _____ Incident occurred in August 1964, when two US destroyers were allegedly torpedoed by North Vietnamese, which led to American assistance in South Vietnam – although many claimed, and still maintain, that this was a "false flag" operation.

    A. Ho Chi Minh

    B. Straits of Malacca

    C. Mekong River

    D. Tet Offensive

    E. Gulf of Tonkin

2. What did opponents in America call the purchase of Alaska from the Russians in 1867, named after the contemporary Republican Party Secretary of State that orchestrated the move?

    A. Putyatin's Madness

    B. Johnson's Fault

    C. Seward's Folly

    D. Sitka's Scandal

    E. Barker's Blunder

3. Which nation did the United States fight against in the War of 1812?

    A. The United Kingdom

    B. Cuba

    C. Japan

    D. Russia

    E. France

4. Which of the following foreign policies accurately represents the 1947 Truman Doctrine?

    A. Providing aid to any country that wanted to rollback its political system

    B. Providing aid to the Midwest to improve their healthcare

    C. Providing aid to Southeast Asian nations so they could compete with India

    D. Providing aid to European countries because they were poor

    E. Providing aid to democratic countries to contain the spread of communism

Social Sciences and History

5. **In May 1790, Rhode Island became the final state to ratify which of the following documents?**

   A. Homestead Act

   B. Constitution of the United States

   C. Civil Rights Act

   D. Emancipation Proclamation

   E. Declaration of Independence

6. **As a result of United States intervention in the Cuban War of Independence (1895-1898), which of the following countries did the United States declare war on in 1898?**

   A. Canada

   B. Russia

   C. France

   D. Spain

   E. The United Kingdom

7. **What event are the Sons of Liberty best known for undertaking?**

   A. The assassination of Archduke Franz Ferdinand of Austria, 1914

   B. The Massacre of Wounded Knee, 1890

   C. The Pueblo Revolt, 1680

   D. The River Run Riot, 2002

   E. The Boston Tea Party, 1773

8. **What was the major result of the American victory against Japan in the Battle of Leyte Gulf, Philippines, in 1944?**

   A. The Japanese retaliated by striking at the American fleet stationed at Pearl Harbor

   B. The Japanese fleet was effectively destroyed, causing them to abandon their occupation of Southeast Asia and crippling their Pacific naval force

   C. The Japanese army decided that Indonesia and Borneo were easier targets, and invaded them the following year in their 'Dutch East Indies campaign'

   D. The Philippines were then divided between America and Japan, allowing each country to exploit resources found in the archipelago

   E. The Japanese fleet escaped to their naval bases to refuel before returning in even greater numbers in 1946

9. What does "virtual representation" mean, in the context of the American War of Independence?

   A. Members of British Parliament claimed to have to the right to speak for and manage the affairs of all British subjects around the world

   B. The claiming of federal land grants by ex-slaves aged 21 years or over

   C. Native American tribes campaigned for their own representatives in the United States government

   D. The United States leadership provided grants of land for third-level educational institutes to train the next generation of politicians

   E. Citizens of the United States wanted the right to vote over the internet and by post

10. Which U.S. president ordered the invasion of the Bay of Pigs, and in which year?

    A. Lyndon B. Johnson, 1964

    B. Harry S. Truman, 1962

    C. John F. Kennedy, 1961

    D. Dwight D. Eisenhower, 1960

    E. Richard M. Nixon, 1963

11. Which event eventually led to the resignation of President Richard Nixon?

    A. The Florida State Voting Recount

    B. The Chappaquiddick Incident

    C. The Watergate Scandal

    D. The Lewinsky Affair

    E. Abu Ghraib prison abuse

12. Which Native American tribe separated from the Shoshone after the Pueblo Revolt (1680), and were famous for their prowess on horseback? They occupied the southwest Great Plains, and today mainly reside in Oklahoma, Texas and New Mexico.

    A. Apache

    B. Wampanoag

    C. Ojibwe

    D. Comanche

    E. Sioux

13. Following the Indian Removal Act (1830), a number of Native American nations were forcibly relocated from their ancestral homelands in the American Southeast to "Indian Territory" west of the Mississippi. By what name is this event known as?

    A. The Quetta Annexation

    B. The Trail of Tears

    C. The Expulsion of the Moriscos

    D. The Highland Clearances

    E. The Santiago de Compostela

14. What did the Thirteenth Amendment to the Constitution, passed in December 1865, accomplish?

    A. Abolition of slavery, except as punishment for a crime

    B. Protected the right to keep and bear arms

    C. The right to be secure against unreasonable searches and seizures

    D. Began electing US Senators by popular vote

    E. Provided the right to trial by jury

15. Which of the following occurred between 1800 and 1900?

    A. George Washington died

    B. New Mexico became the 47th US state

    C. Native Americans given the right to vote

    D. The Wall Street Crash

    E. The *Cross of Gold* speech was delivered by William Jennings Bryan

16. What was the "Dust Bowl", which had a phenomenal influence on the severity of the Great Depression?

    A. An act passed which raised import duties for alcohol, causing widespread protests by those in need of drink

    B. A giant curved dam was built at Grand Rapids, Michigan, which caused major rivers to dry up and the water table to sink

    C. Thousands of banks closed across the country, resulting in them becoming derelict and dusty

    D. A series of dust storms blew across the United States, causing widespread agricultural damage

    E. It is another name for the stock market crash on 'Black Tuesday'

17. Which of the following was not a cause of the period of fear and paranoia during 1919-20 known as the First Red Scare?

    A. The Sedition Act

    B. Senator Joseph McCarthy's anti-communist campaigns

    C. Labor strikes

    D. The Haymarket massacre

    E. Bolshevik Russian Revolution

18. What important Civil Rights Movement incident lasted for over a year from 1955 in Montgomery, Alabama?

    A. A series of church bombings occurred, killing many in the black community

    B. A march was led from Montgomery to Washington, where Martin Luther King gave his "I have a dream" speech

    C. Refusal of the black community to ride on segregated buses

    D. Four black college students engaged in 'sit-ins' at a number of restaurants where black patrons were not served

    E. Riots were held in a local university over the enrolment of the school's first black student, until federal troops were sent to enforce the law

19. Which bilateral conferences occurred between the USA and Soviet Union in the 1970s to reach agreements on the control of nuclear armaments?

    A. The Strategic Arms Limitation Talks

    B. The Committee on Disarmament Conference

    C. The Hague Peace Conference

    D. The Washington Atomic Treaty

    E. The Nuclear Weapons Convention

20. Which Act of Congress was passed in 2001 to assist in the monitoring and detainment of terrorists, and continues to this day?

    A. The Stolen Valor Act

    B. The CAN-SPAM Act

    C. The PROTECT Act

    D. The Risk-Based Security Screening Act

    E. The PATRIOT Act

21. The "Great Famine" of 1845-1852 caused hundreds of thousands of people from which nation to immigrate to the USA?

    A. Germany

    B. Spain

    C. China

    D. Ireland

    E. Mexico

22. What was *Pax Romana*?

    A. A period of peace and stability experienced by those within the Roman Empire

    B. A romantic Roman play about Marc Antony's relationship with Cleopatra

    C. A failed Roman military campaign against Scotland

    D. A network of trade routes that connected Rome with Central Asia

    E. A tax enforced by the Roman Empire

23. The wealth of the Dutch Empire was largely built from shipping and trade to the profitable colonies of the Dutch East India Company, one of the earliest multi-national corporations. Which of the following was a colony of the Dutch East India Company?

    A. Batavia, now Jakarta

    B. Goa

    C. Singapore

    D. Hong Kong

    E. Seychelles

24. Which of the following describes a feudal system?

    A. The king did not own the land, but divided it between his barons into numerous independent states

    B. Knights farmed the land for their barons

    C. Peasants vote to elect their leaders

    D. The church belongs to the people

    E. The noble or lord has power

Social Sciences and History

25. Which individual led armies that created an empire stretching from the Danube in Europe to Egypt, and as far east as India in the 4th century BCE?

    A. Hannibal

    B. Cyrus the Great

    C. Alexander the Great

    D. Qin Shi Huang

    E. Julius Caesar

26. In which Greek tragedy by Sophocles (497 – 406 BCE) does the protagonist inadvertently murder his own father and sleep with his mother, fulfilling a prophecy made by the oracle at Delphi?

    A. The Bacchae

    B. Oedipus the King

    C. Medea

    D. The Iliad

    E. Prometheus Bound

27. Which war took place between Athens and Sparta during the 5th century BCE, and was recorded by Thucydides – considered one of the earliest historians?

    A. War of Pyrrhus

    B. Alexander the Great's campaign

    C. Greco-Persian War

    D. Peloponnesian War

    E. Trojan War

28. Which group of Turks ruled an enormous empire from Mesopotamia to Iran during the time of the First and Second Crusades, before being defeated by the Mongols at the Battle of Köse Dağ (1243)?

    A. Uyghurs

    B. Ottomans

    C. Mamluks

    D. Seljuks

    E. Ayyubids

Social Sciences and History

29. In November 1095 Pope Urban II gave a sermon to the French aristocracy at the Council of Clermont. The following year, what military campaign began?

    A. The First Crusade

    B. The War of the Spanish Succession

    C. The First Balkan War

    D. The conquest of Gaul

    E. The invasion of Northern Germany

30. During the Age of Enlightenment, which event resulted in William of Orange invading England, overthrowing the king, and forever changing the structure of the British monarchy by inextricably linking monarchic with parliamentary power?

    A. The Fronde (1648 - 1653)

    B. The Glorious Revolution (1688)

    C. Pontiac's Rebellion (1763 - 1766)

    D. The Jacobite risings (1688 - 1746)

    E. The Camisard Rebellion (1702 - 1715)

31. Who wrote *The Wealth of Nations* in 1776?

    A. John Keynes

    B. Karl Marx

    C. Irving Fisher

    D. John Locke

    E. Adam Smith

32. Which of the following is an appropriate explanation of humanism, as developed during the Renaissance?

    A. The belief that man can live an ethical and civil life on Earth by studying moral philosophy, history, rhetoric and poetry from Greek and Roman sources

    B. The belief that people as a whole should not be able to read, write, debate, or question how the people are managed

    C. The belief that humans evolved from primates, diverging about 85 million years ago

    D. The belief that we can learn nothing from Classical, pagan works of art, other than how past cultures were hedonistic

    E. The belief that we can trust certain, educated, elite individuals to properly understand the world and promote how we should live

33. **During the early 16th century Pope Leo X sold indulgences in order to pay for the reconstruction of St. Peter's Basilica in Rome. What are indulgences, in this case?**

    A. Beautifully illuminated copies of the Bible

    B. Holders did not have to engage in fasting during Lent

    C. Pardons for one's own sins or the sins of their family

    D. Licences to produce wine

    E. Temporarily allowed monks and nuns to engage in sexual encounters

34. **Influenced by both the American Revolution and Enlightenment thought, what important document advocating "natural, unalienable and sacred" human rights was signed in France in August 1789?**

    A. Rights of Man, by Thomas Paine

    B. Code of Hammurabi

    C. Summa Theologica

    D. Magna Carta

    E. Declaration of the Rights of Man and of the Citizen

35. **The French National Day is July 14th, when it celebrates what event of the French Revolution that occurred in 1789?**

    A. French occupation of Nice

    B. Storming of the Bastille

    C. Napoleon's Egyptian expedition

    D. The fall of Robespierre after the period known as 'the Terror'

    E. Louis XVI beheaded

36. **At which battle did the British destroy Napoleon Bonaparte's fleet in 1805?**

    A. Trafalgar

    B. Somme

    C. Gallipoli

    D. Culloden

    E. Waterloo

Social Sciences and History

37. Which of the following was the most immediate result of the February Revolution in Russia in 1917?

    A. The formation of the USSR

    B. The Grand Duke of Muscovy took power

    C. Peter I (commonly known as 'the Great') responded by modernizing the Russian army

    D. Abdication of Tsar Nicholas II

    E. Execution of the Romanov family

38. In 1917, Vladimir Lenin started an organisation called the Cheka which was dissolved in 1922. What was the Cheka's role?

    A. A group in charge of stimulating peaceful diplomatic relations with the Germans

    B. Build a trans-Siberian railroad to Vladivostok

    C. The governmental department in charge of collectivizing farms

    D. Early Soviet secret police

    E. Radio station primarily used to promote propaganda

39. The Pyramid of Cheops was built by the Pharaoh Khufu during the Old Kingdom of Egypt (3rd millennium BCE) on the Giza Plateau, and is famous around the world as one of the Seven Wonders of the Ancient World. Which of the following monumental structures is also found on the Giza Plateau?

    A. Luxor Temple

    B. Valley of the Kings

    C. Temple of Hatshepsut

    D. Abu Simbel

    E. Great Sphinx

40. In what area of the world did the Second Boer War (1899 – 1910) between the United Kingdom and the Orange Free State take place?

    A. South Africa

    B. Turkey

    C. Argentina

    D. France

    E. Belgium

Social Sciences and History

41. The famous 9th century temple of Borobudur in Java, Indonesia, was a monument for which religion?

A. Islam

B. Daoism

C. Shinto

D. Buddhism

E. Christianity

42. Over 40 countries lay claim UNESCO's World Heritage status from having been involved in the material and cultural movements of the land- and maritime-based Silk Roads. Which of the following countries did the 'Silk Road' not pass through?

A. India

B. Iran

C. Morocco

D. Jordan

E. China

43. What was the "Mandate of Heaven"?

A. The name of Horatio Nelson's flagship, on which he was shot and died during the Napoleonic Wars

B. A plot device used in ancient Greek and Roman plays to suddenly solve or conclude a seemingly unsolvable issue

C. A document nailed to the door of All Saints' Church in Wittenberg by Martin Luther, which is believed to have started the Protestant Reformation

D. An ancient Chinese concept of legitimacy used by the emperors to justify their rule

E. The approval given by the Spanish crown to Christopher Columbus to make his first voyage west

44. Which Chinese admiral embarked with a fleet of over three hundred ships on a series of seven exploratory voyages around Southeast Asia and East Africa the in the early 15th century?

A. Xuanzang

B. Hong Xiuquan

C. Marco Polo

D. Jiang Zemin

E. Zheng He

45. What did the Treaty of Versailles accomplish?

   A. Partitioned the Carolingian Empire

   B. Ended the First World War

   C. Ended the Thirty Years War

   D. Created the Vatican City as an independent state

   E. Ended the Russo-Japanese War

46. The Russo-Japanese War (1904 – 1905) formally ended with the Treaty of Portsmouth. Which of the following is an accurate result of this war?

   A. Russia's victory was met with sympathy and support by countries throughout the rest of East and South-East Asia, as well as confirming Western imperial superiority over non-Western powers.

   B. Japan was awarded the northern part of Sakhalin Island, though had to concede its presence in Port Arthur, Manchuria and Korea to Russia

   C. The Tsar agreed to pay indemnities to Japan, in return for keeping the important strategic location of Port Arthur and the endpoint of the Trans-Siberian Railway

   D. The Meiji Emperor's defeat forced Japan to remove their presence from Manchuria and Korea, causing them to abandon their efforts to establish imperial hegemony in East Asia and undergo a further decade of isolationism

   E. The southern half of Sakhalin Island, Southern Manchuria and Korea were ceded to the Japanese, forcing Russia to withdraw as the country faced internal revolution

47. Francisco Pizarro was a Spanish conquistador that conquered which South American empire in the 16th century?

   A. Incan

   B. Assyrian

   C. Teotihuacan

   D. Mayan

   E. Aztec

48. Which of the following is a result of the 1949 Chinese Communist Revolution?

   A. Political power in China became unified under a stable republic led by Yuan Shikai

   B. Chiang Kai-shek proclaimed Taipei, Taiwan, as the capital of the communist People's Republic of China

   C. It sparked the "Great Leap Forward" the following year, which aimed to transform China into a socialist society

   D. Liu Shaoqi was elected as the first Premier of the People's Republic of China, and spent the following decade establishing diplomatic links with the USA.

   E. Political power in China became divided between two parties: the People's Republic of China led by Mao Zedong and the Kuomintang led by Chiang Kai-shek

49. The Commonwealth Games is an international sporting event that is celebrated every four years by athletes from the Commonwealth of Nations. The Commonwealth of Nations is composed of which of the following?

   A. All members of the League of Nations

   B. Countries that possess one or more UNESCO World Heritage Sites

   C. Former and current territories of the British Empire

   D. Member-countries of the Olympic Council of Asia

   E. All countries in the Arab League

50. When referring to Canada as a realm in the Commonwealth of Nations, which of the following is an ongoing diplomatic link between Canada and the United Kingdom?

   A. The UK is aiding Canada's attempts in becoming a member of the G20 by 2016

   B. Both countries were founding members of the League of Nations

   C. Both countries are members of the Organization of American States

   D. Over the last decade the UK has become Canada's largest source of immigration

   E. Both countries share the same monarch as head of state, Queen Elizabeth II

51. **Debates between Germany and Greece over how to overcome the Greek debt crisis have intensified since 2009, and have worsened since Greece failed to make their International Monetary fund (IMF) repayment in June 2015. One contentious solution pursued by the recent Greek Prime Minister Alexis Tsipras is a €278.7bn payment from Germany, for which of the following reasons?**

    A. To boost Greece's tourism sector, which has been overtaken by Germany's

    B. German taxpayers are amongst the worst in Europe for outstanding tax debts, and are thus hypocrites

    C. Germany has a lower population than Greece, but is much richer and can thus afford to spare the funding

    D. It will let Germany off from funding other potentially indebted governments in the future

    E. Germany owes war reparations as compensation for Nazi activities in Greece during World War II

52. **When you plead the Fifth Amendment, what are you doing?**

    A. Defending your right to vote as an individual aged over 18

    B. Defending your right not to be enslaved

    C. Defending your right to bear arms

    D. Refuse to answer a question to prevent self-incrimination

    E. Refusing to allow an unreasonable search or seizure of property

53. **Why is the constitution known as a "living document"?**

    A. It cannot be amended any more

    B. It was written on vellum (animal hide), rather than paper

    C. It can dynamically change and be edited depending on the current social context

    D. It continues to reflect the values of its initial 39 signatories

    E. It applies to all citizens of the United States

54. **What does "naturalization" mean?**

    A. For a non-citizen to become a recognized citizen of a state

    B. The conquering and subsequent transformation of a nation-state by one of a different political structure, e.g. communism to democracy

    C. The process by which an urban zone becomes redefined as a rural zone

    D. To advocate and practice social nudity

    E. An educational campaign that promotes heterosexuality

55. **What does 'gerrymandering' refer to?**

    A. Illegally tapping communication networks, such as mobile telephones or internet connections, with the intention of blackmailing the victim

    B. It is another word for door-to-door canvassing during a political campaign

    C. Manipulating electoral district boundaries in order to achieve an advantageous result for one party

    D. The annual burning of an effigy in the form on a particularly despised politician, as a form of protest

    E. Bribing or otherwise incentivizing a group of people to vote for a certain official

56. **Which of the following is an example of a welfare state?**

    A. Egypt

    B. Brazil

    C. The United Kingdom

    D. Russia

    E. India

57. **What are "checks and balances", as established by the constitution?**

    A. Ensuring no single branch of government has an unfair advantage or becomes too independent or powerful, by giving other branches the ability to limit the other's actions.

    B. Maintains that all people should be treated equally, regardless of race, color, gender, physical or mental ability, or religion

    C. Gives members of the government freedom to independently implement their policies by providing funding, for which they must apply with a proposal

    D. Guarantees a regular supply of money to the country, by making it illegal to destroy cash or print your own currency

    E. Gives US citizens the right to manage their own banking affairs through web-banking platforms, though not all banks provide this

Social Sciences and History

58. Which of the following most accurately describes a socialist government?

A. A government ruled by those who seek to enforce the will of God

B. Active and controlling role in the economy with many government institutions

C. Government is almost absent, with the individual freedom of the people emphasized, allowing them to make their own economic decisions

D. A prime minister is head of state, in which they can influence the economy for only as long as they remain elected

E. Small groups of leaders elected for their intelligence and wealth, who play a minimal role in society

59. What is "Common Law", when referring to the United States and England?

A. Regulations that restrict a government's ability to make drastic changes to the political system

B. Laws made by collective legislature, resulting in the creation of a formal written statute

C. The resolution of disputes between these two countries at a neutral international court

D. System of courts that applies the law to the "common" people

E. Judicial laws that derive their legitimacy from norms and customs developed gradually over time

60. Which of the following is an accurate description of "Manifest Destiny", as promoted in the USA?

   A. The belief that sovereignty is granted by the people, in exchange for protection afforded to them by the government

   B. The right of the American president to be re-elected, so as to give them an opportunity to complete their policies

   C. The belief that Americans should not be bound by British law

   D. The belief that heaven had granted US presidents the right to rule based on their moral authority

   E. The right of the American government to stretch their power over the entire continent, from coast to coast

61. What did the 1789 Judiciary Act achieve?

   A. Provided federal land grants to adults

   B. Established the federal court system

   C. Introduced the "separate but equal" doctrine

   D. Allowed citizenship in the United States by birth or naturalization

   E. Enabled the direct election of senators

62. What was the major result of the 1965 Voting Rights Act?

   A. Prevented racial discrimination in voting

   B. Gave Native Americans the right to vote

   C. Gave overseas citizens the right to vote

   D. Gave women the right to vote

   E. Abolished property requirements to vote for all men

63. Which of the following describes "suffrage"?

   A. The right to citizenship

   B. The right to education

   C. The right to vote

   D. The right to be free from suffering

   E. The right to free speech

64. Medieval maps of the world are known by what name? They often serve as minor encyclopaedias, with navigational accuracy sacrificed for illustrative classical imagery.

    A. Archaeomaps

    B. Kunyu Quantu

    C. Dymaxion maps

    D. Mappa Mundi

    E. Choropleth maps

65. 'Mercator' is an example of what type of map projection? It provides greater accuracy around the equator, decreasing in accuracy the further away from this central line.

    A. Polyhedral

    B. Cylindrical

    C. Azimuthal

    D. Conic

    E. None of the above

66. The concentric zone model, developed by Ernest Burgess in 1925, is most commonly used to examine what?

    A. Urbanization

    B. Precipitation

    C. Place names

    D. Traffic flow

    E. Death rates

67. When referring to the use of Geographic Information Systems (GIS), which of the following is not true about rasters?

    A. Naturally good at handling image data

    B. Ideal for analysis of landscape

    C. Space is divided into cells of the same size (tessellation)

    D. Data is stored in a matrix

    E. Good for studying clearly bounded entities

68. There have been several proposals throughout history for creating a bridge over which body of water separating Russia from Alaska?

    A. Dardanelles

    B. Bering Strait

    C. Great Belt

    D. Naruto Strait

    E. Alas Strait

Social Sciences and History

69. The contiguous United States are composed of _____.

   A. Alaska, Hawaii, and any overseas territories

   B. 50 U.S. states, the District of Columbia, and any overseas territories

   C. 48 U.S. states and the District of Columbia

   D. 50 U.S. states and the District of Columbia

   E. 52 U.S. states and the District of Columbia

70. Which of these was a result of divergent plate tectonics?

   A. San Andreas Fault

   B. Andes mountain range

   C. The island of Iceland

   D. Japan

   E. The Himalaya mountain range

71. Swash, backwash, prevailing wind, and transportation of sand are all features of which coastal phenomenon?

   A. Melting ice caps

   B. Blowholes

   C. Wave cut platforms

   D. Wave refraction

   E. Longshore drift

72. Afghanistan can be described as going through the second stage of the Demographic Transition Model, otherwise known as the early expanding stage. Which of these are true for this stage?

   A. High birth rate, falling death rate, rising population

   B. Low birth rate, high death rate, falling population

   C. Low birth rate, low death rate, rising population

   D. High birth rate, low death rate, falling population

   E. High birth rate, high death rate, low and stagnant population

73. What name is Southern Italy otherwise known by? The region is widely studied as part of a North-South economic divide in the country, due in part to widespread corruption and violence by the mafia.

   A. Piedmont

   B. Isole

   C. Centro

   D. Mezzogiorno

   E. Settentrione

Social Sciences and History

74. A study is made that estimates changes to network traffic following the widespread adoption of fiber-optic cables. This was in response to local demand for faster internet. What type of spatial analysis is the study likely to use when examining issues of accessibility and connectivity?

    A. Spatial interpolation

    B. Complete spatial randomness

    C. Spatial epidemiology

    D. Spatial interaction

    E. Spatial regression

75. In which country is the caste system prevalent?

    A. Russia

    B. Mexico

    C. Egypt

    D. China

    E. India

76. Which terrestrial biome exhibits these characteristics: permanently frozen soil, low precipitation, and low temperature? Example flora includes shrubs, lichens and mosses. Example fauna includes hares, wolves, and an absence of reptiles.

    A. Mangrove

    B. Temperate coniferous forests

    C. Tundra

    D. Semiarid savanna

    E. Xeric shrub land

77. The current capital city of Turkey has been known by many names since its founding in the 7th century BCE. Which of the following has not been a name of the city?

    A. Byzantium

    B. Constantinople

    C. Istanbul

    D. Stamboul

    E. Alexandria

Social Sciences and History

78. **Which of the following would not normally cause a supply shock?**

    A. Discovery that a certain brand of aspirin causes cancer

    B. Foot and mouth disease hitting a herd of cattle

    C. Adoption of robots providing increased productivity in a car factory

    D. Hurricane Katrina sweeping over an industrial estate

    E. Discovery of a cheaper substitute for gasoline

79. **What does PED stand for, in the economic sense of a commodity's ability to adapt its supply or cost based on changing circumstances?**

    A. Penny Extension Drive

    B. Price Elasticity of Demand

    C. Performance Enhancing Demand

    D. Pressured Economics Directive

    E. Personal Emergency Demand

80. **A market is in equilibrium when:**

    A. Quantity of goods supplied is in excess of the quantity demanded

    B. Quantity of goods supplied is below the quantity demanded

    C. Buyers spend all of their money

    D. Excess demand is zero

    E. Price ceilings stop restricting free market prices

81. **Which of the following is an argument that supports the idea that university students should have to pay for their own fees, rather than the taxpayer?**

    A. The top universities are not under too much pressure, and could comfortably accept on many new students

    B. It encourages the proliferation of less conventional university courses, such as 'Surf Science and Technology'

    C. It will scare off international students, meaning that universities can accept more local students

    D. The state has more than enough money to spare, and should offer subsidies for education

    E. They are deriving private benefit from the experience, and will be the sole ones to gain from the education

82. **Which of the following is not a member of the OPEC?**

    A. Iran

    B. Iraq

    C. Afghanistan

    D. Saudi Arabia

    E. Venezuela

Social Sciences and History

83. The German government suddenly decides to impose a minimum price for Sauerkraut that is below the existing market price. The existing market price was originally higher than the equilibrium price, but what effect will this change have?

    A. Increases supply, as manufacturers are making more of a profit

    B. Decreases supply, as manufacturers are operating on a loss

    C. Causes demand to decrease

    D. Customers now have to pay higher prices for the goods

    E. It has no effect

84. The USA acquires most of its oil from _____.

    A. The USA

    B. Mexico

    C. The United Arab Emirates

    D. Israel

    E. Iraq

85. What is a laissez-faire economic system?

    A. One in which government has a total, authoritarian control over its people

    B. One in which government provides a lot of welfare

    C. One in which members of government are given special privileges and subsidies

    D. One in which government enforces widespread regulations and tariffs

    E. One in which government stays out of economic affairs

86. When we raise the price of a product, the _____ states that this will lower the quantity required of the product.

    A. Law of reflux

    B. Okun's law

    C. Law of demand

    D. Law of profit

    E. Law of quantity

87. Which of the following would not cause changes to a demand curve?

    A. Changes in taste

    B. Changes in the price of the good itself

    C. Changes in consumer incomes

    D. Changes in the price of related goods

    E. Changes in preference

Social Sciences and History

88. A person is late for work, and decides to drive in order to make up time. However, it appears that everybody else has thought of the same thing, and the driver finds that the roads are extremely congested. Which of the following would not be an appropriate description of this shared abuse of public roads – resulting in it being harmful for the group as a whole?

    A. Overexploitation

    B. Zelinsky Model of Migration Transition

    C. Chain reaction

    D. Social trap

    E. Tragedy of the Commons

89. China's per capita water resources are only 28% of the global average, which is one of the lowest levels in the world. The scarcity of water in China today, especially drinking water, has had a devastating effect upon which of the following?

    A. China's annual GDP

    B. growth in China's cities

    C. infant mortality in rural villages

    D. accelerated shrinking of lakes and drying of rivers

    E. all of the above

90. Which psychological model describes the development of long-term interpersonal relationships, such as that between a mother and child, and in particular how humans respond when that relationship is threatened?

    A. Maslow's hierarchy of needs

    B. Kohlberg's stages of moral development

    C. Attachment theory

    D. Triarchic theory of intelligence

    E. Theory of multiple intelligences

91. An individual constantly exaggerates their own self-importance, clearly indicates that they want to be desired by everyone, and at the same time rarely shows empathy for others. These could indicate a _____.

    A. Schizotypal personality disorder

    B. Avoidant personality disorder

    C. Borderline personality disorder

    D. Paranoid personality disorder

    E. Narcissistic personality disorder

Social Sciences and History

92. Which of the following does the brain produce in its normal state when an individual is awake during the day?

    A. Beta waves
    B. Delta waves
    C. Gamma waves
    D. Zeta waves
    E. Theta waves

93. _____ is best known for focusing on the dynamics between the id, ego and superego with their psychoanalytical approach?

    A. Jean Piaget
    B. Sigmund Freud
    C. Carl Rogers
    D. Ivan Pavlov
    E. Kurt Lewin

94. Which of the following is an example of impulsive-aggressive behavior?

    A. Two siblings get into an argument over whose turn it is to play on the video game console, and they resolve the situation by talking it out and reaching a compromise

    B. A school group bully a member of the class by gossiping behind their back, and always pretends to be nice whenever the individual is in their presence

    C. A member of Jane's family always rolls their eyes whenever she says something silly

    D. An individual is very insulted by a statement they overhear, but decide to ignore it and move on

    E. A car driver has to brake suddenly when a cyclist cuts in front. The driver of the car sounds their horn, shouts angrily, and speeds up so as to intimidate the cyclist.

95. Who created a theory of cognitive development that explores the influence childhood has on the development of a person's intelligence?

    A. Ivan Pavlov
    B. Albert Bandura
    C. Jean Piaget
    D. Sigmund Freud
    E. F. Skinner

Social Sciences and History

96. What is a control group?

   A. A group that creates the research plan, and ensures that it stays on track

   B. A group of shareholders that funds research

   C. A group that receives no treatment during an experiment

   D. A group that is studied, but the results of which are ignored in the final synthesis

   E. A group that is complete control over what takes place during an experiment

97. A schoolchild learns that when they receive good grades in class they will be rewarded by their parents with a trip to the cinema, but if they receive poor grades the trip to the cinema is withdrawn. This is an example of:

   A. Innateness theory

   B. Phylogeny

   C. Classical conditioning

   D. Operant conditioning

   E. Ethology

98. An individual is convinced that a slight headache they are experiencing means that they possess a brain tumor. They are not faking the symptoms, but what somatoform disorder may they be experiencing?

   A. Hypochondria

   B. Kleptomania

   C. Dyspareunia

   D. Bulimia nervosa

   E. Erotomania

99. We are able to visualize the world in three dimensions because of which ability?

   A. Nociception

   B. Peripheral vision

   C. Chronoception

   D. Vestibular sense

   E. Depth perception

100. Which theory maintains that people's actions are motivated by their biological impulses?

   A. Drive reduction theory

   B. Disposition deterioration theory

   C. Instinct decline theory

   D. Impulse decrease theory

   E. Motivation collapse theory

Social Sciences and History

101. What is meant by describing someone as being conscientious?

A. They have a tendency to promote a certain point of view above all others

B. They have a tendency to be self-disciplined and organized

C. They have a tendency to exaggerate their own merits or importance

D. They have a tendency to be extremely self-aware, through regular meditation

E. They have a tendency to be lazy and unreliable

102. Which of the following is an example of cultural lag?

A. The technological advancement of smartphones is being readily accepted by global society, resulting in features such as touchscreens, cameras, and access to social networking being made available to a growing number of the world's population.

B. Although their status has changed in recent decades, the rights of women in Saudi Arabia are denounced by some other nations as being extremely limited, although they are considered normal and acceptable by the conservative majority within that nation.

C. A European student is attending an exchange program at a school in Beijing, and feels extremely confused, nervous and disoriented for the first few weeks of living there. This is because they react to elements of Chinese culture differently, such as unusual food, the unfamiliar language and public spitting.

D. Many members of 19th century European imperial powers, such as the British Empire and Dutch Empire, which occupied lands in Asia, Africa and the Americas, believed that the indigenous cultures were largely primitive and would benefit from their colonial presence.

E. The fertilization of a mother's egg occurs in a laboratory environment, using the donated sperm of an unknown male. This is not fully accepted by most of society, and protests occur due to long-established ideas of parenthood, as well as ongoing debates over potential social, psychological, and legal harm that this procedure might cause.

103. Which of the following would not make an appropriate study using a conflict-theory perspective?

   A. How youth crime's relation to mainstream values being imposed on them

   B. How a nation went through stages of feudalism, capitalism and socialism throughout their history

   C. How social cohesion is enforced by institutions in a society

   D. The factors leading to a divide between those who are most wealthy in society and those who primarily engage in labor

   E. How the main economic "classes" of the nation/world create society by clashing

104. In 1991, Clark McPhail's study of collective behavior *The Myth of the Madding Crowd* identified a number of types of convergent and collective behavior – known as his 'assembling perspective'. Which of the following is an example of collective locomotion?

   A. The audience at a conference all facing the speaker

   B. Everybody screams when a roller coaster begins to plunge

   C. A marching band carrying their array of instruments

   D. A congregation speaking *The Lord's Prayer* in church

   E. Jumping for joy when your favorite sports team scores a point

105. Which of the following is a latent function of education?

   A. Taught the duties of a patriotism and citizenship

   B. Identify what your position in society may be after school, based on your talents

   C. Realize the importance of punctuality and self-discipline

   D. Started dating your classmate, who became your life-long partner

   E. Taught the value of discipline by your teacher

106. Sociologists have noticed that in many modern nations gerontocracy has been reduced, changing the social standing of certain groups of people in terms of wealth, prestige, and job opportunities. In a gerontocratic society, who would have the most power and influence?

   A. Children of the previous rulers

   B. The oldest members of society

   C. Younger males

   D. Women who have had at least one child

   E. Nobody has more power – it is shared amongst all members of the adult population

107. **Mothers Against Drunk Driving (MADD) is a national group attempting to change one specific thing about the social structure: to stop drunk driving. What type of social movement is this?**

    A. Resistance movement

    B. Religious movement

    C. Revolutionary movement

    D. Alternative movement

    E. Reform movement

108. **This sociologist's book, *The Elementary Forms of the Religious Life* (1912), studied the role of religion in social life by looking at totemism in Aboriginal Australian communities. Who are they?**

    A. Émile Durkheim

    B. Michel Foucault

    C. Erving Goffman

    D. Daniel Bell

    E. Charles Wright Mills

109. **What social movement started in the 1960s, continued for two decades, and resulted in the formation of the National Organization for Women?**

    A. Second Wave Feminism

    B. Anti-consumerism

    C. Arab Spring

    D. Women's Suffrage Movement

    E. Occupy Wall Street

110. **Which of the following studies would a social epidemiologist be least likely to study?**

    A. Study how people from different countries around the world react to flu germs

    B. Examining health disparities based on gender within a school

    C. Observe how changes in religious beliefs impact the breakdown of the traditional authority of the church

    D. Critically evaluate a popular paper that claims to provide a homeopathic cure for diabetes, by investigating demographics that believe it

    E. How the communal nature of Thanksgiving dinners impact the risk of obesity in a group

111. **A student does not get the required test scores to move on to the next grade; however their teacher decides to move them up anyway in order for them in their intended social group. This is an example of _____.**

    A. Dropping out

    B. Merit promotion

    C. Summer school

    D. Grade retention

    E. Social promotion

112. In August 1942 the Bracero Program was initiated, resulting in the widespread immigration of which "group"?

   A. Irish
   B. Chinese
   C. Polish
   D. Mexicans
   E. Brazilians

113. Which of the following is not the dominant religion in the country?

   A. India – Hinduism
   B. Israel – Judaism
   C. Argentina – Catholicism
   D. Iran – Buddhism
   E. Saudi Arabia – Islam

114. What is the reasoning behind the 'law of superposition', which is the basis of much archaeological and geological investigation?

   A. Anything discovered automatically belongs to the country in which the investigation took place
   B. The age of material remains is indicated by their stratigraphic position, with the bottom layers being the oldest and upper layers being the youngest.
   C. It is a statement indicating the research project's strategy and methods, allowing the researchers to keep focused on specific goals
   D. 'Experts', usually academically trained, are no longer the only ones that may engage in such investigation – increasingly the public are involved
   E. Surveying provides limited information, so it is only through excavation that they can fully understand a site

115. Bronislaw Malinowski was an anthropologist best known for promoting which theoretical approach to social anthropology that emphasizes how cultures exists to meet the cultural and psychological needs of individuals?

   A. Functionalism

   B. Postmodernism

   C. Marxism

   D. Darwinism

   E. Cartesian dualism

116. A survey of an historic landscape is made by a research team. The team is split into smaller groups, who cover a very large area in a short period of time. They use representative sampling strategies, and ensure that nothing on the landscape is touched or disturbed – only recorded. This is an example of:

   A. An intensive, non-intrusive survey

   B. An extensive, intrusive survey

   C. An extensive, non-intrusive survey

   D. An intensive, intrusive survey

   E. None of the above

117. What bias exists in the ways "Asia" has been perceived as distinct from "the West"? Edward Said used this term in his seminal book of the same name to describe how our assumptions of "the East" are actually enduring creations by European scholars, writers and observers during periods of colonial domination – changing how scholars think about power, culture, history and identity formation.

   A. Axiology

   B. Barbarianism

   C. Indology

   D. Orientalism

   E. Occidentalism

118. _____ is a culture's ideas of the origins of the universe, and includes beliefs on how the world and living things were created, our 'place' in the universe, and how the universe 'works'. In some cultures the influences of spiritual, non-corporeal forces play a large role.

   A. Syncretism

   B. Osmosis

   C. Levelling mechanism

   D. Astrology

   E. Cosmology

119. Which of the following approaches believes that one has to study all aspects of a culture in order to fully understand it?

A. Phenomenological approach

B. Cultural Materialistic approach

C. Cultural relativistic approach

D. Functionalist approach

E. Holistic approach

120. Which of the following would anthropologists be least likely to study?

A. the anatomical features of dinosaurs during the Jurassic Period

B. changes in the human body and behavior throughout time

C. major global transformations throughout history, such as the adoption and spread of agriculture, urbanization, and industrialization

D. a country's economic and political system and opportunities provided to various social groups

E. the relationship of a religion's material culture with their theological ideologies

Social Sciences and History

ANSWER KEY

Question Number	Correct Answer	Your Answer	Question Number	Correct Answer	Your Answer	Question Number	Correct Answer	Your Answer
1	E		41	D		81	E	
2	C		42	C		82	C	
3	A		43	D		83	B	
4	E		44	E		84	A	
5	B		45	B		85	E	
6	D		46	E		86	C	
7	E		47	A		87	B	
8	B		48	E		88	B	
9	A		49	C		89	E	
10	C		50	E		90	C	
11	C		51	E		91	E	
12	D		52	D		92	A	
13	B		53	C		93	B	
14	A		54	A		94	E	
15	E		55	C		95	C	
16	D		56	C		96	C	
17	B		57	A		97	D	
18	C		58	B		98	A	
19	A		59	E		99	E	
20	E		60	E		100	A	
21	D		61	B		101	B	
22	A		62	A		102	E	
23	A		63	C		103	C	
24	E		64	D		104	E	
25	C		65	B		105	D	
26	B		66	A		106	B	
27	D		67	E		107	E	
28	D		68	B		108	A	
29	A		69	C		109	A	
30	B		70	C		110	C	
31	E		71	E		111	E	
32	A		72	A		112	D	
33	C		73	D		113	D	
34	E		74	D		114	B	
35	B		75	E		115	A	
36	A		76	C		116	C	
37	D		77	E		117	D	
38	D		78	A		118	E	
39	E		79	B		119	E	
40	A		80	D		120	A	

Western Civilization I: Ancient Near East to 1648

Description of the Examination

The Western Civilization I: Ancient Near East to 1648 examination covers material that is usually taught in the first semester of a two-semester course in Western Civilization. Questions deal with the civilizations of Ancient Greece, Rome, and the Near East; the Middle Ages; the Renaissance and Reformation; and early modern Europe. Candidates may be asked to choose the correct definition of a historical term, select the historical figure whose political viewpoint is described, identify the correct relationship between two historical factors, or detect the inaccurate pairing of an individual with a historical event. Groups of questions may require candidates to interpret, evaluate, or relate the contents of a passage, a map, or a picture to other information, or to analyze and utilize the data contained in a graph or table.

The examination contains approximately 120 questions to be answered in 90 minutes. Some of these are pretest questions that will not be scored. Any time candidates spend on tutorials and providing personal information is in addition to the actual testing time. This examination uses the chronological designations b.c.e. (before the common era) and c.e. (common era). The labels correspond to b.c. (before Christ) and a.d. (anno Domini), which are used in some textbooks.

Knowledge and Skills Required

Questions on the Western Civilization I examination require candidates to demonstrate one or more of the following abilities.

- Ability to understand important factual knowledge of developments in Western Civilization
- Ability to identify the causes and effects of major historical events
- Ability to analyze, interpret, and evaluate textual and graphic historical materials
- Ability to distinguish the relevant from the irrelevant
- Ability to reach conclusions on the basis of facts

The subject matter of the Western Civilization I examination is drawn from the following topics. The percentages next to the main topics indicate the approximate percentage of exam questions on that topic.

8%–10% Ancient Near East
- Political evolution
- Religion, culture, and technical developments in and near the Fertile Crescent

15%–17% Ancient Greece and Hellenistic Civilization
- Political evolution to Periclean Athens
- Periclean Athens through the Peloponnesian Wars
- Culture, religion, and thought of Ancient Greece
- The Hellenistic political structure
- The culture, religion, and thought of Hellenistic Greece

15%–17% Ancient Rome
- Political evolution of the Republic and of the Empire (economic and geographical context)
- Roman thought and culture
- Early Christianity
- The Germanic invasions
- The late empire

23%–27% **Medieval History**
- Byzantium and Islam
- Early medieval politics and culture through Charlemagne
- Feudal and manorial institutions
- The medieval Church
- Medieval thought and culture
- Rise of the towns and changing economic forms
- Feudal monarchies
- The late medieval church

13%–17% **Renaissance and Reformation**
- The Renaissance in Italy
- The Renaissance outside Italy
- The New Monarchies
- Protestantism and Catholicism reformed and reorganized

10%–15% **Early Modern Europe, 1560-1648**
- The opening of the Atlantic
- The Commercial Revolution
- Dynastic and religious conflicts
- Thought and culture

SAMPLE TEST

1. **The Ganges River empties into the:**

    A. Bay of Bengal

    B. Arabian Sea

    C. Red Sea

    D. Arafura Sea

    E. Indian Ocean

2. **The circumference of the earth, which greatly contributed to geographic knowledge, was calculated by:**

    A. Ptolemy

    B. Eratosthenes

    C. Galileo

    D. Strabo

    E. Pythagoras

3. **Which nation colonized most of South America in the 1600s?**

    A. England

    B. France

    C. Spain

    D. The Dutch Republic

    E. Belgium

4. **Which ancient civilization is credited with being the first to develop irrigation techniques through the use of canals, dikes, and devices for raising water?**

    A. The Sumerians

    B. The Egyptians

    C. The Babylonians

    D. The Akkadians

    E. The Hittites

5. **What people group are thought to create some of the world's first cities?**

    A. Egyptians

    B. Semites

    C. Sumerians

    D. Babylonians

    E. Greeks

6. **One of the first ancient civilization to introduce and practice monotheism was the:**

    A. Sumerians

    B. Minoans

    C. Phoenicians

    D. Christians

    E. Hebrews

7. **The "father of political science" is considered to be:**

   A. Aristotle

   B. John Locke

   C. Plato

   D. Thomas Hobbes

   E. Marcus Aurelius

8. **Which early cultural group from 1500 B.C.E. - 300 B.C.E. were known as the greatest sailors?**

   A. Greeks

   B. Persians

   C. Minoans

   D. Phoenicians

   E. Egyptians

9. **Bathtubs, hot and cold running water, and sewage systems with flush toilets were developed by the _____.**

   A. Minoans

   B. Mycenaeans

   C. Phoenicians

   D. Greeks

   E. Sumerians

10. **Geography was first systematically studied by _____.**

    A. the Egyptians

    B. the Greeks

    C. the Romans

    D. the Arabs

    E. the French

11. **Development of a solar calendar, invention of the decimal system, and contributions to the development of geometry and astronomy are all the legacy of:**

    A. The Babylonians

    B. The Persians

    C. The Sumerians

    D. The Egyptians

    E. The Greeks

12. **Which of the following is an example of a direct democracy?**

    A. Elected representatives

    B. Greek city-states

    C. The United States Senate

    D. The United States House of Representatives

    E. The Egyptian priesthood

13. What term is used to describe a complex human society, that began between 8000 B.C.E to 5500 B.C. E, with a high level of cultural and technological development

    A. Lifestyle

    B. Modernism

    C. Civilization

    D. Agricultural Revolution

    E. Barbarianism

14. Which one of the following is not an important legacy of the Byzantine Empire?

    A. It protected Western Europe from various attacks from the East by such groups as the Persians, Ottoman Turks, and Barbarians

    B. It played a part in preserving the literature, philosophy, and language of ancient Greece

    C. It created the Orthodox Church

    D. It kept the legal traditions of Roman government, collecting and organizing many ancient Roman laws

    E. Its military organization was the foundation for modern armies

15. Charlemagne's most important influence on Western civilization is seen today in:

    A. Relationship of church and state

    B. Strong military for defense

    C. The criminal justice system

    D. Education of women

    E. Strong sense of nationalism

16. The "divine right" of kings was the key political characteristic of:

    A. The Age of Absolutism

    B. The Age of Reason

    C. The Age of Feudalism

    D. The Age of Despotism

    E. The Age of Empire

17. Which one of the following is not a reason why Europeans came to the New World?

    A. To find resources in order to increase wealth

    B. To empower Native Americans

    C. To increase a ruler's power and importance

    D. To spread Christianity

    E. To look for alternative shipping routes

18. In Western Europe, the achievements of the Renaissance were unsurpassed and made these countries outstanding cultural centers on the continent. All of the following were accomplishments except:

    A. Invention of the printing press

    B. A rekindling of interest in the learning of classical Greece and Rome

    C. Growth in literature and philosophy

    D. Better military tactics

    E. New techniques applied in art

19. What idea during the Renaissance changed artists and scholars focus from religion to human beings and their interaction with the world?

    A. Realism

    B. Humanism

    C. Individualism

    D. Intellectualism

    E. Surrealism

20. The "father of anatomy" is considered to be:

    A. Vesalius

    B. Servetus

    C. Galen

    D. Harvey

    E. Scipio

21. Which one of the following did not contribute to the early medieval European civilization?

    A. The heritage from the classical cultures

    B. The Christian religion

    C. The influence of the German Barbarians

    D. The spread of ideas through trade and commerce

    E. Feudalism

22. Who is considered to be the most important figure in the spread of Protestantism across Switzerland?

    A. More

    B. Zwingli

    C. Munzer

    D. Leyden

    E. Calvin

23. **The Age of Exploration begun in the 1400s was led by:**

    A. The Portuguese

    B. The Spanish

    C. The English

    D. The Dutch

    E. The French

24. **The Italian born explorer who gave England its claim to North America was:**

    A. Raleigh

    B. Hawkins

    C. Drake

    D. Cabot

    E. Columbus

25. **The societies from _____ suffered from the outcomes of the Renaissance, Enlightenment, Commercial and Industrial Revolutions.**

    A. Asia

    B. Latin America

    C. Africa

    D. Middle East

    E. Europe

26. **The end to hunting, gathering, and fishing of prehistoric people was due to:**

    A. Domestication of animals

    B. Building crude huts and houses

    C. Development of agriculture

    D. Organized government in villages

    E. Scarcity of resources

27. **The ideas and innovations during the Renaissance were spread throughout Europe mainly because of:**

    A. Extensive exploration

    B. Craft workers and their guilds

    C. The invention of the printing press

    D. Increased travel and trade

    E. Warfare

28. **The Roman Empire gave so much to the world, especially the Western world. Of the legacies below which was the most influential, effective, and lasting?**

    A. The language of Latin

    B. Roman law, justice, and political system

    C. Engineering methods

    D. The writings of its poets and historians

    E. Buildings

29. **Which city-states fought in the Peloponnesian Wars?**

    A. Alexandria and Athens

    B. Sparta and Rome

    C. Alexandria and Rome

    D. Sparta and Athens

    E. Athens and Rome

30. **Which of the following was characteristic of Athenian democracy?**

    A. A bicameral legislature

    B. All males could vote in the assembly

    C. Three voting assemblies

    D. Classification of citizens by economic status

    E. Both men and women could vote

31. **The significance of the Norman conquest was that it:**

    A. Was an invasion of Normandy

    B. Was a victory for the British

    C. Kept the French from the British throne

    D. Infused French concepts into English culture

    E. Marked the start of the British Empire

32. **The Byzantine Empire was taken over by the:**

    A. Turks

    B. Mongols

    C. Mughals

    D. Muslims

    E. Latins

33. **The vast majority of people living in Europe during the Middle Ages were:**

    A. Aristocrats

    B. Warriors

    C. Peasants

    D. Noblemen

    E. Knights

34. **What element, more than any, helped the church to dominate in Europe between the ninth and thirteenth centuries?**

    A. The caste system

    B. The class system

    C. Monarchy

    D. Renaissance

    E. Feudalism

35. **Sultan Mehmed II led which group in its capture of Constantinople?**

    A. Byzantines

    B. Ottoman Turks

    C. Suleiman the Magnificent

    D. Visigoths

    E. The Latins

36. **The trade routes in the sub-Sahara connected all of the following areas except:**

    A. India

    B. China

    C. Northern Africa

    D. Western Europe

    E. Eastern Europe

37. **The Catholic Reformation was undertaken to:**

    A. Gain religious tolerance

    B. More opportunities for education

    C. Respond to the Protestant Reformation

    D. Respond to growing criticism

    E. All of the above

38. **Cortés conquered the Aztecs in Mexico with the help of:**

    A. Pizarro

    B. Native American tribes

    C. Montezuma

    D. The Incas

    E. The British

39. **Human settlements began in areas that:**

    A. Had good soil

    B. Offered natural resources

    C. Permitted division of labor

    D. Offered opportunities for animal husbandry

    E. Were already unoccupied

40. **Why was the Fertile Crescent called the "Cradle of Civilization"?**

    A. Agriculture allowed people to remain in one place throughout the year

    B. It had rich agricultural lands

    C. The area developed complex societies

    D. The area hosted the earliest civilizations

    E. It was shaped exactly like a crescent

41. **Which document provides the basis of English constitutional liberties?**

    A. Magna Carta

    B. Hammurabi's Code of Laws

    C. Declaration of Independence

    D. Code of Justinian

    E. The Twelve Tables

42. **How did the Minoans and Mycenaeans differ?**

    A. The Minoans lived in the Peloponnese

    B. The Mycenaeans lived on Crete

    C. The Minoans were traders until about 2700 BCE

    D. The Mycenaeans were warriors and conquerors

    E. They didn't; they were the same group

43. **What revolutionized the trans-Sahara trade in West Africa?**

    A. Silk

    B. Gold

    C. Camels

    D. Slaves

    E. Water bladders

44. **Which of the following is not true about Egypt during ancient times?**

    A. It was occupied by Alexander the Great

    B. It became a Roman province

    C. Its cultural center was Cairo

    D. It became an important center for Christianity

    E. It spawned many architectural marvels

45. **How did politics contribute to the collapse of the Roman Empire?**

    A. Diocletian's reforms encouraged revolution

    B. The "divine-right" monarchy lessened the burden of ruling

    C. Constantine's efforts demoralized the city-states

    D. Landlords controlled more of the large villas and commerce

    E. There were too many treaties with the different Barbarian tribes

46. Which of the following was not an effect of the Crusades?

   A. Increased military authority of the Roman Catholic Church

   B. Establishment of political authority of the Pope

   C. The Spanish Inquisition

   D. Migration of Scandinavian tribes into modern day Germany

   E. The establishment of Latin kingdoms in the Holy Land

47. Which statement is true about colonization in what became Canada in the 1600s?

   A. The Dutch built a plantation society in South America

   B. The British controlled much of Central America

   C. The British controlled the Mississippi

   D. The French controlled most of northern North America, including much of the Great Lake area.

   E. Only large military groups colonized North America

48. Which of the following was not a painter during the Renaissance?

   A. da Vinci

   B. Donatello

   C. el Greco

   D. Montaigne

   E. Botticelli

49. Which ancient king created and distributed one of the oldest set of laws that were cataloged in great detail that include laws on established minimum wage and establishes one of the earliest examples of the presumption of innocence?

   A. Montezuma

   B. Hammurabi

   C. Caesar

   D. Xerxes

   E. Alexander

50. Homer's epic poem, "The Iliad," covered the war between the Trojans and which other group of people?

   A. The Spartans

   B. The Egyptians

   C. The Babylonians

   D. The Greeks

   E. The Amazons

51. The _____ modeled their society and government on Greek ideals.

    A. Corinthians
    B. Romans
    C. Byzantines
    D. Egyptians
    E. Hittites

52. **The war between Hannibal of Carthage and the Romans, led by Scipio Amelianus, was known as:**

    A. The First Punic War
    B. The Second Punic War
    C. The Peloponnesian War
    D. The War of the Alps
    E. The Third Punic War

53. **One lasting effect of the Second Crusade was:**

    A. An increase in power in the Latin Kingdoms
    B. A steady alliance between the Islamic powers and the Crusaders
    C. A decline in Byzantine prestige
    D. An increase in Islamic prestige and power
    E. The establishment of a new Latin kingdom

54. The First Crusade was called by Pope Urban II as an attempt to free the city of _____ from Muslim control.

    A. Jerusalem
    B. Bethlehem
    C. Constantinople
    D. Mecca
    E. Antioch

55. **Which of the following statements about the medieval social structure of feudalism is false?**

    A. Peasants were tied to land owned by their liege lords.
    B. The lands held by the nobility were heredity and could not be taken by the Crown.
    C. Vassals were obliged to provide military service when called upon.
    D. There was a distinct lack of social mobility.
    E. Feudalism declined after the 1500s because of a combination of factors such as warfare, the plague and social unrest.

56. Which of the following religious orders was established to care for pilgrims traveling to the Holy Land?

    A. The Knights Templar

    B. The Franciscans

    C. The Knights Hospitaller

    D. The Red Cross

    E. The Cistercian Monks

57. This queen accompanied her husband, King Louis VII, on the Second Crusade.

    A. Eleanor of Aquitaine

    B. Blanche of Castile

    C. Boudicca

    D. Isabella of France

    E. Isabella of Spain

58. Which crusade temporarily ended the Byzantine Empire and created a Latin Kingdom?

    A. The First Crusade

    B. The Second Crusade

    C. The Third Crusade

    D. The Fourth Crusade

    E. The Fifth Crusade

59. Flying buttresses, large stained glass windows and vaulted ceilings are characteristic of which architectural style?

    A. Neo-classical

    B. Pre-modern

    C. Renaissance

    D. Baroque

    E. Gothic

60. The Bubonic Plague killed what percentage of Europe's population at its peak in 1347?

    A. 13 percent

    B. 25 percent

    C. 33 percent

    D. 49 percent

    E. 65 percent

61. Dante Alighieri's Divine Comedy was written in what language?

    A. Greek

    B. French

    C. Latin

    D. Italian

    E. English

62. The Bayeux Tapestry describes and represents the military victories of _____?

   A. Julius Caesar
   B. William the Conqueror
   C. Edward II of England
   D. Henry I of France
   E. Richard the Lionheart

63. Which of the following was NOT an effect of the Crusades?

   A. Several Latin kingdoms were established
   B. Trade between the Holy Land and Western Europe began to flourish
   C. An exchange of thoughts and ideas began between the European kingdoms and the Islamic territories
   D. Feudalism was strengthened as the number of Crusades rose
   E. Pilgrims and travelers began to move between the Europe and the Middle East

64. The Hundred Years' War was characterized by England's desire to conquer which country:

   A. Spain
   B. France
   C. Portugal
   D. Italy
   E. Byzantium

65. Which English king completed the conquest and incorporation of Wales?

   A. Henry III
   B. Edward I
   C. John
   D. Henry VII
   E. William the Conqueror

66. The Lombards were a Germanic-speaking people who conquered a large portion of Italy in the 700s, ousting which major power from the area?

   A. The Byzantines
   B. The Romans
   C. The Papal States
   D. The French
   E. The Franks

67. **The first Holy Roman Emperor was:**

    A. Constantine the Great

    B. Charlemagne

    C. Lothair I

    D. Louis the German

    E. Drogo of Champagne

68. **The War of the Roses was primarily a fight for:**

    A. Trade rights in Italy

    B. An end of feudalism in England

    C. Succession of the crown of England

    D. English control of the French crown

    E. English control over Scotland

69. **During the Renaissance what is the term for the art form that focused on authentic emotions and life-like proportions?**

    A. Baroque

    B. Realism

    C. Neo-classicism

    D. Surrealism

    E. Impressionism

70. **A popular type of song in the Middle Ages involved multiple people singing the melody one after the other. What was this called?**

    A. Pavan

    B. Carol

    C. Solo

    D. Round

    E. Chant

71. **Which of these emperors was NOT a aspirant contender during the Year of the Four Emperors in 69 CE?**

    A. Galba

    B. Otho

    C. Vitellius

    D. Vespasian

    E. Nero

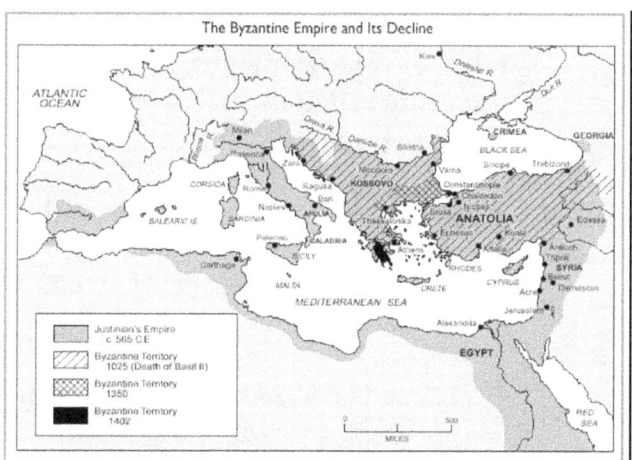

"The Byzantine Empire and its Decline."
All Empires. 2015.
http://www.allempires.com/empires/byzantine1/map09_01.gif.

72. **The dark gray shaded region shows the extent of the Byzantine Empire under which emperor?**

   A. Justinian

   B. Constantine

   C. Manuel I

   D. Zeno

   E. Basil I

73. **The Roman Empire was divided into four sections under which emperor?**

   A. Constantine

   B. Domitian

   C. Diocletian

   D. Tiberius

   E. Augustus

74. **Which of the following is a false statement about women's lives in Rome?**

   A. Women were able to consistently wield large amounts of political power

   B. The role of matriarch was glorified in Roman society

   C. A woman could rule as regent if her son was underage or her husband was absent

   D. Women enjoyed a great deal of social mobility and freedom

   E. There were religious roles that only women could perform

75. **One version of Rome's early history indicates the belief that its earliest founder was a fugitive from what war?**

   A. The Trojan War

   B. The Punic War

   C. The Peloponnesian War

   D. The Greco-Persian Wars

   E. The Corinthian War

76. **This philosopher-emperor was a successful general and author of Stoic Philosophy.**

    A. Nero

    B. Titus

    C. Marcus Aurelius

    D. Augustus

    E. Justinian

77. **Which emperor was not among those classically referred to as the "Five Good Emperors"?**

    A. Nerva

    B. Trajan

    C. Hadrian

    D. Augustus

    E. Antoninus Pius

78. **What was Rome's typical reaction when encountering unknown or opposing religious values in regions it conquered?**

    A. Rome would stamp out any of the native religion and install priests to instruct the new province about Roman ways.

    B. Rome would adopt the religion and gods of the province as its own.

    C. The citizens were offered the option of following Roman religions and gods.

    D. Romans only spread the cult of emperor worship.

    E. Rome would find parallels between the provinces' gods and its own and assume the provinces' gods were incarnations of Roman deities.

79. **The name of the ineffectual and largely ceremonial last emperor of Rome was what?**

    A. Amelianus

    B. Honorius

    C. Theodosius I

    D. Romulus

    E. Valentinian III

80. Rome's early military history involved attacking neighboring cities in Italy to expand its territory. Which war marked the start of expansion outside the borders of Italy?

   A. The Samnite Wars

   B. The First Punic War

   C. The Latin Wars

   D. The Pyrrhic War

   E. The Second Punic War

81. Which of the following was a fact about Roman citizenship?

   A. Both men and women enjoyed the rights of full Roman citizenship.

   B. Slaves could eventually become full citizens after their manumissions.

   C. Residents in Roman territories were automatically granted citizenship.

   D. Roman citizenship was used as a method of influencing nearby territories.

   E. Roman citizenship was not seen as a desirable state.

82. In what year did the western half of the Roman Empire fall?

   A. 284 CE

   B. 312 CE

   C. 372 CE

   D. 454 CE

   E. 476 CE

83. The Crisis of the Third Century was marked by all but what?

   A. Multiple claimants to the throne over a short period of time

   B. Population growth in the Roman Empire

   C. A loss of Roman territory and prestige

   D. Hyperinflation and a weak economy

   E. Breakdown of trade relations across the Roman Empire

84. Which of the following was NOT a social rank in the Roman Empire?

   A. Patrician

   B. Plebian

   C. Equestrian

   D. Slave

   E. Serf

"Arch-of-Titus."*Britannica*.Undefined. 2015.http://www.britannica.com/place/Arch-of-Titus.

85. **The Arch of Titus, seen above, displayed what historical event?**

   A. Julius Caesar's conquest of Gaul

   B. The destruction of the Temple in Jerusalem

   C. The defeat of Hannibal

   D. The conquest of Britannia

   E. The establishment of Roman law

86. **The Greek philosophy of Stoicism was characterized by all but what?**

   A. Focusing on what is said rather than what is done

   B. Focusing on what is done rather than what is said

   C. The application of logic to daily life

   D. The pursuit of a virtuous existence

   E. The belief in self-control and self-determination

87. **The Islamic Golden Age refers to a time of social, military and scientific expansion and cultivation. What marked the end of this period?**

   A. Increasing Christian pressure from Europe and the Mongols from the east

   B. Muslim focus on military matters

   C. Internal revolt and uprisings

   D. A "brain drain" to Europe

   E. An increased focus on religious life

88. **The ancient ruler Sargon the Great conquered Sumerian city-states to form what empire?**

    A. Babylonian

    B. Neo-Assyrian

    C. Akkadian

    D. Hittite

    E. Assyrian

89. **Achievements of the so-called "New Monarchies" included all but what?**

    A. Internal stability

    B. Efficient taxation

    C. A strong focus on nationalism

    D. Increased trade and interaction

    E. Maintaining a standing army

90. **The Commercial Revolution was a period of economic expansion and diversification during the Middle Ages. Which statement can be concluded to be FALSE regarding the Commercial Revolution's effect on society?**

    A. Increased interaction between different kingdoms allowed for more trade

    B. Increased production of goods allowed for the merchant class to grow

    C. Increased competition between the European powers rapidly advanced maritime science

    D. Advances in trade and science did not encourage exploration

    E. Modern banking developed to handle the increased demand for loans and money storage

91. **Who were the Huguenots?**

    A. English Protestants

    B. English Catholics

    C. French Protestants

    D. French Catholics

    E. Dutch Protestants

92. **Which of the following was not a complaint made by Protestants against the Catholic Church?**

    A. The improper selling of indulgences

    B. Churches held too much land

    C. Too much money remaining in the hands of Church officials

    D. The influence of the Church needed to be increased

    E. The Church had become hopelessly corrupt and indulgent

93. **The Reformation in England resulted in which of the following?**

    A. A clear and uncompromising break with the Roman Church

    B. The destruction and dissolution of monasteries

    C. The monarchy immediately adopted Protestantism as the religion of England

    D. All citizens were forced to convert to Protestantism

    E. All Catholic churches in England were eventually dissolved

94. **The man bellow opposed King Henry VIII and the Protestant Reformation in England. What is his name?**

    Birzer, Bradley. "Sir Thomas More, Humanist." *College of Arts and Science, University of Colorado Boulder.* n.d. http://artsandsciences.colorado.edu/ctp/2014/08/the-utopia-of-thomas-more/.

    A. Martin Luther

    B. Thomas Cranmer

    C. Thomas More

    D. Cardinal Wolsey

    E. George Boleyn

95. **Which of the following monarchs was not Protestant?**

    A. Elizabeth I

    B. Mary Tudor

    C. Edward VI

    D. William and Mary

    E. James VI

96. **Early modern Europe was noted for all but which of the following:**

    A. Religious reformation

    B. Religious persecution

    C. A decline in scientific advancement

    D. An increase of exploration and trade

    E. New advancements in philosophy

97. **The Thirty Years' War began as a struggle between which two powers?**

    A. Protestants and Catholics

    B. England and France

    C. England and Germany

    D. Protestants and Huguenots

    E. Spain and France

98. **Which of the following was a result of the Peloponnesian War?**

    A. Sparta lost influence in the Adriatic

    B. Athens gained territory and influence

    C. Sparta gained influence and prestige over Athens

    D. The Peloponnesian League was dissolved

    E. Democracy continued without interruption in Athens

99. **The Persian Wars were a series of engagements between the Greek states and the Persian Empire over fifty years. Who is the primary contemporary source of information during this time?**

    A. Plato

    B. Livy

    C. Herodotus

    D. Plutarch

    E. Aristotle

100. **Which king led the Second Crusade?**

    A. Louis VII of France

    B. Conrad III of Germany

    C. John of England

    D. Richard the Lionheart

    E. Both A and B

101. Sea power was crucial for most of the European powers. In 1588, the English navy defeated the navy of which country, an action that established England as the major rising power in Europe?

   A. France

   B. The Netherlands

   C. Germany

   D. Spain

   E. The Portuguese

102. **The English Civil War resulted from complaints about all of the following except:**

   A. Parliament would not grant Charles I funds

   B. Parliament and the people of England did not support Charles' Catholic bride

   C. Constitutional guarantees were not being made by the king

   D. Parliament did not feel it was being consulted enough by the king

   E. The king's lack of enforcement of Divine Right

103. Nation-states comprised groups of people united by:

   A. Common language

   B. Geography

   C. Traditions

   D. History

   E. All of the above

104. **The Roman Cult of Mithras was made up primarily of whom?**

   A. Women

   B. Slaves

   C. Soldiers

   D. Freemen

   E. Senators

Feitscherg. "Map Gallia Tribes Towns."*wikimedia*.2015.https://commons.wikimedia.org/wiki/File:Map_Gallia_Tribes_Towns.png.

105. **This above Roman province is known as what?**

  A. Britannia

  B. Gaul

  C. Hispania

  D. Londinium

  E. Dacia

106. **In 1492, an edict was issued that expelled Jews from which country?**

  A. England

  B. France

  C. Portugal

  D. Spain

  E. The Netherlands

107. **Baroque art, which gained popularity in the 1600s, can be distinguished by:**

  A. Its return to Greek and Roman styles

  B. Clean, uncomplicated aesthetic

  C. Heavily ornate architecture and paintings

  D. Unemotional figures in paintings

  E. Experimentations with the representation of human form

108. **The Renaissance was a great leap ahead in terms of science, architecture and art. What was another effect of the Renaissance on political culture outside of Italy?**

  A. Independent city-states were established across Europe

  B. Religious thought stagnated

  C. Trade decreased as cities and kingdoms sought to protect their advancements

  D. Monarchies declined in power compared to the Church

  E. Nation-states were created

109. **The Age of Enlightenment emphasized what schools of thought?**

   A. Reason and logic

   B. Emotion

   C. Absolute monarchy

   D. Religion was supreme above science

   E. Isolationism

110. **What is the truest statement about the First and Second Crusades?**

   A. The First Crusade had trouble gathering enough soldiers and pilgrims while the Second Crusade had enough men

   B. The First Crusade increased Muslim power while the Second Crusade decreased it

   C. The First Crusade decreased Muslim power while the Second Crusade increased it

   D. Both crusades were ultimately unsuccessful

   E. Both crusades achieved their objectives

111. **What type of government did Sparta have?**

   A. Oligarchy

   B. Representative democracy

   C. Theocracy

   D. Democracy

   E. Anarchy

112. **Which of the following was NOT a member of the Delian League?**

   A. Neopolis

   B. Athens

   C. Sparta

   D. Byzantium

   E. Chalcedon

113. **New Monarchs achieved all of the following except:**

   A. Increase in power of nobility

   B. The unification of their kingdoms

   C. Creation of national identity

   D. Increase in trade

   E. Creation of a standing army

114. **The type of writing first used in early civilizations was called what?**

   A. Hieroglyphics

   B. Cuneiform

   C. Alphabet

   D. Pictograms

   E. Demotic

115. **Greek political independence ended after the conquest by:**

   A. Alexander the Great

   B. The Romans

   C. The Persians

   D. The Spartans

   E. The Trojans

116. **The body of water surrounding most of the Grecian Islands is called what?**

   A. Black Sea

   B. Indian Ocean

   C. Libyan Sea

   D. Aegean Sea

   E. Mediterranean

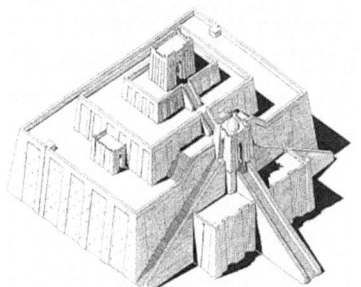

"Ziggurat." *Many Prophets One Message*. undefined. 2014. http://www.manyprophetsonemessage.com/2014/10/14/quran-reveals-lost-knowledge-about-prophet-abraham/.

117. **The above image is called a what?**

   A. Pyramid

   B. Ziggurat

   C. Temple

   D. Burial mound

   E. Obelisk

118. **Which country was least effected by Protestant Reformation?**

   A. France

   B. England

   C. Germany

   D. Spain

   E. Italy

119. **The Anglican Church was considered to be only a partial concession to Protestant pressure because it:**

    A. Reverted back to Catholicism

    B. Maintained Popish ceremonies and décor

    C. Stayed in communication with the Pope

    D. Supported Catholic claims to the throne

    E. Suppressed Protestant supporters

120. **The Roman Inquisition, which was charged with stamping out heresy that resulted from the Protestant Reformation, famously brought which Italian to trial?**

    A. Dante Alighieri

    B. Lucrezia Borgia

    C. Leonardo da Vinci

    D. Michelangelo

    E. Galileo Galilei

Western Civilization I: Ancient Near East to 1648

ANSWER KEY

Question Number	Correct Answer	Your Answer	Question Number	Correct Answer	Your Answer	Question Number	Correct Answer	Your Answer
1	A		41	A		81	D	
2	B		42	D		82	E	
3	C		43	C		83	B	
4	A		44	C		84	E	
5	C		45	C		85	B	
6	E		46	D		86	A	
7	A		47	D		87	A	
8	D		48	D		88	C	
9	A		49	E		89	C	
10	B		50	D		90	D	
11	D		51	B		91	C	
12	B		52	B		92	D	
13	C		53	D		93	B	
14	E		54	A		94	C	
15	A		55	B		95	B	
16	A		56	C		96	C	
17	B		57	A		97	A	
18	D		58	D		98	C	
19	B		59	E		99	C	
20	A		60	C		100	E	
21	D		61	D		101	D	
22	E		62	B		102	E	
23	A		63	D		103	E	
24	D		64	B		104	C	
25	C		65	B		105	B	
26	C		66	A		106	D	
27	C		67	B		107	C	
28	B		68	C		108	E	
29	D		69	B		109	A	
30	B		70	D		110	C	
31	D		71	E		111	A	
32	A		72	A		112	C	
33	C		73	C		113	A	
34	E		74	A		114	B	
35	B		75	A		115	B	
36	D		76	C		116	D	
37	E		77	D		117	B	
38	B		78	E		118	D	
39	B		79	D		119	B	
40	D		80	B		120	E	

Western Civilization II: 1648 to the Present

Description of the Examination

The Western Civilization II: 1648 to the Present examination covers material that is usually taught in the second semester of a two-semester course in Western Civilization. Questions cover European history from the mid-seventeenth century through the post-Second World War period including political, economic, and cultural developments such as Scientific Thought, the Enlightenment, the French and Industrial Revolutions, and the First and Second World Wars. Candidates may be asked to choose the correct definition of a historical term, select the historical figure whose political viewpoint is described, identify the correct relationship between two historical factors, or detect the inaccurate pairing of an individual with a historical event. Groups of questions may require candidates to interpret, evaluate, or relate the contents of a passage, a map, a picture, or a cartoon to the other information, or to analyze and use the data contained in a graph or table.

The examination contains 120 questions to be answered in 90 minutes. Some of these are pretest questions that will not be scored. Any time candidates spend on tutorials and providing personal information is in addition to the actual testing time.

Knowledge and Skills Required

Questions on the Western Civilization II examination require candidates to demonstrate one or more of the following abilities:

- Understanding important factual knowledge of developments in Western Civilization
- Ability to identify the causes and effects of major historical events
- Ability to analyze, interpret, and evaluate textual and graphic materials
- Ability to distinguish the relevant from the irrelevant
- Ability to reach conclusions on the basis of facts

The subject matter of the Western Civilization II examination is drawn from the following topics. The percentages next to the main topics indicate the approximate percentages of exam questions on those topics.

7%–9% **Absolutism and Constitutionalism, 1648–1715**
- The Dutch Republic
- The English Revolution
- France under Louis XIV
- Formation of Austria and Prussia
- The "westernization" of Russia

4%–6% **Competition for empire and economic expansion**
- Global economy of the eighteenth century
- Europe after Utrecht, 1713–1740
- Demographic change in the eighteenth century

5%–7% **The scientific view of the world**
- Major figures of the scientific revolution
- New knowledge of man and society
- Political theory

7%–9% **Period of Enlightenment**
- Enlightenment thought
- Enlightened despotism
- Partition of Poland

Western Civilization II: 1648 to the Present

10%–13% **Revolution and Napoleonic Europe**
- The Revolution in France
- The Revolution and Europe
- The French Empire
- Congress of Vienna

7%–9% **The Industrial Revolution**
- Agricultural and industrial revolution
- Causes of revolution
- Economic and social impact on working and middle class
- British reform movement

6%–8% **Political and cultural developments, 1815–1848**
- Conservatism
- Liberalism
- Nationalism
- Socialism
- The Revolutions of 1830 and 1848

8%–10% **Politics and diplomacy in the Age of Nationalism, 1850–1914**
- The unification of Italy and Germany
- Austria-Hungary
- Russia
- France
- Socialism and labor unions
- European diplomacy, 1871–1900

7%–9% **Economy, culture, and imperialism, 1850–1914**
- Demography
- World economy of the nineteenth century
- Technological developments
- Science, philosophy, and the arts
- Imperialism in Africa and Asia

10%–12% **The First World War and the Russian Revolution**
- The causes of the First World War
- The economic and social impact of the war
- The peace settlements
- The Revolution of 1917 and its effects

7%–9% **Europe between the wars**
- The Great Depression
- International politics, 1919–1939
- Stalin's five-year plans and purges
- Italy and Germany between the wars
- Interwar cultural developments

8%-10% **The Second World War and contemporary Europe**
- The causes and course of the Second World War
- Postwar Europe
- Science, philosophy, the arts, and religion
- Social and political developments

Western Civilization II: 1648 to the Present

SAMPLE TEST

1. What was the initial reason the Thirty Year War began?

   A. Protestantism opposition to Roman Catholicism domination in the Netherlands and Germany

   B. French imperialism over Nordic European countries

   C. Roman Catholicism opposition to Protestantism domination in the Netherlands and Germany

   D. Spanish imperialism over France

   E. Spanish protestant churches revolted

2. What principle was the result of the end of the Thirty Year War at the Treaty of Westphalia in 1648?

   A. That religion was more powerful than politics

   B. National dominion was clearly resilient and remained to serve as the basis for the system on imperialism and colonialism

   C. State sovereignty emerged and serves as the basis for the modern system of nation-states

   D. That state sovereignty could not work

   E. That politics were more powerful than religion

3. What type monarchical government, such as Louis XIV of France government, has absolute power among his or her people, wielding unrestricted political power over the sovereign state and its people?

   A. Tyrannical Monarchism

   B. Constitutional Monarchism

   C. Monarchism

   D. Aristocracy Monarchism

   E. Absolute Monarchism

4. What is a document outlining the fundamental laws and principles that govern a nation.

   A. Judicial Review

   B. Canon Law

   C. Treaty

   D. Parliament document

   E. Constitution

5. **What is the Glorious Revolution?**

    A. Event against King James II (sometimes called the bloodless revolution) that consisted of Whig and Tories forcing him to leave

    B. Religious reformers from Calvinist and Luther sects fight a bloody reformation against Anglicans

    C. French imperialist come to England and displace King James II

    D. French revolutionist come to England and displace King James II

    E. Dutch Republic solidify Catholicism by force.

6. **What was one outcome of the English Revolution?**

    A. Bill of Rights of 1689 created

    B. English sovereignty over the Dutch Republic

    C. English constitution of 1690 created

    D. Parliament created

    E. King James II remained in power

7. **What was one outcome of the War of the Austrian Succession?**

    A. Prussia and France became allies

    B. France and Britain became allies

    C. Prussia became a prominent world leader

    D. Austria lost its sovereignty

    E. The war ended all wars

8. **Define Boyars:**

    A. a member of the old aristocracy in Russia, next in rank to a prince

    B. a member of the Austrian aristocracy

    C. a reformer in the Russian Orthodox church

    D. a member belonging by rank, title, or birth to the aristocracy in the British parliament

    E. an agricultural laborer bound by the feudal system who was tied to working on his lord's estate

9. **Peter the Great revolutionized Russia by**

   A. Introducing communism

   B. Introducing western ideas on education, economy, culture, politics, and military exploits

   C. Allying itself with Nordic countries such as Sweden

   D. Introducing eastern ideas on education, economy, culture, politics, and military exploits

   E. Establishing the Roman Catholic church

10. **What was one main difference between western European powers economies in the 18th century than in the 17th century?**

    A. Wealth is gold and silver

    B. Free trade will create the best world

    C. There was finite amounts of wealth

    D. Mercantilism ideals

    E. Government should control economy

Answer Key

1. A
2. C
3. E
4. E
5. A
6. A
7. C
8. A
9. B
10. B

Please note that this is a sample portion of the CLEP Western Civilization II examination. A complete practice test is available for purchase at Amazon.com and Barnesandnoble.com ISBN 9781607875208.

Biology

Description of the Examination

The Biology examination covers material that is usually taught in a one-year college general biology course. The subject matter tested covers the broad field of the biological sciences, organized into three major areas: molecular and cellular biology, organismal biology, and population biology.

The examination gives approximately equal weight to these three areas. The examination contains approximately 115 questions to be answered in 90 minutes. Some of these are pretest questions that will not be scored. Any time candidates spend on tutorials and providing personal information is in addition to the actual testing time.

Knowledge and Skills Required

Questions on the Biology examination require candidates to demonstrate one or more of the following abilities.

- Knowledge of facts, principles, and processes of biology
- Understanding the means by which information is collected, how it is interpreted, how one hypothesizes from available information, how one draws conclusions and makes further predictions
- Understanding that science is a human endeavor with social consequences

The subject matter of the Biology examination is drawn from the following topics. The percentages next to the main topics indicate the approximate percentage of exam questions on that topic.

33% **Molecular and Cellular Biology**
- Chemical composition of organisms
- Simple chemical reactions and bonds
- Properties of water
- Chemical structure of carbohydrates, lipids, proteins, nucleic acids
- Origin of life

Cells
- Structure and function of cell organelles
- Properties of cell membranes
- Comparison of prokaryotic and eukaryotic cells

Enzymes
- Enzyme-substrate complex
- Roles of coenzymes
- Inorganic cofactors
- Inhibition and regulation

Energy transformations
- Glycolysis, respiration, anaerobic pathways
- Photosynthesis

Cell division
- Structure of chromosomes
- Mitosis, meiosis, and cytokinesis in plants and animals

Chemical nature of the gene
- Watson-Crick model of nucleic acids
- DNA replication
- Mutations
- Control of protein synthesis: transcription, translation, posttranscriptional processing
- Structural and regulatory genes
- Transformation
- Viruses

Biology

34% **Organismal Biology**
- Structure and function in plants with emphasis on angiosperms
- Root, stem, leaf, flower, seed, fruit
- Water and mineral absorption and transport
- Food translocation and storage
- Plant reproduction and development
- Alternation of generations in ferns, conifers, and flowering plants
- Gamete formation and fertilization
- Growth and development: hormonal control
- Tropisms and photoperiodicity

Structure and function in animals with emphasis on vertebrates
- Major systems (e.g., digestive, gas exchange, skeletal, nervous, circulatory, excretory, immune)
- Homeostatic mechanisms
- Hormonal control in homeostasis and reproduction

Animal reproduction and development
- Gamete formation, fertilization
- Cleavage, gastrulation, germ layer formation, differentiation of organ systems
- Experimental analysis of vertebrate development
- Extraembryonic membranes of vertebrates
- Formation and function of the mammalian placenta
- Blood circulation in the human embryo

Principles of heredity
- Mendelian inheritance (dominance, segregation, independent assortment)
- Chromosomal basis of inheritance
- Linkage, including sex-linked
- Polygenic inheritance (height, skin color)

33% **Population Biology**
Principles of ecology
- Energy flow and productivity in ecosystems
- Biogeochemical cycles
- Population growth and regulation (natality, mortality, competition, migration, density, r- and K-selection)
- Community structure, growth, regulation (major biomes and succession)
- Habitat (biotic and abiotic factors)
- Concept of niche
- Island biogeography
- Evolutionary ecology (life history strategies, altruism, kin selection)

Principles of evolution
- History of evolutionary concepts
- Concepts of natural selection (differential reproduction, mutation, Hardy-Weinberg equilibrium, speciation, punctuated equilibrium)
- Adaptive radiation
- Major features of plant and animal evolution
- Concepts of homology and analogy
- Convergence, extinction, balanced polymorphism, genetic drift

- Classification of living organisms
- Evolutionary history of humans

Principles of behavior
- Stereotyped, learned social behavior
- Societies (insects, birds, primates)

Social biology
- Human population growth (age composition, birth and fertility rates, theory of demographic transition)
- Human intervention in the natural world (management of resources, environmental pollution)
- Biomedical progress (control of human reproduction, genetic engineering)

Biology

SAMPLE TEST

1. Which is not true about a cell membrane?

   A. It is made from phospholipids

   B. Both plant and animal cells have a cell membrane.

   C. The cell wall is the same as the cell membrane in plants.

   D. It controls the passage of nutrients within a cell.

   E. It contains embedded proteins that help with passage.

2. Microorganisms use all but which of the following for locomotion?

   A. Pseudopods

   B. Flagella

   C. Cilia

   D. Pili

   E. Villi

3. Which of the following does not possess eukaryotic cells?

   A. Bacteria

   B. Protists

   C. Fungi

   D. Animals

   E. Plants

4. Which of the following groups of organisms is comprised of those with one cell and no nuclear membrane?

   A. Monera

   B. Protista

   C. Fungi

   D. Algae

   E. Plantae

5. Which of these are found on the outside of the rough endoplasmic reticulum?

   A. Vacuoles

   B. Mitochondria

   C. Microfilaments

   D. Ribosomes

   E. Flagella

Biology

6. **Identify the correct sequence of organization of living things.**

   A. cell – organelle – organ – tissue – organ system – organism

   B. cell – tissue – organ – organelle – organ system – organism

   C. organelle – cell – tissue – organ – organ system – organism

   D. organ system – tissue – organelle – cell – organism – organ

   E. organism – organ system – tissue – cell – organelle – organ

7. **Which of these is not a characteristic shared by all living things?**

   A. movement

   B. made of cells

   C. metabolism

   D. reproduction

   E. respond to stimuli

8. **What is the purpose of the Golgi apparatus?**

   A. To break down proteins

   B. To break down fats

   C. To make carbohydrates.

   D. To provide the cell with energy

   E. To sort, modify and package molecules

9. **What do amyloplasts do?**

   A. Store starch in a plant cell

   B. Remove waste in animal cells

   C. Produce green and yellow pigment

   D. Aid in photosynthesis.

   E. Provide energy for metabolism

10. **Which of the following does not belong to the domain Archaea?**

    A. Methanogens

    B. Extreme Halophiles

    C. Thermoacidophiles

    D. Bacteriophiles

    E. Sulfobales

11. **The first cells that evolved on earth were probably of which type?**

    A. autotrophic

    B. eukaryotic

    C. heterotrophic

    D. prokaryotic

    E. endosymbiotic

Biology

12. During which part of photosynthesis is oxygen given off?

    A. light reactions

    B. dark reactions

    C. Krebs cycle

    D. reduction of NAD+ to NADH

    E. phosphorylation

13. Bacteria commonly reproduce by a process called binary fission. Which of the following best defines this process?

    A. Viral vectors carry DNA to new bacteria.

    B. DNA from one bacterium enters another.

    C. DNA doubles and the bacterial cell divides.

    D. DNA from dead cells is absorbed into bacteria.

    E. Bacteria merge with others to form new species.

14. Which tool is best for studying the individual parts of cells?

    A. ultracentrifuge

    B. phase-contrast microscope

    C. CAT scan

    D. electron microscope

    E. light microscope

15. Which of these classifications includes the thermoacidophiles?

    A. Plantae

    B. Animalia

    C. Bacteria

    D. Protista

    E. Archaea

16. Which of the following is not part of the cytoskeleton?

    A. vacuoles

    B. microfilaments

    C. microtubules

    D. intermediate filaments

    E. motor proteins

17. Of what are viruses made?

    A. A protein coat surrounding a nucleic acid.

    B. RNA and protein surrounded by a cell wall.

    C. A nucleic acid surrounding a protein coat.

    D. Protein surrounded by DNA.

    E. A lipid bilayer surrounding a protein coat and RNA.

18. **Which of these are used to classify protists into their major groups?**

    A. Their method of obtaining nutrition.

    B. Their method of reproduction.

    C. Their use of metabolism.

    D. Their form and function.

    E. Their means of locomotion.

19. **Replication of chromosomes occurs during which phase of the cell cycle?**

    A. prophase

    B. interphase

    C. metaphase

    D. anaphase

    E. metaphase

20. **Which of these events occurs during telophase in a plant cell?**

    A. the chromosomes are doubled

    B. a cell plate forms

    C. crossing over occurs

    D. a cleavage furrow develops

    E. spindle fibers become visible

21. **What is the stage of mitosis seen in the diagram?**

    A. anaphase

    B. metaphase

    C. telophase

    D. prophase

    E. interphase

22. **What is the stage of mitosis shown in the diagram?**

    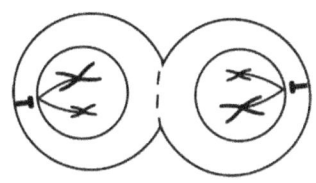

    A. prophase

    B. telophase

    C. anaphase

    D. metaphase

    E. interphase

Biology

23. **What is the stage of mitosis shown in the diagram?**

    A. interphase

    B. metaphase

    C. prophase

    D. telophase

    E. anaphase

24. **Which of the following is a monomer?**

    A. RNA

    B. glycogen

    C. DNA

    D. amino acid

    E. lipid

25. **Which of the following does not affect enzyme rate?**

    A. increase of temperature

    B. amount of substrate

    C. pH

    D. size of the cell

    E. concentration of enzyme

26. **All but which one of the following is true of a cell membrane?**

    A. It contains polar and nonpolar phospholipids.

    B. It only uses active transport to move molecules across it.

    C. It contains cholesterol.

    D. It has proteins imbedded within it.

    E. It is selectively permeable to many substances.

27. **Which of these describes facilitated diffusion?**

    A. It requires energy.

    B. It only happens in plant cells.

    C. It only allows molecules to leave a cell but not to enter it.

    D. It produces a significant amount of energy for the cell.

    E. It needs a transport molecule to pass through the membrane.

28. **What is not true of enzymes?**

    A. They are the most diverse of all proteins.

    B. They act on a substrate.

    C. They work at a wide range of pH.

    D. They are temperature-dependent.

    E. They have specialized functions.

29. Which of these is necessary for diffusion to occur?

    A. carrier proteins

    B. energy

    C. water molecules

    D. a cell membrane

    E. a concentration gradient

30. Which is an example of the use of energy to move a substance through a membrane from areas of low concentration to areas of high concentration?

    A. osmosis

    B. active transport

    C. exocytosis

    D. phagocytosis

    E. facilitated diffusion

31. A plant cell is placed in salt water. What is the resulting movement of water out of the cell called?

    A. facilitated diffusion

    B. diffusion

    C. transpiration

    D. osmosis

    E. active transport

32. What are the monomers of polysaccharides?

    A. Nucleotides

    B. Amino acids

    C. Polypeptides

    D. Fatty acids

    E. Simple sugars

33. Which type of cell would contain the most mitochondria?

    A. muscle cell

    B. nerve cell

    C. epithelial cell

    D. blood cell

    E. bone cell

34. According to the fluid-mosaic model of the cell membrane, of what are membranes composed?

    A. Phospholipid bilayers with proteins embedded in the layers.

    B. One layer of phospholipids with cholesterol embedded in the layer.

    C. Two layers of protein with lipids embedded in the layers.

    D. DNA and fluid proteins with carbohydrates embedded in the layer.

    E. Glycerol and RNA with carbohydrates embedded in the layer.

Biology

35. **Which is the correct statement regarding the human nervous system and the human endocrine system?**

    A. The nervous system maintains homeostasis whereas the endocrine system does not.

    B. Endocrine glands produce neurotransmitters whereas nerves produce hormones.

    C. Nerve signals travel on neurons whereas hormones travel through the blood.

    D. The nervous system involves chemical transmission whereas the endocrine system does not.

    E. The nervous system produces physiological responses whereas the endocrine produces behavioral.

36. **Which process generates the most ATP?**

    A. fermentation

    B. glycolysis

    C. the Calvin cycle

    D. the Krebs cycle

    E. chemiosmosis

37. **Which of these is a function of the cardiovascular system?**

    A. Move oxygenated blood around the body

    B. Oxygenate the blood through gas exchange

    C. Act as an exocrine system

    D. Flush toxins out of the body

    E. Transport signals from the brain

38. **Which of these is not a part of the nervous system?**

    A. brain

    B. spinal cord

    C. axons

    D. venules

    E. cochlea

39. **Organisms need to maintain a constant internal environment to survive. Which of these is a method by which they achieve this?**

    A. respiration

    B. reproduction

    C. depolarization

    D. repolarization

    E. thermoregulation

Biology

40. Which of these controls the body's endocrine mechanisms?

    A. feedback loops

    B. control molecules

    C. neurochemicals

    D. neurotransmitters

    E. behavioral responses

41. What is the gland that regulates the calcium in the body?

    A. Thyroid gland

    B. Parathyroid gland

    C. Hypothalamus

    D. Pituitary gland

    E. Pancreas

42. Which of these steroids is not created in the gonads?

    A. Testosterone

    B. Estrogen

    C. Progesterone

    D. ACTH

    E. FSH

43. What is the most common neurotransmitter?

    A. epinephrine

    B. serotonin

    C. acetyl choline

    D. norepinephrine

    E. oxytocin

44. Food is carried through the digestive tract by a series of wave-like contractions. What is this process is called?

    A. peristalsis

    B. chyme

    C. digestion

    D. absorption

    E. depolarization

45. Which of these must muscles pull on in order to initiate movement?

    A. skin

    B. bones

    C. joints

    D. ligaments

    E. bursa

46. Hormones are essential to the regulation of reproduction. What organ is responsible for the release of hormones for sexual maturity?

    A. pituitary gland

    B. hypothalamus

    C. pancreas

    D. thyroid gland

    E. pineal gland

47. What is the type of muscle in the human body that is voluntary?

    A. Cardiac

    B. Sarcomere

    C. Smooth

    D. Skeletal

    E. Actin

48. The wrist is an example of what kind of joint?

    A. Ball and socket

    B. Pivot

    C. Stationary

    D. Hinge

    E. Gliding

49. What is the waterproofing protein in the skin called?

    A. actin

    B. epidermis

    C. collagen

    D. sebum

    E. keratin

50. What is the muscular adaptation called that is used to move food through the digestive system?

    A. peristalsis

    B. passive transport

    C. voluntary action

    D. bulk transport

    E. endocytosis

51. What is the role of neurotransmitters in nerve action?

    A. to turn off the sodium pump

    B. to turn off the calcium pump

    C. to send impulses to neurons

    D. to send impulses around the body

    E. to send impulses from axon to dendrite

52. **Fats are broken down by which substance?**

    A. bile produced in the gall bladder

    B. lipase produced in the gall bladder

    C. glucagons produced in the liver

    D. amylase produces in the gall bladder

    E. bile produced in the liver

53. **Where does fertilization in humans usually occurs?**

    A. uterus

    B. ovary

    C. fallopian tubes

    D. vagina

    E. epididymis

54. **Which of these is lacking in the dermis layer of skin?**

    A. sweat glands

    B. keratin

    C. hair follicles

    D. blood vessels

    E. living cells

55. **A school age boy had the chicken pox as a baby. Why will he most likely not get this disease again?**

    A. passive immunity

    B. vaccination

    C. antibiotics

    D. active immunity

    E. antigen production

56. **What is any foreign particle called that causes an immune reaction?**

    A. an antigen

    B. a histocompatibity complex

    C. an antibody

    D. a vaccine

    E. a bacteriophage

57. **Which of these statements describes the polymerase chain reaction?**

    A. It is a group of polymerases.

    B. It is a technique for amplifying DNA.

    C. It is a primer for DNA synthesis.

    D. It is a way to synthesize polymerase.

    E. It is a series of genetic mutations.

58. Which part of a DNA nucleotide can vary?

    A. deoxyribose

    B. phosphate group

    C. hydrogen bonds

    D. sugar

    E. nitrogenous base

59. A DNA strand has the base sequence of TCAGTA. Its DNA complement would have which of the following sequences?

    A. ATGACT

    B. TCAGTA

    C. AGUCAU

    D. AGTCAT

    E. TCTGTA

60. Which of these carries amino acids to the ribosome during protein synthesis?

    A. messenger RNA

    B. ribosomal RNA

    C. transfer RNA

    D. DNA

    E. RNA

61. A protein is sixty amino acids in length. This requires a coded DNA sequence of how many nucleotides?

    A. 20

    B. 30

    C. 120

    D. 180

    E. 240

62. A DNA molecule has the sequence of ACTATG. What is the anticodon of this molecule?

    A. UGAUAC

    B. ACUAUG

    C. TGATAC

    D. ACTATG

    E. CTGCGA

63. What is the general term for a change that affects the sequence of bases in a gene?

    A. deletion

    B. polyploid

    C. mutation

    D. duplication

    E. substitution

64. Segments of DNA can be transferred from the DNA of one organism to another through the use of which of the following?

    A. bacterial plasmids

    B. viruses

    C. chromosomes from frogs

    D. plant DNA

    E. Okazaki fragments

65. What is the enzyme that unwinds DNA during replication?

    A. DNAse

    B. DNA replicase

    C. DNA helicase

    D. DNA topoisomerases

    E. DNA polymerase

66. What is a small circular piece of DNA called that contains accessory DNA?

    A. mitochondrial DNA

    B. messenger RNA

    C. transfer DNA

    D. Okazaki fragment

    E. plasmid

67. In DNA, adenine bonds with _____, while cytosine bonds with _____.

    A. thymine/guanine

    B. adenine/cytosine

    C. cytosine/uracil

    D. guanine/thymine

    E. uracil/adenine

68. Which protein structure consists of the coils and folds of polypeptide chains?

    A. secondary structure

    B. quaternary structure

    C. tertiary structure

    D. primary structure

    E. quinary structure

69. What can be said about homozygous individuals?

    A. They have two different alleles.

    B. They are of the same species.

    C. They exhibit the same features.

    D. They have a pair of identical alleles.

    E. They produce identical offspring.

Biology

70. The term "phenotype" refers to which of the following?

A. a condition that is heterozygous

B. the genetic makeup of an individual

C. a condition that is homozygous

D. how the genotype is expressed

E. from which parent the traits were inherited

71. The ratio of brown-eyed to blue-eyed children from the mating of a blue-eyed male to a heterozygous brown-eyed female is expected to be which of the following?

A. 3:1

B. 2:2

C. 1:0

D. 1:2

E. 0:4

72. Which of these defines the Law of Segregation defined by Gregor Mendel?

A. After meiosis, each new cell will contain an allele that is recessive.

B. Only one of two alleles is expressed in a heterozygous organism.

C. The allele expressed is always the dominant allele.

D. Alleles of one trait do not affect the inheritance of alleles on another chromosome.

E. When sex cells form, the two alleles that determine a trait will end up on different gametes.

73. Which of the following is an example of the incomplete dominance that occurs when a white flower is crossed with a red flower?

A. pink flowers

B. red flowers

C. white flowers

D. red and white flowers

E. white and pink flowers

74. A child with type O blood has a father with type A blood and a mother with type B blood. The genotypes of the parents respectively would be which of the following?

    A. AA and BO

    B. AO and BO

    C. AA and BB

    D. AO and OO

    E. OO and AB

75. Crossing over, which increases genetic diversity, occurs during which stage(s) of meiosis?

    A. telophase II in meiosis

    B. metaphase in mitosis

    C. interphase in meiosis

    D. prophase I in meiosis

    E. metaphase II in meiosis

76. ABO blood grouping is an example of which type of allele dominance?

    A. Autosomal dominance

    B. Incomplete dominance

    C. Somatic dominance

    D. Complete dominance

    E. Codominance

77. In a Punnett square with a single trait, what are the ratios of genotypes produced between two heterozygous individuals?

    A. 1:2:2

    B. 2:1:1

    C. 1:1:1

    D. 1:2:1

    E. 2:2:2

78. What is the term for an organism's genetic makeup?

    A. Heterozygote

    B. Genotype

    C. Phenotype

    D. Homozygote

    E. Dominance

79. Which of these represents a genetic engineering advancement in the medical field?

    A. stem cell reproduction

    B. pesticides

    C. degradation of harmful chemicals

    D. antibiotics

    E. gene therapy

Biology

80. Which of the following is not true regarding restriction enzymes?

    A. They aid in transcombination procedures.

    B. They are used in genetic engineering.

    C. They are named after the bacteria in which they naturally occur.

    D. They identify and splice certain base sequences on DNA.

    E. They can be produced by certain lipids during DNA replication.

81. Which of these processes is not one of the modern uses of DNA?

    A. PCR technology

    B. Gene therapy

    C. Cloning

    D. Genetic Alignment

    E. Transgenic organisms

82. Which statement best represents gel electrophoresis?

    A. It isolates fragments of DNA for scientific purposes.

    B. It cannot be used in proteins.

    C. It requires the polymerase chain reaction.

    D. It only separates DNA by size.

    E. It uses different charged particles to color the bands.

83. What is the term that describes the duplication of genetic material into another cell?

    A. replicating

    B. cell duplication

    C. transgenics

    D. genetic restructuring

    E. cloning

84. What does gel electrophoresis use to separate the DNA?

    A. the amount of current

    B. the size of the molecule

    C. the positive charge of the molecule

    D. the solubility of the gel

    E. the source of the DNA

85. Which of these is a result of reproductive isolation?

    A. extinction

    B. migration

    C. fossilization

    D. speciation

    E. radiation

Biology

86. **Which of these is true about natural selection?**

    A. It acts on an individual genotype.

    B. It is not currently happening.

    C. It is only an animal phenomenon.

    D. It acts on the individual phenotype.

    E. It is used to prevent overpopulation.

87. **How does diversity aid a population?**

    A. Individuals are better able to survive.

    B. Mates are attracted to a diverse population.

    C. Potential mates like conformity.

    D. It increases the DNA differences in the population.

    E. It provides possible improvements to the population.

88. **Which statement is not true about diversity?**

    A. Without diversity there would be extinction.

    B. Diversity is increasing all the time.

    C. Fossil evidence supports diversity.

    D. Sexual reproduction encourages more diversity.

    E. Skeletons are too similar to allow for diversity.

89. **Which of these ideas was a major part of Darwin's evolutionary theory?**

    A. Punctualism

    B. Gradualism

    C. Equilibrium

    D. Convergency

    E. Altruism

90. **Which statement is not true about reproductive isolation?**

    A. It prevents populations from exchanging genes.

    B. It can occur by preventing fertilization.

    C. It can result in speciation.

    D. It happens more often on the mainland.

    E. It produces offspring with unique phenotypes

91. **Which idea is true about members of the same species?**

    A. They look identical.

    B. They never change.

    C. They reproduce successfully within their group.

    D. They live in the same geographic location.

    E. They have very dissimilar genotypes.

92. Which of the following factors will affect the Hardy-Weinberg law of equilibrium, leading to evolutionary change?

    A. no mutations

    B. non-random mating

    C. no immigration or emigration

    D. large population

    E. small individual species

93. If a population is in Hardy-Weinberg equilibrium and the frequency of the recessive allele is 0.3, what percentage of the population is expected to be heterozygous?

    A. 9%

    B. 49%

    C. 42%

    D. 21%

    E. 7%

94. Which aspect of science does not support evolution?

    A. comparative anatomy

    B. organic chemistry

    C. comparison of DNA among organisms

    D. analogous structures

    E. embryology

95. In which of these does evolution occurs?

    A. individuals

    B. populations

    C. organ systems

    D. cells

    E. ecosystems

96. Which process contributes most to the large variety of living things in the world today?

    A. meiosis

    B. asexual reproduction

    C. mitosis

    D. alternation of generations

    E. reproductive isolation

97. Which of the following gases was a major part of the primitive Earth atmosphere?

    A. fluorine

    B. methane

    C. oxygen

    D. krypton

    E. argon

98. **What is a major principle of the Endosymbiotic Theory?**

    A. Birds and dinosaurs share a common ancestor.

    B. Animals evolved in close relationships with one another.

    C. Prokaryotes arose from eukaryotes.

    D. Inorganic compounds are the basis of living things.

    E. Eukaryotes arose from very simple prokaryotes.

99. **The wing of a bird, the human arm, and the pectoral fluke of a whale all have the same bone structure. What are these structures called?**

    A. polymorphic structures

    B. homologous structures

    C. vestigial structures

    D. analogous structures

    E. allopatric structures

100. **Which of the following is not an abiotic factor?**

    A. temperature

    B. rainfall

    C. soil quality

    D. predation

    E. wind speed

101. **What is not true about cladistics?**

    A. It is the study of phylogenetic relationships of organisms.

    B. It involves a branching diagram that uses the development of novel traits to separate groups of organisms.

    C. It distinguishes between the relative importance of the traits.

    D. It shows when traits developed with respect to other traits.

    E. It indicates which organisms are most closely related to each other and what their common ancestors were.

102. **If DDT were present in an ecosystem, which of the following organisms would have the highest concentration in its body?**

    A. herring

    B. diatom

    C. zooplankton

    D. salmon

    E. osprey

103. **What eats secondary consumers?**

    A. Producers

    B. Tertiary consumers

    C. Primary consumers

    D. Decomposers

    E. Detritivores

104. **Which statement is true about the water cycle?**

    A. Two percent of the water is fixed and unavailable.

    B. 75% of available water is groundwater.

    C. The water cycle is driven by the ocean currents.

    D. Surface water percolates up from underground springs.

    E. New water is being added into the cycle all the time.

105. **Which statement about the carbon cycle is false?**

    A. Ten percent of all available carbon is in the air.

    B. Carbon dioxide is fixed by glycosylation.

    C. Plants fix carbon in the form of glucose.

    D. Animals release carbon through respiration.

    E. Most atmospheric carbon comes from the decay of dead organisms.

106. **What is the impact of sulfur oxides and nitrogen oxides in the environment when they react with water?**

    A. ammonia

    B. acidic precipitation

    C. sulfuric acid

    D. global warming

    E. greenhouse effect

107. **Which term is not associated with the water cycle?**

    A. precipitation

    B. transpiration

    C. fixation

    D. evaporation

    E. runoff

108. **Which of the following is a density dependent factor that affects a population?**

    A. temperature

    B. rainfall

    C. predation

    D. soil nutrients

    E. wind speed

109. **High humidity and temperature stability are present in which of the following biomes?**

    A. taiga

    B. deciduous forest

    C. desert

    D. tropical rain forest

    E. coniferous forest

110. **Which trophic level has the highest ecological efficiency?**

    A. decomposers

    B. producers

    C. tertiary consumers

    D. secondary consumers

    E. primary consumers

111. **From where does the oxygen created in photosynthesis come?**

    A. carbon dioxide

    B. chlorophyll

    C. glucose

    D. carbon monoxide

    E. water

112. **Which of the following is true of decomposers?**

    A. Decomposers recycle the carbon accumulated in durable organic material.

    B. They take nitrogen out of the soil to use for food.

    C. Decomposers absorb nutrients from the air to maintain their metabolisms.

    D. Decomposers belong to the Genus *Escherichia*.

    E. They are able to use the Sun to produce their own energy.

Biology

113. A clownfish is protected by a sea anemone's tentacles, and in turn, the anemone receives uneaten food from the clownfish. What type of symbiosis is exemplified by this example?

    A. mutualism

    B. parasitism

    C. commensalism

    D. competition

    E. amensalism

114. Which of these is most likely to happen in order for primary succession to occur?

    A. nutrient enrichment

    B. a forest fire

    C. bare rock is exposed after a water table recedes

    D. a housing development is built

    E. a farmer stops cultivating her fields

115. What is the Mendelian law called that states that only one of the two possible alleles from each parent is passed on to the offspring?

    A. The Mendelian Law

    B. The Law of Independent Assortment

    C. The Law of Segregation

    D. The Allele Law

    E. The Law of Dominance and Recessiveness

Biology

ANSWER KEY

Question Number	Correct Answer	Your Answer	Question Number	Correct Answer	Your Answer	Question Number	Correct Answer	Your Answer
1	C		40	A		79	E	
2	E		41	B		80	A	
3	A		42	D		81	D	
4	A		43	C		82	A	
5	D		44	A		83	E	
6	C		45	B		84	B	
7	A		46	B		85	D	
8	E		47	D		86	D	
9	A		48	B		87	E	
10	D		49	E		88	E	
11	D		50	A		89	B	
12	A		51	C		90	D	
13	C		52	E		91	C	
14	D		53	C		92	B	
15	E		54	B		93	C	
16	A		55	D		94	B	
17	A		56	A		95	B	
18	D		57	B		96	A	
19	B		58	E		97	B	
20	B		59	D		98	E	
21	B		60	C		99	B	
22	B		61	D		100	D	
23	E		62	D		101	C	
24	D		63	C		102	E	
25	D		64	A		103	B	
26	B		65	C		104	A	
27	E		66	E		105	B	
28	C		67	A		106	B	
29	E		68	A		107	C	
30	B		69	D		108	C	
31	D		70	D		109	D	
32	E		71	B		110	B	
33	A		72	E		111	E	
34	A		73	A		112	A	
35	C		74	B		113	A	
36	E		75	D		114	C	
37	A		76	E		115	B	
38	D		77	D				
39	E		78	B				

Calculus

Description of the Examination

The Calculus examination covers skills and concepts that are usually taught in a one-semester college course in calculus. The content of each examination is approximately 60% limits and differential calculus and 40% integral calculus. Algebraic, trigonometric, exponential, logarithmic, and general functions are included. The exam is primarily concerned with an intuitive understanding of calculus and experience with its methods and applications. Knowledge of preparatory mathematics, including algebra, geometry, trigonometry, and analytic geometry is assumed.

The examination contains 44 questions, in two sections, to be answered in approximately 90 minutes. Any time candidates spend on tutorials and providing personal information is in addition to the actual testing time.
- Section 1: 27 questions, approximately 50 minutes.
  No calculator is allowed for this section.

- Section 2: 17 questions, approximately 40 minutes.
  The use of an online graphing calculator (non-CAS) is allowed for this section. Only some of the questions will require the use of the calculator.

Graphing Calculator
A graphing calculator is integrated into the exam software, and it is available to students during Section 2 of the exam.

Only some of the questions actually require the graphing calculator. Students are expected to know how and when to make appropriate use of the calculator. The graphing calculator, together with brief video tutorials, is available to students as a free download for a 30-day trial period. Students are expected to download the calculator and become familiar with its functionality prior to taking the exam.

In order to answer some of the questions in the calculator section of the exam, students may be required to use the online graphing calculator in the following ways:
- Perform calculations (e.g., exponents, roots, trigonometric values, logarithms)
- Graph functions and analyze the graphs
- Find zeros of functions
- Find points of intersection of graphs of functions
- Find minima/maxima of functions
- Find numerical solutions to equations
- Generate a table of values for a function

Knowledge and Skills Required

Questions on the exam require candidates to demonstrate the following abilities:
- Solving routine problems involving the techniques of calculus (approximately 50% of the exam)
- Solving nonroutine problems involving an understanding of the concepts and applications of calculus (approximately 50% of the exam)

Calculus

Section I

TIME: 50 Minutes
27 Questions

Directions: Solve each of the following problems without using a calculator. Choose the best answer from those provided. Some questions will require you to enter a numerical answer in the box provided.

Notes:

Figures that accompany questions are intended to provide information useful in answering the questions. All figures lie in a plane unless otherwise indicated. The figures are drawn as accurately as possible EXCEPT when it is stated in a specific question that the figure is not drawn to scale. Straight lines and smooth curves may appear slightly jagged.

Unless otherwise specified, all angles are measured in radians and all numbers used are real numbers.

Unless otherwise specified, the domain of any function f is assumed to be the set of all real numbers x for which $f(x)$ is a real number. The range of f is assumed to be the set of all real numbers $f(x)$, where x is in the domain of f.

In this exam, $\ln(x)$ denotes the natural logarithm of x (the logarithm to the base e).

The inverse of a trigonometric function f may be indicated using the inverse function notation f^{-1} or with the prefix "arc" (e.g, $\sin^{-1}(x)$= arcsin (x)).

SAMPLE TEST

1. If $y = -3x^2 + 2x + 1$, then $\frac{dy}{dx} =$

   A. $-6x$

   B. $-6x + 1$

   C. $-6x + 2$

   D. $-x^3 + x^2$

   E. $-x^3 + x^2 + x$

2. $\int \sin(2x)\,dx =$

   A. $-2\cos(2x) + C$

   B. $-\frac{1}{2}\cos(2x) + C$

   C. $\frac{1}{2}\cos(2x) + C$

   D. $2\cos(2x) + C$

   E. $\frac{1}{2}\sin(2x) + C$

3. $\lim\limits_{x \to \infty} \frac{6x^2 + 2x}{5 - 2x^2} =$

   A. -3

   B. -1

   C. 0

   D. $\frac{6}{5}$

   E. The limit does not exist.

4. The velocity of a particle is constantly increasing, as shown in the table below.

$t\,(s)$	0	1	2	3	4
$v\,(m/s)$	0	2	3	5	7

   Using a Riemann sum with four subdivisions, give an upper bound on the distance traveled (in m).

    m

5. Let f be a function defined over all real numbers, and let c be a real number. If $\lim\limits_{x \to c} f(x) = f(c)$, then which of the following statements MUST be true?

   f is continuous at $x = c$.
   f is differentiable at $x = c$.
   f is integrable at $x = c$.

   A. I only

   B. II only

   C. I and II only

   D. I and III only

   E. I, II and III

6. The graph of a function f is shown in the figure below.

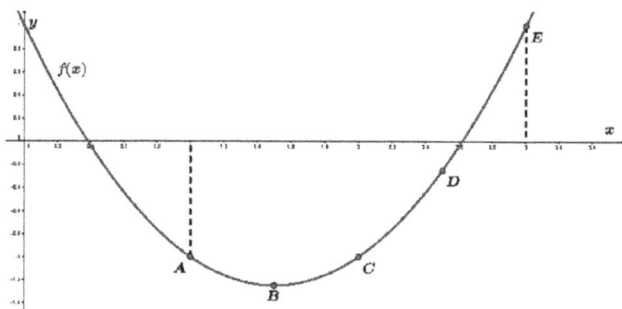

At which of the following points is f' equal to the mean rate of change of f on the interval $[1, 3]$?

A. A

B. B

C. C

D. D

E. E

7. If $y = x^2 \cos(x)$, then $\frac{d^2y}{dx^2} =$

A. $-2\sin(x)$

B. $-2x\sin(x)$

C. $2\cos(x) - 4x\sin(x) - x^2\cos(x)$

D. $2\cos(x) - 4x\sin(x) + x^2\cos(x)$

E. $2\cos(x) + 4x\sin(x) + x^2\cos(x)$

8. The Riemann sum $\sum_{i=1}^{360} \sin\left(\frac{\pi i}{360}\right) \cdot \frac{\pi}{360}$ is an approximation for which of the following integrals?

A. $\int_1^{360} \sin(x)\, dx$

B. $\int_1^{360} \sin(\pi x)\, dx$

C. $\int_0^{\pi} \sin(x)\, dx$

D. $\int_0^{\pi} \sin(\pi x)\, dx$

E. $\int_0^{\pi} \sin(360x)\, dx$

9. If $g(x) = \frac{x}{2x+1}$, then $g'(x) =$

A. $\frac{1}{2}$

B. $\frac{4x+1}{2x+1}$

C. $\frac{4x+1}{(2x+1)^2}$

D. $\frac{1}{2x+1}$

E. $\frac{1}{(2x+1)^2}$

10. Let f and g be differentiable functions on the whole real line, and let $h(x) = f(g(x))$. Use the table of values below to find $h'(1)$.

x	$f(x)$	$f'(x)$	$g(x)$	$g'(x)$
-2	-1	2	-3	0
1	4	5	-2	3

11. If $y = x^x$, then $\frac{dy}{dx} =$

    A. $(\ln(x) + 1)x^x$

    B. $\ln(x) x^x$

    C. x^x

    D. x^{x-1}

    E. $x \ln(x)$

12. Let g be a continuous function on the whole real line, and let $a, b,$ and c be positive constants. $\int_a^b g\left(\frac{x-1}{c}\right) dx$ is equivalent to which of the following integrals?

    A. $\int_{(a-1)/c}^{(b-1)/c} g(u)\, du$

    B. $\frac{1}{c}\int_{(a-1)/c}^{(b-1)/c} g(u)\, du$

    C. $c\int_{(a-1)/c}^{(b-1)/c} g(u)\, du$

    D. $\frac{1}{c}\int_a^b g(u)\, du$

    E. $c\int_a^b g(u)\, du$

13. Let f be differentiable on the whole real line. If $y = -\frac{1}{5}x + \frac{31}{5}$ is normal to the graph of f at $x = 1$, which of the following statements MUST be true?

    I. f is increasing at $x = 1$.

    II. $f'(1) = -\frac{1}{5}$

    III. f is continuous at $x = 1$.

    A. I only

    B. II only

    C. III only

    D. I and II only

    E. I and III only

14. Given $\int_a^b f(x)dx = 4$, $\int_a^c f(x)dx = -2$, and $a < b < c$, evaluate $\int_b^c f(x)dx$.

    \[\quad\quad\quad\quad\]

    If $y = \frac{\sec(x)}{\csc(x)}$, then $\frac{dy}{dx} =$

    A. $-\frac{\sec(x)\tan(x)}{\csc(x)\cot(x)}$

    B. $-\frac{\cos(x)}{\sin(x)}$

    C. $\sec^2(x)$

    D. $-\csc^2(x)$

    E. $\tan(x)$

Calculus

15. The limit $\lim_{h \to 0} \frac{(x+h)^2 - 2(x+h) - x^2 + 2x}{h}$ is equal to the derivative of which of the following functions?

    A. $f(x) = x^2$

    B. $f(x) = x^2 - 2x$

    C. $f(x) = x^2 + 2x$

    D. $f(x) = x - 2$

    E. $f(x) = x + 2$

16. The graph of a twice differentiable function f is shown below.

    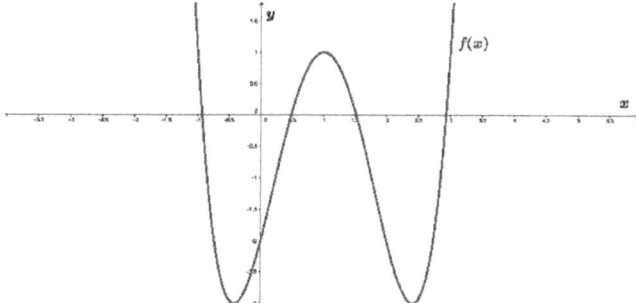

    Which of the following inequalities is true?

    A. $f(1) < f'(1) < f''(1)$

    B. $f(1) < f''(1) < f'(1)$

    C. $f'(1) < f''(1) < f(1)$

    D. $f''(1) < f(1) < f'(1)$

    E. $f''(1) < f'(1) < f(1)$

17. If $y = \arctan(\ln(x))$, then $\frac{dy}{dx} =$

    A. $\frac{1}{(\ln(x))^2 + 1}$

    B. $\frac{1}{(\ln(x))^2 + 1} \cdot \frac{1}{x}$

    C. $\frac{\ln(x)}{(\ln(x))^2 + 1}$

    D. $\frac{1}{\ln(x) + 1}$

    E. $\frac{1}{\ln(x) + 1} \cdot \frac{1}{x}$

18. Below are the graphs of three differentiable functions $f, g,$ and h. Which of the following statements is true?

    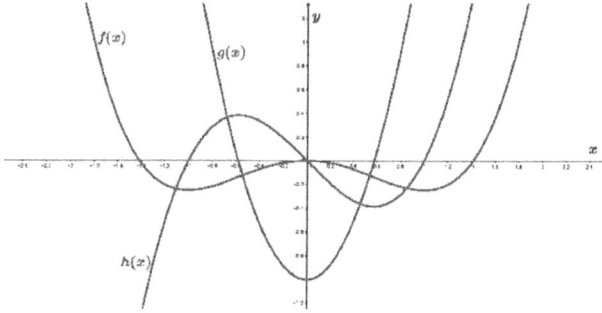

    A. $f'(x) = g(x)$ and $g'(x) = f(x)$

    B. $f'(x) = g(x)$ and $g'(x) = h(x)$

    C. $f'(x) = h(x)$ and $h'(x) = f(x)$

    D. $f'(x) = h(x)$ and $h'(x) = g(x)$

    E. $g'(x) = h(x)$ and $h'(x) = f(x)$

Calculus

19. $\int \cot^2(x)\,dx =$

    A. $-\cot(x) - x + C$

    B. $\cot(x) - x + C$

    C. $\frac{1}{3}\cot^3(x) + C$

    D. $-2\cot^2(x) + C$

    E. $-2\cot^2(x)\csc(x) + C$

20. The graph of $f(t)$ is given below, and $a, b, c, d,$ and e are real numbers.

    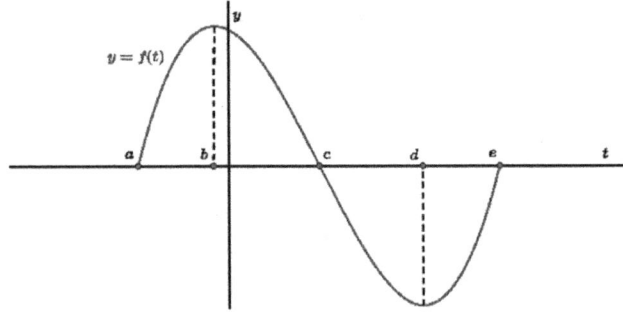

    Let $g(x) = \int_a^x f(t)\,dt$. On which of the following intervals is the graph of g concave up?

    A. (a, b)

    B. (a, c)

    C. $(a, b) \cup (c, d)$

    D. $(a, b) \cup (d, e)$

    E. (b, d)

21. $\int_0^1 \frac{1}{\sqrt{x}}\,dx =$

    A. 2

    B. 1

    C. $\frac{1}{2}$

    D. 0

    E. Undefined

22. Let $f(x) = 2x^3 + 6x^2 + 6x - 1$. Find all values of x for which $f'(x) = f''(x)$.

    A. 0 and 24

    B. -1 and 1

    C. -2 and 2

    D. $-\sqrt{6}$ and $\sqrt{6}$

    E. -6 and 6

Calculus

23. What is the mean value of $f(x) = x^2 + 1$ on the interval $[0, 2]$?

    A. 0

    B. 1

    C. 2

    D. $\frac{7}{3}$

    E. $\frac{14}{3}$

24. $\lim_{x \to 0} \frac{e^{2x}-1}{\tan(3x)}$

    A. $-\infty$

    B. 0

    C. $\frac{2}{3}$

    D. 1

    E. ∞

25. Let $f(x)$ be the following piecewise function.

    $$f(x) = \begin{cases} x^2 - 1 & x \leq 1 \\ 2x + k & x > 1 \end{cases}$$

    Find the value of k for which f is continuous at $x = 1$.

    A. -2

    B. -1

    C. 0

    D. 1

    E. 2

26. Find the real number b such that

    $$\int_1^b \frac{1}{t} dt = -2.$$

    A. e^2

    B. $e^{1/2}$

    C. e^{-2}

    D. $\frac{1}{\sqrt{3}}$

    E. $-\frac{1}{\sqrt{3}}$

Calculus

Section II

TIME: 40 Minutes
17 Questions

Directions: A graphing calculator is available for the questions in this section. Choose the best answer from those provided. Some questions will require you to enter a numerical answer in the box provided.

27. Find the slope at the point $(2, 1)$ on the graph of $x^2 - y^2 - x = 1$.

   A. $-\frac{3}{2}$

   B. -1

   C. 0

   D. 1

   E. $\frac{3}{2}$

28. Find the area of the region bounded by the graphs of $f(x) = (x-1)^3 + 1$ and $g(x) = x$.

   A. 0

   B. $\frac{1}{4}$

   C. $\frac{1}{2}$

   D. $\frac{3}{4}$

   E. 1

29. What is the absolute maximum of the function $f(x) = 2x^3 + 3x^2 - 12x + 4$ on the interval $[0, 2]$?

   A. -3

   B. 4

   C. 8

   D. 24

   E. f has no absolute maximum on $[0,2]$.

30. Find the function $f(x)$ that satisfies both the differential equation $f'(x) = 2x - 3$ and the condition $f(1) = 2$.

   A. $f(x) = x^2 - 3x + 1$

   B. $f(x) = x^2 - 3x + 2$

   C. $f(x) = x^2 - 3x + 3$

   D. $f(x) = x^2 - 3x + 4$

   E. $f(x) = x^2 - 3x + 5$

Calculus

31. Find the area bounded by the x-axis and the graph of f, where $f(x)$ is the following piecewise function.

$$f(x) = \begin{cases} \dfrac{1}{2}x + \dfrac{1}{2} & 0 \le x < 1 \\ \sqrt{1-(x-1)^2} & 1 \le x \le 2 \end{cases}$$

A. $1 + \dfrac{\pi}{2}$

B. $1 + \dfrac{\pi}{4}$

C. $\dfrac{3}{4} + \dfrac{\pi}{2}$

D. $\dfrac{3}{4} + \dfrac{\pi}{4}$

E. $\dfrac{3}{2}$

32. The displacement s of a particle at time $t \ge 0$ is given by the following function.

$$s(t) = \dfrac{1}{20}t^5 - \dfrac{5}{12}t^4 + \dfrac{4}{3}t^3 - 2t^2$$

Assume that all quantities are in SI units. For what values of t (in seconds) is the acceleration of the particle negative?

A. (0,1) only

B. (0,3) only

C. (1,2) only

D. (0,1) ∪ (1,2)

E. (0,1) ∪ (1,3)

33. Use four trapezoids to estimate the area of the region bounded by the graph of $f(x) = \dfrac{1}{x^4+1}$ and the lines $x = 0$, $x = 2$, and $y = 0$. Round your answer to the nearest hundredth.

34. $\lim\limits_{x \to 0^+} x^{\sin(x)} =$

A. -1

B. 0

C. $\dfrac{1}{2}$

D. 1

E. 2

Calculus

35. The acceleration a (in $\frac{m}{s^2}$) of a particle at time $t \geq 0$ (in s) is given by $a(t) = te^{-t^2}$. At $t = 0$ s, the velocity of the particle is $2.5 \frac{m}{s}$. What is the velocity (in $\frac{m}{s}$) of the particle at $t = 2$ s?

A. $2 - \frac{1}{2e^4}$

B. $2 + \frac{1}{2e^4}$

C. $3 - \frac{1}{2e^4}$

D. 3

E. $3 + \frac{1}{2e^4}$

36. Find the equation of the line that passes through the point $(3, 4)$ and that, together with the $x-$ and $y-$axes, forms a triangular region in the first quadrant of minimum area.

A. $3x + 4y - 25 = 0$

B. $3x - 4y + 7 = 0$

C. $4x + 3y - 24 = 0$

D. $4x - 3y = 0$

E. $x + y - 7 = 0$

37. Which of the following inequalities is true?

Let $A = \int_{-1/2}^{1/2} f(x)\, dx$, $B = \int_{-1/2}^{1/2} g(x)\, dx$, and $C = \int_{-1/2}^{1/2} h(x)\, dx$, where $f(x) = \frac{1}{2(x^2+1)}$, $g(x) = \frac{x^2}{x^2+1}$, and $h(x) = e^{-x^2}$

A. $A < B < C$

B. $A < C < B$

C. $B < A < C$

D. $B < C < A$

E. $C < A < B$

38. Let $f(x) = -\frac{1}{3}x^3 - x + 1$. Find any values of x in the interval $[-3, 3]$ at which the instantaneous rate of change of f equals the average rate of change of f on $[-3, 3]$.

A. -3

B. $\pm\sqrt{5}$

C. $\pm\sqrt{3}$

D. $\pm\sqrt{2}$

E. 3

Calculus

39. Consider the region bounded by the graph of $y = 4 - 2x^2$ and the x-axis. Find the area of the largest isosceles triangle that can be inscribed in this region with one vertex at the origin and the base parallel to the x-axis. Round your answer to the nearest hundredth.

    [ ]

40. Which of the following functions is strictly monotonic on its entire domain?

    A. $f(x) = x^3 - 2x$

    B. $f(x) = x^3 - x$

    C. $f(x) = x^3 + x$

    D. $f(x) = x^2 - x$

    E. $f(x) = x^2 + x$

41. The radius of a circle is increasing at a constant rate of $3 \frac{cm}{s}$. At what rate (in $\frac{cm^2}{s}$) is the area of the circle increasing when the radius is $5\ cm$?

    A. 6π

    B. 9π

    C. 10π

    D. 25π

    E. 30π

42. $\lim\limits_{x \to \pi/2} \sec(x) \tan(x) =$

    A. $-\infty$

    B. 0

    C. 1

    D. ∞

    E. The limit does not exist.

43. Find all real numbers c in $[a, b]$ such that $\int_a^b f(x)\, dx = f(c)(b - a)$ if $a = 0, b = 2$, and $f(x) = 3x^2 + 1$.

    A. $\pm \frac{\sqrt{3}}{3}$

    B. $\pm \frac{2\sqrt{3}}{3}$

    C. $\pm \frac{4}{3}$

    D. $\frac{2\sqrt{3}}{3}$

    E. $\frac{4}{3}$

Calculus

ANSWER KEY

Question Number	Correct Answer	Your Answer	Question Number	Correct Answer	Your Answer	Question Number	Correct Answer	Your Answer
1	C		16	B		31	D	
2	B		17	E		32	D	
3	A		18	B		33	A	
4	17		19	D		34	1.07	
5	D		20	A		35	D	
6	C		21	D		36	C	
7	C		22	A		37	C	
8	C		23	B		38	C	
9	E		24	D		39	C	
10	6		25	C		40	2.18	
11	A		26	A		41	C	
12	C		27	C		42	E	
13	E		28	E		43	D	
14	6		29	C		44	D	
15	C		30	C				

Chemistry

Description of the Examination

The Chemistry examination covers material that is usually taught in a one-year college course in general chemistry. Understanding of the structure and states of matter, reaction types, equations and stoichiometry, equilibrium, kinetics, thermodynamics, and descriptive and experimental chemistry is required, as is the ability to interpret and apply this material to new and unfamiliar problems. During this examination, an online scientific calculator and a periodic table are available as part of the testing software.

The examination contains approximately 75 questions to be answered in 90 minutes. Some of these are pretest questions that will not be scored. Any time spent on tutorials and providing personal information is in addition to the actual testing time.

Knowledge and Skills Required

Questions on the Chemistry examination require candidates to demonstrate one or more of the following abilities.

- Recall - remember specific facts; demonstrate straightforward knowledge of information and familiarity with terminology.
- Application - understand concepts and reformulate information into other equivalent terms; apply knowledge to unfamiliar and/or practical situations; use of mathematics to solve chemistry problems.
- Interpretation - infer and deduce from data available and integrate information to draw conclusions, and recognize unstated assumptions.

The subject matter of the Chemistry examination is drawn from the following topics. The percentages next to the main topics indicate the approximate percentage of exam questions on that topic.

Scientific Calculator

A scientific (nongraphing) calculator is integrated into the exam software, and it is available to students during the entire testing time. Students are expected to know how and when to make appropriate use of the calculator. The scientific calculator for the iBT versions of the CLEP exams, together with a brief video tutorial, is available to students as a free download for a 30-day trial period. Students are encouraged to download the calculator and become familiar with its functionality prior to taking the exam.

Students will find the online scientific calculator helpful in performing calculations (e.g., arithmetic, exponents, roots, logarithms).

The eCBT and iBT versions of the scientific calculators look different, but both have the necessary functions that will help the students to answer questions during the exams.

20% Structure of Matter
Atomic theory and atomic structure
- Basics of the atomic theory.
- Atomic masses; determination by chemical and physical means.
- Atomic numbers and mass numbers; isotopes and mass spectroscopy.
- Electron energy levels: atomic spectra, quantum numbers, and atomic orbitals.
- Periodic relationships, including, for example, atomic radii, ionization energies, electron affinities, and oxidation states.

Chemistry

Chemical bonding
- Binding forces
  - Types: covalent, ionic, metallic, macromolecular (or network), dispersion, and hydrogen bonding.
  - Relationships to structure and to properties.
  - Polarity of bonds; electronegativities.
- Geometry of molecules, ions, and coordination complexes: structural isomerism, dipole moments of molecules, and relation of properties to structure.
- Molecular models
  - Valence bond theory, hybridization of orbitals, resonance, and sigma and pi bonds.
  - Other models such as molecular orbitals.
- Nuclear chemistry: nuclear equations, half-lives, and radioactivity; and chemical applications.

19% States of Matter
Gases
- Laws of ideal gases; equations of state for an ideal gas.
- Kinetic-molecular theory:
  - Interpretation of ideal gas laws on the basis of this theory.
  - The mole concept; Avogadro's number.
  - Dependence of kinetic energy of molecules on temperature: Boltzmann distribution.
  - Deviations from ideal gas laws.

Liquids and solids
- Liquids and solids from the kinetic molecular viewpoint.
- Phase diagrams of one-component systems.
- Changes of state, and critical phenomena.
- Crystal structure.

Solutions
- Types of solutions and factors affecting solubility.
- Methods of expressing concentration.
- Colligative properties; for example, Raoult's law.
- Effect of interionic attraction on colligative properties and solubility.

12% Reaction Types
Formation and cleavage of covalent bonds
- Acid-base reactions; concepts of Arrhenius, Brønsted-Lowry, and Lewis; amphoterism.
- Reactions involving coordination complexes.
- Precipitation reactions.

Oxidation-reduction reactions
- Oxidation number.
- The role of the electron in oxidation-reduction.
- Electrochemistry; electrolytic cells, standard half-cell potentials, prediction of the direction of redox reactions, and effect of concentration changes.

10% Equations and Stoichiometry
- Ionic and molecular species present in chemical systems; net-ionic equations.
- Stoichiometry: mass and volume relations with emphasis on the mole concept.
- Balancing of chemical reactions, including those for redox reactions.

Chemistry

7% **Equilibrium**
Concept of dynamic equilibrium, physical and chemical; Le Châtelier's principle; equilibrium constants.

Quantitative treatment
- Equilibrium constants for gaseous reactions in terms of both molar concentrations and partial pressure (K_c, K_p).
- Equilibrium constants for reactions in solutions:
  - Constants for acids and bases; pK; pH.
  - Solubility-product constants and their application to precipitation and dissolution of slightly soluble compounds.
  - Constants for complex ions.
  - Common ion effect and buffers.

4% **Kinetics**
- Concept of rate of reaction.
- Order of reaction and rate constant: their determination from experimental data.
- Effect of temperature change on rate constants.
- Energy of activation; the role of catalysts.
- The relationship between the rate-determining step and a mechanism.

5% **Thermodynamics**
State functions
- First law: heat of formation; heat of reaction; change in enthalpy, Hess's law; heat capacity; heats of vaporization and fusion.
- Second law: free energy of formation; free energy of reaction; dependence of change in free energy on enthalpy and entropy changes.
- Relationship of change in free energy to equilibrium constants and electrode potentials.

14% **Descriptive Chemistry**
The accumulation of certain specific facts of chemistry is essential to enable students to comprehend the development of principles and concepts, to demonstrate applications of principles, to relate fact to theory and properties to structure, and to develop an understanding of systematic nomenclature that facilitates communication.

The following areas are normally included on the examination:
- Chemical reactivity and products of chemical reactions.
- Relationships in the periodic table: horizontal, vertical, and diagonal.
- Chemistry of the main groups and transition elements, including typical examples of each.
- Organic chemistry, including topics such as functional groups and isomerism (may be treated as a separate unit or as exemplary material in other areas, such as bonding).

9% **Experimental Chemistry**
Some experiments are based on laboratory practical work widely performed in general chemistry and ask about the equipment used, observations made, calculations performed, and interpretation of the results. The questions are designed to provide a measure of understanding of the basic tools of chemistry and their applications to simple chemical systems.

Chemistry

SAMPLE TEST

Directions: Read each item and select the best response.

1. A piston compresses a gas at constant temperature. Which gas properties increase?

   I. Average speed of molecules
   II. Pressure
   III. Molecular collisions with container walls per second

   A. I and II

   B. I and III

   C. II and III

   D. I, II, and III

   E. None of the above

2. The temperature of a liquid is raised at atmospheric pressure. Which property of liquids increases?

   A. Critical pressure

   B. Vapor pressure

   C. Surface tension

   D. Viscosity

   E. Boiling Point

3. Potassium crystallizes with two atoms contained in each unit cell. What is the mass of potassium found in a lattice 1.00×10^6 unit cells wide, 2.00×10^6 unit cells high, and 5.00×10^5 unit cells deep?

   A. 85.0 µg

   B. 32.5 µg

   C. 64.9 µg

   D. 130 µg

   E. 130×10^6 µg

4. A gas is heated in a sealed container. Which of the following occur(s)?

   A. Gas pressure rises

   B. Gas density decreases

   C. The average distance between molecules increases

   D. The volume increases

   E. All of the above

5. How many molecules are in 2.20 pg of a protein with a molecular weight of 150 kDa?

   A. 8.83×10^9

   B. 1.82×10^9

   C. 8.83×10^6

   D. 1.82×10^6

   E. 8.83×10^{15}

6. At STP, 20 μL of O_2 contain 5.4×10^{16} molecules. According to Avogadro's hypothesis, how many molecules are in 20 μL of Ne?

   A. 5.4×10^{15}

   B. 1.0×10^{16}

   C. 2.7×10^{16}

   D. 5.4×10^{16}

   E. 1.3×10^6

7. An ideal gas at 50.0 °C and 3.00 atm is enclosed in a 300 cm³ cylinder. The cylinder volume changes by moving a piston until the gas reaches 50.0 °C and 1.00 atm. What is the final volume?

   A. 100 cm³

   B. 450 cm³

   C. 900 cm³

   D. 1.20 dm³

   E. 150.0 cm³

8. 81-butanol, ethanol, methanol, and 1-propanol are all liquids at room temperature. Rank them in order of increasing viscosity.

   A. 1-butanol < 1-propanol < ethanol < methanol

   B. methanol < ethanol < 1-propanol < 1-butanol

   C. methanol < ethanol < 1-butanol < 1-propanol

   D. 1-propanol < 1-butanol < ethanol < methanol

   E. ethanol < methanol < 1-butanol. 1-propanol

9. One mole of an ideal gas at STP occupies 22.4 L. At what temperature will one mole of an ideal gas at 1 atm occupy 31.0 L?

   A. 34.6 °C

   B. 105 °C

   C. 378 °C

   D. 442 °C

   E. 28 °C

Chemistry

10. What pressure is exerted by a mixture of 2.7 g of H_2 and 59 g of Xe at STP in a 50 L container?

    A. 0.69 atm

    B. 0.76 atm

    C. 0.80 atm

    D. 0.97 atm

    E. 27.0 atm

Answer Key

1. C
2. B
3. D
4. A
5. C
6. D
7. C
8. B
9. B
10. C

Please note that this is a sample portion of the CLEP Chemistry examination. A complete practice test is available for purchase at Amazon.com and Barnesandnoble.com ISBN 9781607875239.

College Algebra

Description of the Examination

The College Algebra examination covers material that is usually taught in a one-semester college course in algebra. Nearly half of the test is made up of routine problems requiring basic algebraic skills; the remainder involves solving nonroutine problems in which candidates must demonstrate their understanding of concepts. The test includes questions on basic algebraic operations; linear and quadratic equations, inequalities and graphs; algebraic, exponential and logarithmic functions; and miscellaneous other topics. It is assumed that candidates are familiar with currently taught algebraic vocabulary, symbols and notation. The test places little emphasis on arithmetic calculations. However, an online scientific calculator (nongraphing) will be available during the examination.

The examination contains approximately 60 questions to be answered in 90 minutes. Some of these are pretest questions that will not be scored. Any time candidates spend on tutorials and providing personal information is in addition to the actual testing time.

Knowledge and Skills Required

Questions on the College Algebra examination require candidates to demonstrate the following abilities in the approximate proportions indicated.

- Solving routine, straightforward problems (about 50% of the examination)
- Solving nonroutine problems requiring an understanding of concepts and the applications of skills and concepts (about 50% of the examination)

The subject matter of the College Algebra examination is drawn from the following topics. The percentages next to the main topics indicate the approximate percentage of exam questions on that topic.

25% Algebraic Operations
- Operations with exponents
- Factoring and expanding polynomials
- Operations with algebraic expressions
- Absolute value
- Properties of logarithms

25% Equations and Inequalities
- Linear equations and inequalities
- Quadratic equations and inequalities
- Absolute value equations and inequalities
- Systems of equations and inequalities
- Exponential and logarithmic equations

30% Functions and Their Properties
- Definition, interpretation and representation/modeling (graphical, numerical, symbolic, verbal)
- Domain and range
- Evaluation of functions
- Algebra of functions
- Graphs and their properties (including intercepts, symmetry, transformations)
- Inverse functions

20% Number Systems and Operations
- Real numbers
- Complex numbers
- Sequences and series
- Factorials and Binomial Theorem

College Algebra

SAMPLE TEST

1. **Which of the following is a factor of the expression $9x^2 + 6x - 35$?**

   A. $3x - 5$

   B. $3x - 7$

   C. $x + 3$

   D. $x - 2$

   E. $x - 3$

2. **Given $f(x) = 3x - 2$ and $g(x) = x^2$, determine $g(f(x))$.**

   A. $3x^2 - 2$

   B. $9x^2 + 4$

   C. $9x^2 - 12x + 4$

   D. $3x^3 - 2$

   E. $9x^2 - 36$

3. **Solve for x: $18 = 4 + |2x|$**

   A. $\{-11, 7\}$

   B. $\{-7, 0, 7\}$

   C. $\{-7, 7\}$

   D. $\{-11, 11\}$

   E. $\{-8, 8\}$

4. **Solve for x by factoring: $2x^2 - 3x - 2 = 0$**

   A. $x = (-1, 2)$

   B. $x = (0.5, -2)$

   C. $x = (-0.5, 2)$

   D. $x = (1, -2)$

   E. $x = (-2, 2)$

5. **Which of the following illustrates an inverse property?**

   A. $a + b = a - b$

   B. $a + b = b + a$

   C. $a + 0 = a$

   D. $a + (-a) = 0$

   E. $b - a = 0$

6. **The conjugate of $4 + 5i$ is**

   A. $-4 + 5i$

   B. $4 - 5i$

   C. $4i + 5$

   D. $4i - 5$

   E. $-4 - 5i$

7. **Simplify:** $(6+3i)-(4-2i)$

    A. $2+5i$

    B. $2+i$

    C. $10+5i$

    D. $2-2i$

    E. $10-5i$

8. **Simplify:** $\dfrac{10}{1+3i}$

    A. $-1.25(1-3i)$

    B. $1.25(1+3i)$

    C. $1+3i$

    D. $1-3i$

    E. $10+3i$

9. **Solve** $(2b^3 \cdot b^2)^3$

    A. $3b^9$

    B. $2b^8$

    C. $8b^{15}$

    D. $2b^{18}$

    E. $8b^{18}$

10. **Which of the following is incorrect?**

    A. $(x^2y^3)^2 = x^4y^6$

    B. $m^2(2n)^3 = 8m^2n^3$

    C. $\dfrac{m^3n^4}{m^2n^2} = mn^2$

    D. $(x+y^2)^2 = x^2 + y^4$

    E. $(2s^{-4}w^4)(7sw^{-5}) = \dfrac{14}{s^3w}$

11. **Evaluate** $3^{\frac{1}{2}}\left(9^{\frac{1}{3}}\right)$

    A. $27^{\frac{5}{6}}$

    B. $9^{\frac{7}{12}}$

    C. $3^{\frac{5}{6}}$

    D. $3^{\frac{6}{7}}$

    E. $9^{\frac{12}{7}}$

12. Simplify: $\dfrac{4x^0 y^{-2} z^3}{4x}$

   A. $\dfrac{z^3}{y^2}$

   B. $\dfrac{z^3}{y^2 x}$

   C. $\dfrac{z^2}{y^3}$

   D. $\dfrac{z^3}{x^2 y}$

   E. $z^3 y^2$

13. The exponential equation $2^5 = 32$ can be written as:

   A. $\log_2(5) = 32$

   B. $\log_{10}(32) = 5$

   C. $\log_5(32) = 2$

   D. $\log_2(32) = 5$

   E. $\log_5(2) = 32$

14. Which equation corresponds to the logarithmic statement $\log_x k = m$?

   A. $x^m = k$

   B. $k^m = x$

   C. $x^k = m$

   D. $m^x = k$

   E. $k^x = m$

15. Solve for x: $\log_6(x-5) + \log_6 x = 2$

   A. $x = 9$

   B. $x = 2, x = 7$

   C. $x = 6$

   D. $x = -2, x = -7$

   E. $x = -4, x = -9$

16. Solve for the slope m and y-intercept: $3x + 2y = 14$

   A. $m = \dfrac{2}{3}, y = 5$

   B. $m = -\dfrac{3}{2}, y = 7$

   C. $m = \dfrac{3}{2}, y = -7$

   D. $m = -\dfrac{2}{3}, y = -5$

   E. $m = 2, y = 7$

17. Simplify: $-4(-4x-1) - 4(7x+3)$

   A. $-44x + 16$

   B. $12x - 16$

   C. $44x - 16$

   D. $-12x - 8$

   E. $-11x + 2$

18. Solve $-2x < 5$.

   A. $x < -\dfrac{5}{2}$

   B. $x > -\dfrac{2}{5}$

   C. $x > -\dfrac{5}{2}$

   D. $x > \dfrac{5}{2}$

   E. $x < \dfrac{5}{2}$

19. Solve $10 \leq 3x + 4 \leq 19$.

   A. $2 \leq x \leq 5$

   B. $-2 \leq x \leq 5$

   C. $x \leq 5$

   D. $x \geq 2$

   E. $-5 \leq x \leq -2$

20. Solve for x: $x^2 + 10x - 24 = 0$

   A. $(-5, 12)$

   B. $(-10, 8)$

   C. $(12, 2)$

   D. $(10, 8)$

   E. $(-12, 2)$

21. Find a quadratic equation with roots of 4 and -9.

   A. $x^2 - 5x + 36 = 0$

   B. $x^2 + 5x - 36 = 0$

   C. $4x^2 - 9x - 5 = 0$

   D. $x^2 + 4x - 9 = 0$

   E. $5x^2 - 9x + 4 = 0$

22. Solve: $4800 \leq 200x - 2x^2$

   A. $-40 \leq x \leq 40$

   B. $x \leq 40$

   C. $40 \leq x \leq 60$

   D. $x = 40$

   E. $x = -40$

23. Solve: $|3x + 2| = 4x + 5$

   A. $x = -3$

   B. $x = -1$

   C. $x = 3$

   D. $x = 1$

   E. $x = 6$

College Algebra

24. Solve: $|3x-5|=\frac{1}{2}$

    A. $x=-\frac{11}{6},-\frac{3}{2}$

    B. $x=-\frac{11}{6},\frac{3}{2}$

    C. $x=\frac{11}{6},-\frac{3}{2}$

    D. $x=\frac{11}{6},\frac{3}{2}$

    E. $x=11,\frac{3}{2}$

25. Solve: $2|3x+9|<36$

    A. $x<-9$

    B. $x>3$

    C. $3<x<9$

    D. $-9<x<-3$

    E. $-9<x<3$

26. Solve for x and y:
    $4x+3y=-1$
    $5x+4y=1$

    A. $x=-7, y=9$

    B. $x=7, y=-9$

    C. $x=7, y=9$

    D. $x=-7, y=-9$

    E. $x=y=7$

27. Which point is in the solution set for the system of inequalities below?

    $x-7>1$
    $y<2x-1$

    A. $(-1,-1)$

    B. $(-2,-1)$

    C. $(0,1)$

    D. $(0,-2)$

    E. $(1,1)$

28. Solve: $3^{2x-1}=27$

    A. $x=2$

    B. $x=-3$

    C. $x=-2$

    D. $x=3$

    E. $x=\frac{2}{3}$

29. Solve: $\log_b(x^2)=\log_b(2x-1)$

    A. $x=-2$

    B. $x=1$

    C. $x=-1$

    D. $x=2$

    E. $x=4$

30. Solve: $\log_2(x) + \log_2(x-2) = 3$

    A. $x = 4$

    B. $x = -4, 2$

    C. $x = -4, -2$

    D. $x = 4, -2$

    E. $x = 2$

31. If $f(x) = -3x + 8,$ find $f(5)$.

    A. 23

    B. −23

    C. 7

    D. −7

    E. 21

32. Find the zeros of the function $h(x) = \dfrac{x-9}{x+2}$.

    A. $\{9\}$

    B. $\{-2\}$

    C. $\left\{-\dfrac{9}{2}\right\}$

    D. $\{-2, 9\}$

    E. This function has no zeros.

33. Which number line shows the solution to $7x - 5 \geq 9x - 17$?

    A.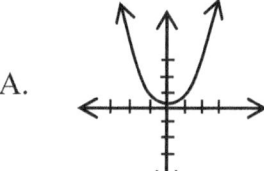

    B.

    C.

    D.

    E.

34. Which graph represents the equation of $y = x^2 + 3x$?

    A.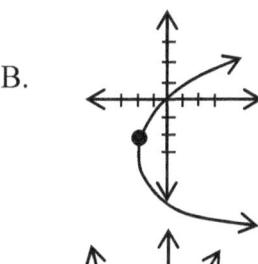

    B.

    C.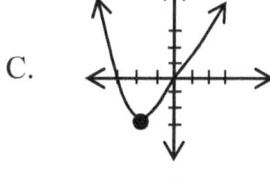

    D.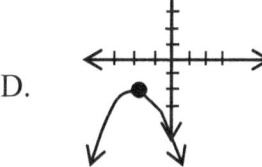

    E.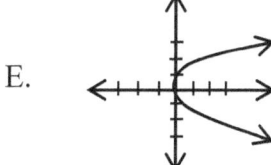

35. Based on the given table, if $y_1 = x^3$, what is the equation for y_2?

x	-2	-1	0	1	2	3
y_1	-8	-1	0	1	8	27
y_2	-18	-11	-10	-9	-2	-17

A. $y_2 = x^5$

B. $y_2 = -x^3$

C. $y_2 = (-x)^3$

D. $y_2 = (x-10)^3$

E. $y_2 = x^3 - 10$

36. Identify the domain and range of the relation:

$$\{(2,-5),(4,31),(11,-11),(-21,3)\}$$

A. Domain is $\{-21\}$, range is $\{-11\}$.

B. Domain is $\{-5, 31, -11, 3\}$, range is $\{2, 4, 11, -21\}$.

C. Domain is $\{11\}$, and range is $\{31\}$.

D. Domain and range are indeterminate.

E. Domain is $\{2, 4, 11, -21\}$, range is $\{-5, 31, -11, 3\}$.

37. Determine the domain of $y = -\sqrt{-2x+3}$.

A. $x = 3$

B. $x \leq \dfrac{3}{2}$

C. $x > \dfrac{3}{2}$

D. $x = 2$

E. $x = 0$

38. For the function $h(x)$ whose graph is shown below, select the domain and range.

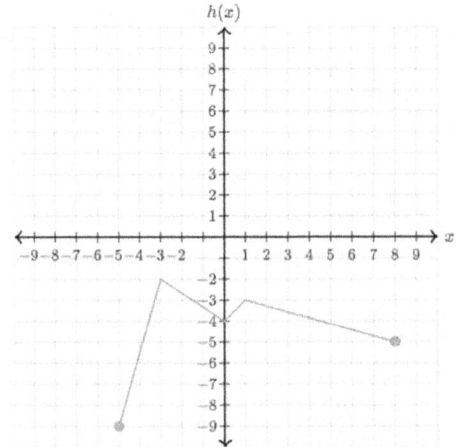

A. Domain is $-5 \leq x \leq 8$, range is $-9 \leq h \leq -2$.

B. Domain is -5, range is -5.

C. Range is $-5 \leq x \leq 8$, domain is $-9 \leq h \leq 2$.

D. Domain is $x \geq -5$, range is $h \geq -9$.

E. Domain is 8, range is -2.

39. Given $f(x) = 3x^2 - 7x + 5,$ find $f(-4)$.

   A. -71
   B. 25
   C. 81
   D. -25
   E. 71

40. For $h(x) = 3x^2 + ax - 1,$ $h(3) = 8,$ find the value of a.

   A. 6
   B. -6
   C. -18
   D. 18
   E. 27

41. Given $f(x) = 3x^2 - 7x + 5,$ find $\dfrac{f(x+h) - f(x)}{h}$

   A. $7h$
   B. $6xh - 7$
   C. $6x + 3h - 7$
   D. $3x + 6h + 7$
   E. $5x$

42. Find the x- and y- intercepts for $5x - 3y = 15$.

   A. $x = 0, y = 0$
   B. $x = -3, y = 5$
   C. $x = -1, y = 5$
   D. $x = -5, y = 3$
   E. $x = 3, y = -5$

43. Which of the figures is a reflection of the triangle shown?

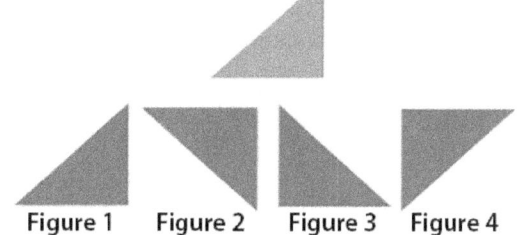

Figure 1   Figure 2   Figure 3   Figure 4

   A. Figure 1 and Figure 4
   B. Figure 4 and Figure 3
   C. Figure 2 and Figure 1
   D. Figures 2, 3 and 4
   E. Figure 1 and Figure 2

College Algebra

44. Name the transformation shown.

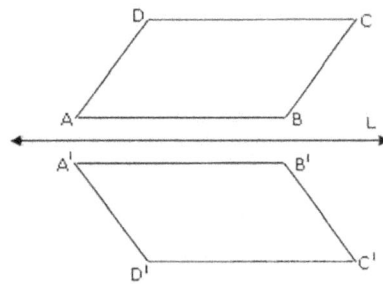

A. Translation

B. Rotation

C. Reflection

D. Dilation

E. Cannot be determined

45. Find the inverse of $y = 3x - 2$.

A. $y = \dfrac{1}{3x-2}$

B. $y = \dfrac{x+2}{3}$

C. $x = \dfrac{y+2}{3}$

D. $y - 3x - 2 = 0$

E. $3x - y - 2 = 0$

46. Find the inverse of
$$f(x) = -\dfrac{1}{3}x + 1$$

A. $f^{-1}(x) = 1$

B. $f^{-1}(x) = 3x$

C. $f^{-1}(x) = 3x - 3$

D. $f^{-1}(x) = -3x + 3$

E. $f^{-1}(x) = x^2$

47. If $f(x) = 3x - 2$ and $g(x) = \dfrac{x}{3} + \dfrac{2}{3}$, which of the following is true:

A. $f(x)$ is the inverse of $g(x)$.

B. $f(x) = g^{-1}(x)$

C. There is no connection between $f(x)$ and $g(x)$.

D. $g(x) = f(x)$

E. A and B

48. Identify the real numbers in the list:
$$1.67, \pi, \sqrt{5}, 0$$

A. All

B. $1.67, \sqrt{5}, 0$

C. $1.67, 0$

D. 0

E. None

College Algebra

49. Which of the following is false?

A. Every rational number is a real number.

B. Every imaginary number is a real number.

C. Every integer is a whole number.

D. Every integer is a real number.

E. Every natural number is positive.

50. Which selection below is NOT a real number?

A. -3

B. $0.6666...$

C. $\dfrac{\pi}{2}$

D. $3+\sqrt{2}$

E. $3i$

51. Simplify $\sqrt{-9}$.

A. -3

B. $-3i$

C. $3i$

D. 3

E. 0

52. Simplify $(i)(2i)(-3i)$.

A. $6i$

B. $-6i^3$

C. $-6i$

D. 0

E. $6i^3$

53. Simplify i^{17}.

A. $17i$

B. i

C. $-17i$

D. $-i$

E. 1

54. List the first four terms of the following sequence, beginning with $n=0$.

$$A_n = \dfrac{(-1)^n}{(n+1)!}$$

A. $\dfrac{1}{2}, 1, \dfrac{3}{2}, 2$

B. $-1, -\dfrac{1}{2}, 0, \dfrac{1}{2}$

C. $0, 1, 2, 3$

D. $1, -\dfrac{1}{2}, \dfrac{1}{6}, -\dfrac{1}{24}$

E. $0, -1, -\dfrac{1}{2}, \dfrac{2}{3}$

College Algebra

55. Expand the following series and find the sum:

$$\sum_{n=0}^{4} 2n$$

A. 20

B. 8

C. 16

D. 4

E. 32

56. Write the series in sigma notation:
$-3+0+9+24+45+72+105$

A. $\sum_{a=0}^{6} 3a^2$

B. $\sum_{a=0}^{6} 3a^2 - 3$

C. $\sum_{a=0}^{6} a^2 - 3$

D. $\sum_{a=1}^{6} 3a^2 - 1$

E. $\sum_{a=0}^{5} a^2 - 3$

57. Find $\dfrac{8!}{6!2!}$

A. $\dfrac{2}{3}$

B. $\dfrac{4}{6}$

C. 28

D. 48

E. 24

58. Expand the binomial $(2x+3y)^4$

A. $16x^4 + 24x^3y + 36x^2y^2 + 54xy^3 + 81y^4$
$2x^4 + 6x^3y + 6x^2y^2 + 6xy^3 + 3y^4$

B. $16x^4 + 81y^4$

C. $16x^4 + 96x^3y + 216x^2y^2 + 216xy^3 + 81y^4$

D. $16x^4 + 24x^3y^3 + 36x^2y^2 + 54xy + 81y^4$

E. $16x^4 + 24x^3y^3 + 36x^2y^2 + 54xy + 81y^4$

59. Evaluate the determinant of the matrix:

$$\begin{pmatrix} -2 & 4 \\ -4 & 3 \end{pmatrix}$$

A. 10

B. −24

C. 4

D. −10

E. 24

College Algebra

60. **Evaluate the determinant of the matrix for** $y = 4$. $\begin{pmatrix} -5y & 3y \\ y-1 & y-3 \end{pmatrix}$

    A. 35

    B. 12

    C. −56

    D. −12

    E. 56

College Algebra

ANSWER KEY

Question Number	Correct Answer	Your Answer	Question Number	Correct Answer	Your Answer
1	A		31	D	
2	C		32	A	
3	C		33	B	
4	C		34	C	
5	D		35	E	
6	B		36	E	
7	A		37	B	
8	D		38	A	
9	C		39	C	
10	D		40	B	
11	C		41	C	
12	B		42	E	
13	D		43	D	
14	A		44	C	
15	A		45	B	
16	B		46	D	
17	D		47	E	
18	C		48	A	
19	A		49	E	
20	E		50	E	
21	B		51	C	
22	C		52	A	
23	B		53	B	
24	D		54	D	
25	E		55	A	
26	A		56	B	
27	D		57	C	
28	A		58	C	
29	B		59	A	
30	A		60	C	

College Mathematics

Description of the Examination

The College Mathematics exam covers material generally taught in a college course for non-mathematics majors and majors in fields not requiring knowledge of advanced mathematics.

The examination contains approximately 60 questions to be answered in 90 minutes. Some of these are pretest questions that will not be scored. Any time test takers spend on tutorials and providing personal information is in addition to the actual testing time.

An online scientific (nongraphing) calculator will be available during the examination. Although a calculator is not necessary to answer most of the questions, there may be a few problems whose solutions are difficult to obtain without using a calculator. Since no calculator is allowed during the examination except for the online calculator provided, is it recommended that prior to the examination you become familiar with the use of the online calculator.

For more information about downloading the practice version of the scientific (nongraphing) calculator, please visit the College Mathematics description on the CLEP website, **clep.collegeboard.org** It is assumed that test takes are familiar with currently taught mathematics vocabulary, symbols, and notation.

Knowledge and Skills Required

Questions on the College Mathematics examination require test takers to demonstrate the following abilities in the approximate proportion indicated.
- Solving routine, straightforward problems (about 50% of the examination)
- Solving nonroutine problems requiring an understanding of concepts and the application of skills and concepts (about 50% of the examination)

The subject matter of the College Mathematics examination is drawn from the following topics. The percentages next to the main topics indicate the approximate percentage of exam questions on that topic.

20% Algebra
- Solving equations, linear inequalities, and systems of linear equations by analytical and graphical methods
- Interpretation, representation, and evaluation of functions: numerical, graphical, symbolic, and descriptive methods
- Graphs of functions: translations, horizontal and vertical reflections, and symmetry about the x-axis, the y-axis, and the origin
- Linear and exponential growth
- Applications

10% Counting and Probability
- Counting problems: the multiplication rule, combinations and permutations
- Probability: union, intersection, independent events, mutually exclusive events, complementary events, conditional probabilities, and expected value
- Applications

15% Data Analysis and Statistics
- Data interpretation and representation: tables, bar graphs, line graphs, circle graphs, pie charts, scatterplots, and histograms

- Numerical summaries of data: mean (average), median, mode, and range
- Standard deviation, normal distribution (conceptual questions only)
- Applications

20% Financial Mathematics
- Percents, percent change, markups, discounts, taxes, profit, and loss
- Interest: simple, compound, continuous interest, effective interest rate, effective annual yield or annual percentage rate (APR)
- Present value and future value
- Applications

10% Geometry
- Properties of triangles and quadrilaterals: perimeter, area, similarity, and the Pythagorean theorem
- Parallel and perpendicular lines
- Properties of circles: circumference, area, central angles, inscribed angles, and sectors
- Applications

15% Logic and Sets
- Logical operations and statements: conditional statements, conjunctions, disjunctions, negations, hypotheses, logical conclusions, converses, inverses, counterexamples, contrapositives, logical equivalence
- Set relationships, subsets, disjoint sets, equality of sets, and Venn diagrams
- Operations on sets: union, intersection, complement, and Cartesian product
- Applications

10% Numbers
- Properties of numbers and their operations: integers and rational, irrational, and real numbers (including recognizing rational and irrational numbers)
- Elementary number theory: factors and divisibility, primes and composites, odd and even integers, and the fundamental theorem of arithmetic
- Measurement: unit conversion, scientific notation, and numerical precision
- Absolute value
- Applications

College Mathematics

SAMPLE TEST

1. Which of the following is closed under division?

   I. $\left\{\frac{1}{3}, 1, 3\right\}$
   II. $\{-1, 1\}$
   III. $\{-1, 0, 1\}$

   A. I only

   B. II only

   C. III only

   D. I and II

   E. II and III

2. Which of the following is always composite if x is an odd positive integer and y is an even positive integer greater than 1?

   A. $x + y$

   B. $|x + y|$

   C. $x + 2y$

   D. $3x + y$

   E. $3xy$

3. Find the LCM of 25, 18, and 24.

   A. 1200

   B. 1800

   C. 2400

   D. 3600

   E. 10,800

4. Solve for x: $|3x| + 6 = 21$

   A. $[9, -5]$

   B. $[-9, 5]$

   C. $[-5, 0, 5]$

   D. $[-5, 5]$

   E. $[-9, 9]$

5. Which graph represents the solution set for $x^2 - 5x > -6$?

   A. ⟵–|–|–⊕–|–|–|–⊕–|–|⟶
         -2   0   2

   B. ⟵–|–⊕–|–|–|–|–|–⊕–|⟶
         -3   0   3

   C. ⟵–|–|–⊕–|–|–|–⊕–|–|⟶
         -2   0   2

   D. ⟵–|–|–|–|–|–|–⊕–⊕–|⟶
                0   2 3

   E. ⟵–|–|–|–|–|–|–⊕–⊕–|⟶
                0   2 3

530

College Mathematics

6. What is the equation of the graph shown below?

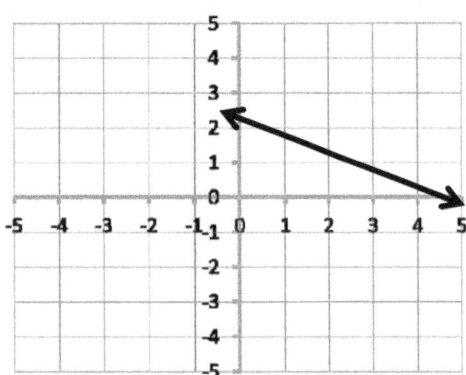

   A. $x + 2y = 4$

   B. $x - 2y = 4$

   C. $2x + y = 4$

   D. $x + 2y = -4$

   E. $x - 2y = -4$

7. Solve the following inequality: $-2x > 4$

   A. $x > -2$

   B. $x < -2$

   C. $x > 2$

   D. $x > -8$

   E. $x < 2$

8. Which equation represents a circle centered on the origin with radius 3?

   A. $x^2 + y^2 = 3$

   B. $x^2 + y^2 = 6$

   C. $x^2 + y^2 = 9$

   D. $x^2 + y^2 = 36$

   E. $x^2 - y^2 = 9$

9. Given that D is a distance, M is a mass, T is a time, and V is a velocity, which of the following units could be used to measure $\frac{MTV}{D}$?

   A. feet

   B. meters

   C. grams

   D. seconds

   E. miles per hour

10. Cubic meters are used to measure which of the following?

    A. Distance

    B. Length

    C. Area

    D. Volume

    E. Mass

11. What figure best describes a data set in which many items are clustered near the median value with a smaller number of values less than or greater than the median at greater distances on each side?

   A. A parabola

   B. A normal curve

   C. A line of best fit

   D. A Cartesian curve

   E. A Newtonian curve

12. If you prove a theorem by showing that an attempt to prove the opposite of the theorem leads to a contradiction, you are using the logical strategy called:

   A. Inductive reasoning

   B. Exhaustive proof

   C. Proof by attraction

   D. Direct proof

   E. Indirect proof

13. Compute the area of the shaded region, given a radius of 7 meters. Point O is the center.

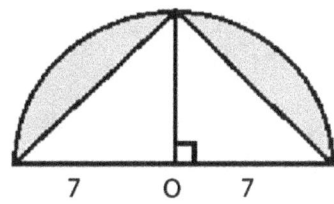

   A. 14.0

   B. 28.0

   C. 55.9

   D. 104.9

   E. 153.9

14. A garden measures 25 m by 40 m, including a circular fishpond with radius 3 m. What is the area of the garden not including the fishpond?

   A. 101.7 m^2

   B. 111.2 m^2

   C. 971.7 m^2

   D. 981.2 m^2

   E. 990.6 m^2

15. The base of cone A has 3 times as great an area as the base of cone B, but the height of cone A is only $\frac{1}{3}$ the height of cone B. Which statement is true?

   A. Cone A has 9 times the volume of cone B.

   B. Cone A has 3 times the volume of cone B.

   C. Cone A and cone B have the same volume.

   D. Cone B has 3 times the volume of cone A.

   E. Cone B has 9 times the volume of cone A.

16. Find the area of the figure depicted below.

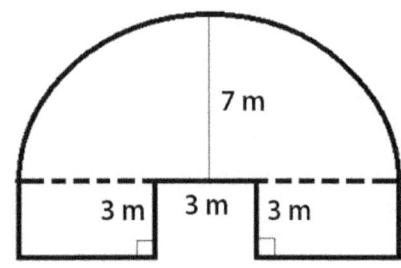

   A. 109.9 m²

   B. 118.9 m²

   C. 142.9 m²

   D. 144.9 m²

   E. 186.9 m²

17. State the domain of the function $f(x) = \dfrac{2x-14}{x^2-9}$.

   A. $x \neq 3$

   B. $x \neq 3, 7$

   C. $x \neq 3, -3$

   D. $x \neq 7$

   E. $x = 3, -3, 7$

18. Which of the following is a factor of the expression $6x^2 - 5x - 14$?

   A. $3x+7$

   B. $6x+7$

   C. $6x-7$

   D. $6x-5$

   E. $x+2$

19. Solve for x by factoring:
$$x^2 + x - 6 = 0$$

   A. $x = (-3, 2)$

   B. $x = (3, -2)$

   C. $x = (-6, 1)$

   D. $x = (6, -1)$

   E. no real solutions

College Mathematics

20. Which of the following is equivalent to $\sqrt[b]{x^a}$?

   A. $x^{\frac{a}{b}}$

   B. $x^{\frac{b}{a}}$

   C. $a^{\frac{x}{b}}$

   D. $b^{\frac{x}{a}}$

   E. $a^{\frac{b}{x}}$

22. Given $f(x) = 2x+1$ and $g(x) = x^2 - 1$, determine $g(f(x))$.

   A. $4x^2 + 4x - 1$

   B. $4x^2 + 4x + 1$

   C. $4x^2$

   D. $4x^2 - 1$

   E. $4x^2 + 4x$

23. Compute the median for the following data set:
    {9, 11, 18, 13, 12, 21}

   A. 12

   B. 12.5

   C. 13

   D. 14

   E. 15.5

21. Which graph represents the equation $y = x^2 + 3x$?

   A.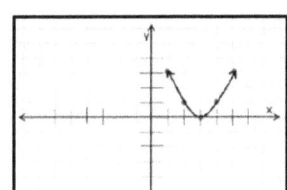

   B.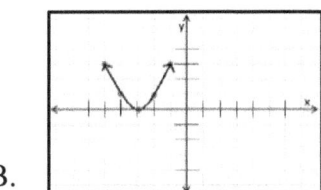

   C.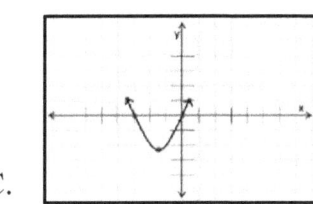

   D.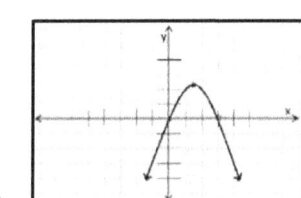

   E.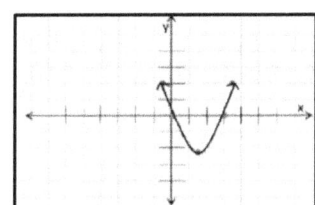

24. What would be the best measure of central tendency for the following collection of high temperatures on 10 successive days?
{27, 24, 33, 24, 36, 65, 34, 30, 28, 29}

    A. Mean

    B. Either mean or median

    C. Median

    D. Mode

    E. Either median or mode

25. If the correlation between two variables is zero, the association between the two variables is

    A. Negative linear

    B. Positive linear

    C. Quadratic

    D. Direct variation

    E. Random

26. Which of the following is not a valid method of collecting statistical data?

    A. Random sampling

    B. Systematic sampling

    C. Volunteer response

    D. Weighted sampling

    E. Cylindrical sampling

27. A jar contains 3 red marbles and 7 green ones. What is the probability that a marble picked at random from the jar will be red?

    A. $\dfrac{1}{3}$

    B. $\dfrac{1}{7}$

    C. $\dfrac{3}{7}$

    D. $\dfrac{3}{10}$

    E. $\dfrac{7}{10}$

28. A die is rolled several times. What is the probability that a 6 will not appear before the fourth roll of the die?

    A. $\dfrac{125}{216}$

    B. $\dfrac{625}{1296}$

    C. $\dfrac{1}{2}$

    D. $\dfrac{5}{6}$

    E. $\dfrac{1}{216}$

29. There is a 30% chance of rain this Saturday and a 30% chance of rain on Sunday as well. What is the chance of rain on both days?

   A. 9%

   B. 30%

   C. 49%

   D. 60%

   E. 70%

30. Which equation matches the data in the table?

x	3	4	5	6
y	7	8	9	10

   A. $y = 2x - 1$

   B. $y = 2x + 1$

   C. $y = -x + 10$

   D. $y = x + 4$

   E. $y = x - 4$

31. Which table could be generated by the equation $y = x^2 + 2x - 1$?

   A.
x	1	2	3	4
y	2	5	8	11

   B.
x	1	2	3	4
y	4	9	16	25

   C.
x	1	2	3	4
y	1	5	11	19

   D.
x	1	2	3	4
y	2	7	13	21

   E.
x	1	2	3	4
y	2	7	14	23

College Mathematics

32. The fees charged by a parking garage are as follows:

Hours	1	2	3	4	5
Fee	$12	$19	$26	$33	$40

How would you summarize the fees charged?

A. $12 an hour

B. $5 plus $7 per hour

C. $15 an hour with a $3 discount

D. $4 plus $8 per hour

E. $3 plus $9 per hour

33. Which of the following is a solution to $x^2 + 4x + 4 = 25$?

A. 2

B. −2

C. −7

D. −3

E. 5

34. Solve the following system of equations:
$$2x + y = 8$$
$$4x + 2y = 20$$

A. $x = 2, y = 4$

B. $x = 3, y = 1$

C. $x = 4, y = 0$

D. no solutions

E. an infinite number of solutions

35. If an initial deposit of $10,000 is made to a savings account with interest compounded continuously at an annual rate of 6%, how much money is in the account after 5 years?

A. $13,498.59

B. $3498.59

C. $13,382.26

D. $3,382.26

E. $13,000.00

36. A dance team comes prepared with a tango, a waltz, a disco number, a salsa routine, and a ballet selection. In how many different orders can they present their routines?

   A. 5

   B. 25

   C. 120

   D. 625

   E. 3125

37. You can choose 3 selections from a buffet table with 8 dishes. How many different plates can you choose?

   A. 6

   B. 24

   C. 56

   D. 336

   E. 6561

38. Leah has 4 blouses, 3 skirts, and 6 pairs of shoes. How many different outfits can she dress herself in?

   A. 12

   B. 13

   C. 24

   D. 72

   E. 720

39. Hiroshi surveys his classmates to find what percent of them come to school on the bus, by car, by subway, by bicycle, or on foot. What is the best way to display his results?

   A. A line graph

   B. A box plot

   C. A stem-and-leaf plot

   D. A scatterplot

   E. A circle graph

40. Which equation could be used as a line of best fit for the scatterplot below?

   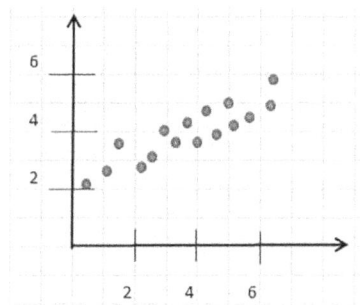

   A. $y = \dfrac{1}{2}x + 2$

   B. $y = 2x + 2$

   C. $y = -2x + 2$

   D. $y = \dfrac{1}{2}x - 2$

   E. $y = \dfrac{1}{2}x + 2$

41. To find the standard variation of a data set, you first compute the square of the distance of each data item from the mean of all the data items. Then what do you do?

   A. Add all the squared distances and take the square root of the result.

   B. Find the mean of the squared distances and take the square root of the result.

   C. Multiply the squared distances and take the nth root of the result.

   D. Multiply the square root of the sum of the squared distances by the mean of the squared distances.

   E. Multiply the sum of the squared distances by the square root of the mean of the squared distances.

42. In which data set is the mode greater than the median?

   A. {9,11,11,12,14}

   B. {13,15,17,19,21}

   C. {8,11,12,12,19}

   D. {9,9,9,14,20}

   E. {7,11,13,14,14}

43. Of the 200 students in the junior class, 8% are in the Spanish Club. How many juniors are in the Spanish Club?

   A. 4

   B. 8

   C. 16

   D. 20

   E. 25

44. When Olga bought a boat for $1750, she paid an excise tax of $78.75. What was the percent of the tax?

   A. 4.5%

   B. 5.5%

   C. 6.3%

   D. 7%

   E. 7.5%

45. A bank account pays 5% interest yearly. How large an amount would have to be deposited to earn $75 interest in a year?

   A. $375

   B. $875

   C. $1200

   D. $1500

   E. $3750

College Mathematics

46. A stock previously trading at $96 a share is now trading at $88 a share. What is the percent of change in the value of the stock?

A. −8%

B. −8.3%

C. −12%

D. −12.5%

E. −16%

47. The admission price to tour the Haunted House has been changed from $25 to $30. What is the percent of change in the admission price?

A. 5%

B. 16.7%

C. 20%

D. 25%

E. 30%

48. Eileen's Bakery had expenses of $62,500 last year and sales of $68,750. What was the profit as a percent of the expenses?

A. 6.25%

B. 10%

C. 12%

D. 15%

E. 16.7%

49. Tim's Typewriters had expenses of $26,200 last year and sales of $19,912. What was the loss as a percent of the expenses?

A. 7%

B. 8%

C. 16.7%

D. 20%

E. 24%

50. A stock that had been selling at $30 a share increased its share price by 20%. Later in the day the same stock suffered a 20% decrease in its share price. What was the price at the end of the day?

A. $24

B. $28.80

C. $30

D. $33

E. $36

College Mathematics

51. A sweater is marked "25% off." The sale price is $36. What was the price before the discount?

   A. $27

   B. $32

   C. $40

   D. $45

   E. $48

52. The sum of $1440 is deposited in a bank which pays 6% simple interest per year. After how many years will there be $1872 in the account?

   A. 2.5 years

   B. 3 years

   C. 4 years

   D. 5 years

   E. 8 years

53. A bank pays 5% interest on deposits, compounded yearly. If $14,000 is deposited, how much will be in the account 3 years later?

   A. $14,350

   B. $15,435

   C. $16,100

   D. $16,206.75

   E. $17,500

54. Which statement is logically equivalent to the following: If it's raining, my roof is leaking.

   A. If my roof isn't leaking, it isn't raining.

   B. If my roof is leaking, it's raining.

   C. If it isn't raining, my roof isn't leaking.

   D. If my roof is leaking, it's not raining

   E. If it's raining, my roof isn't leaking.

College Mathematics

55. What is the union of set A and set B?

    Set A: {2,4,5,9,11}
    Set B: {3,5,8,11,13}

    A. {2,3,4,5,5,8,9,11,11,13}

    B. {2,3,4,5,8,9,11,13}

    C. {5,11}

    D. {2,3,4,8,9,13}

    E. {5,9,13,20,24}

56. What is the intersection of set A and set B?

    Set A: {1,3,7,9,10,12,14}
    Set B: {1,4,7,8,11,12,15}

    A. {1,1,3,4,7,7,8,9,10,11,12,12,14,15}

    B. {1,3,4,7,8,9,10,11,12,14,15}

    C. {1,7,12}

    D. {1,1,7,7,12,12}

    E. {3,4,8,9,10,11,14,15}

57. Which statement is NOT implied by the Venn diagram below?

    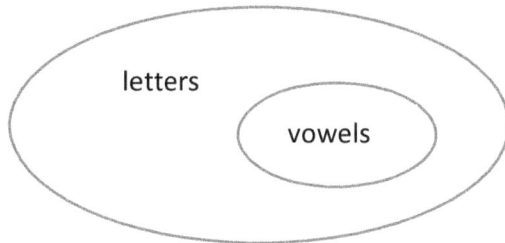

    A. No vowels are not letters.

    B. All vowels are letters.

    C. Some letters are vowels.

    D. Some letters are not vowels.

    E. Some vowels are not letters.

58. A total of 150 students have signed up for musical activities. There are 82 students in the choir and 80 students in the band. How many students are in both the band and the choir?

    A. 12

    B. 24

    C. 42

    D. 70

    E. 162

College Mathematics

59. Chris's older brother Mike is 2 years younger than Florence. When Tom's younger sister Rhoda was 8, Chris was 3. Florence is not older than Rhoda. Name the five people in ascending order of age.

   A. Tom, Rhoda, Florence, Mike, Chris

   B. Tom, Florence, Rhoda, Mike, Chris

   C. Chris, Mike, Florence, Rhoda, Tom

   D. Chris, Mike, Rhoda, Florence, Tom

   E. Chris, Rhoda, Mike, Florence, Tom

60. Disprove the following statement by offering a counterexample: "Multiplying two numbers together produces a larger number than either of the two original numbers."

   A. $\sqrt{2} \times \sqrt{2}$

   B. 1.25×1.78

   C. -3×-3

   D. 0.5×0.6

   E. -0.8×-0.3

College Mathematics

ANSWER KEY

Question Number	Correct Answer	Your Answer	Question Number	Correct Answer	Your Answer
1	B		31	E	
2	E		32	B	
3	B		33	C	
4	D		34	D	
5	E		35	A	
6	A		36	C	
7	B		37	C	
8	C		38	D	
9	C		39	E	
10	D		40	A	
11	B		41	B	
12	E		42	E	
13	B		43	C	
14	C		44	A	
15	C		45	D	
16	A		46	B	
17	C		47	C	
18	B		48	B	
19	A		49	E	
20	A		50	B	
21	E		51	E	
22	B		52	D	
23	C		53	D	
24	C		54	A	
25	E		55	B	
26	E		56	C	
27	D		57	E	
28	A		58	A	
29	A		59	C	
30	D		60	D	

Natural Sciences

Description of the Examination

The Natural Sciences examination covers a wide range of topics frequently taught in introductory courses surveying both biological and physical sciences at the freshman or sophomore level. Such courses generally satisfy distribution or general education requirements in science that usually are not required of nor taken by science majors. The Natural Sciences exam is not intended for those specializing in science; it is intended to test the understanding of scientific concepts that an adult with a liberal arts education should have. It does not stress the retention of factual details; rather, it emphasizes the knowledge and application of the basic principles and concepts of science, the comprehension of scientific information, and the understanding of issues of science in contemporary society.

The primary objective of the examination is to give candidates the opportunity to demonstrate a level of knowledge and understanding expected of college students meeting a distribution or general education requirement in the natural sciences. An institution may grant up to six semester hours (or the equivalent) of credit toward fulfillment of such a requirement for satisfactory scores on the examination. Some may grant specific course credit, on the basis of the total score for a two-semester survey course covering both biological and physical sciences.

The examination contains approximately 120 questions to be answered in 90 minutes. Some of these are pretest questions that will not be scored. Any time candidates spend on tutorials and providing personal information is in addition to the actual testing time.

Knowledge and Skills Required

The Natural Sciences examination requires candidates to demonstrate one or more of the following abilities in the approximate proportions indicated.

- Knowledge of fundamental facts, concepts, and principles (about 40 percent of the examination)
- Interpretation and comprehension of information (about 20 percent of the examination) presented in the form of graphs, diagrams, tables, equations, or verbal passages
- Qualitative and quantitative application of scientific principles (about 40 percent of the examination), including applications based on material presented in the form of graphs, diagrams, tables, equations, or verbal passages; more emphasis is given to qualitative than quantitative applications

Topical Specifications:

50%	**Biological Science**
10%	**Origin and evolution of life, classification of organisms**
10%	**Cell organization, cell division, chemical nature of the gene, bioenergetics, biosynthesis**
20%	**Structure, function, and development in organisms; patterns of heredity**
10%	**Concepts of population biology with emphasis on ecology**
50%	**Physical Science**
7%	**Atomic and nuclear structure and properties, elementary particles, nuclear reactions**
10%	**Chemical elements, compounds and reactions, molecular structure and bonding**
12%	**Heat, thermodynamics, and states of matter; classical mechanics; relativity**

4%	**Electricity and magnetism, waves, light, and sound**
7%	**The universe: galaxies, stars, the solar system**
10%	**The Earth: atmosphere, hydrosphere, structure features, geologic processes, and history**

The examination includes some questions that are interdisciplinary and cannot be classified in one of the listed categories. Some of the questions cover topics that overlap with those listed previously, drawing on areas such as history and philosophy of science, scientific methods, science applications and technology, and the relationship of science to contemporary problems of society, such as environmental pollution and depletion of natural resources. Some questions are laboratory oriented.

Natural Sciences

SAMPLE TEST

1. **According to scientists, what is the estimate age of the Earth?**

    A. 4.5 million years

    B. 4.5 billion years

    C. 450 million years

    D. 1.000 million years

    E. 10.000 million years

2. **The first cells that evolved on earth were probably of which type?**

    A. Autotrophic

    B. Eukaryotic

    C. Similar to viruses

    D. Prokaryotic

    E. Endosymbiotic

3. **What is a major principle of the Endosymbiotic Theory?**

    A. Birds and dinosaurs share a common ancestor.

    B. Animals evolved in close relationships with one another.

    C. Prokaryotes arose from eukaryotes.

    D. Inorganic compounds are the basis of living things.

    E. Eukaryotes arose from very simple prokaryotes.

4. **According to Oparin & Haldane's theory, the primitive atmosphere was composed by**

    A. Hydrogen, methane, water, ammonia

    B. Oxygen, methane, water, ammonia

    C. Oxygen and carbonic gas

    D. Oxygen, carbonic gas, nitrogen

    E. Hydrogen, methane, water, ozone

5. **Which of these is true about natural selection?**

    A. It acts on an individual genotype

    B. It is not currently happening

    C. It is only an animal phenomenon

    D. It acts on the individual phenotype

    E. It is used to prevent overpopulation

6. **Which of these is a result of reproductive isolation?**

    A. Extinction

    B. Migration

    C. Fossilization

    D. Speciation

    E. Radiation

Natural Sciences

7. Which of these is NOT a prezygotic barrier?

   A. Geographical isolation

   B. Hybrid sterility

   C. Temporal isolation

   D. Mechanical isolation

   E. Behavioral isolation

8. Which mode of natural selection favors the more common phenotypes?

   A. Directional selection

   B. Positive selection

   C. Stabilizing selection

   D. Diversifying selection

   E. Disruptive selection

9. Which phylum accounts for 85% of all animal species?

   A. Nematoda

   B. Chordata

   C. Arthropoda

   D. Cnidaria

   E. Annelida

10. The scientific name of humans is *Homo sapiens*. Choose the proper classification beginning with kingdom and ending with order

    A. Animalia, Vertebrata, Mammalia, Primates, Hominidae

    B. Animalia, Vertebrata, Chordata, Mammalia, Primates

    C. Animalia, Chordata, Vertebrata, Mammalia, Primates

    D. Chordata, Vertebrata, Primate, *Homo, sapiens*

    E. Chordata, Primates, Hominidae, *Homo, sapiens*

11. Which of the following animals is coelomate?

    I. Flatworms
    II. Earthworms
    III. Crickets

    A. I only

    B. II only

    C. III only

    D. I and III

    E. II and III

12. Heterotrophic organisms that have cell walls with chitin are classified as

   A. Plants

   B. Bacteria

   C. Fungi

   D. Animals

   E. Protists

13. Of what are viruses made?

   A. A protein coat surrounding a nucleic acid

   B. RNA and protein surrounded by a cell wall

   C. A nucleic acid surrounding a protein coat

   D. Protein surrounded by DNA

   E. A lipid bilayer surrounding a protein coat and RNA

14. According to the fluid-mosaic model of the cell membrane, membranes are composed of

   A. A phospholipid bilayer with proteins embedded in the layers

   B. One layer of phospholipids with cholesterol embedded in the layer

   C. Two layers of protein with lipids embedded in the layers

   D. DNA and fluid proteins

   E. Two layers of phospholipids and DNA

15. Which of the following is not part of the cytoskeleton?

   A. Vacuoles

   B. Microfilaments

   C. Microtubules

   D. Intermediate filaments

   E. Motor proteins

16. Bacteria commonly reproduce by a process called binary fission. Which of the following best defines this process?

   A. Viral vectors carry DNA to new bacteria

   B. DNA from one bacterium enters another

   C. DNA doubles and the bacterial cell divides

   D. DNA from dead cells is absorbed into bacteria

   E. Bacteria merge with others to form new species

17. What is the stage of mitosis shown in the diagram?

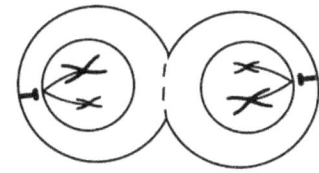

   A. Prophase
   B. Telophase
   C. Anaphase
   D. Metaphase
   E. Interphase

18. Crossing over, which increases genetic diversity, occurs during which stage of meiosis?

   A. Telophase II in meiosis
   B. Metaphase in mitosis
   C. Interphase in meiosis
   D. Prophase I in meiosis
   E. Metaphase II in meiosis

19. What is the enzyme that unwinds DNA during replication?

   A. DNAse
   B. Replicase
   C. DNA helicase
   D. DNA topoisomerases
   E. DNA polymerase

20. Which part of a DNA nucleotide can vary?

   A. Deoxyribose
   B. Phosphate group
   C. Hydrogen bonds
   D. Sugar
   E. Nitrogenous base

21. Which of these describes facilitated diffusion?

   A. It requires energy
   B. It only happens in plant cells
   C. It only allows molecules to leave a cell but not to enter it
   D. It produces a significant amount of energy for the cell
   E. It needs a transport molecule to pass through the membrane

22. During which part of photosynthesis is oxygen given off?

   A. Light reactions
   B. Dark reactions
   C. Krebs cycle
   D. Reduction of NAD+ to NADH
   E. Phosphorylation

23. **During the Krebs cycle, 8 carrier molecules are formed. What are they?**

    A. 3 NADH, 3 FADH, 2 ATP

    B. 6 NADH and 2 ATP

    C. 4 $FADH_2$ and 4 ATP

    D. 6 NADH and 2 $FADH_2$

    E. 4 NADH and 4 $FADH_2$

24. **In the comparison of respiration to photosynthesis, which statement is true?**

    A. Oxygen is a waste product in photosynthesis but not in respiration

    B. Glucose is produced in respiration but not in photosynthesis

    C. Carbon dioxide is formed in photosynthesis but not in respiration

    D. Water is formed in respiration but not in photosynthesis

    E. Carbon dioxide and water are formed in photosynthesis

25. **Identify the correct sequence of organization of living things**

    A. Cell – organelle – organ – tissue – organ system – organism

    B. Cell – tissue – organ – organelle – organ system – organism

    C. Organelle – cell – tissue – organ – organ system – organism

    D. Organ system – tissue – organelle – cell – organism – organ

    E. Organism – organ system – tissue – cell – organelle – organ

26. **Bird wings, human arms, and the flipper of whales have the same bone structure and different functions. These are called**

    A. Polymorphic structures

    B. Homologous structures

    C. Vestigial structures

    D. Analogous structures

    E. Primitive structure

27. **Parts of the nervous system include all but the following**

    A. Brain

    B. Spinal cord

    C. Axons

    D. Venules

    E. Glial cells

28. Which of the following best completes the statement below? Peristalsis and the movement of the iris are possible due to the action of _____ muscles.

    A. Skeletal

    B. Smooth

    C. Cardiac

    D. Striated

    E. Voluntary

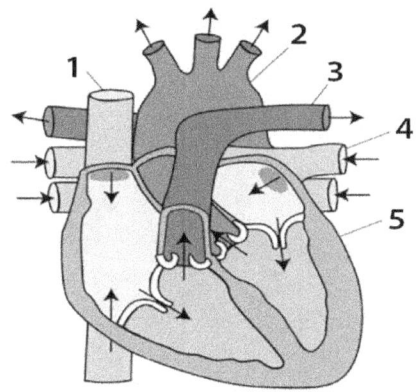

29. Consider the heart illustration above, with arrows indicating the direction of blood flow. Which number indicates the aorta?

    A. 1

    B. 2

    C. 3

    D. 4

    E. 5

30. Microorganisms use all but which of the following for locomotion?

    A. Pseudopods

    B. Flagella

    C. Cilia

    D. Pili

    E. Villi

31. Which of these is a function of the cardiovascular system?

    A. Move oxygenated blood around the body

    B. Oxygenate the blood through gas exchange

    C. Act as an exocrine system

    D. Flush toxins out of the body

    E. Transport signals from the brain

32. Which of these steroids is not created in the gonads?

    A. Testosterone

    B. Estrogen

    C. Progesterone

    D. ACTH

    E. FSH

33. **The role of neurotransmitters in nerve action is**

    A. To turn off the sodium pump

    B. To turn off the calcium pump

    C. To send impulses to neurons

    D. To send impulses to the body

    E. To maintain the membrane polarized

34. **Which of the following is NOT a function of the vertebrate skin?**

    A. Respiration

    B. Protection

    C. Sensation

    D. Regulation of temperature

    E. Regulation of reproduction

35. **Homeostatic mechanisms in the body do NOT include**

    A. Thermoregulation

    B. Excretion

    C. Respiration

    D. Osmoregulation

    E. Hemostasis

36. **What controls gas exchange on the bottom of a plant leaf?**

    A. Stomata

    B. Epidermis

    C. Collenchyma and schlerenchyma

    D. Palisade mesophyll

    E. Trichomes

37. **Hormones are essential to the regulation of reproduction. What organ is responsible for the release of hormones for sexual maturity?**

    A. Thymus gland

    B. Hypothalamus

    C. Pancreas

    D. Thyroid gland

    E. Cerebellum

38. **Fertilization in humans usually occurs in the**

    A. Uterus

    B. Ovary

    C. Fallopian tubes

    D. Vagina

    E. Cervix

39. After sea turtles hatch on the beach, they start the journey to the ocean. This is due to

    A. Learned behavior
    B. Territoriality
    C. The tide
    D. Innate behavior
    E. Feeding strategy

40. What is any foreign particle called that causes an immune reaction?

    A. An antigen
    B. A histocompatibity complex
    C. An antibody
    D. A vaccine
    E. A bacteriophage

41. What is (are) the germ layer(s) missing in diploblastic animals?

    A. Ectoderm only
    B. Mesoderm only
    C. Endoderm only
    D. Ectoderm and mesoderm
    E. Endoderm and mesoderm

42. What is the order of the stages that happen after fertilization?

    A. Blastula – gastrulation – neurulation – organogenesis – cleavage
    B. Cleavage – neurulation – gastrulation – organogenesis – blastula
    C. Cleavage – blastula – gastrulation – neurulation – cell growth
    D. Cell growth – gastrulation – blastula – neurulation – organogenesis
    E. Cleavage – blastula – gastrulation – neurulation – organogenesis

43. What is the general term for a change that affects the sequence of bases in a gene?

    A. Deletion
    B. Polyploidy
    C. Mutation
    D. Duplication
    E. Substitution

44. **What can be said about homozygous individuals?**

    A. They have two different alleles

    B. They are of the same species

    C. They exhibit the same features

    D. They have a pair of identical alleles

    E. They produce identical offspring

45. **In a Punnett square with a single trait, what are the ratios of genotypes produced between two heterozygous individuals?**

    A. 1:2:2

    B. 2:1:1

    C. 1:1:1

    D. 1:2:1

    E. 2:2:2

46. **A child with type O blood has a father with type A blood and a mother with type B blood. The genotypes of the parents respectively would be which of the following?**

    A. AA and BO

    B. AO and BO

    C. AA and BB

    D. AO and OO

    E. OO and BO

47. **Which of these defines the Law of Segregation defined by Gregor Mendel?**

    A. After meiosis, each new cell will contain an allele that is recessive.

    B. Only one of two alleles is expressed in a heterozygous organism.

    C. The allele expressed is always the dominant allele.

    D. Alleles of one trait do not affect the inheritance of alleles on another chromosome.

    E. When sex cells form, the two alleles that determine a trait will end up on different gametes.

48. **Hemophilia and color-blindness are examples of**

    A. Lethal alleles

    B. Codominance system

    C. Sex-linked traits

    D. Incomplete dominance

    E. Nondisjunction

49. Which of the following is NOT an abiotic factor?

    A. Temperature
    B. Rainfall
    C. Soil quality
    D. Predation
    E. Wind speed

50. An experiment was performed to measure the growth of bacteria at different temperatures. The cultures were kept on a 12 hour light/dark cycle and given the same amount of nutrients. Which of these is the independent variable?

    A. Growth of number of colonies
    B. Amount of nutrients
    C. Type of bacteria used
    D. Light duration
    E. Temperature

51. Which term is not associated with the water cycle?

    A. Precipitation
    B. Transpiration
    C. Fixation
    D. Evaporation
    E. Infiltration

52. Which trophic level has the highest ecological efficiency?

    A. Decomposers
    B. Producers
    C. Tertiary consumers
    D. Secondary consumers
    E. Primary consumers

53. What is NOT true about competition?

    A. May occur between very different species
    B. It is usually asymmetric, affecting one species more than the other
    C. It increases the amount of available resources
    D. May affect the abundance of competitors
    E. Competition is a common process in natural communities

54. Which of the following is true about parasites?

    I. All parasites are facultative
    II. Parasites can be either ecto- or endoparasites
    III. Parasites increase their hosts' fitness
    IV. Parasites always kill their hosts

    A. I only
    B. II only
    C. I and II
    D. I, II and III
    E. I, II, III and IV

55. A clownfish is protected by a sea anemone's tentacles, and in turn, the anemone receives uneaten food from the clownfish. What type of symbiosis is exemplified by this example?

    A. Mutualism
    B. Parasitism
    C. Commensalism
    D. Competition
    E. Amensalism

56. Since the industrial revolution, the size of the human population has been

    A. Decreasing
    B. Stable
    C. Increasing slowly
    D. Changing randomly
    E. Increasing exponentially

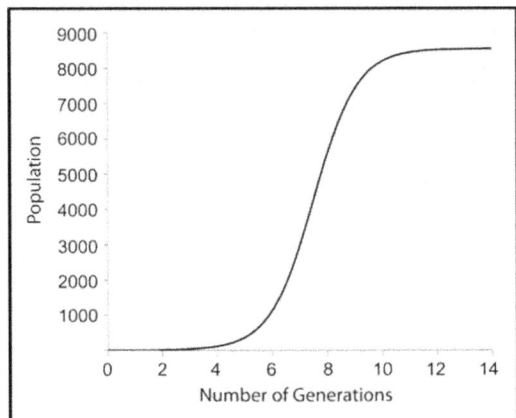

57. According to the graphic above, what is the approximate population size after 8 generations?

    A. 1000
    B. 2000
    C. 6000
    D. 8000
    E. 12000

Natural Sciences

58. **Xerophytes are more commonly found in which biome?**

    A. Temperate forests

    B. Tropical forests

    C. Oceans

    D. Deserts

    E. Grasslands

59. **Which zone of the ocean receives no light and has the lowest temperatures?**

    A. Intertidal

    B. Pelagic

    C. Abyssal

    D. Euphotic

    E. Epipelagic

60. **Which biome is the most prevalent on Earth?**

    A. Marine

    B. Desert

    C. Savanna

    D. Tundra

    E. Lakes and rivers

61. **How many neutrons are there in $^{60}_{27}Co$?**

    A. 27

    B. 33

    C. 60

    D. 87

    E. 14

62. **Which of the following can be determined from the periodic table?**

    I. The number of protons
    II. The number of neutrons
    III. The number of isotopes of that atom
    IV. The number of valence electrons

    A. I only

    B. I and II

    C. I, II, and III

    D. I, II, III, IV

    E. I, II and IV

63. **When a radioactive material emits an alpha particle only, its atomic number**

    A. Decreases

    B. Increases

    C. Remains unchanged

    D. Changes randomly

    E. Approaches zero

64. The terrestrial composition of an element is 50.7% as a stable isotope with an atomic mass of 78.9 u and 49.3% as a stable isotope with an atomic mass of 80.9 u. What is the atomic mass of the element?

    A. 79.0 u

    B. 79.8 u

    C. 79.9 u

    D. 80.8 u

    E. 80.0 u

65. Moving down a column on the Periodic Table

    I. The atomic radius increase
    II. Ionization energy increase
    III. Protons are added
    IV. Metallic characteristics increase

    A. I only

    B. III only

    C. I and II

    D. III and IV

    E. I, II, III

66. Which of the following quantum numbers are needed to define the position of the electrons in an element?

    A. Principal, circular, magnetic and electromagnetic

    B. Principal, angular momentum, magnetic, and spin

    C. Angular, magnetic, electronic, spin

    D. Primary, angular momentum, magnetic, and spin

    E. Principal only

67. $^{3}_{1}H$ decays with a half-life of 12 years. Twenty four years ago, 3.0 g of pure $^{3}_{1}H$ were placed in sealed container. How many grams of $^{3}_{1}H$ remain?

    A. 0.38 g

    B. 0.75 g

    C. 1.5 g

    D. 0.125 g

    E. 3.0 g

Natural Sciences

68. Write a balanced nuclear equation for the emission of an alpha particle by polonium-209

    A. $^{209}_{84}Po \rightarrow {}^{205}_{81}Po + {}^{4}_{2}He$

    B. $^{209}_{84}Po \rightarrow {}^{205}_{82}Po + {}^{4}_{2}He$

    C. $^{209}_{84}Po \rightarrow {}^{209}_{85}Po + {}^{0}_{-1}He$

    D. $^{209}_{84}Po \rightarrow {}^{205}_{82}Po + {}^{4}_{2}He$

    E. $^{209}_{84}Po \rightarrow {}^{209}_{83}Po + {}^{4}_{2}He$

69. Based on trends in the periodic table, which of the following properties would you expect to be greater for Rb than for K?

    I. Density
    II. Melting point
    III. Ionization energy
    IV. Oxidation number in a compound with chlorine

    A. I only

    B. I, II, and III

    C. II and III

    D. I and IV

    E. I, II, III, and IV

70. According to the periodic table, which list contains only metals?

    A. Li, Cd, Ca, S

    B. Li, Cd, Ca, He

    C. Li, Cd, Ca, Pb

    D. Li, C, Ca, He

    E. Ca, Fe, F, Pb

71. Which of the following are the properties of noble gases?

    I. They are colorless and odorless under STP
    II. They have little tendency to gain or lose electrons
    III. High melting points
    IV. Full valence electron shells

    A. I and II

    B. I and III

    C. II and III

    D. I, II and IV

    E. I, II, III and IV

72. The temperature of a liquid is raised at atmospheric pressure. Which property of liquids increases?

    A. Critical pressure

    B. Vapor pressure

    C. Surface tension

    D. Viscosity

    E. Boiling Point

73. Osmotic pressure is the pressure required to prevent _____ from flowing from low to high _____ concentration across a semipermeable membrane.

    A. solute, solute
    B. solute, solvent
    C. solvent, solute
    D. solvent, solvent
    E. ions, solute

74. Consider the reaction between iron and hydrogen chloride gas

    Fe(s) + 2HCl(g) → FeCl$_2$(s) + H$_2$(g)

    7 moles of iron and 10 moles of HCl react until the limiting reagent is consumed. Which statements are true?

    I. HCl is the excess reagent
    II. HCl is the limiting reagent
    III. 7 moles of H$_2$ are produced
    IV. 2 moles of the excess reagent remain

    A. I and III
    B. I and IV
    C. II and III
    D. II and IV
    E. II, III and IV

75. 1-butanol, ethanol, methanol, and 1-propanol are all liquids at room temperature. Rank them in order of increasing viscosity.

    A. 1-butanol < 1-propanol < ethanol < methanol
    B. methanol < ethanol < 1-propanol < 1-butanol
    C. methanol < ethanol < 1-butanol < 1-propanol
    D. 1-propanol < 1-butanol < ethanol < methanol
    E. ethanol < methanol < 1-butanol < 1-propanol

76. List the following scientists in chronological order, from earliest to most recent, with respect to their most significant contribution to atomic theory

    I. John Dalton
    II. Niels Bohr
    III. J. J. Thomson
    IV. Ernest Rutherford

    A. I, III, II, IV
    B. I, III, IV, II
    C. I, IV, III, II
    D. III, I, II, IV
    E. I, II, III, IV

77. **Which statement about acids and bases is NOT true?**

    A. All strong acids ionize in water.

    B. All Lewis acids accept an electron pair.

    C. All Brønsted bases use OH⁻ as a proton acceptor.

    D. All Arrhenius acids form H^+ ions in water.

    E. The reaction of an acid with a base is called neutralization reaction.

78. **Why does $CaCl_2$ have a higher normal melting point than NH_3?**

    A. Covalent bonds are stronger than London dispersion forces.

    B. Covalent bonds are stronger than hydrogen bonds.

    C. Ionic bonds are stronger than London dispersion forces.

    D. Ionic bonds are stronger than hydrogen bonds.

    E. Covalent Bonds are stronger than Ionic Bonds.

79. **Which intermolecular attraction explains the following trend in straight-chain alkanes?**

Condensed structural formula	Boiling point (°C)
CH_4	-161.5
CH_3CH_3	-88.6
$CH_3CH_2CH_3$	-42.1
$CH_3CH_2CH_2CH_3$	-0.5
$CH_3CH_2CH_2CH_2CH_3$	36.0
$CH_3CH_2CH_2CH_2CH_2CH_3$	68.7

    A. London dispersion forces

    B. Dipole-dipole interactions

    C. Hydrogen bonding

    D. Ion-induced dipole interactions

    E. Covalent bonds

80. **Which substance is most likely to be a gas at STP?**

    A. SeO_2

    B. F_2

    C. $CaCl_2$

    D. I_2

    E. H_2O

81. **A calorie is the amount of heat energy that will**

    A. Raise the temperature of one gram of water from 14.5° C to 15.5° C.

    B. Lower the temperature of one gram of water from 16.5° C to 15.5° C

    C. Raise the temperature of one gram of water from 32° F to 33° F

    D. Cause water to boil at two atmospheres of pressure.

    E. Raise the temperature of 100 mL of water from 14.5° C to 15.5° C.

82. **Heat transfer by electromagnetic waves is termed**

    A. Conduction

    B. Convection

    C. Radiation

    D. Phase Change

    E. Warming

83. **What is temperature?**

    A. Temperature is a measure of the conductivity of the atoms or molecules in a material

    B. Temperature is a measure of the kinetic energy of the atoms or molecules in a material

    C. Temperature is a measure of the relativistic mass of the atoms or molecules in a material

    D. Temperature is a measure of the angular momentum of electrons in a material

    E. Temperature is the amount of heat of a material

84. **Which statement about reactions is true?**

    A. All spontaneous reactions are exothermic and cause an increase in entropy.

    B. An endothermic reaction that increases the order of the system cannot be spontaneous.

    C. A reaction can be non-spontaneous in one direction and also non-spontaneous in the opposite direction.

    D. Melting snow is an exothermic process.

    E. Thermodynamic Functions are dependent on the reaction pathway.

Natural Sciences

85. If the internal energy of a system remains constant, how much work is done by the system if 1 kJ of heat energy is added?

    A. 0 kJ

    B. -1 kJ

    C. 1 kJ

    D. 3.14 kJ

    E. 0.5 kJ

86. When KNO₃ dissolves in water, the water grows slightly colder. An increase in temperature will _____ the solubility of KNO₃.

    A. Increase

    B. Slightly decrease

    C. Have no effect on

    D. Have an unknown effect on

    E. Highly decrease

87. Which phase may be present at the triple point of a substance?

    I. Gas
    II. Liquid
    III. Solid
    IV. Supercritical fluid

    A. I, II, and III

    B. I, II, and IV

    C. II, III, and IV

    D. I, II, III, and IV

    E. I and III

88. The normal boiling point of water on the Kelvin scale is closest to

    A. 100 K

    B. 112 K

    C. 212 K

    D. 273 K

    E. 373 K

89. A few minutes after opening a bottle of perfume, the scent is detected on the other side of the room. What law relates to this phenomenon?

    A. Graham's law

    B. Dalton's law

    C. Boyle's law

    D. Avogadro's law

    E. Charles' law

Natural Sciences

90. The magnitude of a force is

    A. Directly proportional to mass and inversely to acceleration
    B. Inversely proportional to mass and directly to acceleration
    C. Directly proportional to both mass and acceleration
    D. Inversely proportional to both mass and acceleration
    E. Independent of the mass

91. When acceleration is plotted versus time, the area under the graph represents

    A. Moment in time
    B. Distance
    C. Velocity
    D. Acceleration
    E. Mass

92. A needle floating in a tray of water demonstrates the property of

    A. Specific Heat
    B. Surface Tension
    C. Oil-Water Interference
    D. Archimedes' Principle
    E. Metal density

93. Heat is added to a pure solid at its melting point until it all becomes liquid at its freezing point. Which of the following occur?

    I. Intermolecular attractions are weakened.
    II. The kinetic energy of the molecules does not change.
    III. The freedom of the molecules to move about increases.

    A. I only
    B. II only
    C. III only
    D. I, II and III
    E. I and III

94. Which statement about thermochemistry is true?

    A. Particles in a system move about less freely at high entropy.
    B. Water at 100° C has the same internal energy as water vapor at 100° C.
    C. A decrease in the order of a system corresponds to an increase in entropy.
    D. At its sublimation temperature, dry ice has higher entropy than gaseous CO_2.
    E. A decrease in the order of a system corresponds to a decrease in entropy.

95. A semi-conductor allows current to flow

    A. Never
    B. Always
    C. As long as it stays below a maximum temperature
    D. When a minimum voltage is applied
    E. Only when a high voltage is applied

96. What is the direction of the magnetic field at the center of the loop of current (I) shown below (i.e., at point A)?

    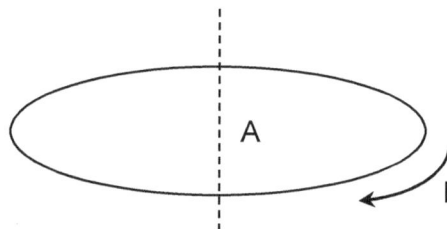

    A. Down, along the axis (dotted line)
    B. Up, along the axis (dotted line)
    C. The magnetic field is oriented in a radial direction
    D. The direction is random
    E. There is no magnetic field at point A

97. An electromagnetic wave propagates through a vacuum. Independent of its wavelength, it will move with constant

    A. Acceleration
    B. Velocity
    C. Induction
    D. Sound
    E. Frequency

98. A light bulb is connected in series with a rotating coil within a magnetic field. Which actions can increase the brightness of the light?

    I. Rotating the coil more rapidly
    II. Using more loops in the coil
    III. Using a different color wire for the coil
    IV. Using a stronger magnetic field

    A. I only
    B. II only
    C. I, II and IV
    D. I, II and III
    E. I, II, III and IV

Natural Sciences

99. Rainbows are created by

A. Reflection, dispersion, and recombination

B. Reflection, resistance, and expansion

C. Reflection, compression, and specific heat

D. Reflection, refraction, and dispersion

E. Reflection, refraction and recombination

100. The Sun is a

A. Asteroid

B. Star

C. Planet

D. Satellite

E. Giant planet

101. The nucleus of comets is made of

A. Gases only

B. Dust only

C. Solid rocks

D. Ice and gases

E. Ice, dust and rocky particles

102. What is the warmest planet of the Solar System?

A. Mars

B. Saturn

C. Earth

D. Venus

E. Jupiter

103. The mass of the Milky Way is mainly composed by

A. Dark matter

B. Stars

C. Planets

D. Dust

E. Asteroids

104. The light that reaches the planets originates in the

A. Dwarf planets

B. Black holes

C. Asteroids

D. Moons

E. Stars

Natural Sciences

105. In 2015, the *New Horizons* spacecraft flew by Pluto, a dwarf planet of the Solar System. How many moons does Pluto have?

A. Pluto doesn't have moons.

B. Two moons

C. Three moons

D. Four moons

E. Five moons

106. Geostationary satellites are often used by communications. Their orbital period is ____ Earth's rotational period, and their direction of rotation is ____

A. Shorter than – the same as Earth's

B. Longer than – opposite to Earth's

C. Equal to – the same as Earth's

D. Shorter than – opposite to Earth's

E. Longer than – the same as Earth's

107. Which list shows only terrestrial planets?

A. Earth, Mercury, Jupiter, and Mars

B. Earth, Mercury, Venus, and Mars

C. Jupiter, Saturn, Neptune, and Uranus

D. Earth, Mercury, Neptune, and Uranus

E. Earth, Mercury, Venus, and Uranus

108. Why Mars is called "the red planet"?

A. Its waters are rich in sulfur compounds

B. Its waters are rich in iron compounds

C. Due to gases present in the atmosphere

D. Iron oxides in its surface give a reddish appearance

E. Its surface is rich in sulfur compounds

109. Which layer of the atmosphere contains the ozone layer?

A. Stratosphere

B. Thermosphere

C. Mesosphere

D. Troposphere

E. Ionosphere

110. What is the most abundant gas in our atmosphere?

A. Oxygen

B. Nitrogen

C. Helium

D. Argon

E. Carbonic dioxide

111. Which process adds oxygen to the atmosphere?

    A. Respiration

    B. Ultraviolet light

    C. Weathering of rocks

    D. Photosynthesis

    E. Movements of air masses

112. What is the impact of sulfur oxides and nitrogen oxides in the environment when they react with water?

    A. Ammonia

    B. Acidic precipitation

    C. Carbonic acid

    D. Global warming

    E. Greenhouse effect

113. Most of Earth's freshwater is

    A. Available for human consumption

    B. Found in rivers and lakes

    C. Found in the groundwater

    D. Found in the clouds and atmosphere

    E. Trapped in the form of ice

114. Which of the following statements about groundwater is true?

    I. Groundwater is a renewable resource
    II. Groundwater cannot be replaced by sea water
    III. Groundwater never flows to the surface of the Earth

    A. I only

    B. II only

    C. III only

    D. I and II

    E. I, II and III

115. What are the current Era, Period and Epoch we are living in, respectively?

    A. Cenozoic, Quaternary, Holocene

    B. Mesozoic, Quaternary, Holocene

    C. Mezozoic, Quaternary, Pleistocene

    D. Cenozoic, Neogene, Holocene

    E. Cenozoic, Neogene, Eocene

116. What is the main element present in the Earth's core?

    A. Carbon

    B. Sulfur

    C. Iron

    D. Cobalt

    E. Manganese

117. **The lava released by volcanoes during eruption originates in**

    A. The Earth's inner mantle

    B. The volcano itself

    C. The Earth's outer core

    D. The Earth's inner core

    E. Magma chambers

118. **Which statement about the carbon cycle is NOT true?**

    A. Ten percent of all available carbon is in the air.

    B. Carbon dioxide is fixed by glycosylation.

    C. Plants fix carbon in the form of glucose.

    D. Animals release carbon through respiration.

    E. Most atmospheric carbon comes from the decay of dead organisms.

119. **The supercontinent Pangea was fragmented due to which geological process?**

    A. Sedimentation

    B. Erosion

    C. Chemical weathering

    D. Plate tectonics

    E. Meteorite impact

120. **Which statement(s) about fossils is (are) true?**

    I. Only animals with bones can become fossils
    II. There are insect fossils found in amber
    III. The fossil's age can be estimated by radiometric aging
    IV. The fossil's age can be estimated by stratigraphy

    A. I only

    B. II only

    C. I and II

    D. II, III and IV

    E. I, II, III and IV

Natural Sciences

ANSWER KEY

Question Number	Correct Answer	Your Answer	Question Number	Correct Answer	Your Answer	Question Number	Correct Answer	Your Answer
1	B		41	B		81	A	
2	D		42	E		82	C	
3	E		43	C		83	B	
4	A		44	D		84	B	
5	D		45	D		85	C	
6	D		46	B		86	A	
7	B		47	E		87	A	
8	C		48	C		88	E	
9	C		49	D		89	A	
10	C		50	E		90	C	
11	E		51	C		91	C	
12	C		52	B		92	B	
13	A		53	C		93	D	
14	A		54	B		94	C	
15	A		55	A		95	D	
16	C		56	E		96	A	
17	B		57	C		97	B	
18	D		58	D		98	C	
19	C		59	C		99	D	
20	E		60	A		100	B	
21	E		61	B		101	E	
22	A		62	E		102	D	
23	D		63	A		103	A	
24	A		64	C		104	E	
25	C		65	E		105	E	
26	B		66	B		106	C	
27	D		67	B		107	B	
28	B		68	D		108	D	
29	B		69	A		109	A	
30	E		70	C		110	B	
31	A		71	D		111	D	
32	D		72	B		112	B	
33	A		73	C		113	E	
34	E		74	D		114	D	
35	C		75	B		115	A	
36	A		76	B		116	C	
37	B		77	C		117	E	
38	C		78	D		118	B	
39	D		79	A		119	D	
40	A		80	B		120	D	

Precalculus

Description of the Examination

The Precalculus examination assesses student mastery of skills and concepts required for success in a first-semester calculus course. A large portion of the exam is devoted to testing a student's understanding of functions and their properties. Many of the questions test a student's knowledge of specific properties of the following types of functions: linear, quadratic, absolute value, square root, polynomial, rational, exponential, logarithmic, trigonometric, inverse trigonometric, and piecewise-defined. Questions on the exam will present these types of functions symbolically, graphically, verbally, or in tabular form. A solid understanding of these types of functions is at the core of all precalculus courses, and it is a prerequisite for enrolling in calculus and other college-level mathematics courses.

The examination contains approximately 48 questions, in two sections, to be answered in 90 minutes. Any time candidates spend on tutorials and providing personal information is in addition to the actual testing time.

- Section 1: 25 questions, 50 minutes. The use of an online graphing calculator (non-CAS) is allowed for this section. Only some of the questions will require the use of the calculator.
- Section 2: 23 questions, 40 minutes.
- **No calculator is allowed for this section.**

Although most of the questions on the exam are multiple-choice, there are some questions that require students to enter a numerical answer.

Graphing Calculator

A graphing calculator is integrated into the exam software, and it is available to students during Section 1 of the exam.

Only some of the questions actually require the graphing calculator. Students are expected to know how and when to make appropriate use of the calculator. The graphing calculator, together with brief video tutorials, is available to students as a free download for a 30-day trial period. Students are expected to download the calculator and become familiar with its functionality prior to taking the exam.
In order to answer some of the questions in the calculator section of the exam, students may be required to use the online graphing calculator in the following ways:
- Perform calculations (e.g., exponents, roots, trigonometric values, logarithms)
- Graph functions and analyze the graphs
- Find zeros of functions
- Find points of intersection of graphs of functions
- Find minima/maxima of functions
- Find numerical solutions to equations
- Generate a table of values for a function

Knowledge and Skills Required

Questions on the examination require candidates to demonstrate the following abilities in the approximate proportions indicated.
- Recalling factual knowledge and/or performing routine mathematical manipulation
- Solving problems that demonstrate comprehension of mathematical ideas and/or concepts

Precalculus

- Solving non-routine problems or problems that require insight, ingenuity, or higher mental processes

The subject matter of the Precalculus examination is drawn from the following topics. The percentages next to the topics indicate the approximate percentage of exam questions on that topic.

20% Algebraic Expressions, Equations, and Inequalities
- Ability to perform operations on algebraic expressions
- Ability to solve equations and inequalities, including linear, quadratic, absolute value, polynomial, rational, radical, exponential, logarithmic, and trigonometric
- Ability to solve systems of equations, including linear and nonlinear

15% Functions: Concept, Properties, and Operations
- Ability to demonstrate an understanding of the concept of a function, the general properties of functions (e.g., domain, range), function notation, and to perform symbolic operations with functions (e.g., evaluation, inverse functions)

30% Representations of Functions: Symbolic, Graphical, and Tabular
- Ability to recognize and perform operations and transformations on functions presented symbolically, graphically, or in tabular form
- Ability to demonstrate an understanding of basic properties of functions and to recognize elementary functions (linear, quadratic, absolute value, square root, polynomial, rational, exponential, logarithmic, trigonometric, inverse trigonometric, and piecewise-defined functions) that are presented symbolically, graphically, or in tabular form

10% Analytic Geometry
- Ability to demonstrate an understanding of the analytic geometry of lines, circles, parabolas, ellipses, and hyperbolas

15% Trigonometry and its Applications*
- Ability to demonstrate an understanding of the basic trigonometric functions and their inverses and to apply the basic trigonometric ratios and identities (in right triangles and on the unit circle)
- Ability to apply trigonometry in various problem-solving contexts

10% Functions as Models
- Ability to interpret and construct functions as models and to translate ideas among symbolic, graphical, tabular, and verbal representations of functions

Precalculus

* Note that trigonometry permeates most of the major topics and accounts for more than 15 percent of the exam. The actual proportion of exam questions that requires knowledge of either right triangle trigonometry or the properties of the trigonometric functions is approximately 30-40 percent.

Precalculus

SAMPLE TEST

PART 1: THE FOLLOWING QUESTIONS CAN BE ANSWERED WITH THE AID OF A CALCULATOR.

1. Which of the following is not a solution to this system of equations?

$$\begin{cases} y = x^2 \\ y = x + 12 \end{cases}$$

   A. (4, 16)

   B. (-3, 9)

   C. (-3, 4)

   D. (4, -3)

   E. Neither C or D is s solution to the system

2. Solve $\sqrt{n^2 + 16} = 3n$

   A. 2

   B. ±2

   C. ±$\sqrt{2}$

   D. ±$\frac{4}{3}$

   E. No Real Solution

3. Solve for x such that $0 \leq x \leq 2\pi$.
   $\frac{1}{2}\sin 2x - \frac{\sqrt{2}}{4} = 0$

   A. $\left\{\frac{\pi}{4}\right\}$

   B. $\left\{\frac{\pi}{8}\right\}$

   C. $\left\{\frac{\pi}{8}, \frac{\pi}{4}\right\}$

   D. $\left\{\pm\frac{\pi}{8}, \pm\frac{\pi}{4}\right\}$

   E. $\left\{\frac{\pi}{8}, \frac{3\pi}{8}, \frac{9\pi}{8}, \frac{11\pi}{8}\right\}$

4. Find the solution to the system of equations. $\begin{cases} 4x + 2y = 18 \\ y = -2x + 9 \end{cases}$

   A. No solution

   B. Infinitely many solutions

   C. (2, 1)

   D. (9, 18)

   E. (0, 0)

Precalculus

5. If $h(x) = \frac{3x+4}{x}$ for all real values of $x \neq 0$, find $h^{-1}(x)$

   A. $h^{-1}(x) = \frac{-3x-4}{x}$

   B. $h^{-1}(x) = \frac{x}{3x+4}$

   C. $h^{-1}(x) = \frac{4}{x-3}$

   D. $h^{-1}(x) = \left(\frac{1}{x}\right)(3x+4)$

   E. None of the above represent $h^{-1}(x)$

6. What values of x will keep this function defined over all Real numbers?
   $f(x) = \sqrt{3 - 2x}$

   A. $\left\{x \middle| x \leq \frac{3}{2}\right\}$

   B. $\left\{x \middle| x \geq \frac{2}{3}\right\}$

   C. $\left\{x \middle| -\frac{3}{2} \leq x \leq \frac{3}{2}\right\}$

   D. $\left\{x \middle| x \neq \frac{3}{2}\right\}$

   E. All Real numbers, x

7. Which function below does not represent an even function?

   A. $f(x) = 5x^4$

   B. $g(x) = x^2 + 5$

   C. $h(x) = 6x^3$

   D. $q(x) = \cos(x)$

   E. $t(x) = \frac{x^2}{x^4+1}$

8. Based on the given table, if $y_1 = x^3$, what is the equation for y_2?

X	-2	-1	0	1	2	3
y_1	-8	-1	0	1	8	27
y_2	-18	-11	-10	-9	-2	-17

   A. $y_2 = x^5$

   B. $y_2 = -x^3$

   C. $y_2 = (-x)^3$

   D. $y_2 = (x - 10)^3$

   E. $y_2 = x^3 - 10$

Precalculus

9. **Which choice below makes a true statement regarding the minimum of $f(x) = (x+2)(x-3)(x-12)$?**

   A. The minimum value is -2.

   B. The minimum value is equal to zero.

   C. The minimum value is less than zero.

   D. The minimum value occurs between $x = -2$ and $x = 3$.

   E. Choice C and D are both true statements.

10. **Find the zeros of the function $h(x) = \frac{x-9}{x+2}$.**

    A. {9}

    B. {-2}

    C. $\left\{-\frac{9}{2}\right\}$

    D. {-2, 9}

    E. This function has no zeros.

Answer Key

1. E
2. C
3. E
4. B
5. C
6. A
7. C
8. E
9. C
10. A

Please note that this is a sample portion of the CLEP Precalculus examination. A full practice test is available for purchase at Amazon.com and Barnesandnoble.com ISBN 9781607875345

Financial Accounting

Description of the Examination

The Financial Accounting examination covers skills and concepts that are generally taught in a first-semester undergraduate financial accounting course. Colleges may award credit for a one-semester course in financial accounting.

The exam contains approximately 75 questions to be answered in 90 minutes. Some of these are pretest questions that will not be scored. Any time candidates spend on tutorials or providing personal information is in addition to the actual testing time.

Knowledge and Skills Required

Questions on the Financial Accounting examination require candidates to demonstrate one or more of the following abilities.

- Familiarity with accounting concepts and terminology
- Preparation, use and analysis of accounting data and financial reports issued for both internal and external purposes
- Application of accounting techniques to simple problem situations involving computations
- Understanding the rationale for Generally Accepted Accounting Practices and Procedures

The subject matter of the Financial Accounting examination is drawn from the following topics. The percentages next to the main topics indicate the approximate percentage of exam questions on that topic.

20-30% **General Topics**
- Generally Accepted Accounting Principles
- Rules of Double-Entry Accounting/Transaction Analysis/Accounting Equation
- The Accounting Cycle
- Business Ethics
- Purpose of, Presentation of, and Relationships Between Financial Statements
- Forms of Business

20-30% **The Income Statement**
- Presentation Format Issues
- Recognition of Revenues and Expenses
- Cost of Goods Sold
- Elasticity
- Irregular Items
- Profitability Analysis

30-40% **The Balance Sheet**
- Cash and Internal Controls
- Valuation of Accounts and Notes Receivable (including bad debts)
- Valuation of Inventories
- Acquisition and Disposal of Long-Term Assets
- Depreciation/Amortization/Depletion
- Intangible Assets
- Accounts and Notes Payable
- Long-Term Liabilities
- Owner's Equity
- Preferred and Common Stock
- Retained Earnings
- Liquidity, Solvency, Activity Analysis

5-10%	**The Statement of Cash Flows** • Indirect Method • Cash Flow Analysis • Operating, Financing and Investing Activities	
1-5%	**Miscellaneous** • Investments • Contingent Liabilities	

SAMPLE TEST

1. **Sale – March**
   Delivery - April
   Payment – May
   Warranty – 1 Year
   Warranty expense reported in:

   A. March

   B. April

   C. March of the following year

   D. April of the following year

   E. When the warranty ends

2. **Amortization of prepaid insurance appears on:**

   A. Balance sheet only

   B. Balance sheet and cash flows statement

   C. Balance sheet and income statement

   D. Income statement and cash flows statement

   E. Cash flows statement and balance sheet

3. **Starting inventory - $1,000**
   Purchases - $15,000
   Ending inventory - $2,000
   COGS - $____ :

   A. 12,000

   B. 16,000

   C. 14,000

   D. 17,000

   E. 15,000

4. **Which of the following appears separately, net of income tax, on an income statement:**

   A. Gross Profit

   B. Loss on Discontinued Operations

   C. Gain on Sale of a Truck

   D. Interest Expense

   E. Tax expense

Financial Accounting

5. Business loan worth $1 million
   Interest rate is 0%
   Repayment period is 10 years
   Payments are made annually
   This is recorded as:

   A. A current liability of $1 million

   B. A long-term liability of $1 million

   C. Current liability of $100,000 and a long-term liability of $900,000

   D. Note payable of $100,000 and bond payable of $900,000

   E. Long-term liability of $100,000 and current liability of $900,000

6. Which of the following appears as a cash flow from investing activities:

   A. Revenues from the sale of goods

   B. Paying interest to bondholders

   C. Paying a dividend to preferred shareholders

   D. Sale of machinery for scrap

   E. COGS

7. The government agency which regulates financial reporting of publicly-traded companies is:

   A. IRS

   B. FASB

   C. AICPA

   D. SEC

   E. DoD

8. The professional organization which issues accounting credentials is:

   A. FASB

   B. AICPA

   C. IRS

   D. SEC

   E. DoD

9. The organization is charge of establishing GAAP is:

   A. IRS

   B. FASB

   C. AICPA

   D. SEC

   E. FBI

Financial Accounting

10. **The accounting equation states:**

    A. Assets = Liabilities + Equity

    B. Equity = Liabilities - Assets

    C. Equity = Liabilities + Assets

    D. Assets = Equity − Liabilities

    E. Assets = Equity/Liabilities

Answer Key

1. B
2. C
3. C
4. B
5. C
6. C
7. D
8. B
9. B
10. A

Please note that this is a sample portion of the CLEP Financial Accounting examination. A complete practice test is available for purchase at Amazon.com and Barnesandnoble.com
ISBN 9781607875383

Information Systems

Description of the Examination

The Information Systems examination covers material that is usually taught in an introductory college-level business information systems course. Questions test knowledge, terminology, and basic concepts about information systems as well as the application of that knowledge. The examination does not emphasize the details of hardware design and language-specific programming techniques. References to applications such as word processing or spreadsheets do not require knowledge of a specific product. The focus is on concepts and techniques applicable to a variety of products and environments. Knowledge of arithmetic and mathematics equivalent to that of a student who has successfully completed a traditional first-year high school algebra course is assumed.

The examination contains approximately 100 questions to be answered in 90 minutes. Some of these are pretest questions and will not be scored. The time candidates spend on tutorials and providing personal information is in addition to the actual testing time.

Note: Prior to October 2015, this examination was called Information Systems and Computer Applications.

Knowledge and Skills Required

Questions on the Information Systems examination require candidates to demonstrate knowledge of the following content. The percentages next to each main topic indicate the approximate percentage of exam questions on that topic.

10% Office Applications
- Productivity software (word processing, spreadsheet, presentation package, end-user database package)
- Operating systems (memory management, file management, interfaces, types of OS)
- Office systems (e-mail, conferencing, collaborative work, document imaging, system resources)

15% Internet and World Wide Web
- Internet and other online services and methods (World Wide Web, protocol, Web search engines, Web bots, intranet, cloud computing, communications, push/pull technology, W3C)
- Web browsers (URLs, protocols, standards, history, cookies, resource allocation)
- Web technologies (HTML, XML, JavaScript)
- Website development (analysis, design, functionality, accessibility)

15% Technology Applications
- Specialized systems (knowledge management, expert systems, TPS/OLTP, DSS, GIS, BI, workflow management, project management)
- E-commerce/E-business (EDI, standards, tools, characteristics, types of transactions, business models)
- Enterprise-wide systems (ERP, CRM, SCM)
- Data management (data warehousing, data mining, networking, security, validation, migration, storage, obsolescence)

- Business strategies (competition, process reengineering, process modeling, TQM, Web 2.0)
- Information processing methods (batch, real-time, transaction)

15% Hardware and Systems Technology
- Devices (processing, storage, input and output, telecommunications, networking)
- Functions (computer, telecommunications, network hardware)
- Network architectures (local area, wide area, VPN, enterprise)
- Computer architectures (mainframe, client/server, operating systems)
- Wireless technologies (Wi-Fi, cellular, satellite, mobile, GPS, RFID)

10% Software Development
- Methodologies (prototyping, SDLC, RAD, CASE, JAD, Agile)
- Processes (feasibility, systems analysis, systems design, end-user development, project management)
- Implementation (testing, training, data conversion, system conversion, system maintenance, post-implementation activities, post-implementation review, documentation)
- Standards (proprietary, open source)
- User interface design
- Development and purpose of standards

10% Programming Concepts and Data Management
- Programming logic (Boolean, arithmetic, SQL)
- Methodologies (object-oriented, structured)
- Data (concepts, types, structures, digital representation of data)
- File (types, structures)
- Database management systems (relational, hierarchical, network, management strategies)

25% Social and Ethical Implications and Issues
- Economic effects (secure transactions, viruses, malware, cost of security)
- Privacy concerns (individual, business, identity theft)
- Property rights (intellectual, legal, ownership of materials, open-source software)
- Effects of information technology on jobs (ergonomics, virtual teams, telecommuting, job design)
- Technology's influence on workforce strategies (globalization, virtual teams, telecommuting, outsourcing, insourcing)
- Careers in IS (responsibilities, occupations, career path, certification)
- Computer security and controls (system application, personal computer, disaster recovery)
- Social networking (benefits, risks, ethics, technology, Web 2.0)

Information Systems

SAMPLE TEST

1. What does a .gif picture file stand for?

   A. Graphical Interface Format

   B. Graphics Interior Format

   C. Graphical Interchanging Format

   D. Graphics Interchange Format

   E. Giant Interface Format

2. It allows you to personalize your document, protect your document, and identify the ownership of the document.

   A. Picture background

   B. Confidential

   C. Watermark

   D. Washout

   E. Identity Pin

3. The acronym USB stands for?

   A. Universal Series Bus

   B. Universal Serial Bus

   C. Union Series Bus

   D. Unified Serial Bus

   E. Universal Station Bus

4. There is a huge system of interconnected networks on the Internet. What are *networks*?

   A. Two or more computers connected together

   B. Programs that go on searches

   C. Groups of programmers

   D. Television stations

   E. A group of software

5. Which of the following is *not* a unique feature of e-commerce technology?

   A. interactivity

   B. social technology

   C. global broadcasting

   D. richness

   E. Universal standards

6. Inadequate database capacity is an example of the _____ dimension of business problems.

   A. technology

   B. organizational

   C. people

   D. management

   E. serial

7. **When is the best time to secure dedicated backup servers, networks and either hot sites or redundant and independent sites?**

    A. As soon as possible after a disaster declared

    B. Prior to any disaster

    C. Prior to establishing the disaster recovery planning team

    D. Once "business as usual" is established after a disaster is declared.

    E. Once other financial concerns have been taken care of.

8. **What do *directories* do?**

    A. List the information you search for

    B. List addresses and phone numbers

    C. List information by categories

    D. List information for librarians

    E. Confuse those searching for information.

9. **Interactivity in the context of e-commerce can be described as the**

    A. ability to physically touch and manipulate a product.

    B. complexity and content of a message.

    C. ability of consumers to create and distribute content.

    D. establishing of a portal to buy products.

    E. enabling of two-way communication between consumer and merchant.

10. **Who often performs system testing and acceptance testing respectively?**

    A. Senior programmers and professional testers.

    B. Technical system testers and potential customers.

    C. Independent test team and users of the system.

    D. Development team and customers of the system.

    E. Customers of the system and the technical team.

11. Which of the problems below best characterizes a result of software failure?

    A. Damaged reputation
    B. Lack of methodology
    C. Inadequate training
    D. Regulatory compliance
    E. Poor management

12. _____ computing refers to applications and services that run on a distributed network using virtualized resources.

    A. Distributed
    B. Cloud
    C. Soft
    D. Parallel
    E. Hard

13. Which test support tool can be used to enforce coding standards?

    A. Static analysis tool
    B. Performance testing tool
    C. Test comparator
    D. Test management tool
    E. Enforcement tool

14. What are the three main search expressions, or operators, recognized by Boolean logic?

    A. FROM, TO, WHOM
    B. AND, OR, NOT
    C. SEARCH, KEYWORD, TEXT
    D. AND, OR, BUT
    E. AND, TO, BUT

15. Which of the following statements about meta-search engines is NOT true?

    A. Meta-search engines scan multiple search engines simultaneously.
    B. Meta-search engines are a waste of time because they provide very few results.
    C. Meta-search engines provide results based on the keyword(s) submitted.
    D. Meta-search engines can save time, but you shouldn't rely on them exclusively.
    E. Meta-search engines take input from a user and simultaneously send out queries to a third party search engine for results.

16. This is programming that protects the resources of a private network from users from other networks.

    A. Cybernetics
    B. Firewall
    C. Server-side include
    D. Intranet
    E. Server protection

17. What test can be conducted for off-the-shelf software to get market feedback?

    A. Beta testing
    B. Usability testing
    C. Alpha testing
    D. COTS testing
    E. Trial and error testing

18. When the computer is started, a bootstrap or Initial Program Load (IPL) begins testing the system. Where is this bootstrap program stored?

    A. RAM
    B. ROM
    C. hard drive
    D. virtual memory
    E. DNS

19. A software robot that systematically searches the Web is a:

    A. search engine
    B. web rabbit
    C. weblog
    D. spider
    E. net catch

20. What principle is best described when test designs are written by a third-party?

    A. Exploratory testing
    B. Independent testing
    C. Integration testing
    D. Interoperability testing
    E. Designer testing

21. What should a software developer use to document each variable in a software solution?

    A. Data dictionary
    B. Data file
    C. Data flow diagram
    D. Structured data types
    E. Data notebook

Information Systems

22. While compiling a program the following error message occurred:

    unexpected '=' in code line 57

    What is the most likely cause of this message?

    A. Line 57 causes an incorrect output.

    B. A global variable has not been initialized.

    C. Line 57 was missing.

    D. The syntax rules of the programming language have not been followed.

    E. The incorrect logical or arithmetic operator has been used in a calculation.

23. **Antivirus software**

    A. needs to be installed only when your computer is networked.

    B. needs to be installed once you have detected a virus on your computer.

    C. needs to be updated regularly in order to ensure protection from newly created viruses.

    D. works quickest when you install multiple antivirus programs from different companies.

    E. Needs to be reinstalled daily.

24. The maximum amount of data that can be transmitted electronically during a given period of time is known as

    A. frequency.

    B. broadband.

    C. fiber-optic.

    D. broadwidth

    E. bandwidth.

25. **One of the purposes of software requirements specifications (SRS) is to provide**

    A. the breakdown of a problem into its component parts.

    B. instructions of users, describing how to use the new solution.

    C. instructions to programmers on how the new program works.

    D. evaluation criteria to ensure solution requirements have been met.

    E. brainstorming of a program's most desired features.

26. **Which one of the following techniques would capture data to measure the *effectiveness* of a software solution?**

    A. Surveying users

    B. Measuring average login time

    C. Running the network under load

    D. Timing the execution of a process

    E. Measuring average wait time

27. **The most appropriate data structure to store information about customer orders on a computer's hard drive is a**

    A. file.

    B. character.

    C. one-dimensional array.

    D. two-dimensional array.

    E. document

28. **A validation check used to ensure that entered data is a number is called**

    A. a type check.

    B. a range check.

    C. a character check.

    D. an existence check.

    E. a calculation check.

29. **Network technicians can use error logs to measure the**

    A. speed of a network.

    B. usability of a network.

    C. reliability of a network.

    D. maintainability of a network.

    E. redundancy of a network.

30. **Who founded Google?**

    A. Sergei Zuckerberg and Larry King

    B. Louis Page and Sergei Rockmonanov

    C. Larry Page and Sergei Brin

    D. Mark Zuckerberg and Steve Balmer

    E. Louis Page and Steve Balmer

31. **Which of the following tags allows loading malicious code (often in the form of JavaScript applet) onto an otherwise trusted page?**

    A. <script>

    B. <!-->

    C. <iframe>

    D. <section>

    E. <header>

Information Systems

32. **Data management technology consists of the**

    A. physical hardware and media used by an organization for storing data.

    B. detailed, preprogrammed instructions that control and coordinate the computer hardware components in an information system.

    C. software governing the organization of data on physical storage media.

    D. hardware and software used to transfer data.

    E. hardware that connects the user to the data.

33. **The hardware and software used to transfer data in an organization is called**

    A. data management technology.

    B. networking and data management technology.

    C. data and telecommunications technology.

    D. networking and telecommunications technology.

    E. data management and hardware management.

34. **Sociologists study information systems with an eye to understanding**

    A. how systems affect individuals, groups and organizations.

    B. how human decision makers perceive and use formal information.

    C. how new information system changes the control and cost structures within the firm.

    D. the production of digital goods.

    E. why consumers buy products.

35. **Which of the following would NOT be used as an input for an information system?**

    A. digital dashboard

    B. handheld computer

    C. bar-code scanner

    D. cell phone

    E. iPad

36. **Which field of study focuses on both a behavior and technical understanding of information systems?**

    A. sociology

    B. operations research

    C. economics

    D. management information systems

    E. research management

37. **The computer's hardware is controlled by the**

    A. CPU

    B. random access memory (RAM)

    C. operating system

    D. keyboard

    E. mouse

38. **Which of the following is not an example of a digital modem?**

    A. modem connected to a television cable

    B. modem connecting to a wireless network

    C. modem connecting to a public telephone network

    D. modem connecting to a DSL telephone line

    E. modem connecting to an Ethernet cable.

39. **The first application in what came to be called office automation was**

    A. word processing.

    B. email.

    C. facsimile (fax).

    D. electronic calendaring.

    E. database management

40. **What is WPA/WPA-2 PSK?**

    A. WPA/WPA2 PSK uses a pre-shared key for access to he wireless network.

    B. A protection check that validates the connecting client.

    C. A special attack on WPA/WPA-2 wireless networks.

    D. A method to protect wireless access points from DoS (denial of service) attacks.

    E. A new encryption method that will replace AES.

41. **Malicious software performing unwanted and harmful actions in disguise of a legitimate and useful program is known as**

    A. adware

    B. a computer worm

    C. a Trojan horse

    D. spyware

    E. hoax

Information Systems

42. **Systems analysts are**

    A. highly trained technical specialists who write computer software instructions.

    B. specialists who translate business problems and requirements into information requirements and systems.

    C. employees who head the formal security function for an organization.

    D. senior managers in charge of the information systems function in a firm.

    E. employees who oversee programmers.

43. **_____ are online communities for expanding users' business or social contacts by making connections through their mutual business or personal connections.**

    A. Wikis

    B. Virtual worlds

    C. Social networking

    D. Email

    E. Bookmarking tools

44. **Buying or selling goods over the Internet is called**

    A. e-commerce

    B. e-business

    C. an intranet

    D. an extranet

    E. computer business

45. **A _____ allows individuals at two or more locations to communicate simultaneously through two-way video and audio transmissions.**

    A. videotape

    B. wiki

    C. blog

    D. videoconference

    E. social media account

46. **Because the Internet lowers barriers to entry in most industries, it**

    A. decreases the threat of new entrants.

    B. increases the threat of new entrants.

    C. makes it easier to build customer loyalty.

    D. increases supplier power.

    E. increases the number of brick and mortar stores.

Information Systems

47. Gathering "competitive intelligence"

A. is good business practice.

B. is illegal.

C. is considered unethical.

D. minimizes the need to obtain information in the public domain.

E. is a waste of time.

48. Which of the following is considered to be social software?

A. an iPad

B. Google Alerts

C. a Dell PC

D. an iPhone

E. Mac computers

49. An app on a smartphone is labeled as _____.

A. a device

B. social software

C. a wiki

D. a connection

E. hardware

50. Which of the following constitutes four types of social publishing sites?

A. social networking sites, message boards, forums, and wikis

B. microsharing sites, media sharing sites, and social bookmarking and news sites

C. reviews and ratings, deal sites and deal aggregators, social shopping markets and social storefronts

D. the Internet, social software, devices and social media users

E. blogs, smart phones, news sites, forums

51. Which of the following is considered to be social software?

A. an app

B. an iPad

C. a Sony digital camera

D. an iPhone

E. a Dell computer

52. To which of the following zones of social media do Facebook applications apply?

    A. social community only

    B. social publishing only

    C. social entertainment and social commerce

    D. social commerce and social publishing

    E. social community, publishing, entertainment and commerce

53. In computer security, the part of malware code responsible for performing malicious action is referred to as

    A. payload

    B. header

    C. frame

    D. preamble

    E. footer

54. The _____ includes esteem in its measure of the value that people exchange.

    A. horizon revolution

    B. digital native

    C. reputation economy

    D. network effect

    E. network revolution

55. The process social media users undergo to categorize content according to their own folksonomy is labeled as _____.

    A. crowdsourcing

    B. tagging

    C. cloud computing

    D. blogging

    E. E-chatting

56. Web 2.0:

    A. is a one-way communications device.

    B. provides limited availability to users.

    C. is an interactive social system of users and senders.

    D. cannot be accessed on devices like smartphones.

    E. is outdated technology.

57. A _____ protects against an attack in which one party generates a message for another party to sign.

    A. data authenticator

    B. strong hash function

    C. weak hash function

    D. digital signature

    E. data signature

Information Systems

58. **Harnessing collective knowledge to solve problems and complete tasks is labeled as _____.**

    A. crowdsourcing

    B. tagging

    C. cloud computing

    D. blogging

    E. face timing

59. **Social media are:**

    A. anything that involves delivering hosted services online.

    B. the means to harness the collective knowledge of a crowd to solve problems and complete tasks;

    C. the online means of communication, conveyance, collaboration, and cultivation among interconnected and interdependent networks.

    D. people who share their views about a product or service even though they're not affiliated with the company.

    E. a one-way communication device.

60. **On average, _____ of all possible keys must be tried in order to achieve success with a brute-force attack.**

    A. one-fourth

    B. half

    C. wo-thirds

    D. three-fourths

    E. four-fifths

61. **The purpose of a _____ is to produce a "fingerprint" of a file, message, or other block of data.**

    A. secret key

    B. digital signature

    C. keystream

    D. hash function

    E. digital file

62. **The idea that the program instructions and data are both stored in memory while being processed is known as the**

    A. processing concept.

    B. stored program concept

    C. data-instruction concept

    D. memory-data-instruction concept

    E. memory-processing concept.

63. As a matter of necessity, network interfaces must conform to standard agreements, known as _____, for messages to be understood by both computers during a message exchange between a pair of computers.

    A. protocols

    B. I/O services

    C. device controllers

    D. Ethernet standards

    E. networks

64. The components of an individual computer system consist of processing hardware, input devices, output devices, storage devices,

    A. and application programs.

    B. and operating system software.

    C. application software and operating system software.

    D. application software, file storage, and data processing.

    E. file storage and data processing.

65. What is the only requirement for data to be manipulated and processed by a computer?

    A. The data type must be numeric.

    B. The data must be represented in binary form.

    C. The data type must be alphanumeric, graphic, sound or color.

    D. The size of the data must be smaller than the capacity of the hard drive.

    E. The data type must be alphanumeric.

66. The main memory, often known as primary storage, working storage, or RAM (for random access memory), holds

    A. data.

    B. program instructions.

    C. program instructions and data.

    D. program instructions, data, and instructions for booting the computer.

    E. None of the above.

67. Many of the internal OS services are provided by the _____ module, which contains the most important operating system processing functions.

   A. CPU

   B. root

   C. kernel

   D. central

   E. functioning

68. A development methodology that focuses on the processes as the core of the system is said to be _____.

   A. action-oriented

   B. structure-oriented

   C. process-centered

   D. object-oriented

   E. nature-oriented

69. Which of the following computer applications would best help a teacher keep records of students' academic information in a format that would allow complex searches using logical operators such as AND, OR, and NOT?

   A. utility

   B. database

   C. spreadsheet

   D. word processing

   E. text file

70. The primary advantage of defining styles when creating a word processing document is that they:

   A. allow page breaks to be set automatically.

   B. provide a template for the placement of text and images.

   C. automatically create text boxes and allow text to be wrapped.

   D. facilitate formatting of the text elements in the document.

   E. reduce errors in typing.

Information Systems

71. It is most appropriate to use a vector graphics program rather than a bitmapped graphics program when creating:

    A. images that will be saved in a file format for the Web.

    B. an image that contains small decorative type.

    C. images that will be used in print products.

    D. an image that can be enlarged with no loss of quality.

    E. the image does not need to be saved.

72. Which of the following is a function of a plug-in?

    A. allowing a Web browser to execute files that are in formats the Web browser would normally not recognize

    B. decreasing the amount of time required for a Web browser to display multimedia files

    C. providing site visitors with greater control over how the files are displayed

    D. checking multimedia files for viruses before displaying them in the Web browser

    E. allowing users to modify others websites

73. A person designing a Web page is most likely to use JavaScript for which of the following applications?

    A. to play a sound file when the user clicks on a sound icon

    B. to allow the user to send an email to the Webmaster

    C. to print and save information entered in forms by users

    D. to pause and play video clips and animations

    E. to allow the visitor to leave the site quickly.

74. How can the risk of unauthorized computer system access be reduced?

    A. By installing anti-spam software.

    B. By using a firewall.

    C. By setting up a WAN.

    D. By encrypting all data stored in the system.

    E. By creating a password.

75. A user wants to detect and clean a virus-infected file as it is opened. Which of the following would best achieve this?

    A. Schedule a local virus scan.

    B. Utilize a real-time virus scan.

    C. Perform a scheduled network virus scan.

    D. Perform a complete virus scan of all hard disks.

    E. Reinstall virus protection software.

76. Which of the following is a feature or characteristic of macros?

    A. They can be hyperlinked to a file.

    B. They can be saved as a separate file.

    C. They can only be used to carry viruses.

    D. They can be embedded in spreadsheet.

    E. They cause viruses to spread.

77. The _____ provides the physical mechanisms to input and output data, to manipulate and process data, and to electronically control the various input, output and storage components.

    A. data

    B. network

    C. computer hardware

    D. computer software

    E. Internet

78. Which of the following is NOT an HTML container element?

    A. <region>

    B. <section>

    C. <footer>

    D. <aside>

    E. <header>

79. Which of the following is the most common operating system used by webservers?

    A. Windows

    B. Mac OS

    C. Android

    D. Linux

    E. System 7

Information Systems

80. When does a written work receive protection under U.S. copyright laws?

    A. When the work is written down.

    B. When the author first comes up with the idea for the work.

    C. When the work is published.

    D. When the work is registered with the U.S. Copyright Office.

    E. When the work is notarized.

81. A _____ is created by using a secure hash function to generate a hash value for a message and then encrypting the hash code with a private key.

    A. digital signature

    B. keystream

    C. one way hash function

    D. secret key

    E. protected message

82. Web addresses are called Uniform Resource Locators (URLs). A URL is a text string that specifies an Internet address and the method by which the address can be accessed. The protocol component of a URL identifies

    A. the name of the server on which the page resides.

    B. the site owner's registered site.

    C. the type of server and Internet service being used.

    D. the organization type.

    E. where the owner resides.

83. The work performed by an individual computer system within an IT system can be characterized by

    A. hardware and software.

    B. input, storage and output.

    C. storage, processing and output.

    D. input, processing and output.

    E. input, storage and software.

84. In what ways can cookies be useful for Web site developers?

   A. Cookies give developers access to Web site visitors' hard drive files.

   B. Cookies inform the Web site manager about visitors' preferences.

   C. Cookies are dangerous and should never be used in Web development.

   D. Cookies enable developers to convey their preferences to Web site users.

   E. Cookies allow users to access the website's backend.

85. Mike receives an email message from a friend that contains a zip file. He opens the file and later notices that his email application has sent a copy of that zip to each person in his address book without his commanding it to do so. What event has most likely occurred?

   A. Mike has accidently sent a mass email to everyone on in his address book.

   B. A virus has infected Mike's computer.

   C. A hacker has taken over Mike's computer.

   D. Mike's email application has malfunctioned and must be replaced.

   E. Mike was logged into the wrong email account.

86. Harmful programs used to disrupt computer operation, gather sensitive information, or gain access to private computer systems are commonly referred to as

   A. adware

   B. malware

   C. computer viruses

   D. spyware

   E. worm

87. Which tag must appear within an HTML table?

   A. <tr>

   B. <th>

   C. <caption>

   D. <tc>

   E. <tb>

Information Systems

88. What is the correct definition of a block level tag?

    A. A block level tag is a HTML element that affects one or more paragraphs.

    B. A block level tag affects an individual character or word.

    C. A block level tag does not require a paragraph break before the tag is used.

    D. A block level tag creates a table border.

    E. A block level tag places the paragraph into a block format.

89. Which of the following refers to the characteristic features of an advertising-supported software?

    A. Unsolicited or undesired electronic messages

    B. A worm that infiltrates the computer's operating system

    C. Commonly referred to as malware

    D. Malicious program that sends copies of itself to other computers on the network

    E. Commonly referred to as adware

90. This is an application program that provides a way to look at and interact with all the information on the World Wide Web.

    A. Line Checker

    B. Browser

    C. Access Provider

    D. Avatar

    E. Social Media

91. Which technology enables business to create multimedia applications to deliver their messages?

    A. Push technology

    B. Pull technology

    C. Media access technology

    D. Neo-Web technology

    E. Customer support initiative

92. You are a member of a Web design team. Which member of the team is responsible for developing the overall plan of the Web site?

   A. Web analyst
   B. Web Designer
   C. Web Architect
   D. Web Manager
   E. Systems Manager

93. Which of the following technologies manages the process of resolving URLs to official IP addresses?

   A. Domain Name System (DNS)
   B. File Transfer Protocol (FTP)
   C. Internet Service Providers (ISP)
   D. Simple Network Management Protocol (SNMP)
   E. Post Office Protocol (POP3)

94. Which of the following retains the information it's storing when the power to the system is turned off?

   A. RAM
   B. DRAM
   C. DIMM
   D. CPU
   E. ROM

95. You are setting up a new email client application, which of the follow pieces of information will you provide that will handle outgoing mail messages?

   A. Post Office Protocol (POP3)
   B. Simple Mail Transfer Protocol (SMTP)
   C. Internet Message Access Protocol (IMAP)
   D. Transmission Control Protocol (TCP)
   E. File Transfer Protocol (FTP)

96. Which of the following is NOT true about Open Source Software?

   A. Open Source Software is developed primarily by inexperienced students.
   B. Open Source Software is typically developed through a collaborative process.
   C. "Freeware" or "shareware" are not the same as open source software.
   D. Open Source Software is commercial software.
   E. There is a lot of Open Source Software available.

Information Systems

97. Which of the following image types typically supports transparency?

A. BMP and JPEG

B. PNG and BMP

C. PNG and GIF

D. JPEG and GIF

E. JPEG and BMP

98. Which of the following do search engines expect you to use when making complex searches for information?

A. Radical Inquiries

B. Spiders

C. SMS text messages

D. SQL statements

E. Boolean values

99. You have been asked to help implement a Web marketing campaign. Which of the following tools will best help you ensure that this project is completed on time?

A. A spreadsheet program

B. An email application

C. A Gantt chart

D. A social networking site such as LinkedIn

E. A relational database

100. Who owns the user data found on social networking sites such as Facebook and Twitter?

A. The user who created the data

B. The social networking site

C. The W3C or similar third party who ensures user privacy

D. The group of users with whom the user has communicated.

E. Everyone. It is part of Creative Commons.

Information Systems

ANSWER KEY

Question Number	Correct Answer	Your Answer	Question Number	Correct Answer	Your Answer	Question Number	Correct Answer	Your Answer
1	D		35	A		69	B	
2	C		36	A		70	D	
3	B		37	C		71	D	
4	A		38	C		72	A	
5	C		39	A		73	D	
6	A		40	A		74	B	
7	B		41	C		75	B	
8	C		42	B		76	D	
9	E		43	C		77	C	
10	C		44	A		78	D	
11	A		45	D		79	D	
12	B		46	B		80	D	
13	A		47	A		81	A	
14	B		48	B		82	C	
15	B		49	B		83	D	
16	B		50	A		84	B	
17	A		51	A		85	B	
18	B		52	E		86	B	
19	D		53	A		87	A	
20	B		54	C		88	A	
21	A		55	B		89	E	
22	D		56	C		90	A	
23	C		57	D		91	A	
24	E		58	A		92	C	
25	C		59	C		93	A	
26	A		60	B		94	E	
27	A		61	C		95	B	
28	A		62	B		96	A	
29	C		63	A		97	C	
30	C		64	C		98	E	
31	C		65	B		99	C	
32	D		66	B		100	B	
33	A		67	C				
34	A		68	C				

Introductory Business Law

Description of the Examination

The Introductory Business Law examination covers material that is usually taught in an introductory one-semester college course in the subject. The examination places not only major emphasis on understanding the functions of contracts in American business law, but it also includes questions on the history and sources of American law, legal systems and procedures, agency and employment, sales, and other topics.
The examination contains approximately 100 questions to be answered in 90 minutes. Some of these are pretest questions that will not be scored. Any time candidates spend on tutorials or providing personal information is in addition to the actual testing time.

Knowledge and Skills Required

Questions on the test require candidates to demonstrate one or more of the following abilities in the approximate proportions indicated.

- Knowledge of the basic facts and terms (about 30-35 percent of the examination)
- Understanding of concepts and principles (about 30-35 percent of the examination)
- Ability to apply knowledge to specific case problems (about 30 percent of the examination)

The subject matter of the Introductory Business Law examination is drawn from the following topics. The percentages next to the main topics indicate the approximate percentages of exam questions on those topics.

5%–10% History and Sources of American Law/Constitutional Law

5%–10% American Legal Systems and Procedures

25%–35% Contracts
- Meanings of terms
- Formation of contracts
- Capacity
- Consideration
- Joint obligations
- Contracts for the benefit of third parties
- Assignment/delegation
- Statute of frauds
- Scopes and meanings of contracts
- Breach of contract and remedies
- Bar to remedies for breach of contract
- Discharge of contracts
- Illegal contracts
- Other

25%–30% Legal Environment
- Ethics
- Social responsibility of corporations
- Government regulation/administrative agencies
- Environmental law
- Securities and antitrust law
- Employment law
- Creditors' rights
- Product liability
- Consumer protection
- International business law

10%–15% Torts

5%–10% Miscellaneous

SAMPLE TEST

1. **What is the "supreme law of the land?"**

    A. Congress

    B. The Supreme Court

    C. The President

    D. The Constitution

    E. The Senate

2. **Legislative law is called _____ law.**

    A. statutory

    B. common

    C. judge-made

    D. executive

    E. codified

3. **What part of the government makes rules and regulations that have the force and effect of law?**

    A. Congress

    B. The President

    C. The Supreme Court

    D. Administrative agencies

    E. The House of Representatives

4. **Court-made law is called _____.**

    A. legal law

    B. common law

    C. administrative law

    D. legislative law

    E. codified law

5. **Stare decisis means _____.**

    A. "let the decision stand"

    B. precedent

    C. codification

    D. "jurisdictional authority"

    E. the authority of the court to hear a case

6. **An ordinance is an example of _____ law.**

    A. federal

    B. state

    C. local

    D. territorial

    E. global

7. Colonists settled Plymouth, Jamestown, and Massachusetts Bay Colony in the 1600s. They brought with them the concepts of laws from their home country. From which country is our common law derived?

   A. France

   B. Holland

   C. England

   D. Spain

   E. Germany

8. The criminal code is an example of _____.

   A. statutory law

   B. executive law

   C. common law

   D. civil law

   E. judicial law

9. What is the source of law that results when Congress approved an agreement with another country?

   A. Civil law

   B. Treaty

   C. Criminal law

   D. Administrative law

   E. International

10. Pedestrian is injured when crossing a street. The driver insists that the pedestrian crossed the street while the light was red. Pedestrian claims the light was green. Pedestrian suffers a broken leg and back injuries and misses a month of work. In order to resolve the issue, pedestrian sues driver. Which type of law will be applied to the case?

    A. Administrative law

    B. Civil law

    C. Criminal law

    D. Statutory law

    E. Agency law

11. What is the trial court for the federal court system called?

    A. Circuit court

    B. Appeals court

    C. District court

    D. Chancery court

    E. Criminal court

12. For how long are federal judges appointed?

    A. Five years

    B. Life

    C. Ten years

    D. Two years

    E. During good behavior

Introductory Business Law

13. Which court will first hear a dispute between two states?

    A. State trial court

    B. Federal trial court

    C. State appellate court

    D. Federal court of appeals

    E. U.S. Supreme Court

14. The state's highest court of appeals ruled against a defendant on his claim that his constitutional rights were violated. If he wants to take the case to the U.S. Supreme court, what is the first filing his attorney must make?

    A. Complaint

    B. Writ of Certiorari

    C. Writ of Mandamus

    D. Counterclaim

    E. Reply

15. Store owner wants to collect an unpaid account. What is the first pleading the owner must file in court?

    A. Cross-claim

    B. Deposition

    C. Answer

    D. Complaint

    E. Summons

16. What is the burden of proof for the prosecution in a criminal case?

    A. Precedent

    B. Beyond a Reasonable Doubt

    C. Stare Decisis

    D. Nolo contendre

    E. Preponderance of the evidence

17. What is the term for the power of a court to hear a case?

    A. Venue

    B. Jurisdiction

    C. Arraignment

    D. Docketing

    E. Voir Dire

18. When is a summary judgment granted?

    A. When the plaintiff fails to appear

    B. When the defendant fails to appear

    C. When interrogatories are not answered

    D. When there is no genuine issue of material fact

    E. When all issues have been decided

19. What is another name for jury selection?

    A. Voir dire

    B. Stare decisis

    C. Depositions

    D. The appellate process

    E. Subpoena duces tecum

20. What are written questions propounded by one party to another party to be answered by the second party under oath prior to trial?

    A. Depositions

    B. Interrogatories

    C. Voir Dire

    D. Cross-claims

    E. Counterclaims

21. What is the rule that states a common law acceptance must be identical in reverse to a common law offer?

    A. Identical Rule

    B. Common Law Offer Rule

    C. Common Law Acceptance Rule

    D. Mirror Image Rule

    E. Exactness Rule

22. What is the term that indicates the parties have the legal ability to enter into a contract?

    A. Capacity

    B. Competency

    C. Adulthood

    D. Intent

    E. Majority

23. What is the term that defines a situation in which a landlord gives to a relative the power to receive rents that are normally paid to the landlord?

    A. Delegation

    B. Authorization

    C. Assignment

    D. Transfer

    E. Intent

24. Which statue requires transactions involving real estate to be in writing?

    A. Parol Evidence Rule

    B. Doctrine of Promissory Estoppel

    C. Doctrine of Plain Meaning

    D. Statute of Limitations

    E. Statute of Frauds

Introductory Business Law

25. What is the person making an offer called?

    A. Offeree

    B. Offeror

    C. Beneficiary

    D. Assignor

    E. Assignee

26. Who is the delegee?

    A. The person to whom a contractual duty is delegated

    B. The person who delegates a contractual duty

    C. The person who assigns a contract.

    D. The person to whom a contract is assigned.

    E. The person to whom the mirror image rule applies.

27. What is the benefit that must be bargained for in contract law?

    A. Offer

    B. Consideration

    C. Acceptance

    D. Mutual promises

    E. Remedies

28. Which element listed below is NOT applicable to a misrepresentation?

    A. Reliance

    B. Knowledge of falsity

    C. Material fact

    D. Statement of fact

    E. Intent to deceive

29. What does "force majure" mean?

    A. Commercial frustration of a contract

    B. The impossibility of performing a contract

    C. A reason for imposing damages

    D. An unexpected event of nature that allows parties not to perform a contract

    E. A major reason for requiring the performance of a contract

30. Which of the following is NOT an element of undue influence?

    A. A superior and subservient relationship

    B. An opportunity to influence

    C. Duress

    D. Vulnerable person

    E. Suspicious transaction

Introductory Business Law

31. Buyer has always wanted to purchase Seller's farm and has made offers to purchase several times. However, Seller has always turned Buyer down. Both are at a party, enjoying the refreshments. Seller tells Buyer to write out an agreement. Buyer writes out the terms on a paper napkin. Seller and Buyer sign the napkin. Buyer takes the money (in cash) to Seller. Seller refuses to deliver the property and says he did not have any intent to sell his family farm and that the "agreement" was a joke. What element of contract law is applicable to the "agreement"?

    A. Offer

    B. Acceptance

    C. Formation

    D. Consideration

    E. Capacity

32. Owner of property has drawn up plans for a subdivision. He has complied with all government requirements. He advertises the acre lots as "ready for well-drilling and building" upon signing closing papers. Buyer of lot contracts with well-driller who, after doing some testing, finds the water table too low for a well. Buyer wants his money back. On what basis would a refund be proper?

    A. Unilateral mistake

    B. Mutual mistake

    C. Lack of consideration

    D. No meeting of the minds

    E. Undue influence

33. What is the purpose of awarding contract damages?

    A. To put the person in a better position than he was in before the breach

    B. To put the person in the position he would have been in had the breach not occurred

    C. To punish the person causing the harmful breach

    D. To order the breaching party to specifically perform

    E. To halt the harmful behavior

34. What type of remedy is available to a purchaser who wants a court to order the seller to deliver property that he/she sold to the buyer?

   A. Injunction

   B. Damages

   C. Specific Performance

   D. Recission

   E. Liquidated damages

35. Which statement is NOT correct about liquidated damages?

   A. They must be reasonable.

   B. The parties need to agree that liquidated damages will be awarded.

   C. Liquidated damages are awarded for anticipatory breach.

   D. They must be stated as a specific amount.

   E. They may be determined by a percentage or by another agreed-upon method.

36. For which type of remedy must irreparable harm be shown?

   A. Liquidated damages

   B. Damages at law

   C. Specific performance

   D. Recission

   E. Injunction

37. According to the common law "mailbox rule" when is an offer accepted?

   A. When the offer is sent

   B. When the offer is received

   C. When the time is agreed upon

   D. When any method of acceptance is used

   E. When the acceptance is delivered by the agreed upon method

38. All of the following are examples of termination of a contract sale of real estate EXCEPT:

   A. completion

   B. breach

   C. operation of law

   D. recission

   E. death of a party

39. Buyer and Seller sign a purchase agreement for the sale/purchase of a house that sits on ½ acre. Buyer moves into the house and begins to use the shed that is on the property at the edge of the property line. Seller tells buyer to stop using the shed because the shed had not been part of the deal. What rule of law would prevent the buyer from arguing that the parties had meant to include the shed in the real estate transaction?

   A. mutual mistake

   B. parol evidence

   C. specific performance

   D. promissory estoppel

   E. injunction

40. Builder and homeowner enter into a contract for builder to construct an addition to a home that includes a 16' x 24' family room. Builder sends homeowner his last invoice for ½ the agreed-upon price. Homeowner refuses to pay because he argues that contractor breached their contract. Homeowner shows builder that the size of the family room is only 15'5" x 23'9". What doctrine would permit builder to be paid?

   A. Substantial performance

   B. Substantial breach

   C. No meeting of the minds

   D. Promissory estoppel

   E. Mutual mistake

41. Bob has his Rav 4 for sale. Sue offers him $9,000. Bob says, "No, but I will take $11,000." What is Bob's response?

   A. A revocation

   B. A rejection

   C. An offer

   D. A counter-offer

   E. Agreement

42. Jim, a college student, began selling used vehicles. A customer looks at a 1990 Ford Mustang convertible. Jim tells the customer that the car is in A-1 condition. How would you classify Jim's statement?

   A. Puffing

   B. Misrepresentation

   C. Fraudulent

   D. A statement made under duress

   E. A mistake

43. Daughter tells her elderly parents that she will move into their house care for them if they give her the house. A few days later, the parents contact their lawyer and add a codicil to their will, bequeathing the house to their daughter when they die. One week later, daughter has not moved in but her parents are killed in an airplane crash. She is devastated about their deaths but begins moving into the house. Her brother objects to her being given the house and argues that the house should be sold and proceeds divided equally as they are the only heirs. What is his argument?

    A. Fraud on the part of his sister

    B. Duress caused by his sister

    C. Undue influence of his sister

    D. Misrepresentation by his sister

    E. She should be promissorily estopped from getting the house.

44. A racing enthusiast purchases a horse to enter races. When he gets the horse to the stable, he learns the horse is great with foal (pregnant). Pregnant horses don't race. Seller learns of the pregnancy and wants the horse returned because pregnant horses are more valuable and expensive than racing horses. What will seller argue to try to get the horse returned?

    A. Benefit of the bargain

    B. Illegal contract

    C. Void contract

    D. Mutual mistake

    E. Unilateral mistake

45. Pet owner hired an artist to paint a portrait of her cat. Artist has an opportunity to go on vacation and wants a friend, who is also a painter, to finish the portrait. Cat owner objects. Can the artist have the friend finish the picture?

    A. Yes, if the painter agrees.

    B. Yes, regardless of whether the cat owner agrees. The task is assignable

    C. Yes, regardless of whether the cat owner agrees. The task is delegable

    D. No, because the pet hisses at the substitute painter

    E. No, because it is a personal service contract that is not delegable without approval

46. Aimee enters into a contract to purchase a $35,000.00 car. She is 17 years old but looks like she is 18 (an adult). She drives the car twice and decides she does not like the car. Can she avoid the contract?

    A. Yes, because she is a minor

    B. Yes, because she does not like the way the car handles

    C. No, because she looks like an adult

    D. No, because she has ratified the contract by driving the car

    E. No, if the car is a necessary

47. Which of the following is an example of an illegal contract?

    A. A contract a merchant enters into with a malt manufacturer for the purchase of alcoholic beverages during Prohibition

    B. A contract a merchant enters into for the purchase of alcoholic beverages to be sold in a county that, before delivery of the product, declares the products may not be sold in the county.

    C. A contract entered into that requires shipment of items to be delivered to a non-existent street number

    D. A contract entered into for delivery of hazardous products that are not permitted to be shipped by rail, as the contract provides.

    E. A contract to purchase an item that becomes illegal to manufacture after the date of the agreement.

48. What is another term for an illegal contract?

    A. Enforceable

    B. Unenforceable

    C. Avoidable

    D. Voidable

    E. Void

Introductory Business Law

49. **Which of the following is an example of a third-party beneficiary contract?**

    A. One party to a contract delegates performance to a third party

    B. One party to a contract asks the advice of a third party before signing the contract

    C. One party to a contract purchases a life insurance policy and names a relative as beneficiary

    D. One party leases a property with a right of first refusal to purchase the property from a subsequent purchaser

    E. One party donates the proceeds of a contract to a charity after receiving payment under the contract

50. **To what does the "plain meaning" rule apply?**

    A. Statutory construction

    B. Offers

    C. Acceptances

    D. Consideration

    E. Damages

51. **Which of the following is an example of a violation of business ethics?**

    A. Making a mistake in the addition of business expenses

    B. Charging a customer a price from a two-year-old price guide that is less than the price stated for a product on an updated guideline sent the day before the sale

    C. Exercising your judgment for a "return policy" for an outdated item where the company has no stated policy

    D. Submitting an "hours worked" sheet that included thirty-additional minutes because you forgot to time one of your work days.

    E. Contacting your manager to assist in solving a business-related issue when you have the authority to solve such problems on your own.

52. When might "moonlighting" be an ethical violation for a business employee?

   A. It is not an ethical violation.

   B. It is an ethical violation if the employee exceeds 40 work hours per week.

   C. It is an ethical violation if the employee arrives only five minutes ahead of the required time to begin work for the second job.

   D. It is an ethical violation if the employee's work performance becomes poor.

   E. It is only a violation if both employers raise the issue.

53. What does "corporate social responsibility" mean?

   A. A company must provide its employees breaks during the day for social gatherings.

   B. A company's officers are responsible for helping new employees find housing and community information.

   C. A company must provide scheduled times for employees to take "personal days" off work.

   D. A company has a duty to maintain a balance between the economy and the ecosystems.

   E. A company must communicate, through its officers, to its employees new laws regarding workplace safety.

54. Which of the following statements about corporate social responsibility is INCORRECT?

   A. It is an ethical framework.

   B. The concept applies to society as a whole.

   C. Active social responsibility is acting in a way to avoid engaging in socially harmful acts.

   D. Active social responsibility is performing activities that directly advance social goals

   E. Social responsibility can be either active or passive.

55. What is considered the "fourth" branch of government?

   A. Congress

   B. Executive Branch

   C. Administrative Agency

   D. Judicial Branch

   E. The Senate

56. Which of the following statements about administrative agencies is INCORRECT?

   A. Rules and regulations of administrative agencies have the force and effect of law.

   B. Administrative agencies are created by Congress.

   C. The Internal Revenue Service is an example of an administrative agency.

   D. An objection to an administrative rule can be brought in the judicial branch of government.

   E. Administrative law is considered a branch of public law.

57. Which of the following statements about securities law is INCORRECT?

   A. Securities laws are an example of a regulatory scheme.

   B. U.S. corporate securities are regulated at the federal level.

   D. The purpose of securities laws is to inform people about buying and selling stocks.

   E. Securities laws govern the purchase of stock of private corporations.

58. Of what type of law is greenhouse gas regulation an example?

   A. Environmental law

   B. Real estate law

   C. Business law

   D. Mining law

   E. Social responsibility law

59. Which federal agency helps regulate entities in meeting federal environmental requirements?

   A. Department of Justice

   B. Environmental Protection Agency

   C. Federal Trade Commission

   D. Department of Agriculture

   E. Consumer Protection Agency

60. What was the first major federal anti-trust law?

   A. Robinson Patman Act

   B. Sherman Antitrust Act

   C. Clayton Antitrust Act

   D. Federal Trade Commission Act

   E. Celler-Kefauver Antimerger Act

61. A company that sells copy machines requires purchasers to buy copy paper from them. This is an example of what kind of antitrust violation?

    A. Horizontal restraint

    B. Vertical restraint

    C. Merger

    D. Tying arrangement

    E. Price fixing

62. What rule does a court use to determine whether there has been price-fixing in a restraint of trade case?

    A. Rule of reason

    B. Per se rule

    C. Collateral estoppel

    D. Promissory estoppel

    E. Cease and desist

63. Title VII of the Civil Rights of 1964 prohibits unlawful employment discrimination based on all of the following EXCEPT _____.

    A. race

    B. national origin

    C. age

    D. religion

    E. sex

64. Which statement is correct about employment law?

    A. Employment law excludes hours and wages issues and OSHA issues.

    B. Employment law excludes age and disabilities issues.

    C. Employment law excludes family leave issues.

    D. Employment law excludes collective bargaining.

    E. Employment law excludes worker's compensation issues.

65. Creditors' rights are protected in bankruptcy filings in all of the following ways EXCEPT _____.

    A. Filing a proof of claim

    B. Attending a meeting of creditors

    C. Objecting to a plan of reorganization

    D. Filing suit against the debtor

    E. Objecting to discharge

66. How may creditors protect their rights to collect a judgment if a debtor refuses to pay a judgment?

    A. Garnishee wages

    B. Apply the Fair Debt Collection Act

    C. File suit

    D. They have no recourse.

    E. File a showing of contempt

67. To whom is the Fair Debt Collection Act directed?

    A. Parties collecting their own debts

    B. Collectors of debts of third parties

    C. Creditors

    D. Debtors

    E. Courts

68. Which of the following is NOT an example of a consumer debt?

    A. A student loan

    B. Unpaid taxes

    C. Purchase of a refrigerator on a credit card

    D. Car loan

    E. Pledge to charity

69. Which is one of the more often used ways to resolve issues of international business transactions?

    A. Mediation

    B. Arbitration

    C. Litigation

    D. The International Court of Justice

    E. The European Union

70. Which statement is INCORRECT about a defective product?

    A. The defective product must cause injury.

    B. The defective product must have been defective when it left the manufacturer.

    C. The defective product must have been in the stream of commerce.

    D. The defective product cannot result in liability for a retailer.

    E. The defect in the defective product cannot always be observed.

71. **What does a warranty of "merchantability" mean?**

    A. The product can be sold on the open market.

    B. The product is fit for a particular purpose.

    C. The product is fit for ordinary purposes.

    D. The warranty is to be written on the box or label before sale.

    E. The warranty is stated to the purchaser.

72. **A product that is dangerous needs to have a warning. What statement is INCORRECT about warnings?**

    A. Failure to warn is a breach of duty.

    B. The warning must be conspicuous.

    C. The warning must be made large enough.

    D. The warning can be spoken.

    E. The warning must be in writing.

73. **Which of the following is an example of an express warranty?**

    A. The fact that a coffee pot is expected to make coffee

    B. The fact that a tool with attachments will perform as thought

    C. The fact that a lawn mower will cut grass

    D. The fact that an electric toothbrush holds size AA batteries

    E. The fact that an electric mixer can be repaired at no cost for a period of sixty days

74. **Why is strict liability imposed on manufacturers in product liability cases?**

    A. Because there has been negligence

    B. Because there has been a breach of warranty

    C. Because there is a deep pocket.

    D. Because of the goal of punishing the manufacturer

    E. Because of the goal of negligence litigation

75. "Manufacturer will repair or replace item within one year of purchase if a defect or malfunction occurs. Manufacturer will not compensate purchaser for any loss arising from defect or malfunction." The preceding statement is an example of a(n) _____.

   A. Warranty

   B. Implied warranty

   C. Express warranty

   D. Limited Warranty

   E. Breach of warranty

76. What is the "egg shell" theory?

   A. The wrongdoer takes the victim the way he/she finds the victim.

   B. The plaintiff's weaknesses must be exposed.

   C. The defendant's weaknesses must be exposed.

   D. There is a fracture in the plaintiff's case.

   E. The plaintiff has a thin chance of success.

77. Which of the following is NOT an element of battery?

   A. An unconsented to or rude touching

   B. Touching the person or something close to him/her, such as a cane or hat

   C. Intent to touch

   D. Intent to harm

   E. Resulting harm

78. Which of the following is NOT an element of assault?

   A. Putting a person in fear

   B. The element of fear is subjective

   C. An intent to put a person in fear

   D. Touching a person or something close to the person

   E. The fear of imminent harm

79. If you are attending a pool party in the backyard of a friend and you see a two-year-old step into the pool and sink to the bottom, who, sitting around the pool, has a legal duty to try to save the child?

    A. You

    B. A neighbor

    C. A babysitter

    D. A family friend

    E. The caterer

80. Which of the following is an example of an ultrahazardous or abnormally dangerous activity?

    A. Mink farming

    B. Baseball

    C. Mining

    D. Snow plowing

    E. Reforestation

81. Which of the following is an example of a situation in which vicarious liability is imposed?

    A. Workmen's compensation cases

    B. Intentional torts cases

    C. A driver's negligence due to hitting a pedestrian with the driver's own vehicle

    D. Emotional distress cases

    E. Battery cases

82. Nominal damages are likely to be awarded in which type of case?

    A. Assault

    B. Negligence

    C. Interference with contractual relations

    D. Battery

    E. Trespass

83. Which is NOT an element of negligence?

    A. Duty

    B. Breach of duty

    C. Legal cause

    D. Injury

    E. Damages

84. Upon what does proximate cause depend?

    A. Negligence

    B. Foreseeability

    C. Legal cause

    D. "But for" cause

    E. Respondeat superior

85. **Most states would deny a bystander the right to recover damages for the negligent infliction of emotional distress based on what rule?**

    A. The foreseeability rule

    B. The impact rule

    C. The privity rule

    D. The proximate cause rule

    E. The Discovery rule

86. **In which situation might punitive damages be imposed?**

    A. A personal injury case where the driver injured a pedestrian who was crossing the street while the light was red.

    B. A case where a driver on a 'frolic and detour' caused injury to a bicyclist

    C. A case where a person sued for negligent infliction of emotional distress.

    D. A case where a retailer falsely imprisons a suspected shoplifter

    E. A case where a business sells a faulty tool from an overseas manufacturer

87. **In which situation would respondeat superior apply?**

    A. An independent contractor causing damages to a yard while digging a ditch

    B. An employee who, while driving a company truck backs into a car

    C. A driver, driving her own car, injures a pedestrian

    D. A biker who injures a jogger

    E. The owner of a company who damages the company car of her way to work

88. **Which is NOT correct about conversion?**

    A. The owner is deprived of the possession personal property.

    B. The converter deprives the owner of the ownership of the property.

    C. The converter may intend to return the property.

    D. The converter may have also committed a criminal act of conversion.

    E. Converting property is an intentional tort.

89. Where a lawnmower has no warning about the dangers of use, what element of negligence applies to the lack of warning?

    A. Injury

    B. Causation

    C. Breach of duty

    D. Duty

    E. Damages

90. What term is applicable when an employee is running an errand for the employer and decides to take her own mail to the post office?

    A. Negligence

    B. Intentional tort

    C. Independent contractor

    D. Respondeat superior

    E. Frolic and detour

91. Which article of the Uniform Commercial Code applies to sales of goods?

    A. Article 2

    B. Article 2A

    C. Article 3

    D. Article 4

    E. Article 9

92. Which of the following statements about "goods" is INCORRECT?

    A. Goods are movable at the time of identification to the contract for sale.

    B. Goods include the unborn young of animals.

    C. Goods may be existing and/or identified before any interest in them can pass.

    D. Specially manufactured goods are defined as "goods."

    E. Money is a "good" that is defined as the "price that is to be paid."

93. Mark asks Sue to sell his iPod. She agrees. He gives her a plastic grocery bag with the iPod in it. Sue asks Tom if he is interested in buying Mark's iPod. Tom indicates he is. When he looks in the bag, he finds a case for the iPod in addition to the iPod. Tom indicates he is only interested in the purchase/sale if the case is included. If Sue sells both items together and Mark tells her that the case was not to be sold, what is Sue's argument to support the sale of the case?

    A. She had express authority to sell the case.

    B. She had apparent authority to sell the case.

    C. She had implied authority to sell the case.

    D. She had actual authority to sell the case.

    E. She was acting as a gratuitous agent.

94. Which of the following is an example of a fiduciary duty in the area of agency law?

    A. Pay wages

    B. Act on behalf of the principal

    C. Be controlled by the principal

    D. Be loyal

    E. Discharge duties in a timely manner

95. Which is a key element in determining whether a person is an employee or an independent contractor?

    A. Does the employer pay the person doing work for him?

    B. Does the employer have control over how the person's work is done?

    C. Does the employer pay taxes for the worker's income?

    D. Is there an agreement between the parties?

    E. Is there a past work history between the parties?

96. What generally happens to a partnership when a partner dies?

    A. The partnership is dissolved.

    B. The partnership continues with the remaining partners.

    C. The partnership allows a new partner to purchase the deceased partner's shares.

    D. The partnership becomes a sole proprietorship is there is only one remaining partner.

    E. The partnership's future is determined by the remaining partner(s).

Introductory Business Law

97. If a person wants to invest money into a partnership but does not want to be involved in the decision-making process, what type of partnership should that person form?

    A. General partnership

    B. Limited liability company

    C. Limited liability partnership

    D. Limited partnership

    E. Sole proprietorship

98. What is one of the main advantages of a corporate form of business organization?

    A. The tax structure

    B. Owning shares of stock

    C. Having a board of directors

    D. Having a bylaws

    E. Limited liability

99. Which of the following provides the written guidance for the operation of a corporation?

    A. Articles of Incorporation

    B. Bylaws

    C. Board of Directors

    D. Officers

    E. Corporate employee manual

100. What is the type of lawsuit that is filed by an injured party when a corporation is alleged to be an alter-ego of the sole shareholder?

    A. A derivative suit

    B. A suit to dissolve the corporation

    C. A suit for punitive damages

    D. A suit for an accounting

    E. A suit to pierce the corporate veil

Introductory to Business Law

ANSWER KEY

Question Number	Correct Answer	Your Answer
1	D	
2	A	
3	D	
4	B	
5	A	
6	C	
7	C	
8	A	
9	B	
10	B	
11	C	
12	E	
13	E	
14	B	
15	D	
16	B	
17	B	
18	D	
19	A	
20	B	
21	D	
22	A	
23	C	
24	E	
25	B	
26	A	
27	B	
28	E	
29	D	
30	C	
31	C	
32	B	
33	B	
34	C	

Question Number	Correct Answer	Your Answer
35	D	
36	E	
37	B	
38	E	
39	B	
40	A	
41	D	
42	A	
43	C	
44	D	
45	E	
46	E	
47	A	
48	E	
49	C	
50	A	
51	D	
52	D	
53	D	
54	C	
55	C	
56	D	
57	E	
58	A	
59	B	
60	B	
61	D	
62	B	
63	C	
64	D	
65	D	
66	A	
67	B	
68	B	

Question Number	Correct Answer	Your Answer
69	B	
70	D	
71	C	
72	D	
73	E	
74	C	
75	D	
76	A	
77	D	
78	D	
79	C	
80	C	
81	A	
82	E	
83	E	
84	B	
85	B	
86	D	
87	B	
88	B	
89	C	
90	E	
91	A	
92	C	
93	C	
94	D	
95	B	
96	A	
97	D	
98	E	
99	B	
100	E	

Principles of Management

Description of the Examination

The Principles of Management examination covers material that is usually taught in an introductory course in the essentials of management and organization. The fact that such courses are offered by different types of institutions and in a number of fields other than business has been taken into account in the preparation of this examination. It requires a knowledge of human resources and operational and functional aspects of management.

The examination contains approximately 100 questions to be answered in 90 minutes. Some of these are pretest questions that will not be scored. Any time candidates spend on tutorials and providing personal information is in addition to the actual testing time.

Knowledge and Skills Required

Questions on the Principles of Management examination require candidates to demonstrate one or more of the following abilities in the approximate proportions indicated.

- Specific factual knowledge, recall, and general understanding of purposes, functions, and techniques of management (about 10 percent of the exam)
- Understanding of and ability to associate the meaning of specific terminology with important management ideas, processes, techniques, concepts, and elements (about 40 percent of the exam)
- Understanding of theory and significant underlying assumptions, concepts, and limitations of management data, including a comprehension of the rationale of procedures, methods, and analyses (about 40 percent of the exam)
- Application of knowledge, general concepts, and principles to specific problems (about 10 percent of the exam)

The subject matter of the Principles of Management examination is drawn from the following topics. The percentages next to the main topics indicate the approximate percentage of exam questions on that topic.

15-25%   **Organization and Human Resources**
- Personnel Administration
- Human Relations and Motivation
- Training and Development
- Performance Appraisal
- Organizational Development
- Legal Concerns
- Workforce Diversity
- Recruiting and Selecting
- Compensation and Benefits
- Collective Bargaining

10-20%   **Operational Aspects of Management**
- Operations Planning and Control
- Work Scheduling
- Quality Management
- Information Processing and Management
- Strategic Planning and Analysis
- Productivity

45-55%   **Functional Aspects of Management**
- Planning
- Organizing
- Leading
- Controlling
- Authority
- Decision Making

- Organization Charts
- Leadership
- Organizational Structure
- Budgeting
- Problem Solving
- Group Dynamics and Team Functions
- Conflict Resolution
- Communication
- Change
- Organizational Theory
- Historical Aspects

10-20% **International Management and Contemporary Issues**
- Value Dimensions
- Regional Economic Integration
- Trading Alliances
- Global Environment
- Social Responsibilities of Business
- Ethics
- Systems
- Environment
- Government Regulation
- Management Theories and Theorists
- E-Business
- Creativity and Innovation

SAMPLE TEST

1. **According to equity theory:**

   A. (Employee B's rewards/Employee A's input) = (Employee A's rewards/Employee B's input)

   B. (Employee A's rewards/Employee A's input) = (Employee B's rewards/Employee B's input)

   C. (Employee A's rewards/Employee B's input) = (Employee B's rewards/Employee A's input)

   D. (Employee A's rewards/Employee A's input) > (Employee B's rewards/Employee B's input)

   E. (Employee A's rewards/Employee A's input) < (Employee B's rewards/Employee B's input)

2. **Productivity is:**

   A. Input*Output

   B. Input/Output

   C. Output/Input

   D. (Output-Input)/Output

   E. (Input-Output)/Input

3. **The use of a neutral third party tasked with resolving a dispute but who doesn't have the authority to enforce the outcome is known as:**

   A. Mediation

   B. Conciliation

   C. Arbitration

   D. Bargaining

   E. Litigation

4. **___ is not one of Porter's five forces of environmental scanning:**

   A. Bargaining power of suppliers

   B. Regulation of governments

   C. Bargaining power of customers

   D. Threat of new entrants

   E. Threat of substitutes

5. ___ is an example of ethnocentrism:

   A. Opening a wholly-foreign owned enterprise before attempting licensing

   B. Mistranslations of promotional materials

   C. Managing team dynamics in foreign offices as in home offices

   D. Using the same asset management analytics in each global office

   E. Structuring a business by functional division rather than geography

6. ___ is an example of the maintenance group role:

   A. Making acquisition decisions for upcoming projects

   B. Collecting feedback on an internal policy change

   C. Alleviating office friction during end of fiscal year

   D. Playing "Devil's Advocate"

   E. Scheduling project milestones in line with final deadline

7. The highest degree of group autonomy is found in ___ groups:

   A. Traditional

   B. Semi-autonomous

   C. Cross-functional

   D. Self-managed

   E. Virtual

8. A management method training employees on the operations of the company and the role of their primary function within it:

   A. Job enlargement

   B. Job rotation

   C. Job enrichment

   D. Job reengineering

   E. Job intensification

9. **Equity theory requires the use of objective measurements of input because:**

   A. So that employees know what to expect in their rewards

   B. The endowment effect means each person values their own contributions more than equivalent contributions by others

   C. So that inputs and outputs can be readily calculated

   D. To set a prediction reference point relative to actual outcomes

   E. To set a reference point for negotiations in future exchanges

10. **What type of plan is this "Over the next 5 years we will expand the total market by targeting previously untouched demographics":**

    A. Strategic

    B. Tactical

    C. Operational

    D. Project

    E. Contingency

11. **Who is in charge of establishing operational plans:**

    A. Middle managers

    B. First-line managers

    C. Executive managers

    D. Financial managers

    E. Shift managers

12. **The best contingency plans:**

    A. Deviate from the optimal plan at the point of change, preserving the value of the previous steps

    B. Are fully established plans wholly separate from the optimal plan

    C. Set alternatives for each step which feed back into the optimal plan

    D. Should be pursued simultaneously to the optimal plan

    E. Should only be developed if the optimal plan fails

13. **In change management, all the following are part of the unfreezing process except:**

    A. Surveying employees about their jobs and how they can be improved

    B. Quantify the operational, competitive, and financial impact of elements to be changed

    C. Reinforcing the negative aspects of current methods in the minds of the staff

    D. Communicating controlled isolation of the problem with plans for improvement that doesn't extend into the rest of the organization

    E. Implementing new policies

14. **At 6σ, the ideal goal of Six Sigma quality management, there are ____ DPMO with a ____ percentage yield:**

    A. 0.019, 99.9999981

    B. 3.4, 99.99966

    C. 233, 99.977

    D. 6,210, 99.38

    E. 66,807, 93.3

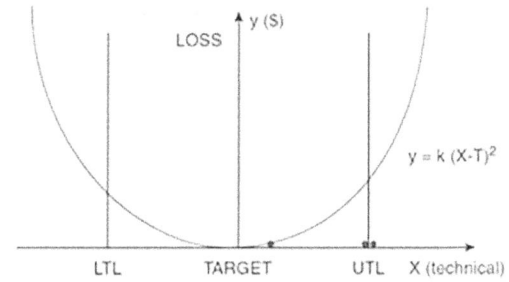

15. **The Taguchi Loss Function states:**

    A. Deviations from target specifications create a loss which increases exponentially and must not exceed upper and lower limits

    B. Quality management operations must be effective enough to be financially viable, but not to the point that its costs exceed its benefits

    C. The defective parts per million opportunities will increase the costs of fixing/reconstructing defective output more than the costs of preventing them

    D. Increasing losses create deviations from planned growth rates which become unsustainable at upper and lower limits

    E. Losses are a function of parabolic curves

16. $100,000 earned at complete project
    Planned 10 week deadline, linear PV
    $60,000 EV at 5 weeks
    What is the SPI:

    A. 120%

    B. 83%

    C. 10%

    D. -10%

    E. 100%

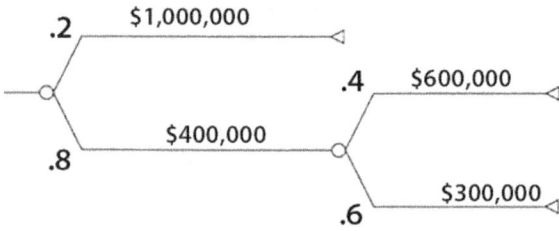

17. The adjusted values at the 2nd node of this decision tree are:

    A. -$200,000, $100,000

    B. $240,000, $180,000

    C. $300,000, -$300,000

    D. $200,000, $320,000

    E. $240,000, $300,000

Severity	Probability	Frequent	Likely	Occasional	Seldom	Unlikely
		A	B	C	D	E
Catastrophic	I	E	E	H	H	M
Critical	II	E	H	H	M	L
Moderate	III	H	M	M	L	L
Negligible	IV	M	L	L	L	L

18. In the management of a fire department, the risk to individual staff members is:

    A. None

    B. Low (L)

    C. Moderate (M)

    D. High (H)

    E. Extreme (E)

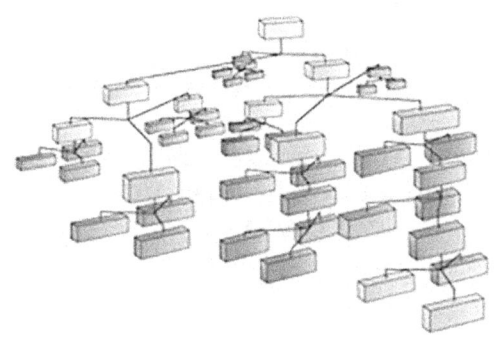

19. Models such as this are most commonly used to depict:

    A. Organizational hierarchy

    B. Product portfolio

    C. Subsidiary structure

    D. Capital assets

    E. Team motivation drivers

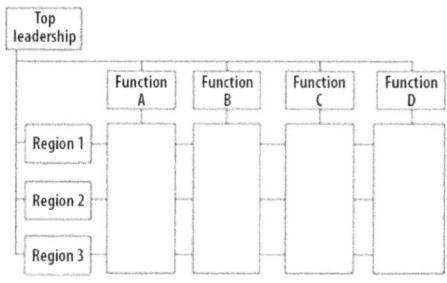

20. This represents:

    A. Divisional management

    B. Matrix management

    C. Micromanagement

    D. Tight matrix

    E. Organizational spreadsheet

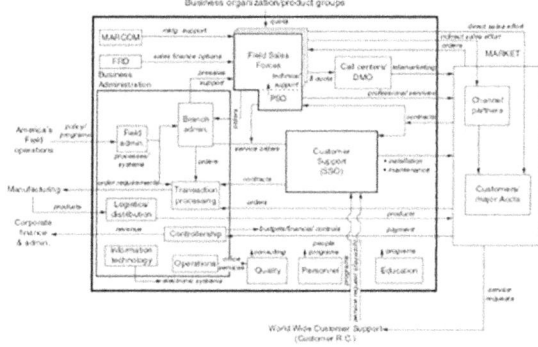

21. This is called ____ which represents ____:

    A. Process flowchart, dynamic operations of an organization

    B. Organizational structure, management hierarchy

    C. Schematic diagram, an electrical circuit

    D. Organizational structure, dynamic operations of an organization

    E. Process flowchart, management hierarchy

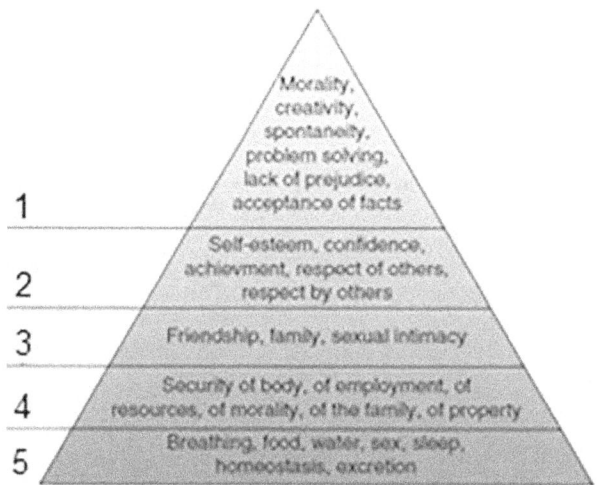

22. In Maslow's Hierarchy of Needs, self-actualization is found at:

    A. 1

    B. 2

    C. 3

    D. 4

    E. 5

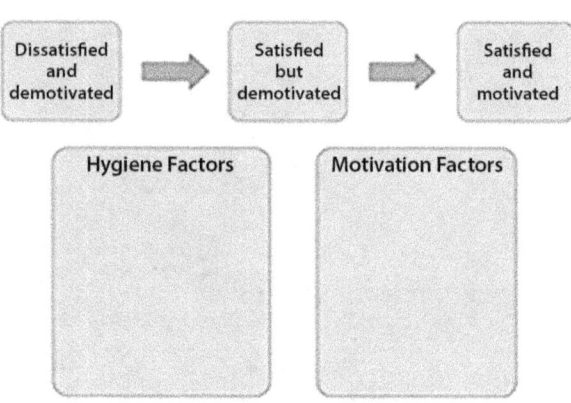

23. In Herzberg's Two-Factor Theory of Motivation, ____ is a hygiene factor and ____ is a motivator:

    A. Wages, prestige

    B. Responsibility, working conditions

    C. Promotions, job security

    D. Sense of purpose, clear expectations

    E. Recognition, professional relationships

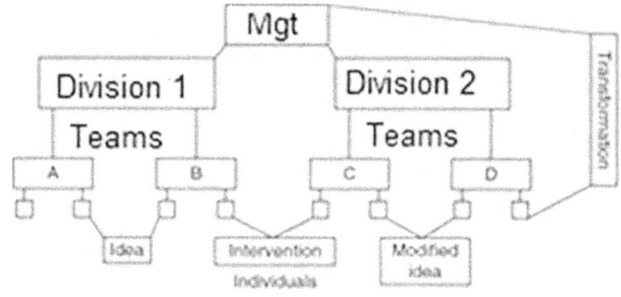

24. This graph illustrates:

    A. Structure of authority

    B. Team-based project management

    C. Organizational decision making process

    D. Bottom-up communication

    E. The flow of information in managing continuous improvement

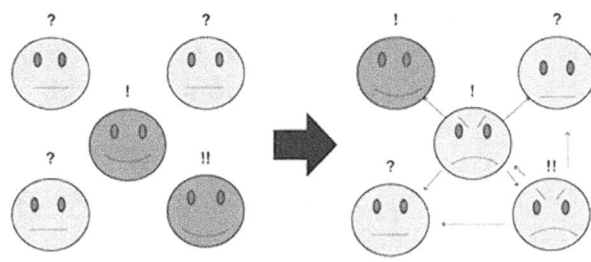

25. **This diagram on conflict creation illustrates the need for:**

    A. Clear direction and dissemination of information from management

    B. The need for arbitration during the decision making process

    C. Multiple styles of negotiations

    D. Constructive forms of persuasion

    E. Team development programs

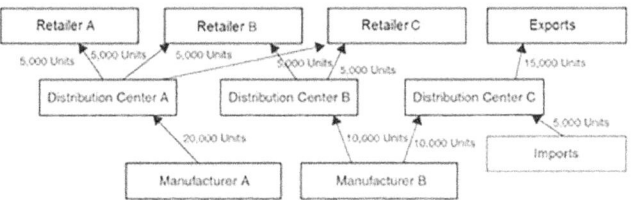

26. **Which manufacturer has the lowest-risk supply chain:**

    A. Manufacturer B because 100% of their production has multiple channels to the end consumer

    B. Manufacturer A because their primary distribution center sells to 50% more retailers than 2nd highest

    C. Manufacturer A because they are not competing with foreign imports

    D. Manufacturer B because they have domestic and foreign sales

    E. Both manufacturers A and B have equal risk of disrupted supply chains

27. ___ is a form of ___ given to first-line managers, though ___ is often reserved for middle management:

   A. Reward authority, legitimate power, coercive authority

   B. Personal power, legitimate power, positional authority

   C. Referent authority, personal power, coercive authority

   D. Reward authority, personal power, coercive authority

   E. Coercive authority, legitimate power, positional authority

28. ___ is acquired by being charismatic or motivational, rather than having any formal power:

   A. Expert authority

   B. Referent authority

   C. Positional authority

   D. Reward authority

   E. Coercive authority

29. Compartmentalization of operations to prevent interaction and communication is typically used to:

   A. This is never done in a healthy organization

   B. To create an immersive environment during job rotation training

   C. To prevent interaction between men and women in some highly orthodox cultures

   D. To prevent conflict with competing individuals or teams

   E. Prevent any person from having access to the whole of proprietary information

30. The point in the team development process in which members conflict with each other as they establish roles and culture is called:

   A. Forming

   B. Storming

   C. Norming

   D. Performing

   E. Adjourning

31. The point in which a manager will most likely need to validate the credentials of a member is:

    A. Adjourning

    B. Forming

    C. Storming

    D. Norming

    E. Performing

32. According to Kohlberg's Stages of Moral Development, how should a manager address an individual at Stage 4:

    A. Emphasize conditioning systems of reward and punishment

    B. Emphasize personal gain to be earned in negotiated terms

    C. Emphasize the importance of policies and organizational authority

    D. Emphasize the mutual benefits of constructed operations and dynamics

    E. Emphasize conforming to organizational roles and cultures as a means of acceptance

33. According to Kohlberg's Moral Development, how should a manager address an individual at Stage 3:

    A. Emphasize conforming to organizational roles and cultures as a means of acceptance

    B. Emphasize the importance of policies and organizational authority

    C. Emphasize the mutual benefits of constructed operations and dynamics

    D. Emphasize conditioning systems of reward and punishment

    E. Emphasize personal gain to be earned in negotiated terms

34. Motivation is mathematically represented as:

    A. (Expectancy*Value)/(1+Impulsiveness*Delay)

    B. Expectancy*Value

    C. (Expectancy*Value)/(1+Impulsiveness)

    D. Expected Value – Expected Costs

    E. Expected Value/(Impulsiveness*Delay)

35. The negotiating style which includes offering either fake or inconsequential concessions in order to gain on those things which matter to you is called:

    A. Accommodating

    B. Avoiding

    C. Collaborating

    D. Competing

    E. Compromising

36. The negotiating style which involves intentionally keeping negotiations on aspects which are not issues of conflict in order to draw the other person in is called:

    A. Collaborating

    B. Competing

    C. Avoiding

    D. Accommodating

    E. Compromising

37. Employees each produce 10 units per day, units sell for $100 each with a total cost of $90 per unit entirely composed of labor. If it takes 5 days to train a new employee, what is the turnover cost:

    A. $5,000

    B. $4,500

    C. $500

    D. $450

    E. $0

38. Per day, experienced staff produce 500 units and earn $100.
    Per day, new staff produce 300 units and earn $50.
    Training takes 5 days and each unit produced is worth $1
    The calculation to analyze the wage productivity differential is:

    A. $(500/100)n - ((300/50)n-250)$

    B. $(300/50)n-250)-(500/100)n$

    C. $(100/500)n-(300/50)n$

    D. $(500/100)n-(300/50)n$

    E. $(500-300)n/100-250$

39. Setup costs = $10
    Demand = 100
    Production cost = $20
    Interest rate = 100%
    EOQ is:

    A. 5

    B. 10

    C. 50

    D. 100

    E. 500

COSTS	IN-HOUSE	OUTSOURCED
Billing department costs	$118,000	$4,000
Software and hardware costs	$7,500	$500
Direct claim processing costs	$3,600	$122,500
Software and hardware costs	$5,500	$2,000
% of billings collected	60%	70%
Collections	$1,370,900	$1,623,000
Collections costs	$129,100	$127,000
Collections, net of costs		

40. **Decide whether to outsource:**

    A. Do not outsource to prevent losing $254,200

    B. Outsource to gain $254,200

    C. Do both to gain $254,200

    D. End function completely to prevent losing $254,200

    E. Panic

41. **It is best to use an authoratarian leadership style when:**

    A. During skill development programs

    B. When interpersonal conflict begins to hinder basic work functions

    C. When seeking input for revision of internal policies

    D. When managing skilled experts working in creative conditions

    E. During times of crisis when change must be rapid

42. **A pacesetting leadership style intended to facilitate the staff's activities is best used when:**

    A. When managing skilled experts working in creative conditions

    B. When seeking input for revision of internal policies

    C. When interpersonal conflict begins to hinder basic work functions

    D. During times of crisis when change must be rapid

    E. During skill development programs

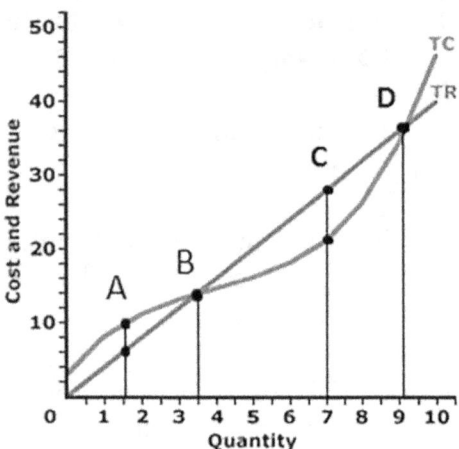

43. For profit-maximizing firms efficiency is optimized at __ and for revenue-maximizing firms at ___:

   A. B, C

   B. D, C

   C. C, D

   D. C, B

   E. B, D

44. Under generic competitive conditions, productive efficiency is achieved at:

   A. MC=FC

   B. FC=AC

   C. VC=FC

   D. MC=AC

   E. MC=TC

45. Which is not a type of team dysfunction:

   A. Groupthink

   B. Interpersonal conflict

   C. Freeriding

   D. Comprehensive input

   E. Lack of individualization

46. Analysis paralysis typically results from:

   A. Lack of decisive confidence

   B. Too much information

   C. Too little information

   D. Too much or too little information

   E. Rapidly changing business environment

47. The shareholder wealth maximization model is concerned with:

   A. Increasing current profitability

   B. Increasing the value of company equity

   C. Maximizing the value that the company creates for those which it influences

   D. Increasing company revenue growth

   E. Increasing NPV of company investments

48. **Which of the following is not a stakeholder:**

    A. Competitors

    B. Shareholders

    C. Employees

    D. Customers

    E. Partners

49. **Agency problems result from:**

    A. Executives who manage a company in a manner contrary to that which benefits the shareholders

    B. Executives who manage a company in a manner contrary to that which benefits the stakeholders

    C. Contradictions between the benefits of the shareholders and stakeholders

    D. Managers who embezzle money from the company

    E. Inefficient functions such as bid rigging and nepotism

50. **A short organization is one which has:**

    A. Few degrees of management with a larger volume of staff per manager

    B. More degrees of management with a lower volume of staff per manager

    C. Few degrees of management with a lower volume of staff per manager

    D. More degrees of management with a with a larger volume of staff per manager

    E. Few degrees of management with higher staff empowerment

51. **SIPOC analysis includes each except:**

    A. Competitors

    B. Supplier

    C. Inputs

    D. Processes

    E. Outputs

52. According to Lean-Six Sigma, the 8 sources of waste include everything except:

    A. Defects

    B. Overproduction

    C. Non-utilized talent

    D. Overtime

    E. Inventory-in-process

53. The most integrated way to create a direct presence within a foreign market is through:

    A. WFOE

    B. Licensing

    C. Joint venture

    D. Exporting

    E. Outsourcing

54. In SWOT, ___ is an example of "W" and ___ is an example of "O":

    A. Small HR pool in area, small population leading to insufficient revenues

    B. Efficient inventory management, cost-leader strategy from low costs

    C. Low brand recognition, cult following with potential for niche market strategy

    D. High materials costs, price competition

    E. Unique product, lack of sustainable advantage due to no IP registration

55. Something must be ___ and ___ to maintain a sustainable competitive advantage:

    A. Valuable, exchangeable

    B. Unsubstitutable, irreplaceable

    C. Rare, inimitable

    D. Rare, exchangeable

    E. Valuable, irreplaceable

56. ___ is the person who influences decisions by using indirect information to guide other to come to the desired conclusion:

   A. Idea planters

   B. Predictors

   C. Trend setters

   D. Persuaders

   E. Negotiators

57. **According to JIT ___:**

   A. Reserve inventory should always be held to account for variations from predicted sales volume

   B. The only reserve inventory to be held is that which will be used in the next month

   C. The only reserve inventory to be held is that which will be used biweekly

   D. The only reserve inventory to be held is that which will be used in the next week

   E. No reserve inventory should be held

58. How is PESTEL different in a global environment than a domestic one:

   A. Economical factors must include a corrective index to account for different economic structures

   B. Sociocultural factors become impossible to predict in foreign nations

   C. The interaction between nations creates dynamics more complex than both nations by themselves

   D. You must include political factors

   E. There is no difference

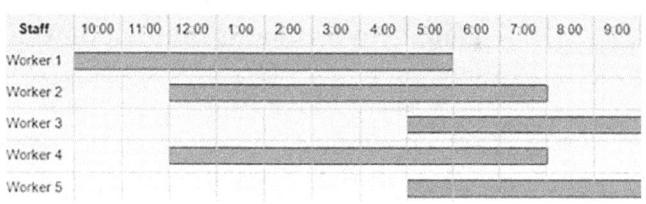

59. What does this say about operations:

A. Open from 10am-9pm with a shift change at 7pm and mornings are busier than evening

B. Open from 10am-9pm with a shift change at 5pm and mornings are busier than evenings

C. A one-day project starting at 10am with a deadline of 9pm has up to 5 workers on it at any time

D. One person opens at 10am, 2 people close at 9pm, and there are 4 employees to the manager

E. The period of 5pm-7pm is the busiest, requiring the most people

60. Decentralization requires ____ in order to ____:

A. Decreased authority in first-line management, empower employees

B. Increased authority in middle management, maintain control

C. Increased authority in first-line management, be responsive to customers

D. Empowerment of middle management, make decisions

E. Centralization, maintain order

61. The Foreign Corrupt Practices Act:

A. Bans the bribing of domestic officials by US or foreign citizens

B. Bans the bribing of domestic officials by foreigners, and holds foreign corporations listed domestically to SEC laws

C. Bans US citizens from banning foreign officials or domestic officials

D. Bans the bribing of foreign officials, bans the bribing of domestic officials by foreigners

E. Bans the bribing of foreign officials, and holds foreign corporations listed domestically to SEC laws

62. **According to _____, management involves using the scientific method to break-down each function into rigid specializations in a mass-production environment:**

   A. Henri Fayol

   B. David Aaker

   C. FW Taylor

   D. Charon Drotter

   E. Max Weber

63. **Henry Ford, founder of the Ford Motor Company, paid twice the standard salary because:**

   A. It allowed employees to purchase the products they were making

   B. Paying standard wages gave people little incentive to stay, creating huge turnover costs

   C. To attract highly-skilled workers

   D. To increase aggregate demand using the income effect

   E. To motivate employees to be more productive

64. **According to ____, management must include participative setting of objectives:**

   A. Frederick Herzberg

   B. Geert Hoftsede

   C. Abraham Maslow

   D. FW Taylor

   E. Peter Drucker

65. **Lower wages do not lead to higher employment because:**

   A. Fewer people are willing to work at a given price level despite their need to survive

   B. Companies will never hire more people than they need to meet production demand, regardless of wage level

   C. Lower wages cause greater per-person output

   D. Higher employment requires higher price levels to increase supply

   E. Unions prevent labor negotiations

66. According to Blanchard and Hersey, the ___ management style is used when employees are most developed, and ___ when they are least developed:

   A. Coaching, directing

   B. Delegating, supporting

   C. Coaching, supporting

   D. Delegating, directing

   E. Directing, delegating

67. The 20-70-10 rule states:

   A. Employees in the bottom 70% of productivity must be replaced, those in the top 10% supported, and the remaining 20% coached

   B. Employees get 10% of their skills from training, 70% from working, and the remaining 20% from work socialization

   C. Employees in the bottom 20% of productivity must be replaced, those in the top 10% supported, and the remaining 70% coached

   D. Employees in the bottom 10% of productivity must be replaced, those in the top 20% supported, and the remaining 70% coached

   E. Employees get 70% of their skills from training, 10% from working, and the remaining 20% from work socialization

68. According to Hofstede, the degree to which a culture values gain and achievement over social cohesion is called:

   A. Indulgence

   B. Masculinity

   C. Individualism

   D. Time orientation

   E. Power distance

69. Hofstede and GLOBE share which cultural dimension:

   A. Uncertainty avoidance

   B. Gender egalitarianism

   C. Performance orientation

   D. In-group collectivism

   E. Humane orientation

70. According to the original Civil Rights Act of 1964, it was legal to discriminate employment based on:

   A. Disability

   B. Gender

   C. Race

   D. Religion

   E. Color

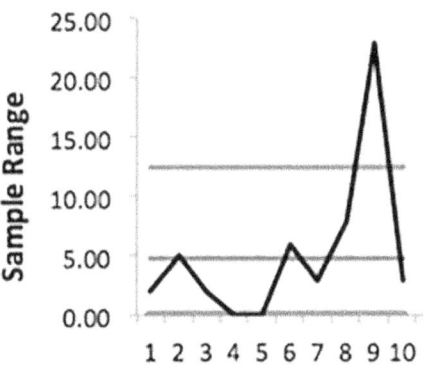

71. In statistical process control, this is typical of:

A. A systematic flaw causing consistent variability

B. An anomalous or temporary flaw in the production cycle

C. Volatile production growth

D. Seasonal production variations

E. Normal production quality

72. A behavior is considered unlawful harassment when:

A. The behavior is not appropriate in the workplace

B. An individual perceives the behavior as offensive

C. It is persistent or severe enough to make the workplace intimidating

D. The behavior breaks other laws

E. The behavior is socially inappropriate

73. A company is held liable for harassment within the workplace when:

A. Companies are never held liable, only people

B. It fails to act on any harassment brought to its attention

C. It fails to provide workplace equality training during orientation

D. It fails to act on harassment brought to its attention, or immediately when supervisors harass

E. Companies are always immediately liable for what happens

74. ____ is not a type of compensation:

A. Wages

B. Insurance benefits

C. Flex time

D. 401(k) matching

E. Pensions

75. **Each limits the bargaining power of individual employees except:**

    A. The high cost of developing new skills relative to low income

    B. Government regulation

    C. The majority of labor does not have the savings to survive for extended negotiations or job search

    D. Low skill requirements for those jobs most vulnerable

    E. Lack of equivalent access to legal and PR resources

76. **Performance appraisals must be all except:**

    A. Performed regularly

    B. Clear and specific

    C. Objectively measured

    D. Strict

    E. Individualized

77. **Which is not a tool used to create a cohesive virtual environment:**

    A. Instant messaging

    B. Cloud computing

    C. Database management systems

    D. Collaborative workspace

    E. Video conferencing

78. **____ is not one of the reasons workplace diversity is important:**

    A. Different perspectives increases innovation and improves idea pool

    B. Larger labor pools increase total labor potential

    C. Affirmative action requires special consideration for underrepresented groups

    D. Demographic equivalence improves responsiveness to changing markets

    E. Workplace diversity expands market size and/or market share

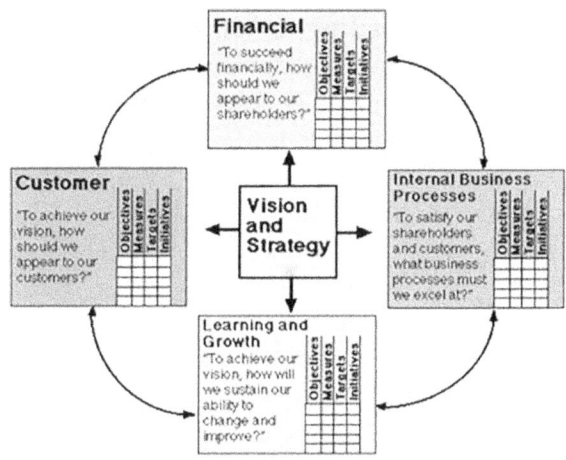

79. This is ____, which ____:

   A. Balanced scorecard, evaluates the degree to which different functions are prepared to pursue a strategy initiative before execution

   B. Balanced scorecard, assesses the degree to which operations support the overall strategy

   C. Balanced scorecard, calculates the resource utilization of different functions dedicated to a strategic initiative

   D. Strategic operations chart, defines the way in which organizational operations must function to achieve strategic goals

   E. Strategy control graph, assesses the degree to which operations support the overall strategy

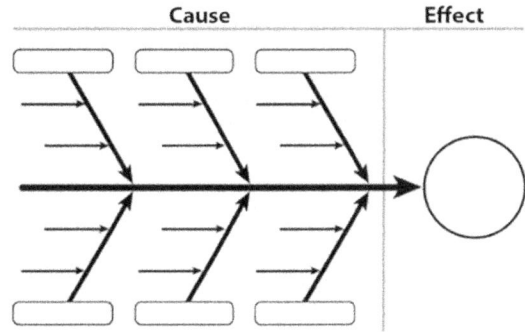

80. This is ____ :

   A. Causal loop diagram

   B. Cause-effect graph

   C. Why-because analysis

   D. Ishikawa diagram

   E. Causal diagram

81. In a corporation, top management is hired by:

   A. Board of directors

   B. Shareholders

   C. Stakeholders

   D. Executives

   E. Front-line management

82. In a corporation, board of directors is hired by:

   A. Board of directors

   B. Shareholders

   C. Stakeholders

   D. Executives

   E. Front-line management

83. **The four functions of management does not include:**

    A. Planning

    B. Organizing

    C. Marketing

    D. Leading

    E. Controlling

84. **According to Mintzberg, the role of the manager which involves communicating information to people outside the organization is:**

    A. Disseminator

    B. Spokesperson

    C. Monitor

    D. Figurehead

    E. Liaison

85. **According to Mintzberg, the role of the manager which includes networking within and outside the organization is:**

    A. Liaison

    B. Spokesperson

    C. Figurehead

    D. Disseminator

    E. Monitor

86. **According to Mintzberg, the role of the manager which involves defending the interests of the business is:**

    A. Disturbance handler

    B. Entrepreneur

    C. Negotiator

    D. Resource allocator

    E. Leader

87. **Which are traditionally listed as part of the managerial skill set:**

    A. Technical skills, human skills

    B. Human skills, marketing skills

    C. Conceptual skills, accounting skills

    D. Technical skills, marketing skills

    E. Human skills, accounting skills

88. **___ refers to those actions and behaviors which people believe to be important:**

    A. Morals

    B. Principles

    C. Beliefs

    D. Values

    E. Ethics

89. Setting goals does not:

    A. Function has a comprehensive plan
    B. Provide guidance and direction
    C. Create a foundation for organized planning
    D. Establish challenging milestones to motivate staff
    E. Provide a method for evaluating performance

90. The official parameters set by an organization outlining an activity or response is called:

    A. Regulations
    B. Rules
    C. Procedures
    D. Laws
    E. Norms

91. Which type of grand strategy can involve selling current business units:

    A. entrenchment
    B. Global
    C. Growth
    D. Stability
    E. Business

92. According to the rational model, the decision-making process includes everything except:

    A. Assess options
    B. Determine the point of acceptable satisficing
    C. Make decision
    D. Define the problem
    E. Evaluate results

93. Which is a potential disadvantage of group decision-making:

    A. Greater error recognition
    B. Improved morale through participation
    C. Greater acceptance of decision by staff
    D. Diffusion of responsibility
    E. Expanded knowledge pool

94. Techniques teams can use to stimulate creative problem solving include everything except ___, which is typically used by individuals:

    A. Brainstorming
    B. Delphi technique
    C. Cross-fertilization
    D. Nominal group technique
    E. Devil's advocacy

95. **Fast, repetitive production environments are facilitated by a ____, and creative environments of dynamic challenges by a ____:**

   A. Industrial system, organic system

   B. Mechanistic system, organic system

   C. Natural system, Mechanistic system

   D. Industrial system, natural system

   E. Mechanistic system, mechanistic system

96. **Horizontal organizations are unique because:**

   A. They formed as a result of horizontal integration with other organizations

   B. They have a small number of employees per manager

   C. They emphasize functional integration and personal empowerment over hierarchy

   D. They give greater authority to employees than management

   E. They are the inverse of vertical organizations

97. **Perceptual errors in leadership do not include:**

   A. Halo effect

   B. Strictness or leniency

   C. Expectancy effect

   D. Projection effect

   E. Selective perception

98. **Which type of team is best when highly specialized operations are involved:**

   A. Dysfunctional team

   B. Cross-functional team

   C. Functional team

   D. Vertical team

   E. Project

99. **What type of team is best for executive operations:**

   A. Dysfunctional team

   B. Cross-functional team

   C. Functional team

   D. Vertical team

   E. Project team

100. Groupthink is:

A. A form of group brainstorming

B. The collective culture of an organization

C. The aggregate knowledge set of a team

D. The innovation created in large groups of highly specialized people

E. A state in which conformity takes priority over critical thought

Principles of Management

ANSWER KEY

Question Number	Correct Answer	Your Answer	Question Number	Correct Answer	Your Answer	Question Number	Correct Answer	Your Answer
1	B		36	C		71	B	
2	C		37	A		72	C	
3	C		38	A		73	D	
4	B		39	B		74	C	
5	C		40	B		75	B	
6	C		41	E		76	D	
7	D		42	A		77	C	
8	B		43	C		78	C	
9	B		44	D		79	B	
10	A		45	D		80	D	
11	B		46	A		81	A	
12	C		47	B		82	B	
13	E		48	A		83	C	
14	B		49	A		84	B	
15	A		50	A		85	A	
16	A		51	A		86	C	
17	B		52	D		87	A	
18	E		53	A		88	D	
19	A		54	C		89	A	
20	B		55	C		90	C	
21	A		56	A		91	A	
22	A		57	E		92	B	
23	A		58	C		93	D	
24	E		59	B		94	C	
25	A		60	C		95	B	
26	A		61	E		96	C	
27	A		62	C		97	B	
28	B		63	B		98	C	
29	E		64	E		99	B	
30	B		65	B		100	E	
31	B		66	D				
32	C		67	C				
33	A		68	B				
34	A		69	A				
35	E		70	A				

Principles of Marketing

Description of the Examination

The Principles of Marketing examination covers the material that is usually taught in a one-semester introductory course in marketing. Such a course is usually known as Basic Marketing, Introduction to Marketing, Fundamentals of Marketing, Marketing, or Marketing Principles. The exam is concerned with the role of marketing in society and within a firm, understanding consumer and organizational markets, marketing strategy planning, the marketing mix, marketing institutions, and other selected topics, such as international marketing, ethics, marketing research, services and not-for-profit marketing. The candidate is also expected to have a basic knowledge of the economic/demographic, social/cultural, political/legal, and technological trends that are important to marketing.

The examination contains approximately 100 questions to be answered in 90 minutes. Some of these are pretest questions that will not be scored. Any time candidates spend on tutorials and providing personal information is in addition to the actual testing time.

Knowledge and Skills Required

The subject matter of the Principles of Marketing examination is drawn from the following topics in the approximate proportions indicated. The percentages next to the main topics indicate the approximate percentage of exam questions on that topic.

8-13% **Role of Marketing in Society**
* Ethics
* Nonprofit Marketing
* International Marketing

17-24% **Role of Marketing in a Firm**
* Marketing Concept
* Marketing Strategy
* Marketing Environment
* Marketing Decision System
* Marketing research
* Marketing Information System

22-27% **Target Marketing**
* Consumer Behavior
* Segmentation
* Positioning
* B2B Markets

40-50% **Marketing Mix**
* Produce and Service Management
* Branding
* Pricing Policies
* Distribution Channels and Logistics
* Integrated Marketing Communications and Promotion
* Marketing Application in e-Commerce

Principles of Marketing

SAMPLE TEST

1. **In marketing, commercialization is:**

   A. The development of commercial ads

   B. The point at which a new product is launched onto the market

   C. The point at which a new product is tested in a small market before wider launch

   D. The point at which research is performed for the production of a new product

   E. A shift of social values toward material goods

2. **When performing market research, primary research is ____ but ____ then secondary research:**

   A. Easier to find, subject to interpretation

   B. Less detailed, cheaper

   C. More detailed, more expensive

   D. More detailed, cheaper

   E. Less detailed, more expensive

3. **The least integrated way to create a direct presence within a foreign market is through:**

   A. Wholly-owned subsidiaries

   B. Joint ventures

   C. Franchising

   D. Licensing

   E. Exporting

4. **____ is a restriction which prevents the importing of particular goods:**

   A. Tariff

   B. Quota

   C. Credit restriction

   D. Exchange control

   E. Embargo

5. **Success in marketing relies on:**

   A. Executive partnerships

   B. Production efficiency

   C. Customer satisfaction

   D. Assertive staff

   E. Constant innovation

6. **During what stage of the product lifecycle should a marketer build product awareness:**

   A. Decline

   B. Maturity

   C. Introduction

   D. Growth

   E. Replacement

7. **When demand is highly elastic:**

   A. Seasonal fluctuations are very strong

   B. Price will change very slowly in response to a change in demand

   C. Price will change quickly in response to a change in demand

   D. It will change quickly in response to a change in price

   E. It will change very slowly in response to a change in price

8. **The 4 P's of the marketing mix are:**

   A. Product, price, promotion, placement

   B. Product, price, place, promotion

   C. Produce properly priced products

   D. Product, promotion, placement, profit

   E. Product, price, place, profit

9. **A company operating at low PED will benefit most from a ___ strategy:**

   A. Price leader

   B. Penetration

   C. Niche

   D. 2nd mover

   E. Premium pricing

10. **A company operating at high PED will benefit most from a ___ strategy:**

    A. Price leader

    B. Premium pricing

    C. Niche

    D. 2nd mover

    E. Penetration

Answer Key

1. B
2. C
3. C
4. E
5. C
6. C
7. D
8. B
9. E
10. A

Please note that this is a sample portion of the CLEP Principles of Marketing examination. A complete practice test is available for purchase at Amazon.com and Barnesandnoble.com
ISBN 9781607875475

XAMonline
The CLEP Specialist
Individual Sample Tests in ebook format with full explanations

eBooks

All 33 CLEP sample tests are available as ebook downloads from retail websites such as **Amazon.com** and **Barnesandnoble.com**

American Government	9781607875130
American Literature	9781607875079
Analyzing and Interpreting Literature	9781607875086
Biology	9781607875222
Calculus	9781607875376
Chemistry	9781607875239
College Algebra	9781607875215
College Composition	9781607875109
College Composition Modular	9781607875437
College Mathematics	9781607875246
English Literature	9781607875093
Financial Accounting	9781607875383
French	9781607875123
German	9781607875369
History of the United States I	9781607875178
History of the United States II	9781607875185
Human Growth and Development	9781607875444
Humanities	9781607875147
Information Systems	9781607875390
Introduction to Educational Psychology	9781607875451
Introductory Business Law	9781607875420
Introductory Psychology	9781607875154
Introductory Sociology	9781607875352
Natural Sciences	9781607875253
Precalculus	9781607875345
Principles of Macroeconomics	9781607875406
Principles of Microeconomics	9781607875468
Principles of Marketing	9781607875475
Principles of Management	9781607875468
Social Sciences and History	9781607875161
Spanish	9781607875116
Western Civilization I	9781607875192
Western Civilization II	9781607875208

TO ORDER  XAMonline.com or amazon or BARNES&NOBLE BOOKSELLERS

XAMonline
CLEP
Full Study Guides

CLEP College Algebra
ISBN: 9781607875598
Price: $34.95

CLEP Biology
ISBN: 9781607875314
Price: $34.95

CLEP Analyzing and
Interpreting Literature
ISBN: 9781607875260
Price: $34.95

CLEP College Composition
and Modular
ISBN: 9781607875277
Price: $19.99

CLEP College Mathematics
ISBN: 9781607875321
Price: $34.95

CLEP Psychology
ISBN: 9781607875291
Price: $34.95

CLEP Spanish
ISBN: 9781607875284
Price: $34.95

TO ORDER — **X** XAMonline.com or amazon or **BARNES & NOBLE** BOOKSELLERS

XAMonline
CLEP Subject Series
Collection by Topic
Sample Test Approach

CLEP Literature
ISBN: 9781607875833
Price: $34.95

CLEP Foreign Language
ISBN: 9781607875772
Price: $34.95

CLEP History
ISBN: 9781607875789
Price: $34.95

CLEP Sociology
ISBN: 9781607875796
Price: $34.95

CLEP Science
ISBN: 9781607875802
Price: $34.95

CLEP Mathematics
ISBN: 9781607875819
Price: $34.95

CLEP Business
ISBN: 9781607875826
Price: $34.95

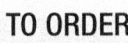 or  or

XAMonline
CLEP Favorites
Collection by Topic
Sample Test Approach

CLEP Five Favorites
ISBN: 9781607875765
Price: $24.95

CLEP Military Favorites
ISBN: 9781607875512
Price: $24.95

 or  or BARNES & NOBLE BOOKSELLERS